THE LEGEND OF ZELDA™

FOUR SWORDS

FOUR SWORDS ADVENTURES — THE GAME

The Legend of Zelda™: *Four Swords* was released for the Nintendo Game Cube in 2004. The Game Boy Advance could also be used as a controller and connected to the Game Cube in order to play. The game was known for its multiplayer mode that allowed up to four players to take the roles of different-colored Links and work together to complete the game.

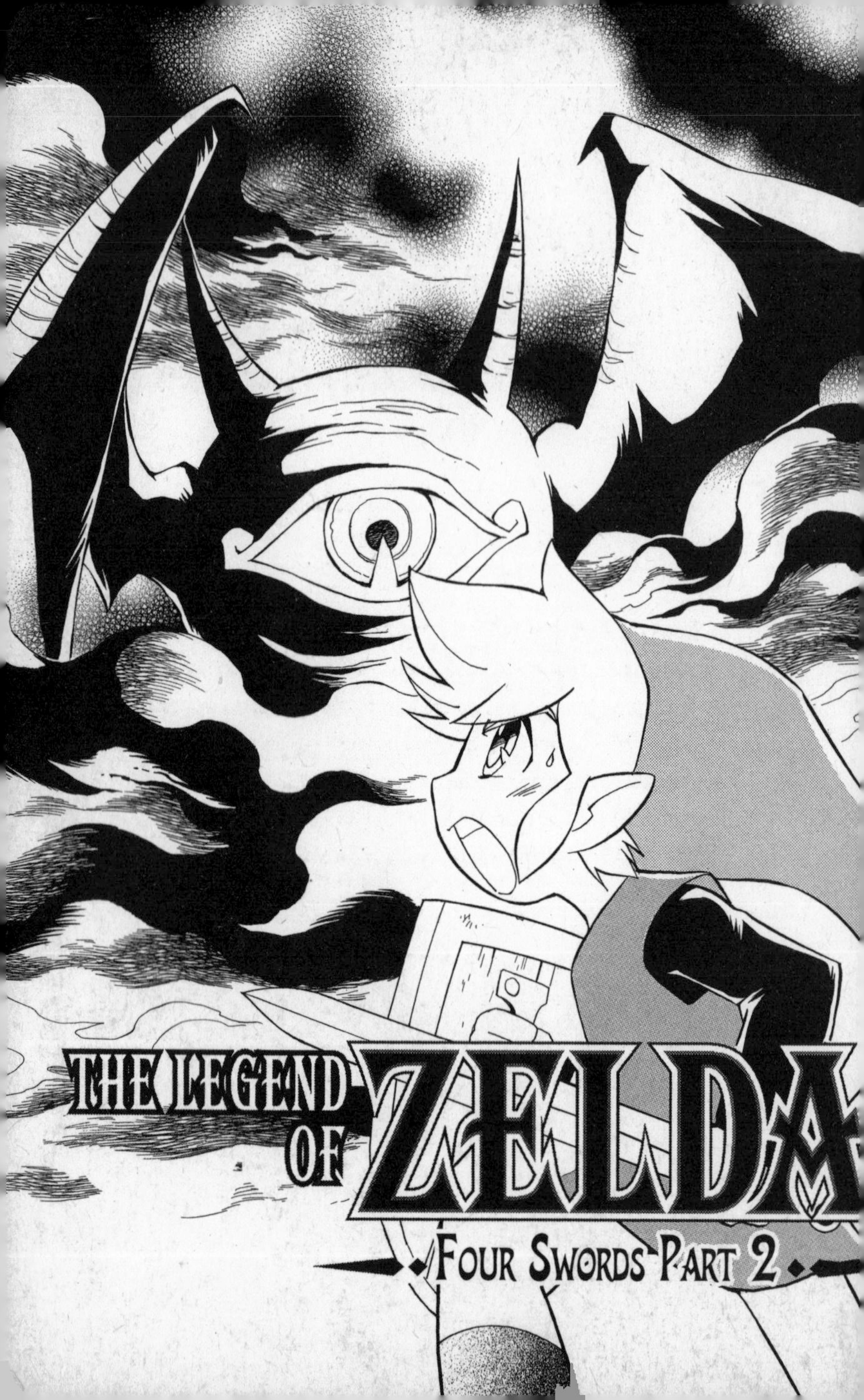
THE LEGEND OF ZELDA
FOUR SWORDS PART 2

THE LEGEND OF ZELDA™ FOUR SWORDS PART 2

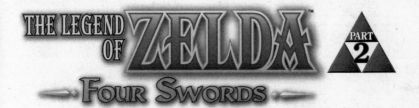

CONTENTS

FOUR SWORDS PART 2

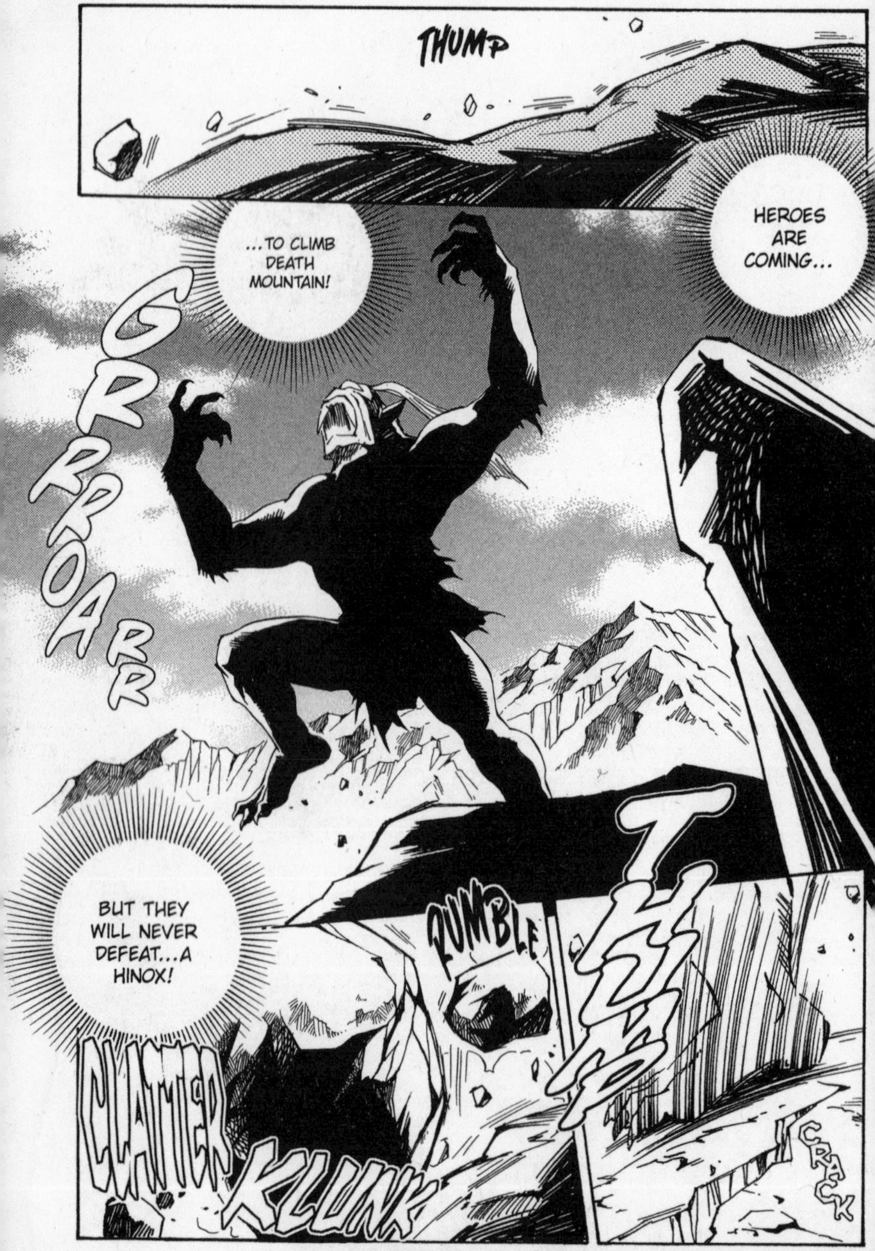
THUMP
HEROES ARE COMING...
...TO CLIMB DEATH MOUNTAIN!
GRRROARRR
BUT THEY WILL NEVER DEFEAT...A HINOX!
THUMP
CRACK
RUMBLE
CLATTER
KLUNK

CHAPTER 7 CLIMB DEATH MOUNTAIN!

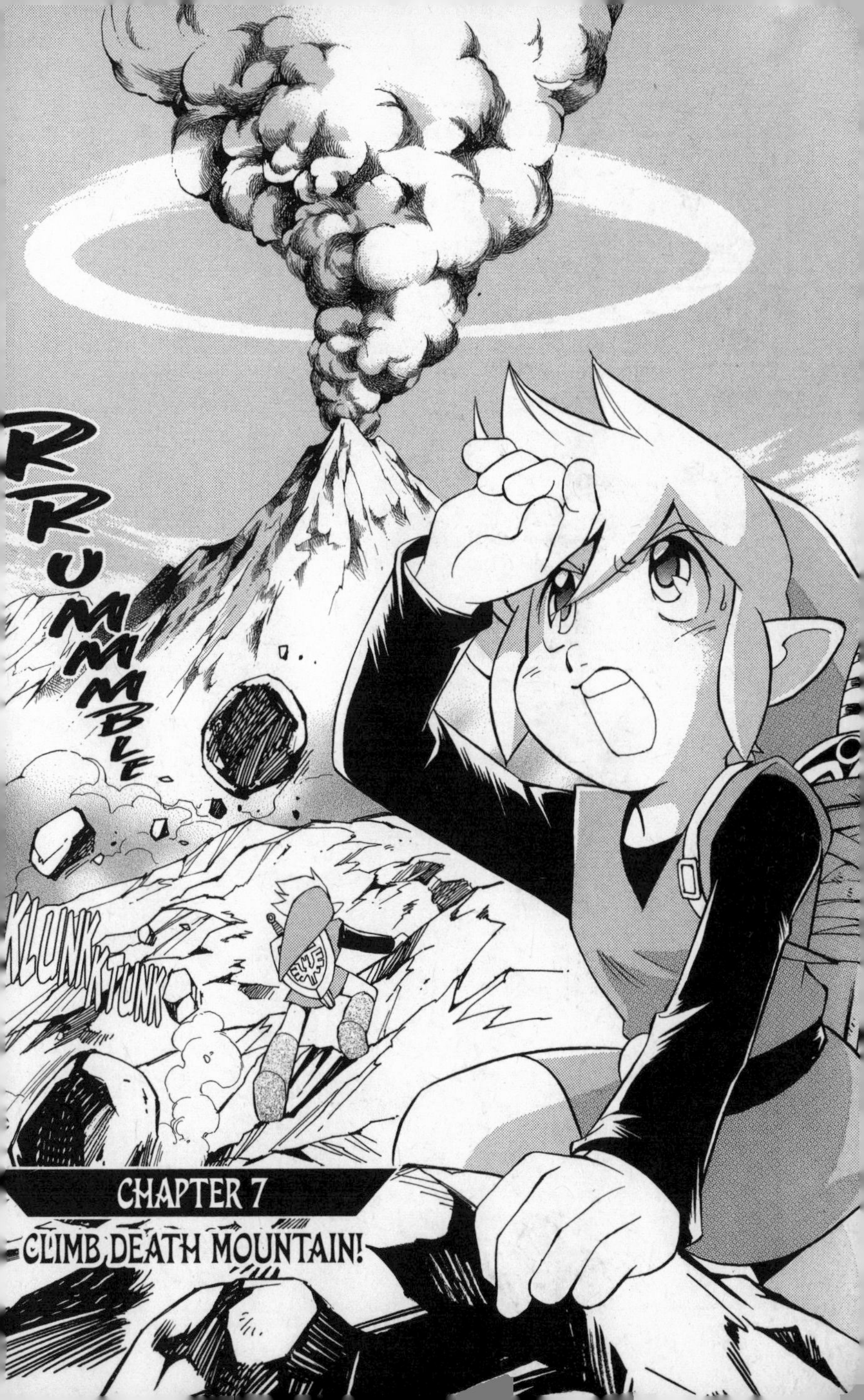
RRRUMMMMBLE
KLUNK TUNK
CHAPTER 7
CLIMB DEATH MOUNTAIN!

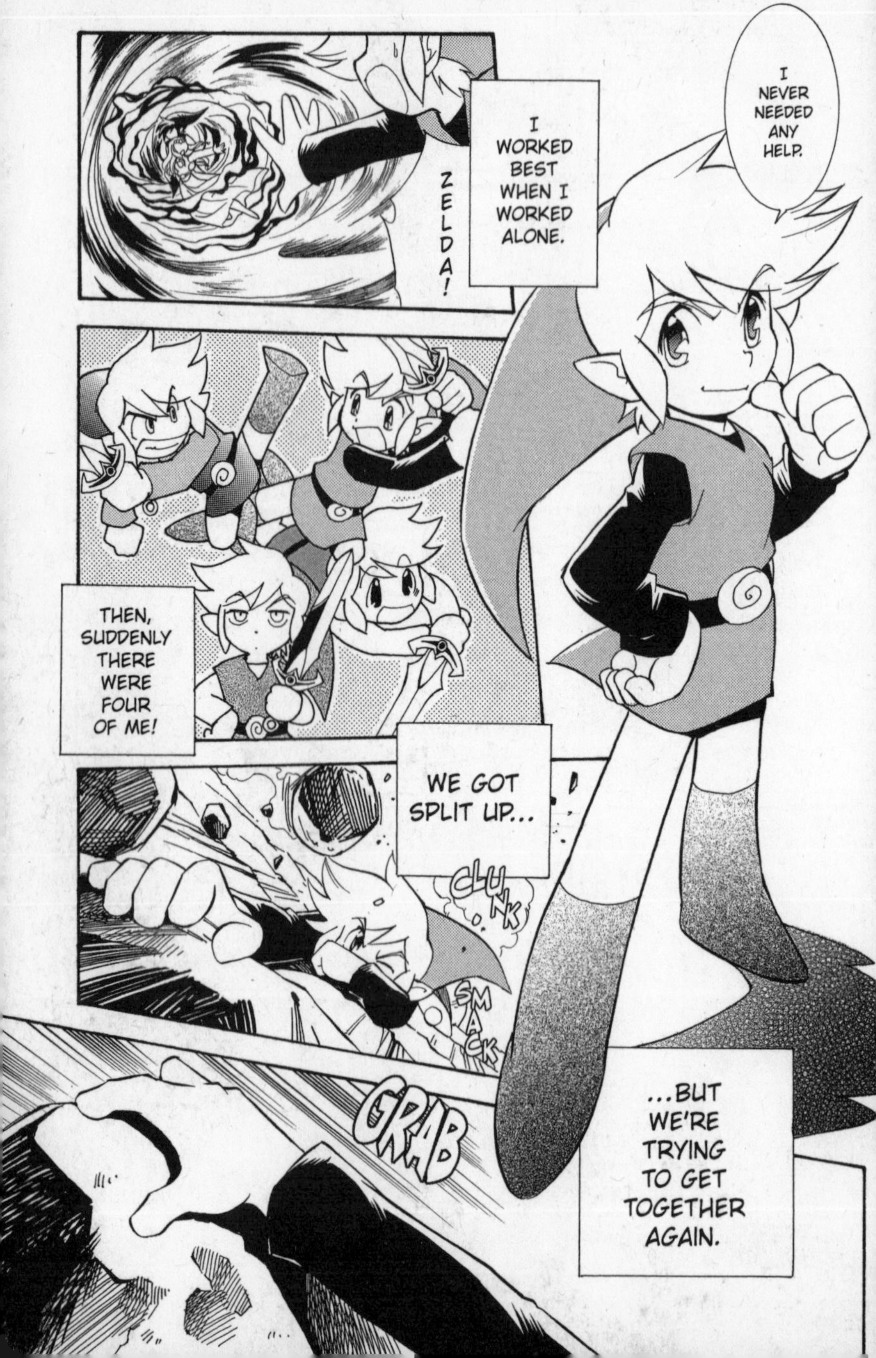

I NEVER NEEDED ANY HELP.
I WORKED BEST WHEN I WORKED ALONE.
ZELDA!
THEN, SUDDENLY THERE WERE FOUR OF ME!
WE GOT SPLIT UP...
CLUNK
SMACK
GRAB
...BUT WE'RE TRYING TO GET TOGETHER AGAIN.

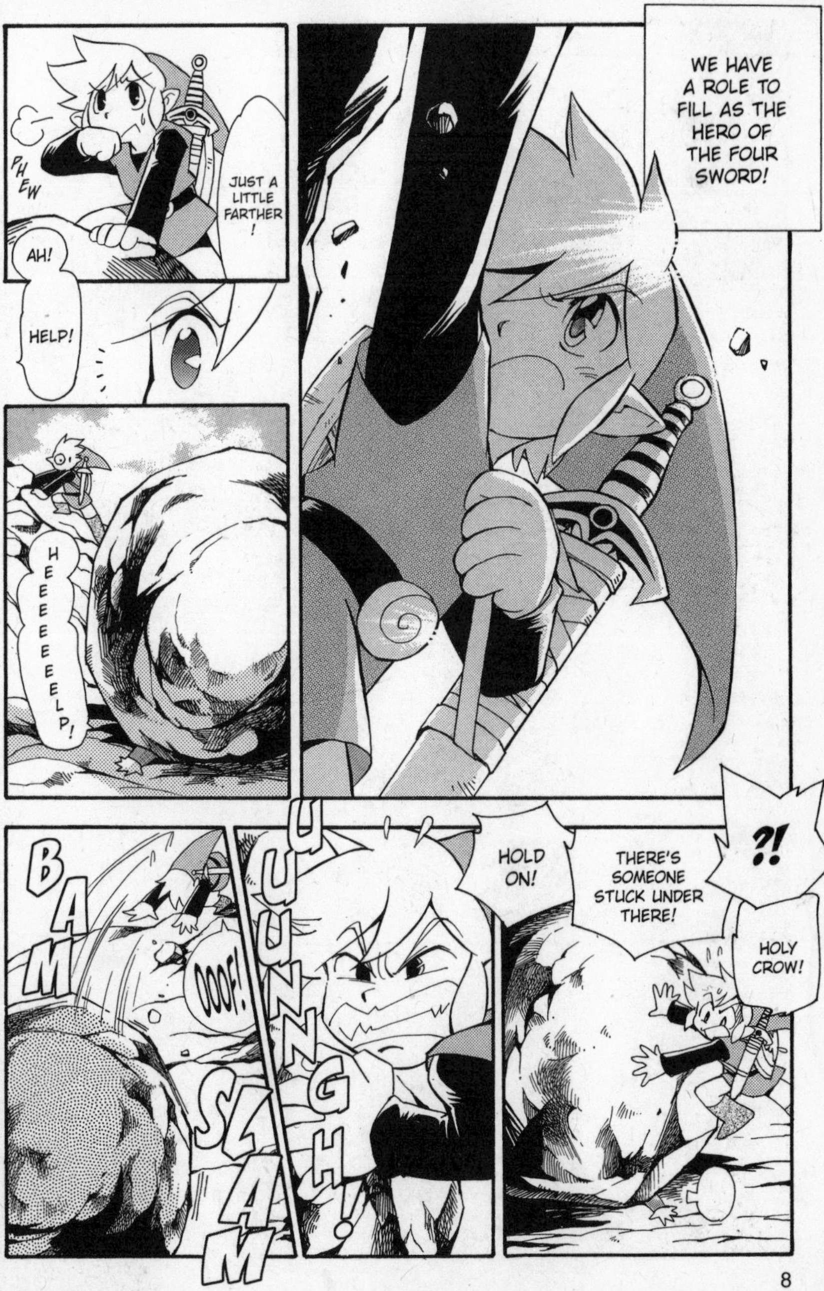
WE HAVE A ROLE TO FILL AS THE HERO OF THE FOUR SWORD!
PHEW
JUST A LITTLE FARTHER!
AH!
HELP!
HEEEEEEEELP!
?!
HOLY CROW!
THERE'S SOMEONE STUCK UNDER THERE!
HOLD ON!
UUUNNGH!
BAM
DOOF!
SLAM

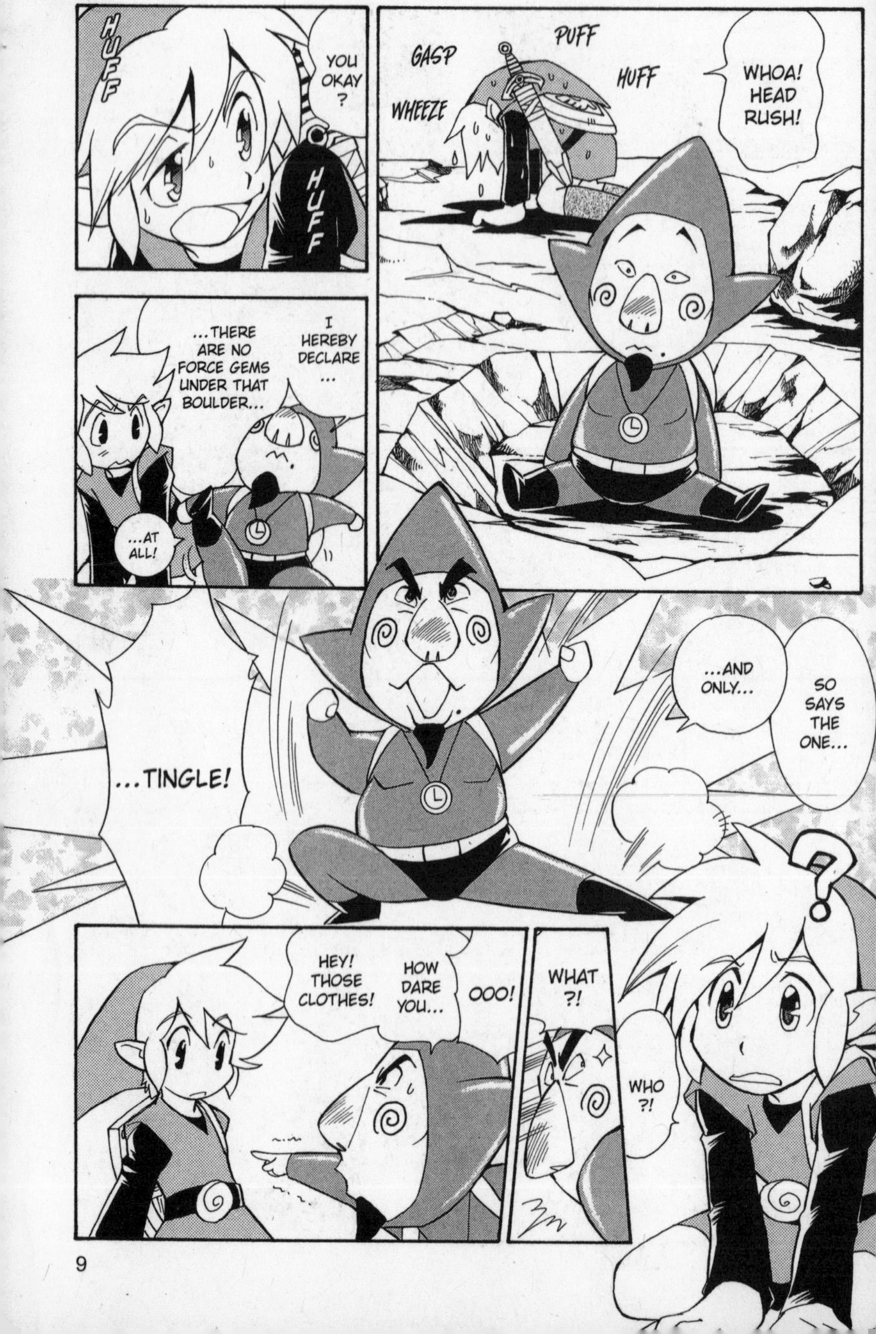
PUFF
GASP
HUFF
WHEEZE
WHOA! HEAD RUSH!
HUFF
YOU OKAY?
HUFF
I HEREBY DECLARE...
...THERE ARE NO FORCE GEMS UNDER THAT BOULDER...
...AT ALL!
SO SAYS THE ONE...
...AND ONLY...
...TINGLE!
?
WHO ?!
WHAT ?!
OOO!
HOW DARE YOU...
HEY! THOSE CLOTHES!

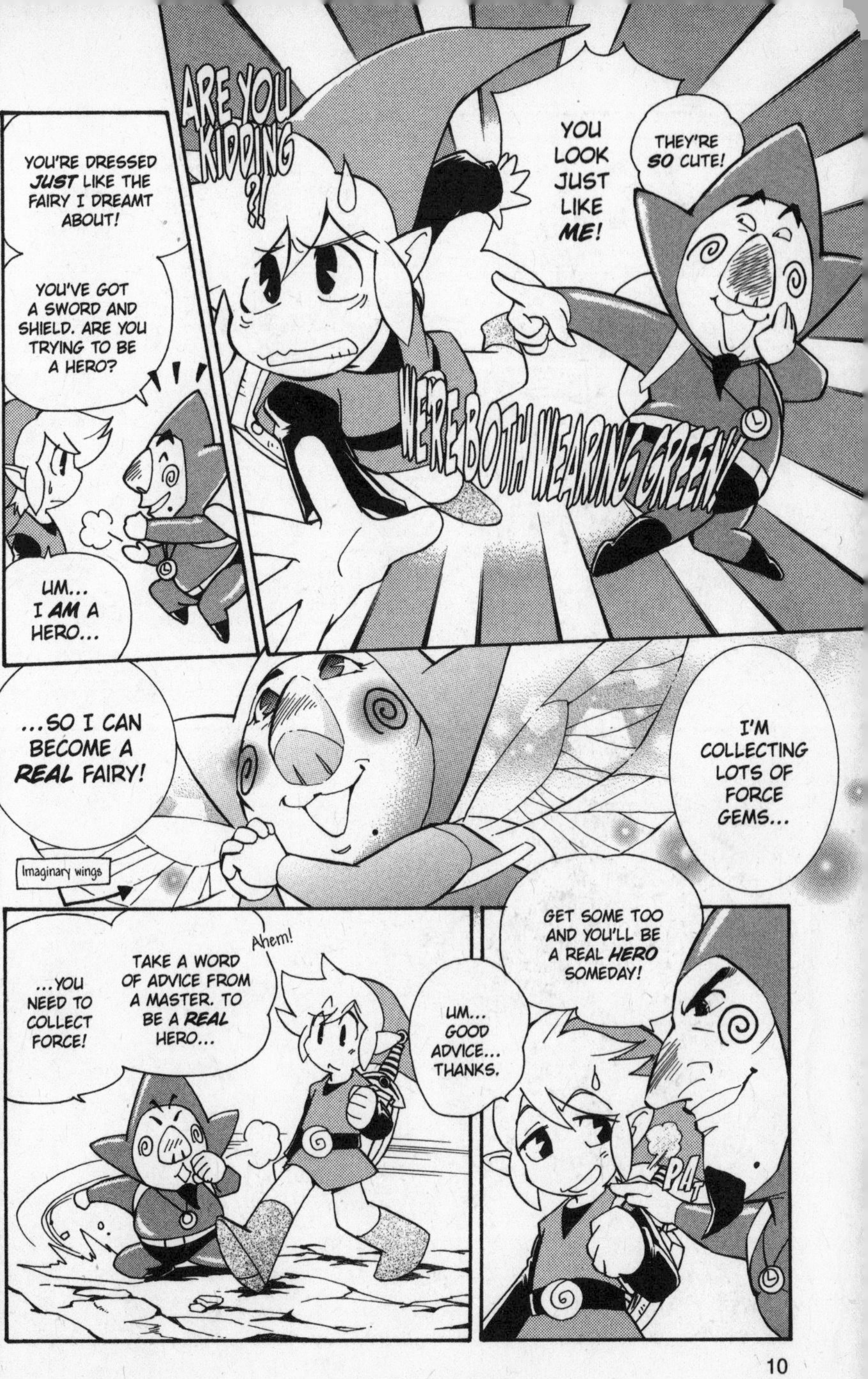
THEY'RE SO CUTE!
YOU LOOK JUST LIKE ME!
ARE YOU KIDDING?!
WE'RE BOTH WEARING GREEN!
YOU'RE DRESSED JUST LIKE THE FAIRY I DREAMT ABOUT!
YOU'VE GOT A SWORD AND SHIELD. ARE YOU TRYING TO BE A HERO?
UM... I AM A HERO...
I'M COLLECTING LOTS OF FORCE GEMS...
...SO I CAN BECOME A REAL FAIRY!
Imaginary wings
GET SOME TOO AND YOU'LL BE A REAL HERO SOMEDAY!
UM... GOOD ADVICE... THANKS.
PAT
Ahem!
TAKE A WORD OF ADVICE FROM A MASTER. TO BE A REAL HERO...
...YOU NEED TO COLLECT FORCE!

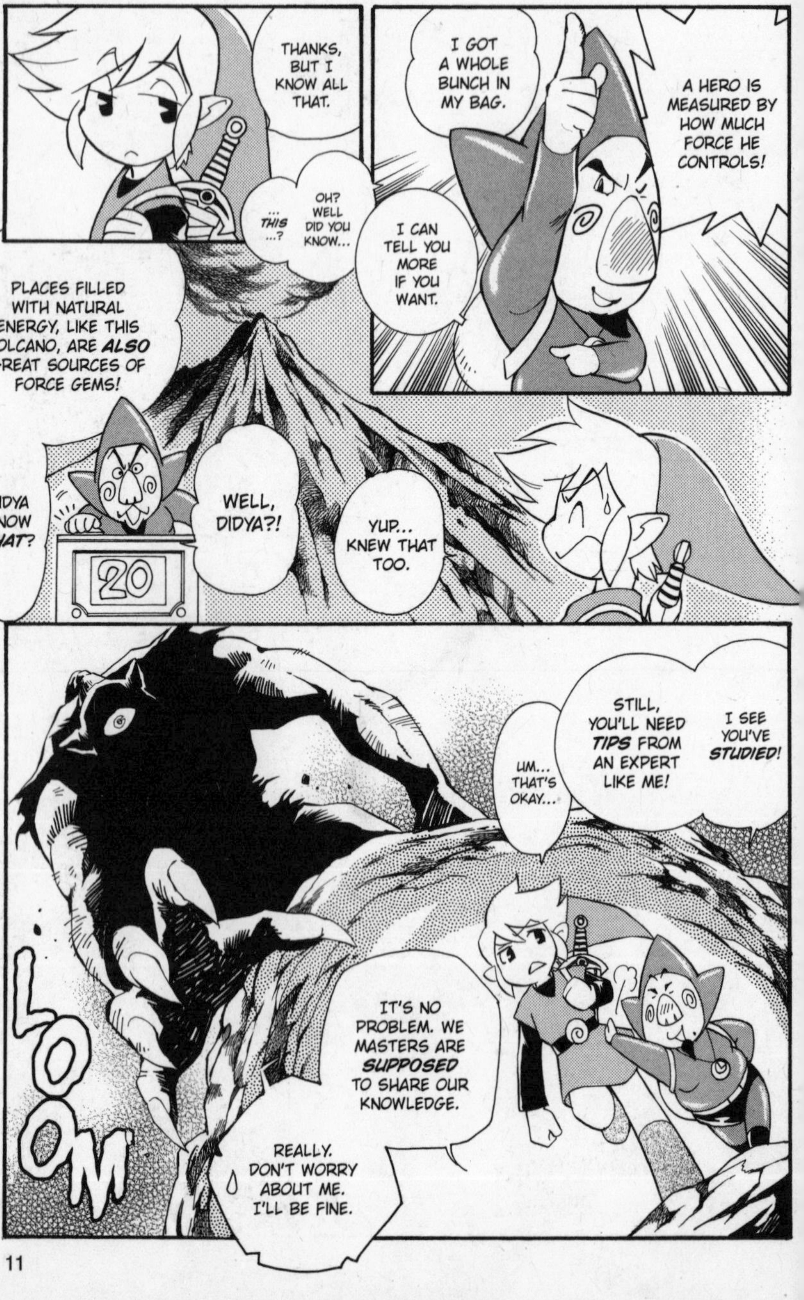
I GOT A WHOLE BUNCH IN MY BAG.
A HERO IS MEASURED BY HOW MUCH FORCE HE CONTROLS!
I CAN TELL YOU MORE IF YOU WANT.
THANKS, BUT I KNOW ALL THAT.
OH? WELL DID YOU KNOW...
...THIS...?
PLACES FILLED WITH NATURAL ENERGY, LIKE THIS VOLCANO, ARE *ALSO* GREAT SOURCES OF FORCE GEMS!
DIDYA KNOW *THAT*?
WELL, DIDYA?!
20
YUP... KNEW THAT TOO.
I SEE YOU'VE *STUDIED*!
STILL, YOU'LL NEED *TIPS* FROM AN EXPERT LIKE ME!
UM... THAT'S OKAY...
IT'S NO PROBLEM. WE MASTERS ARE *SUPPOSED* TO SHARE OUR KNOWLEDGE.
REALLY. DON'T WORRY ABOUT ME. I'LL BE FINE.
LOOM

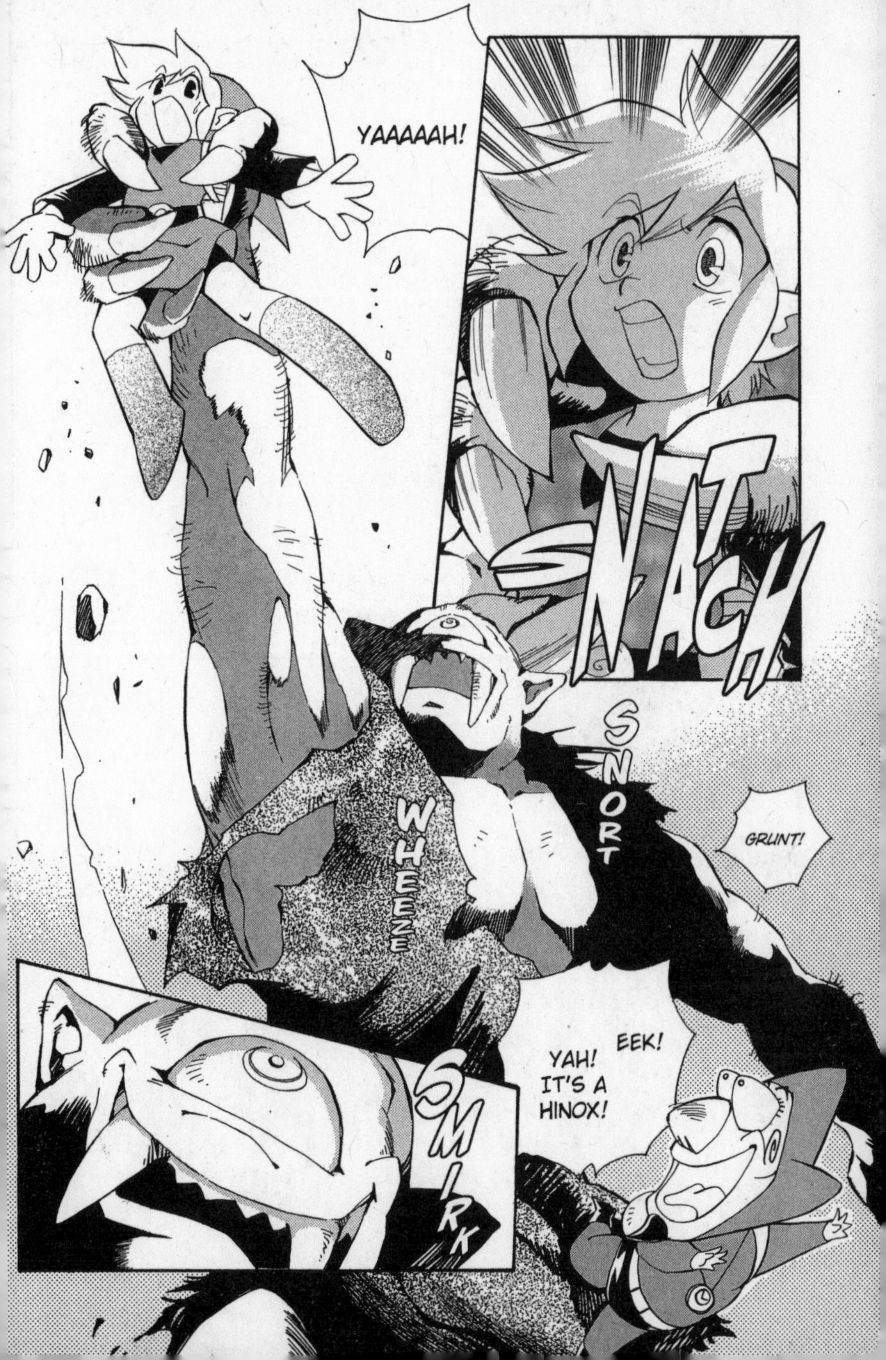
SNATCH
YAAAAAH!
SNORT
WHEEZE
GRUNT!
EEK!
YAH! IT'S A HINOX!
SMIRK

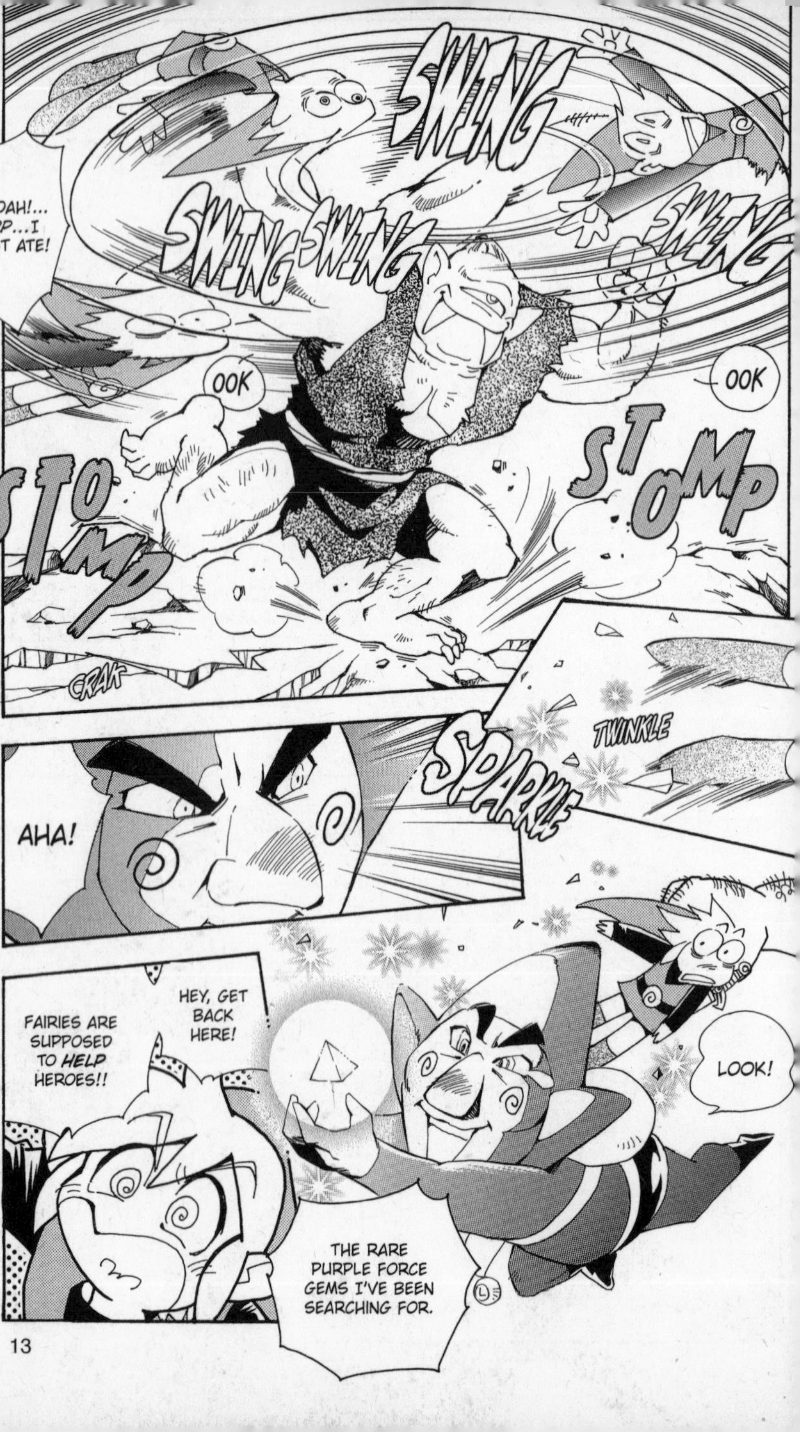
SWING
SWING
OOK
STOMP
SWING SWING
WHOAH!... URP...I JUST ATE!
OOK
STOMP
CRAK
TWINKLE
SPARKLE
AHA!
LOOK!
THE RARE PURPLE FORCE GEMS I'VE BEEN SEARCHING FOR.
HEY, GET BACK HERE!
FAIRIES ARE SUPPOSED TO *HELP* HEROES!!

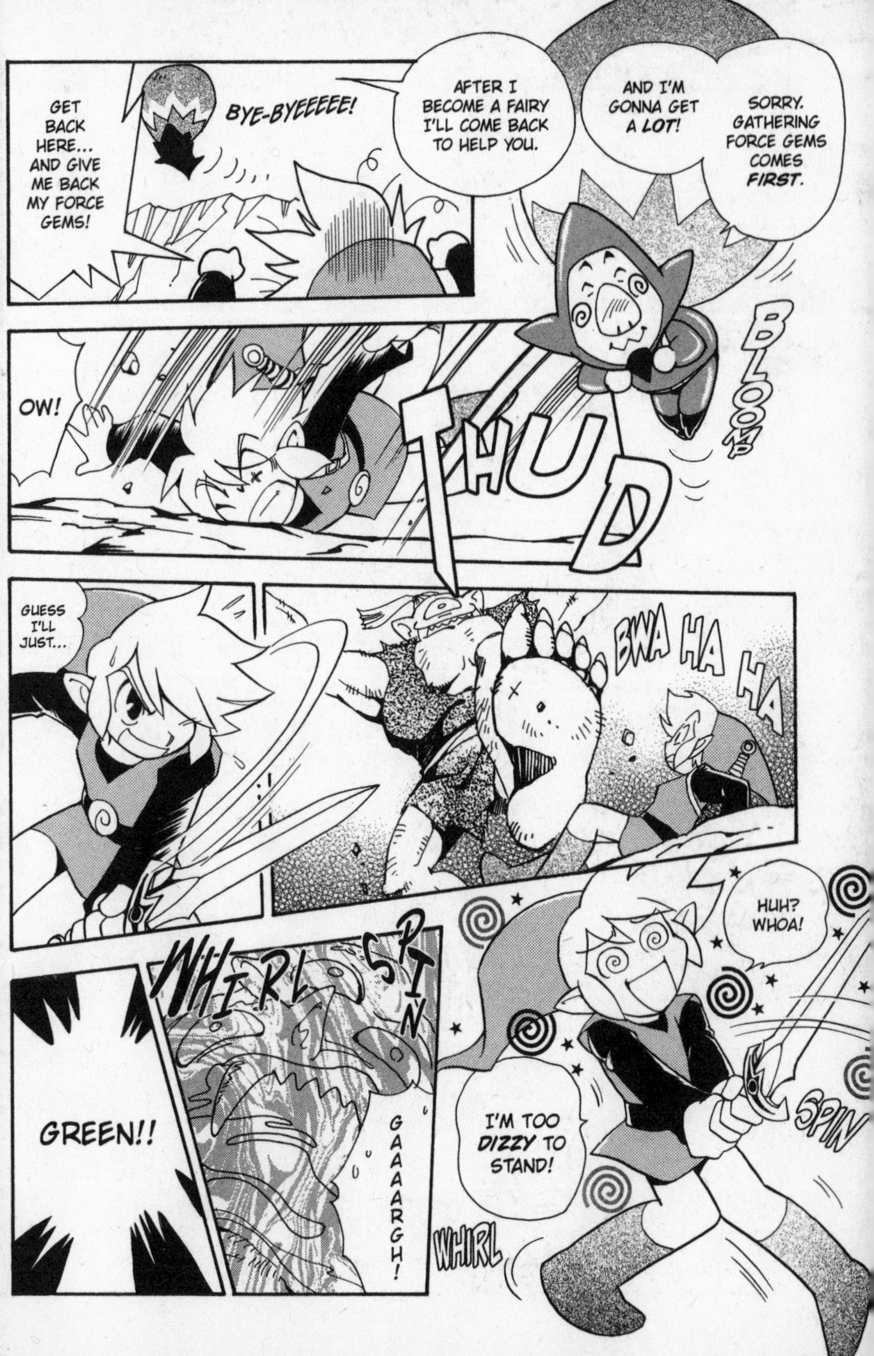
SORRY. GATHERING FORCE GEMS COMES FIRST.
AND I'M GONNA GET A LOT!
AFTER I BECOME A FAIRY I'LL COME BACK TO HELP YOU.
BYE-BYEEEEE!
GET BACK HERE... AND GIVE ME BACK MY FORCE GEMS!
BLOOMP
THUD
OW!
BWA HA HA HA
GUESS I'LL JUST...
HUH? WHOA!
SPIN
I'M TOO DIZZY TO STAND!
WHIRL
WHIRL SPIN
GAAAAARGH!
GREEN!!

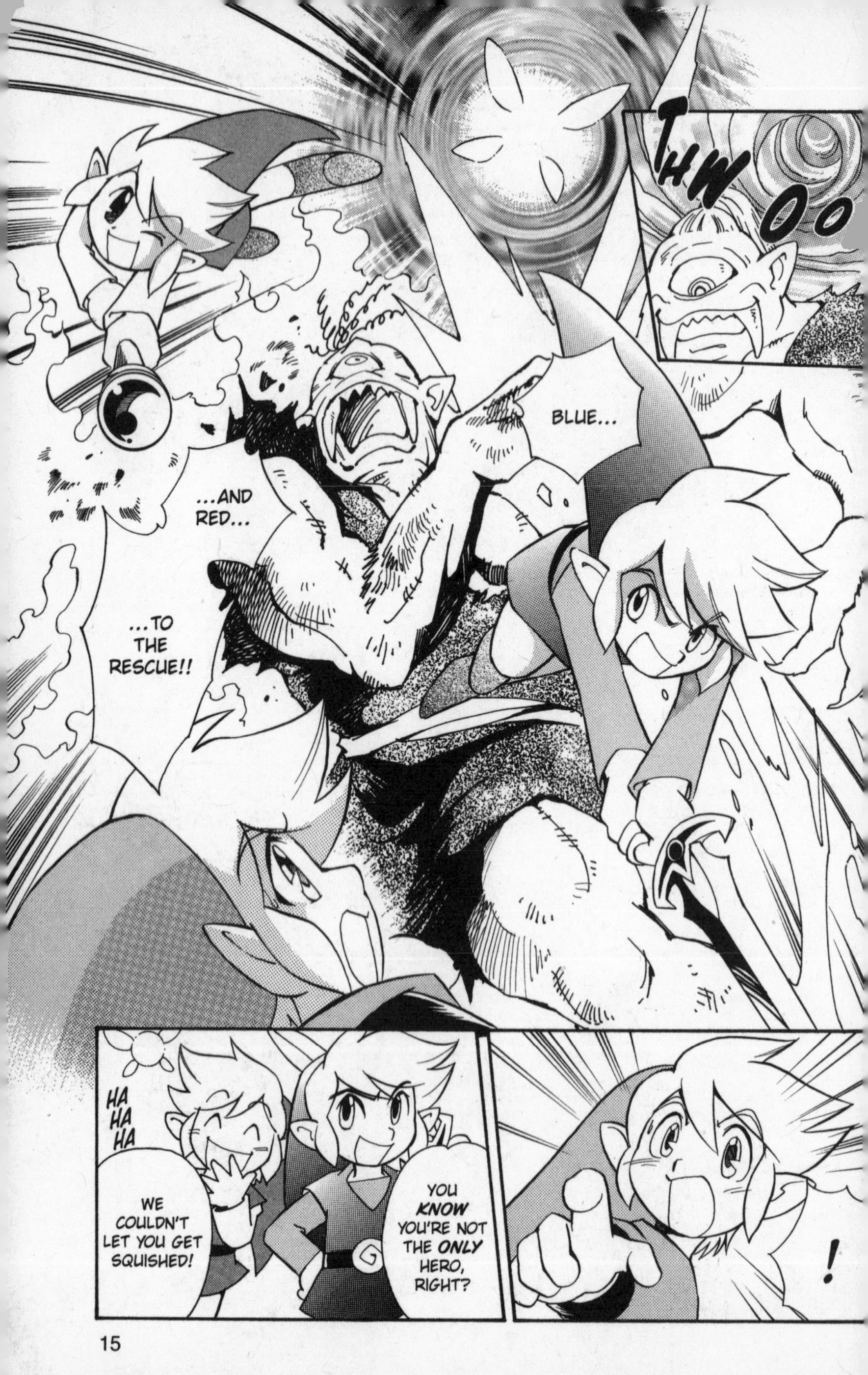
THWOOO
BLUE...
...AND RED...
...TO THE RESCUE!!
!
YOU KNOW YOU'RE NOT THE ONLY HERO, RIGHT?
HA HA HA
WE COULDN'T LET YOU GET SQUISHED!

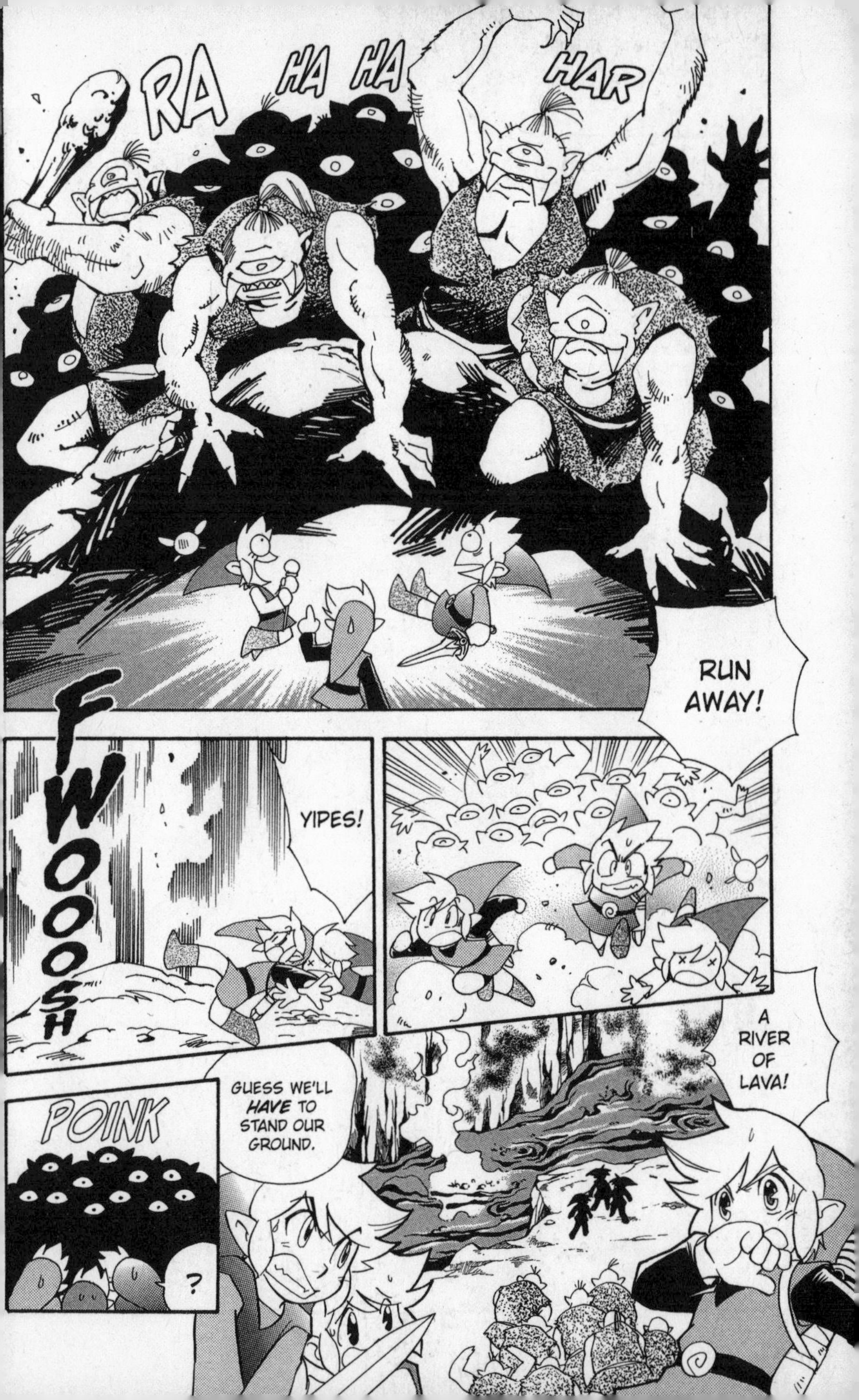
RA HA HA HAR
RUN AWAY!
FWOOOOSH
YIPES!
A RIVER OF LAVA!
GUESS WE'LL *HAVE* TO STAND OUR GROUND.
POINK
?

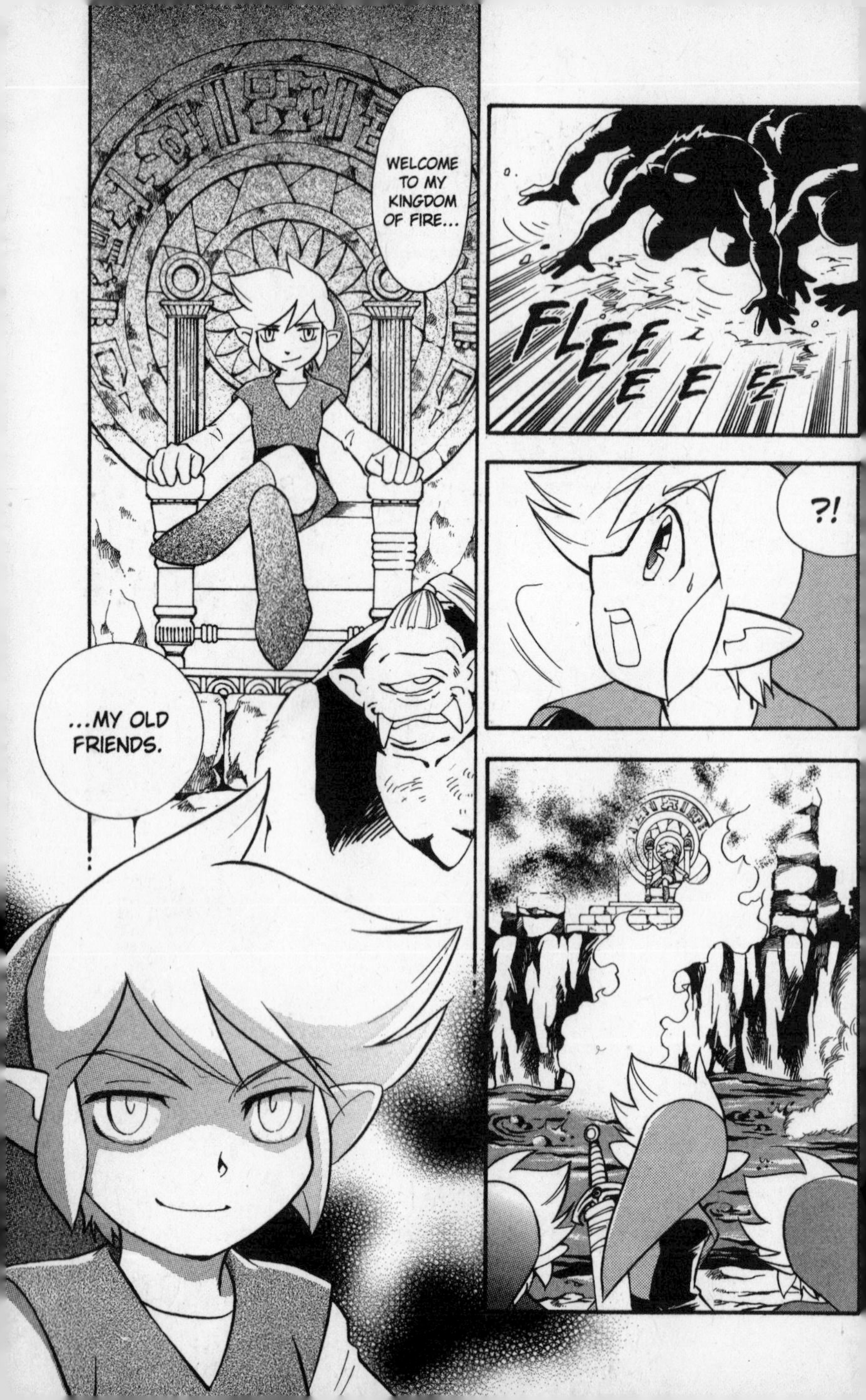
FLEEEEEEEE
?!
WELCOME TO MY KINGDOM OF FIRE...
...MY OLD FRIENDS.

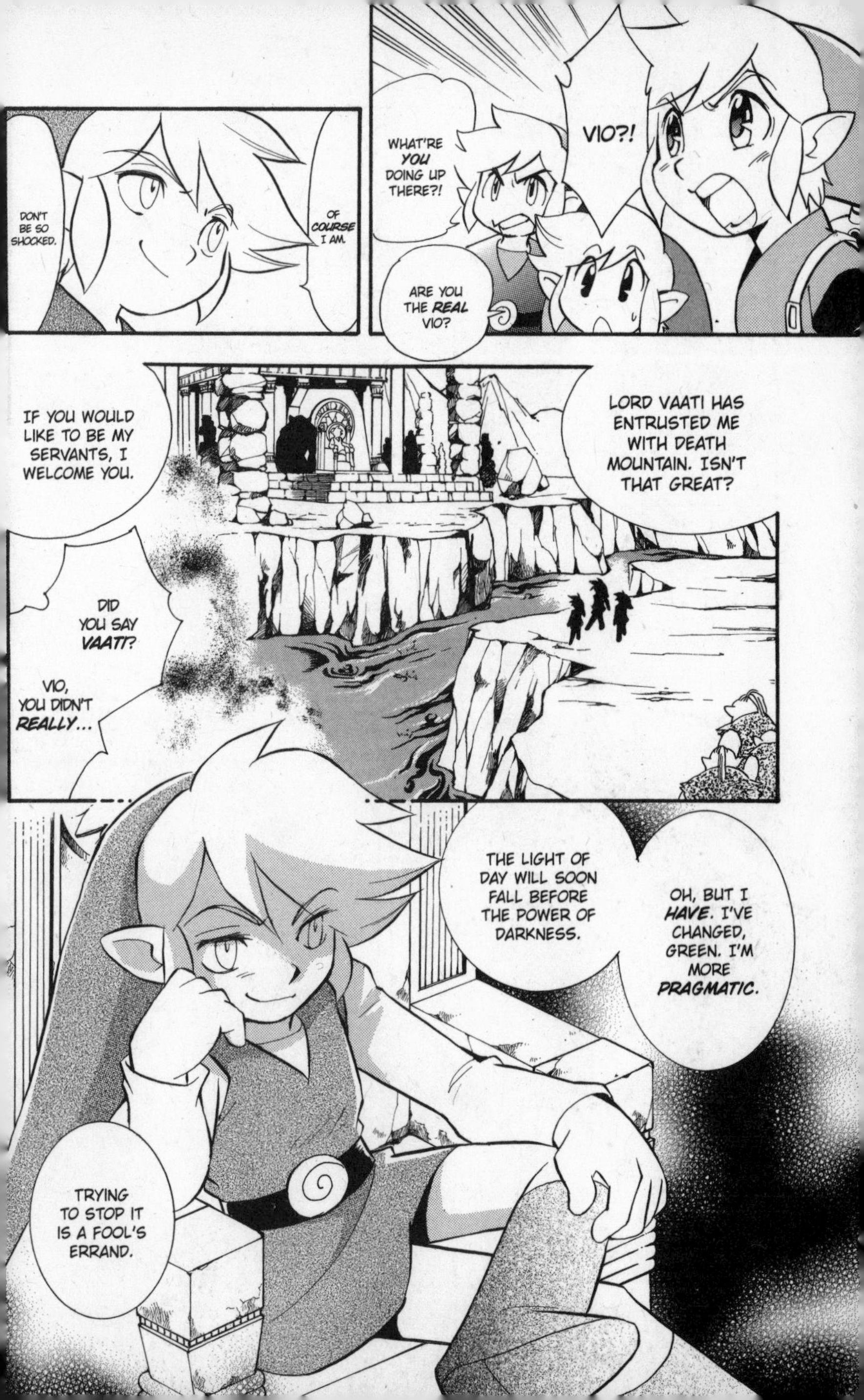
VIO?!
WHAT'RE YOU DOING UP THERE?!
ARE YOU THE REAL VIO?
OF COURSE I AM.
DON'T BE SO SHOCKED.
LORD VAATI HAS ENTRUSTED ME WITH DEATH MOUNTAIN. ISN'T THAT GREAT?
IF YOU WOULD LIKE TO BE MY SERVANTS, I WELCOME YOU.
DID YOU SAY VAATI?
VIO, YOU DIDN'T REALLY...
OH, BUT I HAVE. I'VE CHANGED, GREEN. I'M MORE PRAGMATIC.
THE LIGHT OF DAY WILL SOON FALL BEFORE THE POWER OF DARKNESS.
TRYING TO STOP IT IS A FOOL'S ERRAND.

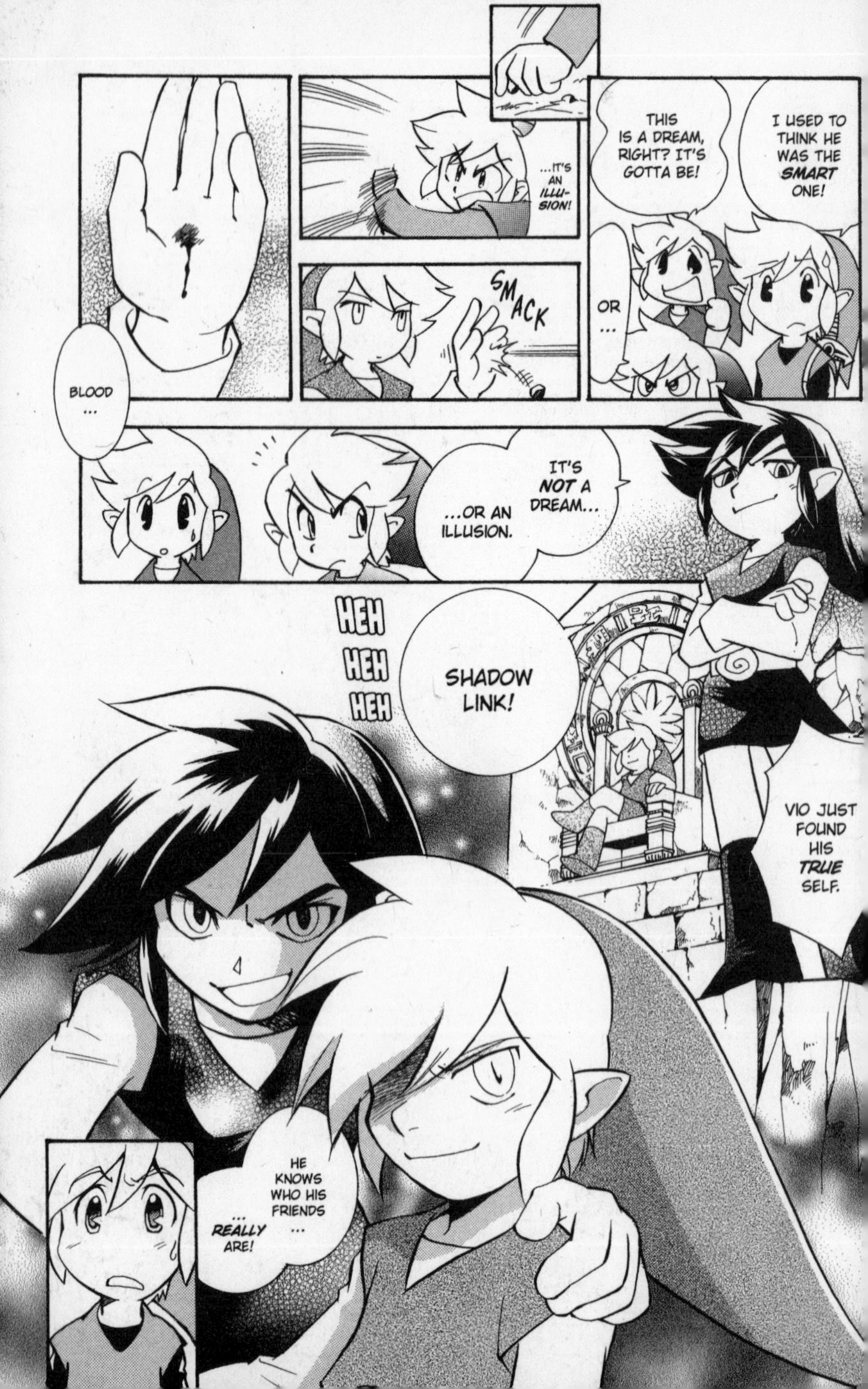

I USED TO THINK HE WAS THE SMART ONE!
THIS IS A DREAM, RIGHT? IT'S GOTTA BE!
OR ...
...IT'S AN ILLUSION!
SMACK
BLOOD ...
IT'S NOT A DREAM...
...OR AN ILLUSION.
SHADOW LINK!
HEH HEH HEH
VIO JUST FOUND HIS TRUE SELF.
HE KNOWS WHO HIS FRIENDS ... REALLY ARE!

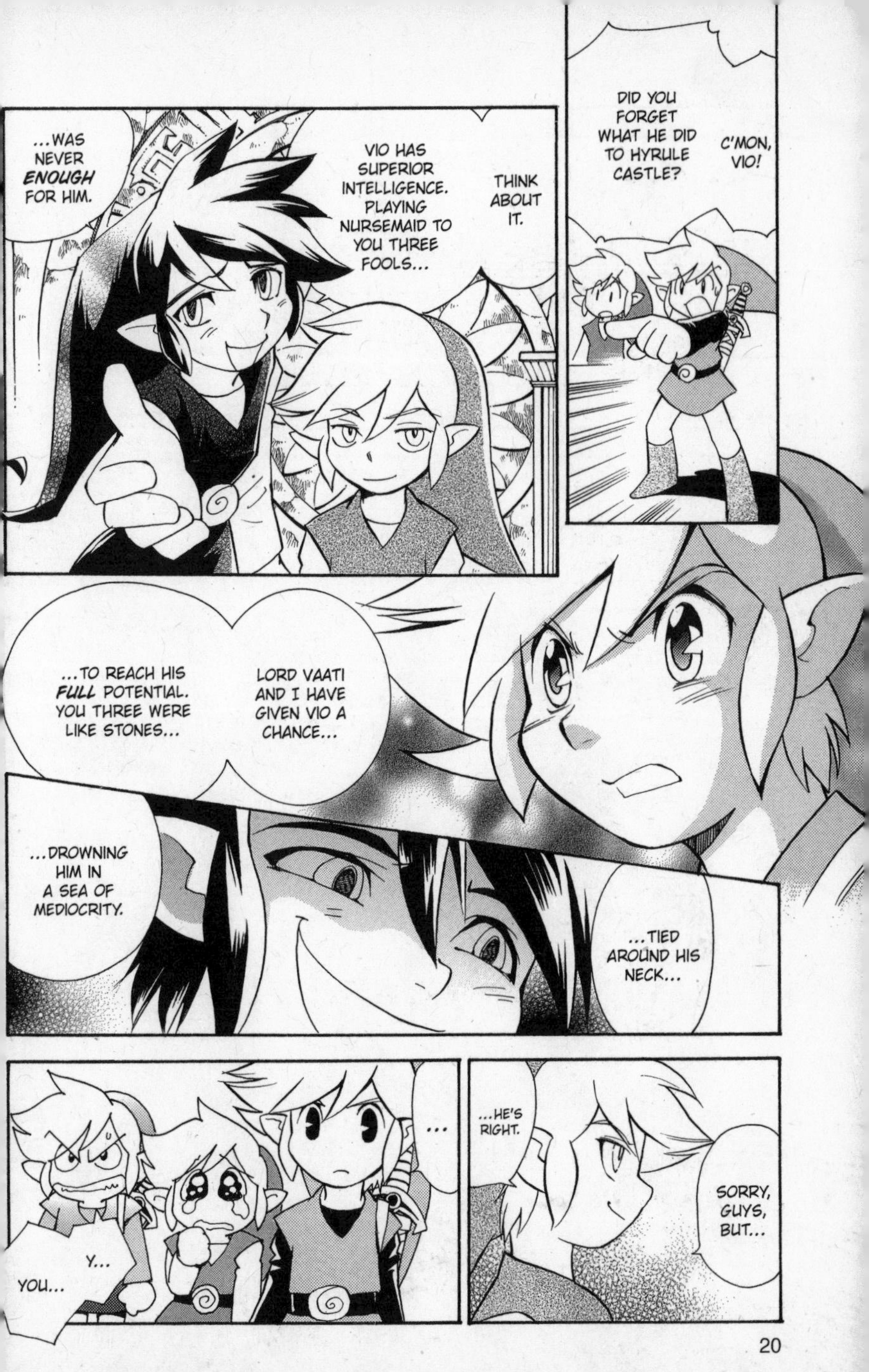
C'MON, VIO!
DID YOU FORGET WHAT HE DID TO HYRULE CASTLE?
THINK ABOUT IT.
VIO HAS SUPERIOR INTELLIGENCE. PLAYING NURSEMAID TO YOU THREE FOOLS...
...WAS NEVER **ENOUGH** FOR HIM.
LORD VAATI AND I HAVE GIVEN VIO A CHANCE...
...TO REACH HIS **FULL** POTENTIAL. YOU THREE WERE LIKE STONES...
...TIED AROUND HIS NECK...
...DROWNING HIM IN A SEA OF MEDIOCRITY.
SORRY, GUYS, BUT...
...HE'S RIGHT.
...
Y...
YOU...

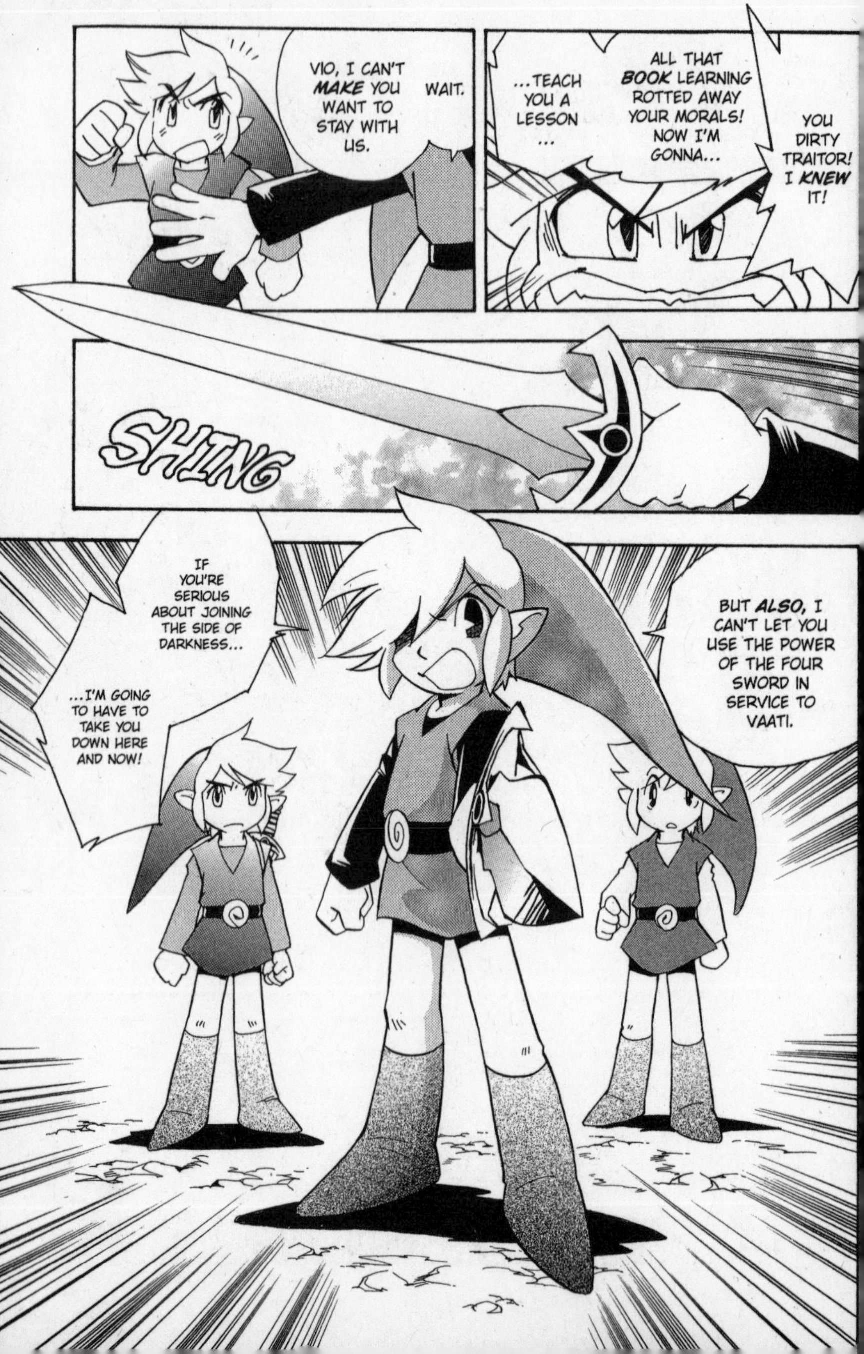
YOU DIRTY TRAITOR! I **KNEW** IT!
ALL THAT **BOOK** LEARNING ROTTED AWAY YOUR MORALS! NOW I'M GONNA...
...TEACH YOU A LESSON ...
WAIT.
VIO, I CAN'T **MAKE** YOU WANT TO STAY WITH US.
SHING
BUT **ALSO,** I CAN'T LET YOU USE THE POWER OF THE FOUR SWORD IN SERVICE TO VAATI.
IF YOU'RE SERIOUS ABOUT JOINING THE SIDE OF DARKNESS...
...I'M GOING TO HAVE TO TAKE YOU DOWN HERE AND NOW!

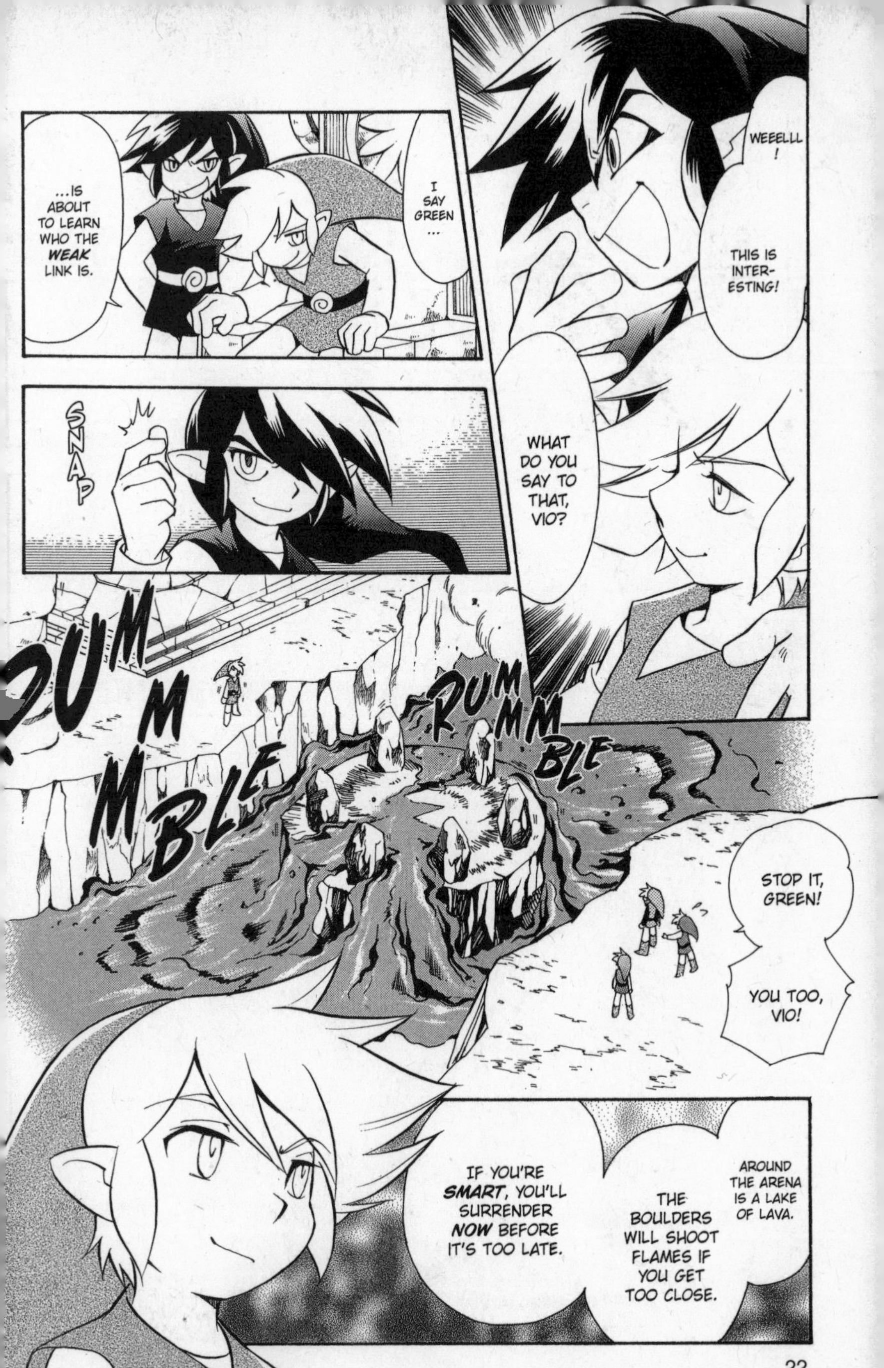
WEEELLL!
THIS IS INTERESTING!
WHAT DO YOU SAY TO THAT, VIO?
I SAY GREEN...
...IS ABOUT TO LEARN WHO THE **WEAK** LINK IS.
SNAP
RUMMMBLE
RUMMMBLE
STOP IT, GREEN!
YOU TOO, VIO!
AROUND THE ARENA IS A LAKE OF LAVA.
THE BOULDERS WILL SHOOT FLAMES IF YOU GET TOO CLOSE.
IF YOU'RE **SMART**, YOU'LL SURRENDER **NOW** BEFORE IT'S TOO LATE.

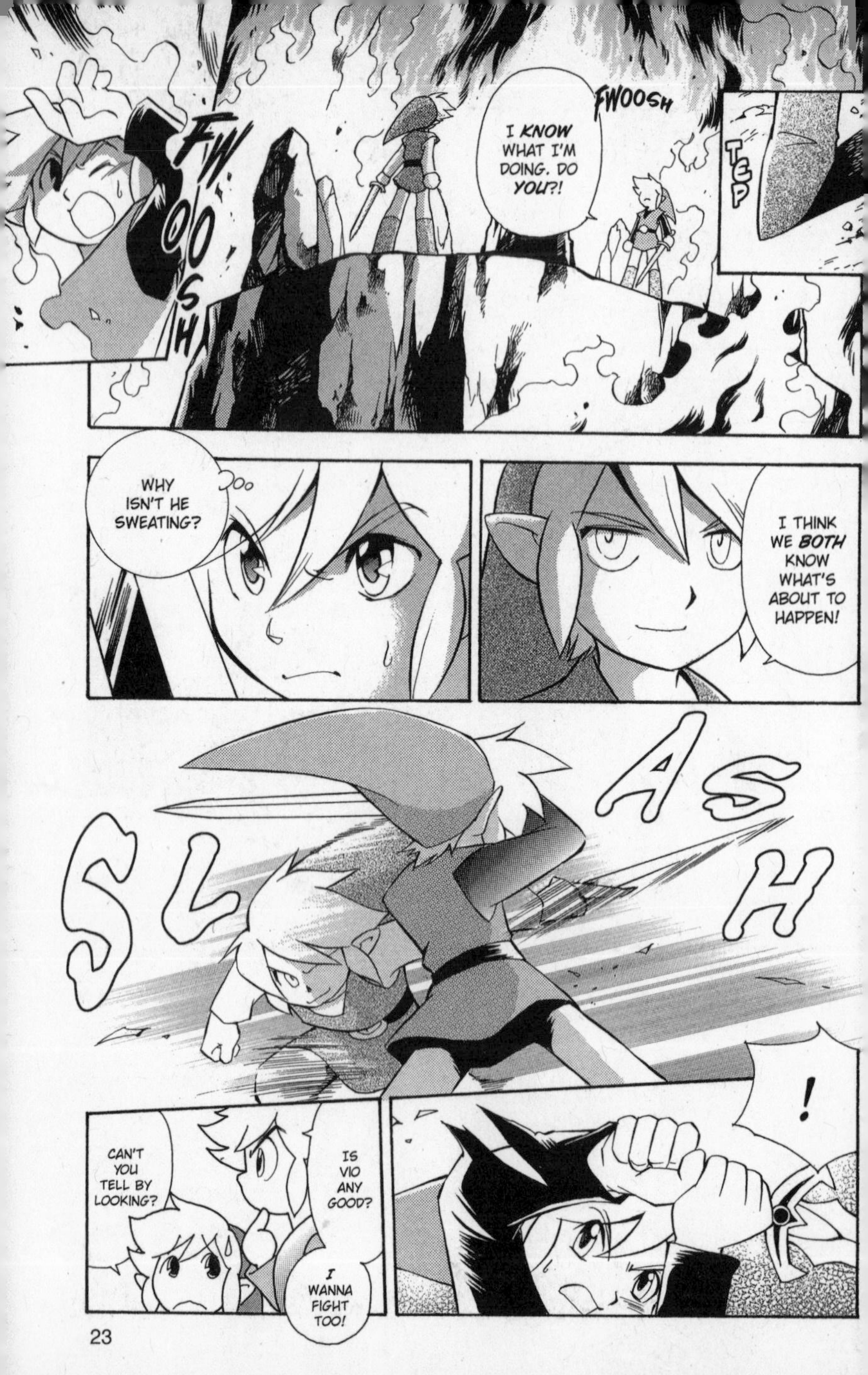
TEP
FWOOSH
I *KNOW* WHAT I'M DOING. DO *YOU*?!
FWOOOSH
I THINK WE *BOTH* KNOW WHAT'S ABOUT TO HAPPEN!
WHY ISN'T HE SWEATING?
SLASH
!
IS VIO ANY GOOD?
CAN'T YOU TELL BY LOOKING?
I WANNA FIGHT TOO!

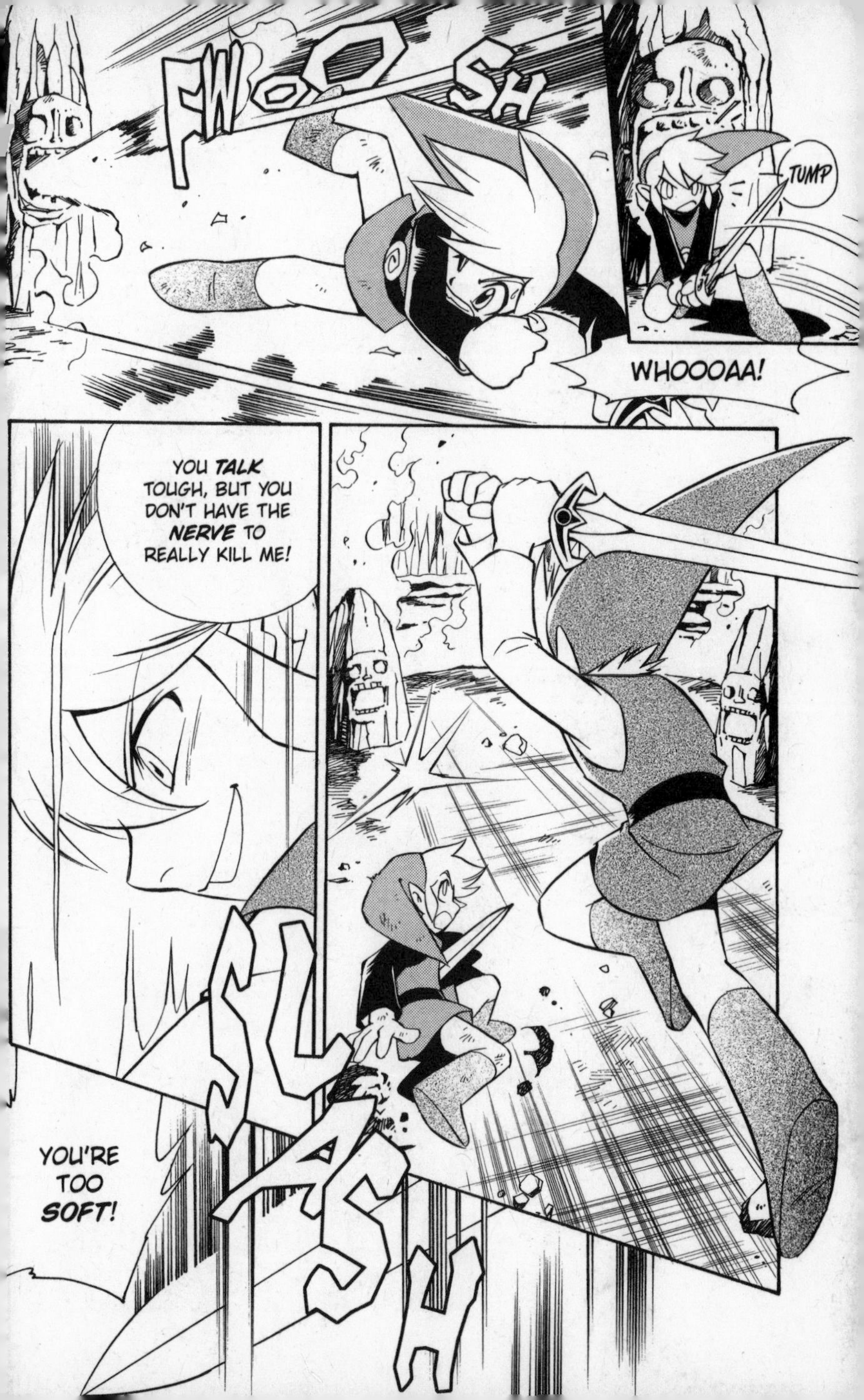

TUMP
FWOOSH
WHOOOAA!
SLASH
YOU TALK TOUGH, BUT YOU DON'T HAVE THE NERVE TO REALLY KILL ME!
YOU'RE TOO SOFT!

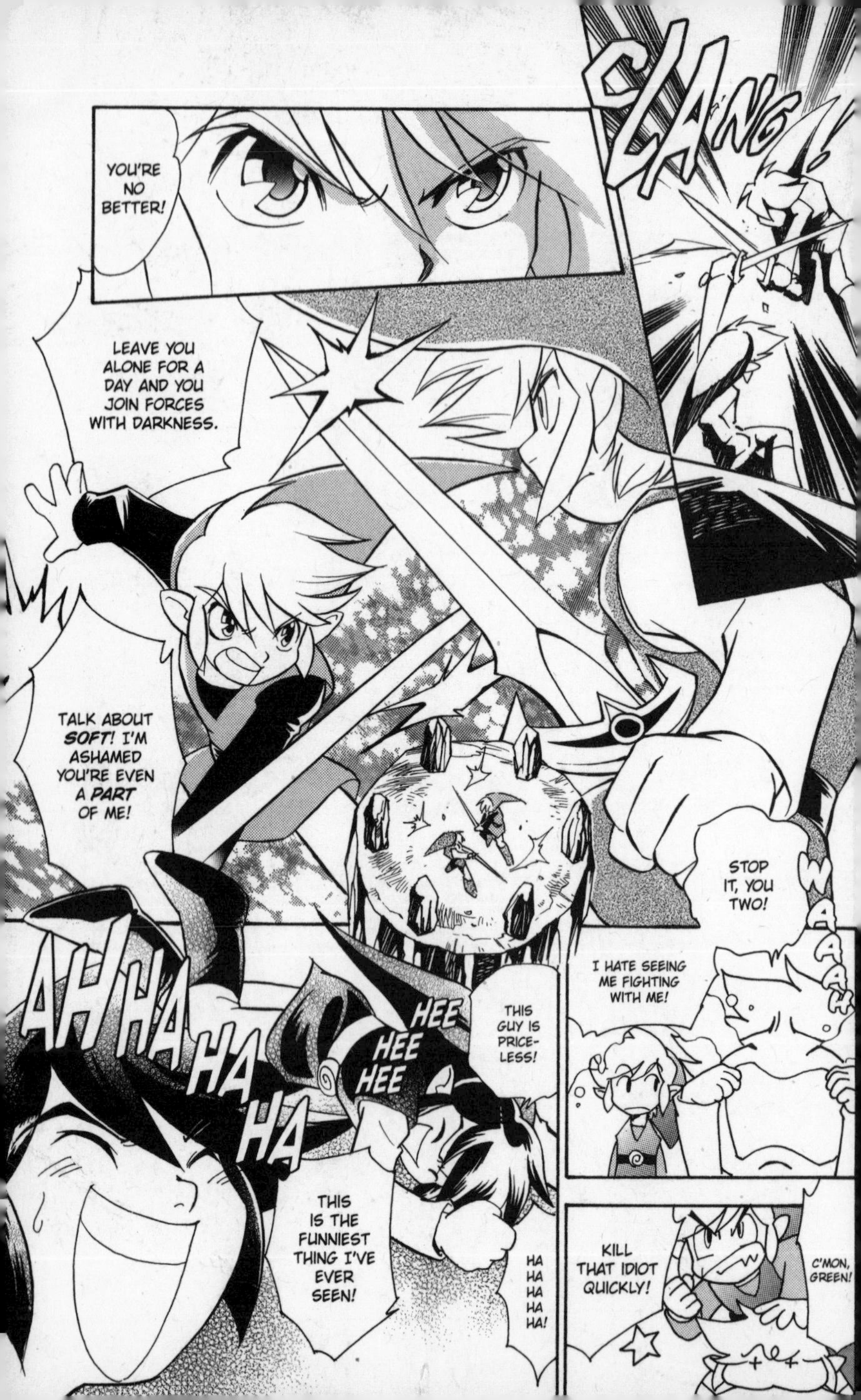
CLANG!
YOU'RE NO BETTER!
LEAVE YOU ALONE FOR A DAY AND YOU JOIN FORCES WITH DARKNESS.
TALK ABOUT **SOFT**! I'M ASHAMED YOU'RE EVEN A ***PART*** OF ME!
STOP IT, YOU TWO!
WAAAAH
I HATE SEEING ME FIGHTING WITH ME!
C'MON, GREEN!
KILL THAT IDIOT QUICKLY!
AH HA HA HA HA
HEE HEE HEE
THIS GUY IS PRICELESS!
THIS IS THE FUNNIEST THING I'VE EVER SEEN!
HA HA HA HA HA!

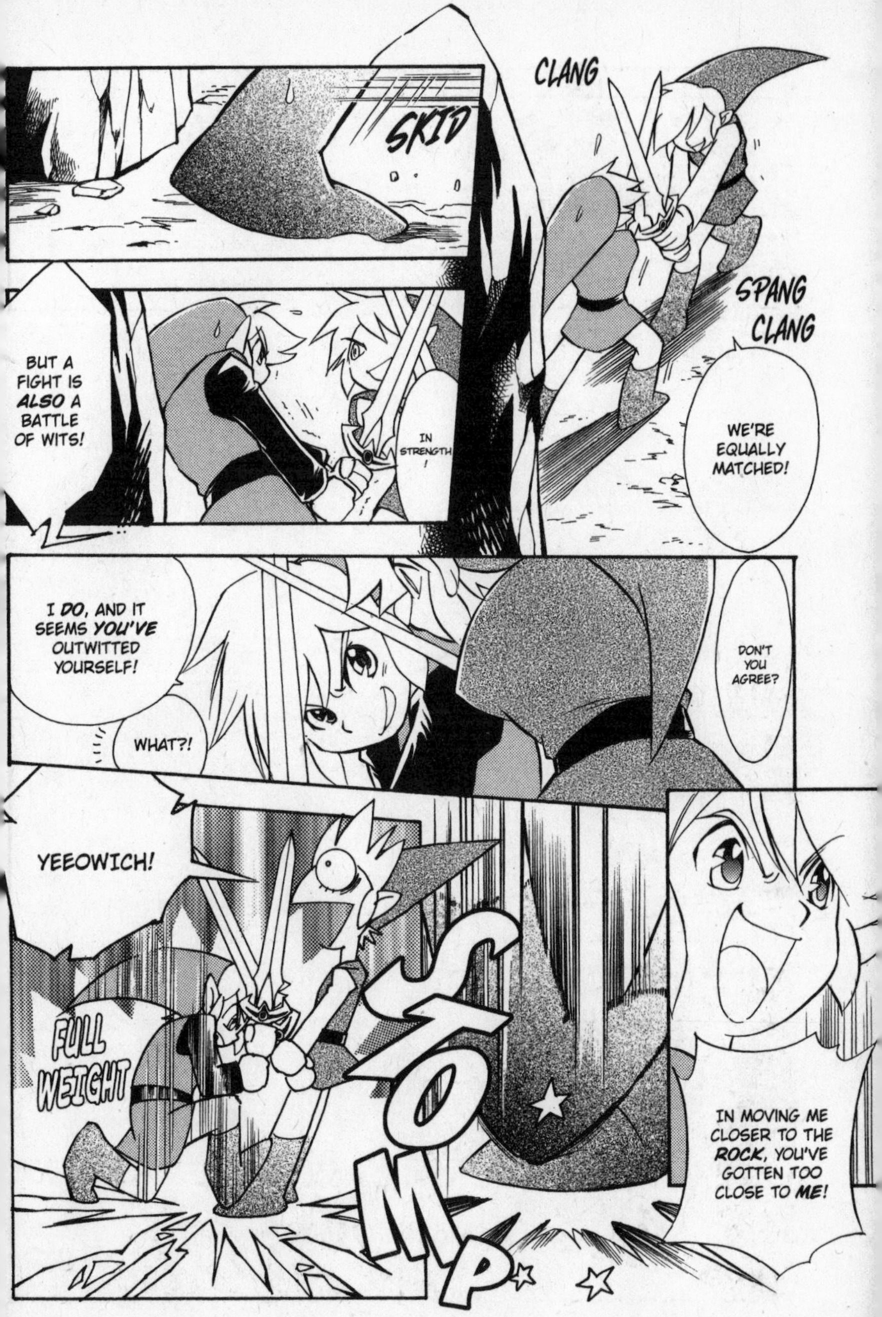
CLANG
SPANG CLANG
WE'RE EQUALLY MATCHED!
SKID
IN STRENGTH!
BUT A FIGHT IS ALSO A BATTLE OF WITS!
DON'T YOU AGREE?
I DO, AND IT SEEMS YOU'VE OUTWITTED YOURSELF!
WHAT?!
IN MOVING ME CLOSER TO THE ROCK, YOU'VE GOTTEN TOO CLOSE TO ME!
STOMP
FULL WEIGHT
YEEOWICH!

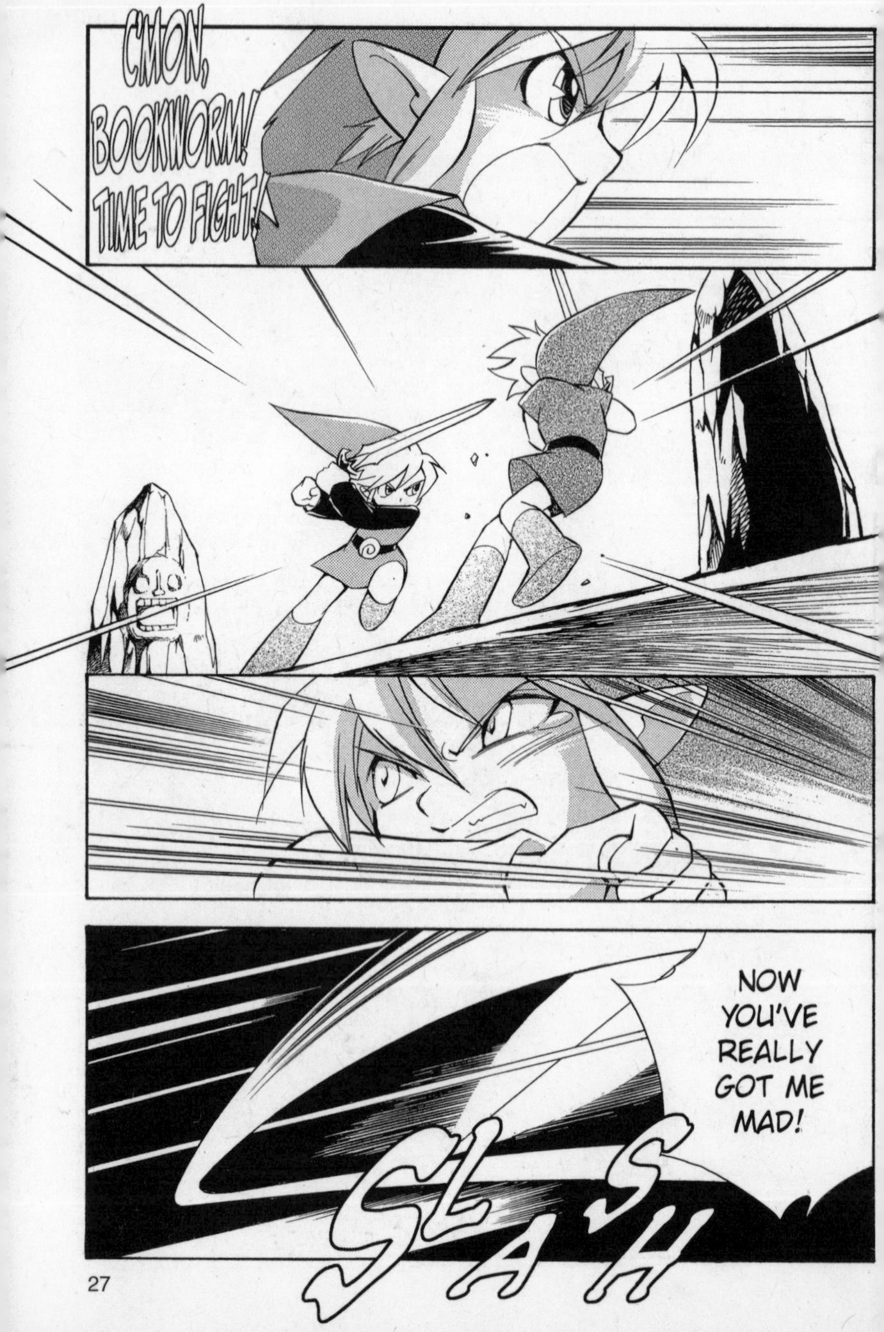
C'MON, BOOKWORM! TIME TO FIGHT!
NOW YOU'VE REALLY GOT ME MAD!
SLASH

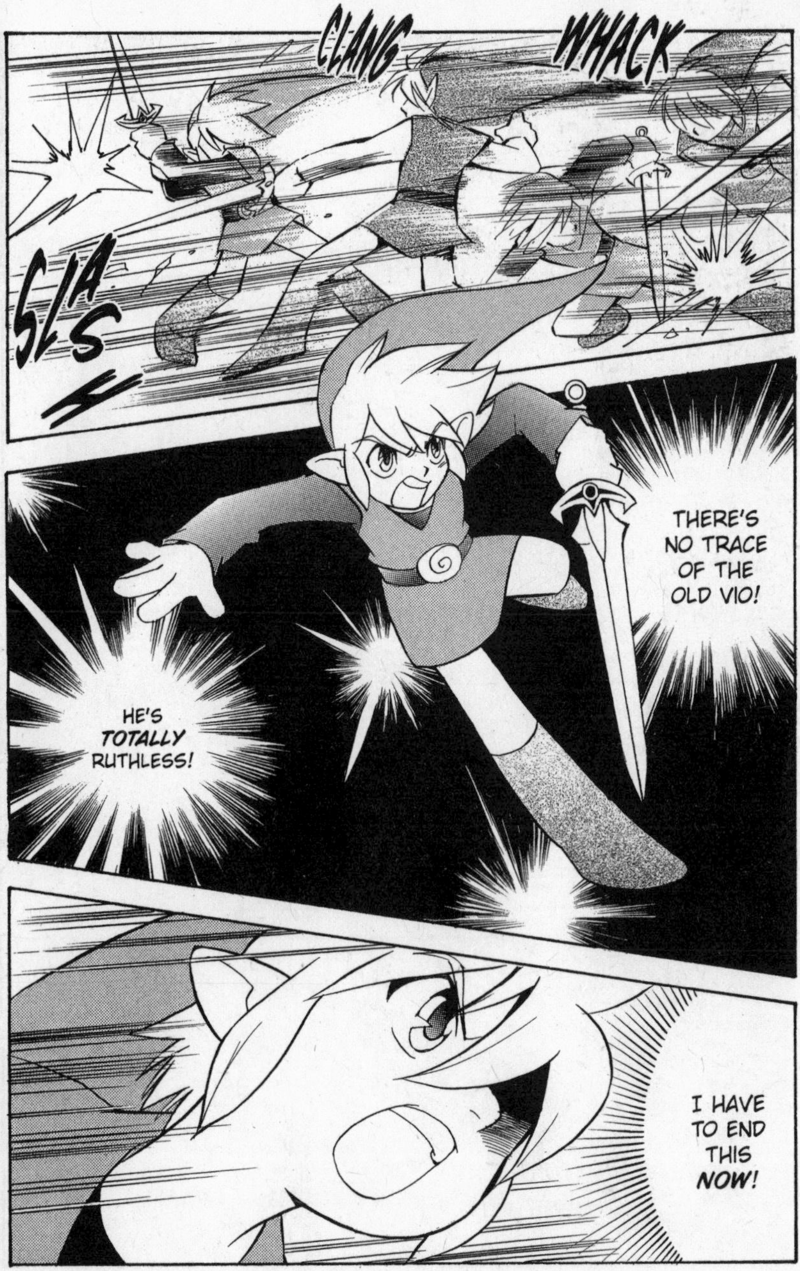
WHACK
CLANG
SLASH
THERE'S NO TRACE OF THE OLD VIO!
HE'S *TOTALLY* RUTHLESS!
I HAVE TO END THIS ***NOW!***

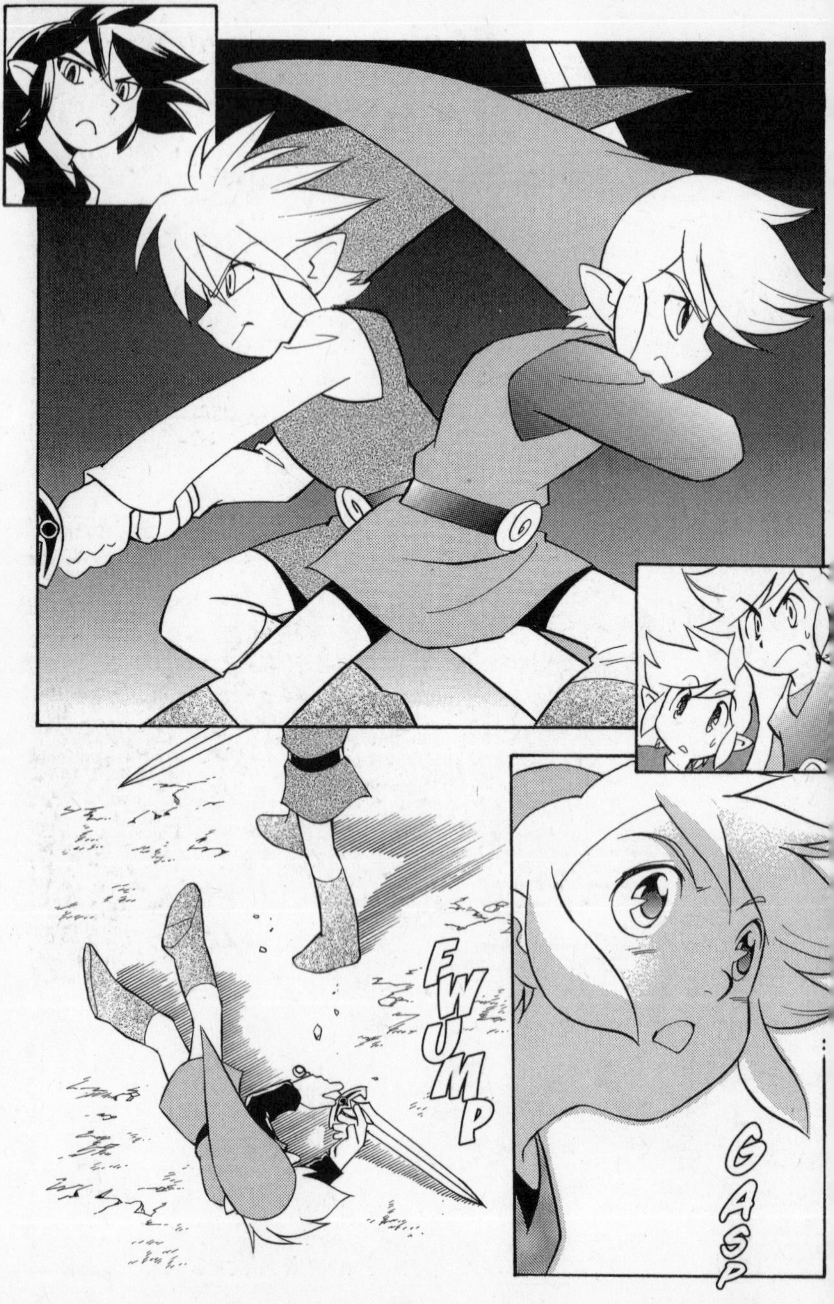
GASP
FWUMP

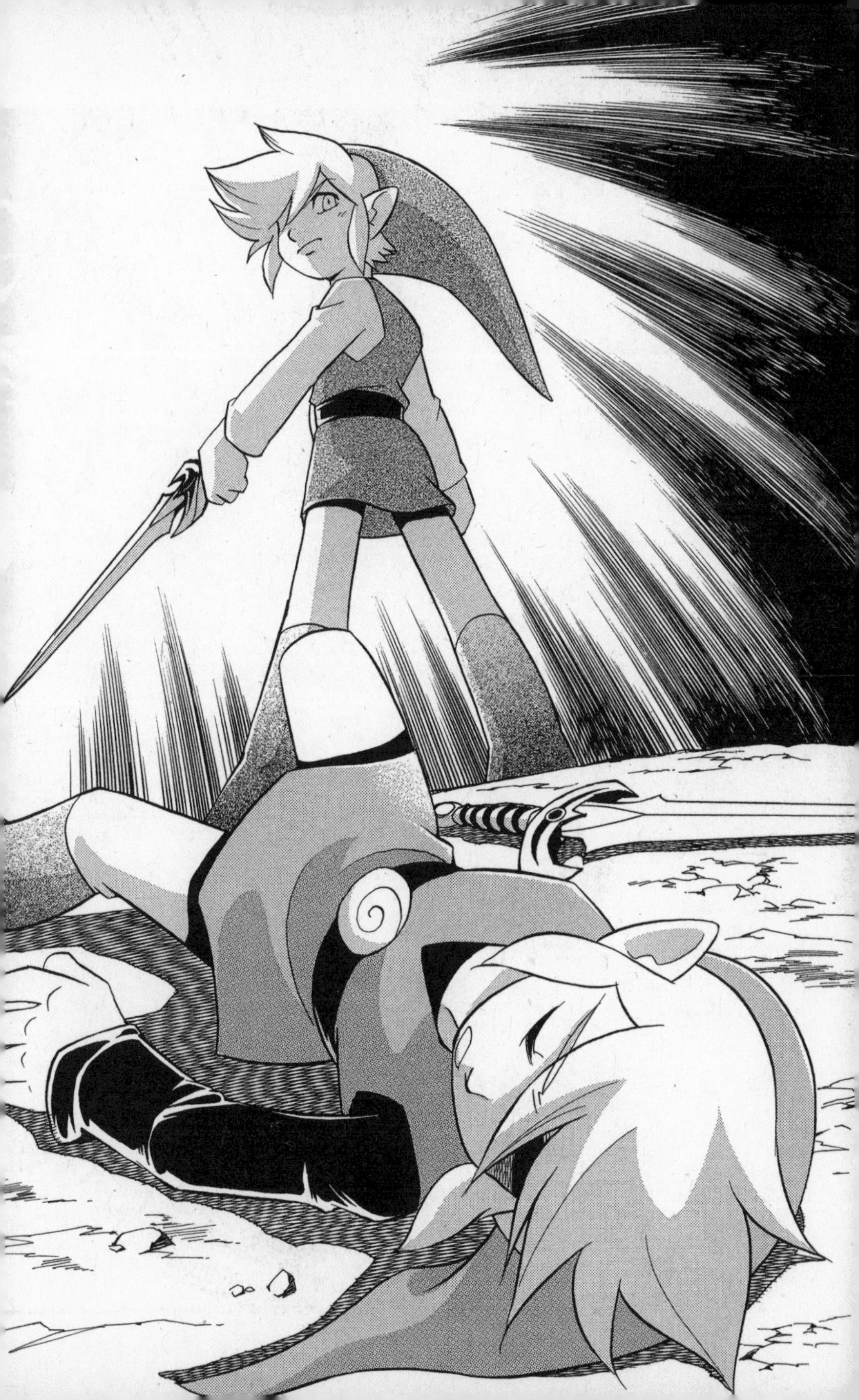

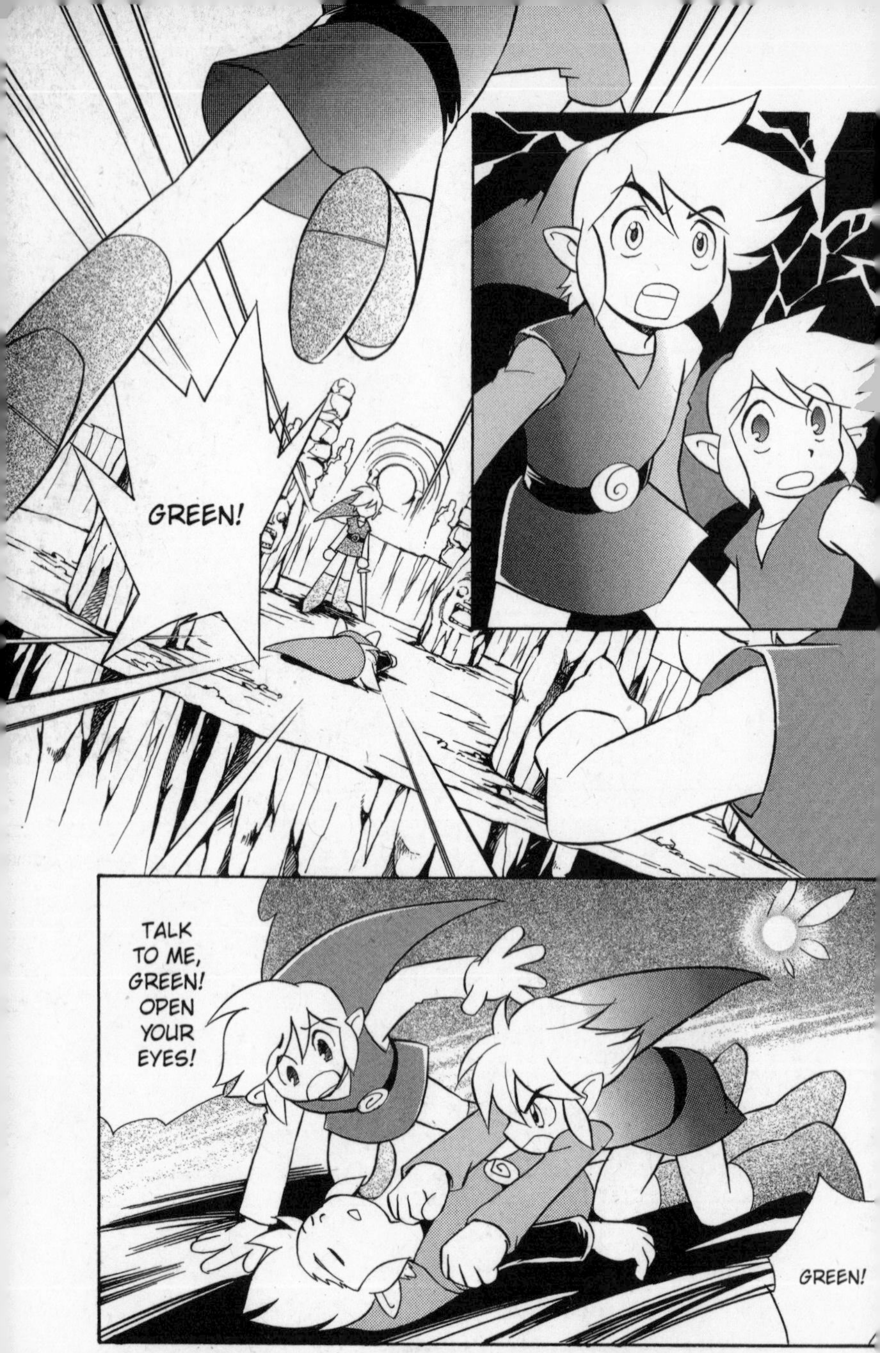
GREEN!
TALK TO ME, GREEN! OPEN YOUR EYES!
GREEN!

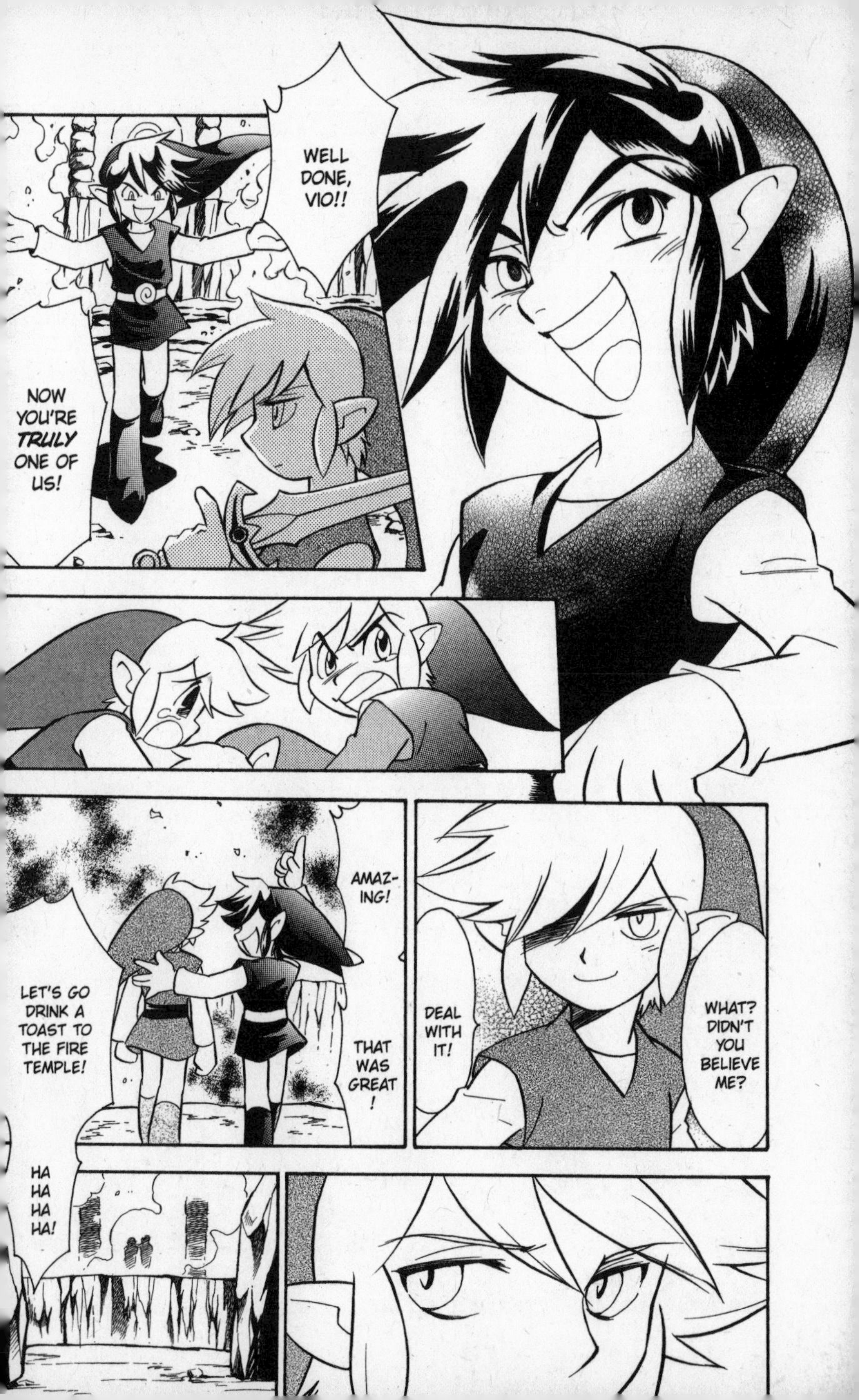
WELL DONE, VIO!!
NOW YOU'RE ***TRULY*** ONE OF US!
WHAT? DIDN'T YOU BELIEVE ME?
DEAL WITH IT!
AMAZ-ING!
THAT WAS GREAT!
LET'S GO DRINK A TOAST TO THE FIRE TEMPLE!
HA HA HA HA!

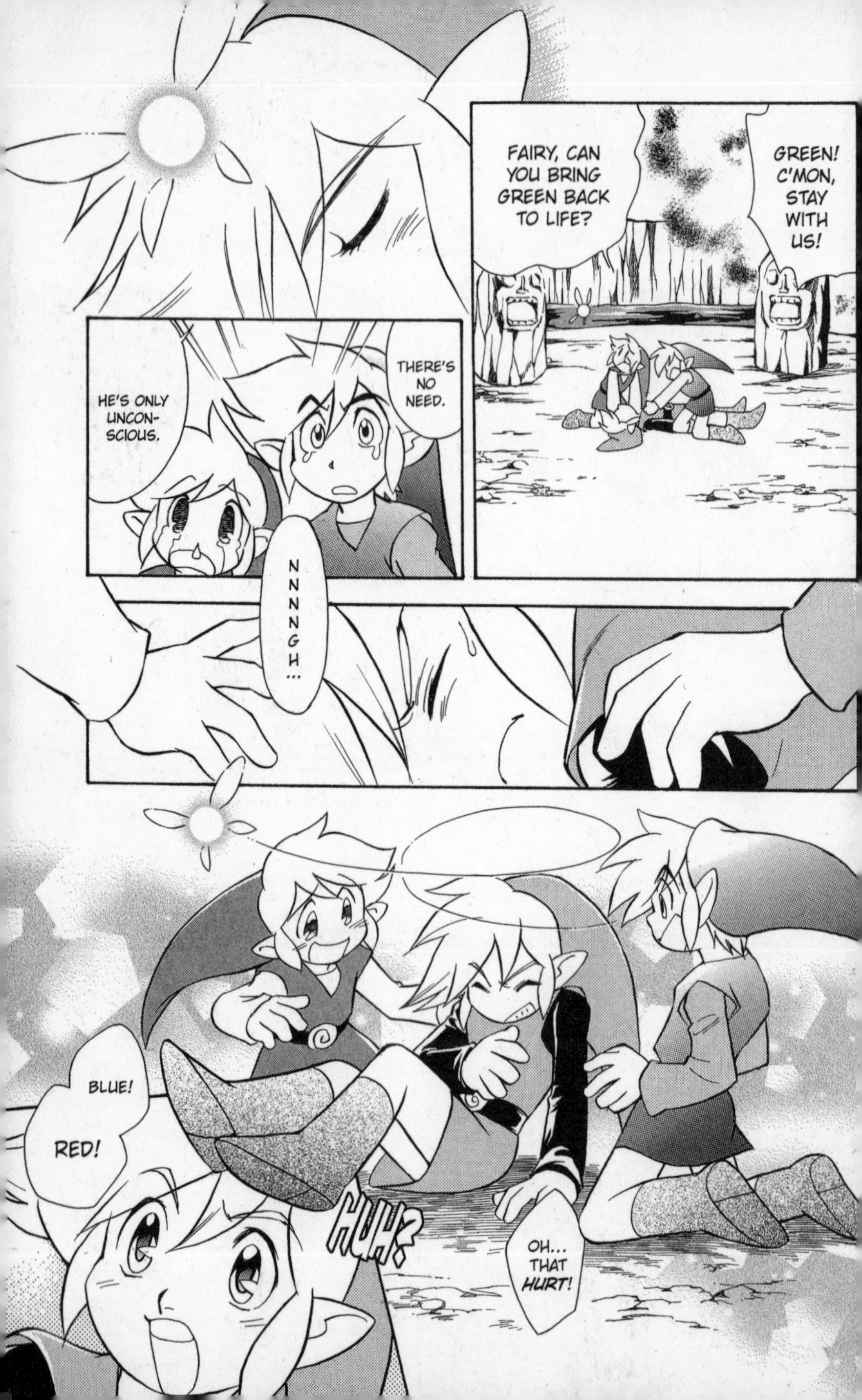
GREEN! C'MON, STAY WITH US!
FAIRY, CAN YOU BRING GREEN BACK TO LIFE?
THERE'S NO NEED.
HE'S ONLY UNCONSCIOUS.
NNNNGH...
OH... THAT *HURT*!
HUH?
BLUE!
RED!

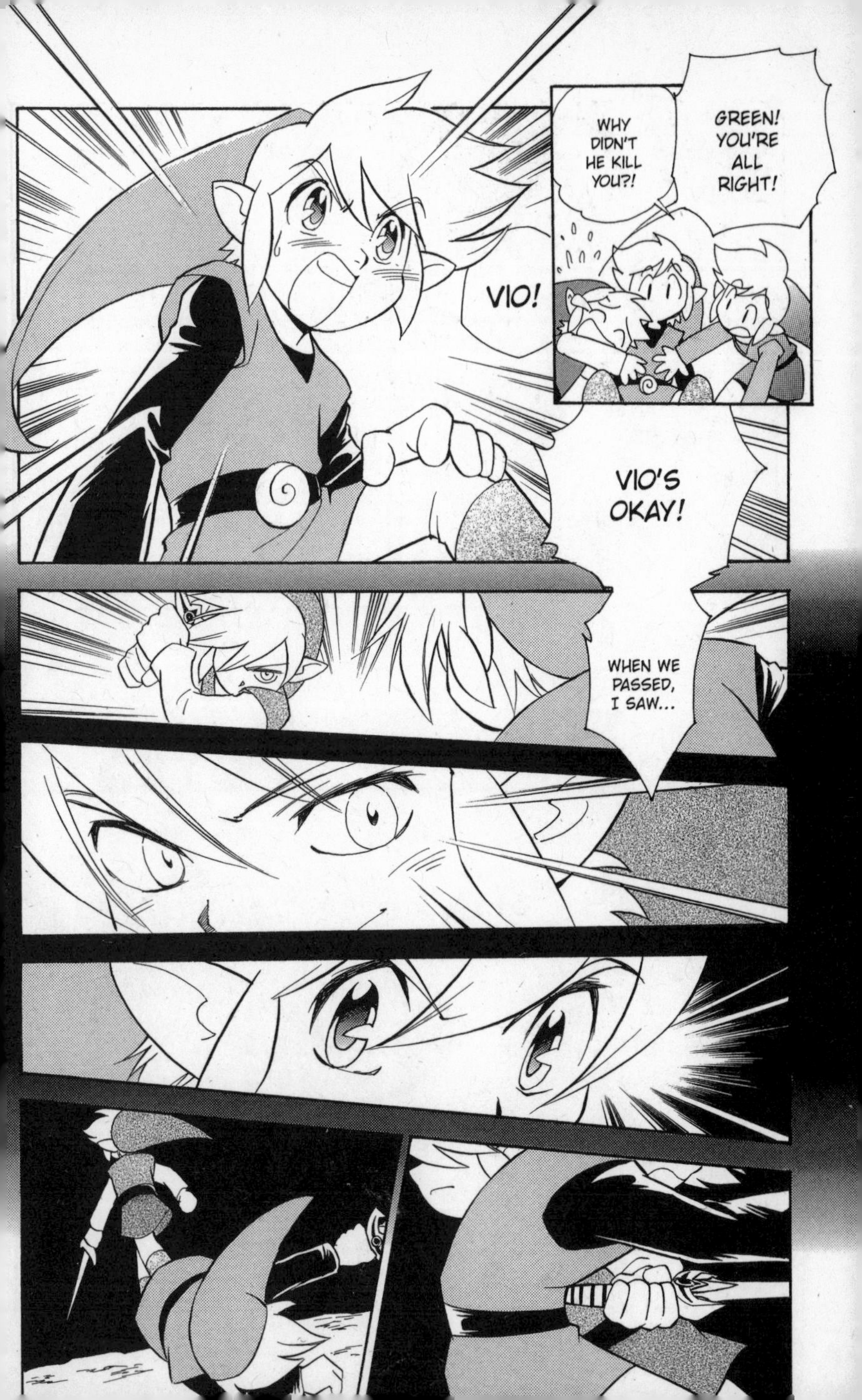
GREEN! YOU'RE ALL RIGHT!
WHY DIDN'T HE KILL YOU?!
VIO!
VIO'S OKAY!
WHEN WE PASSED, I SAW...

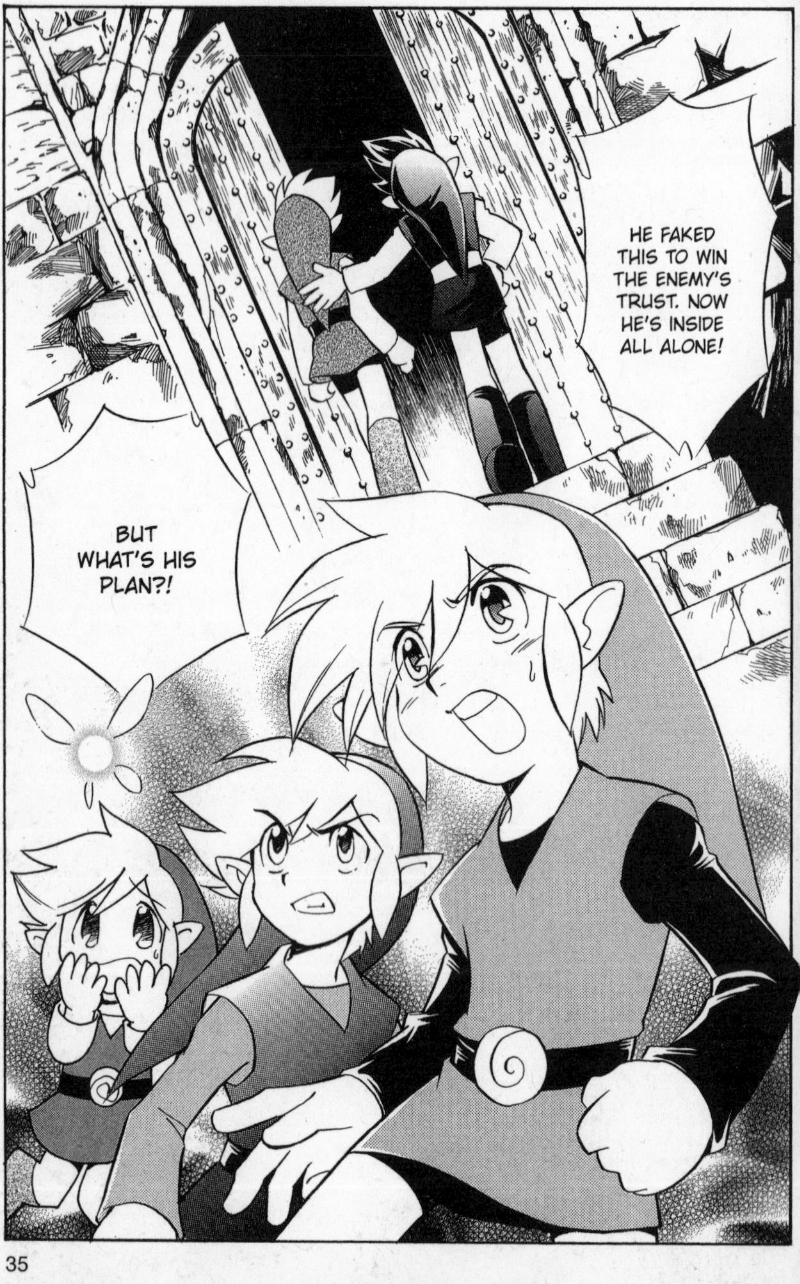
HE FAKED THIS TO WIN THE ENEMY'S TRUST. NOW HE'S INSIDE ALL ALONE!
BUT WHAT'S HIS PLAN?!

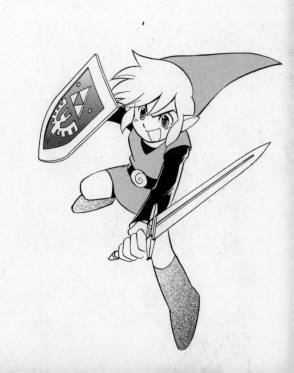

CHAPTER 8 SAD SHADOW LINK

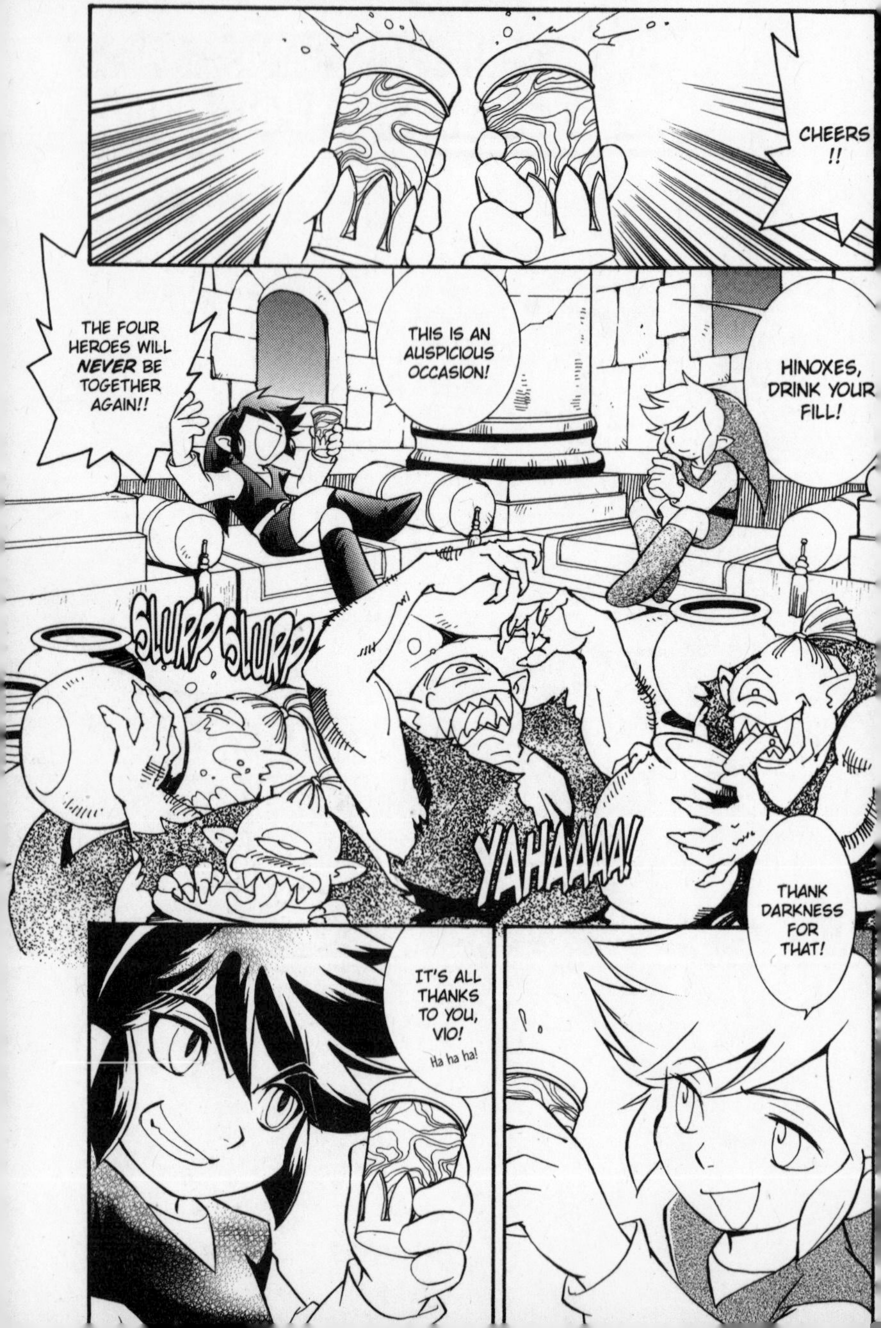
CHEERS!!
HINOXES, DRINK YOUR FILL!
THIS IS AN AUSPICIOUS OCCASION!
THE FOUR HEROES WILL *NEVER* BE TOGETHER AGAIN!!
SLURP SLURP
YAHAAAA!
THANK DARKNESS FOR THAT!
IT'S ALL THANKS TO YOU, VIO!
Ha ha ha!

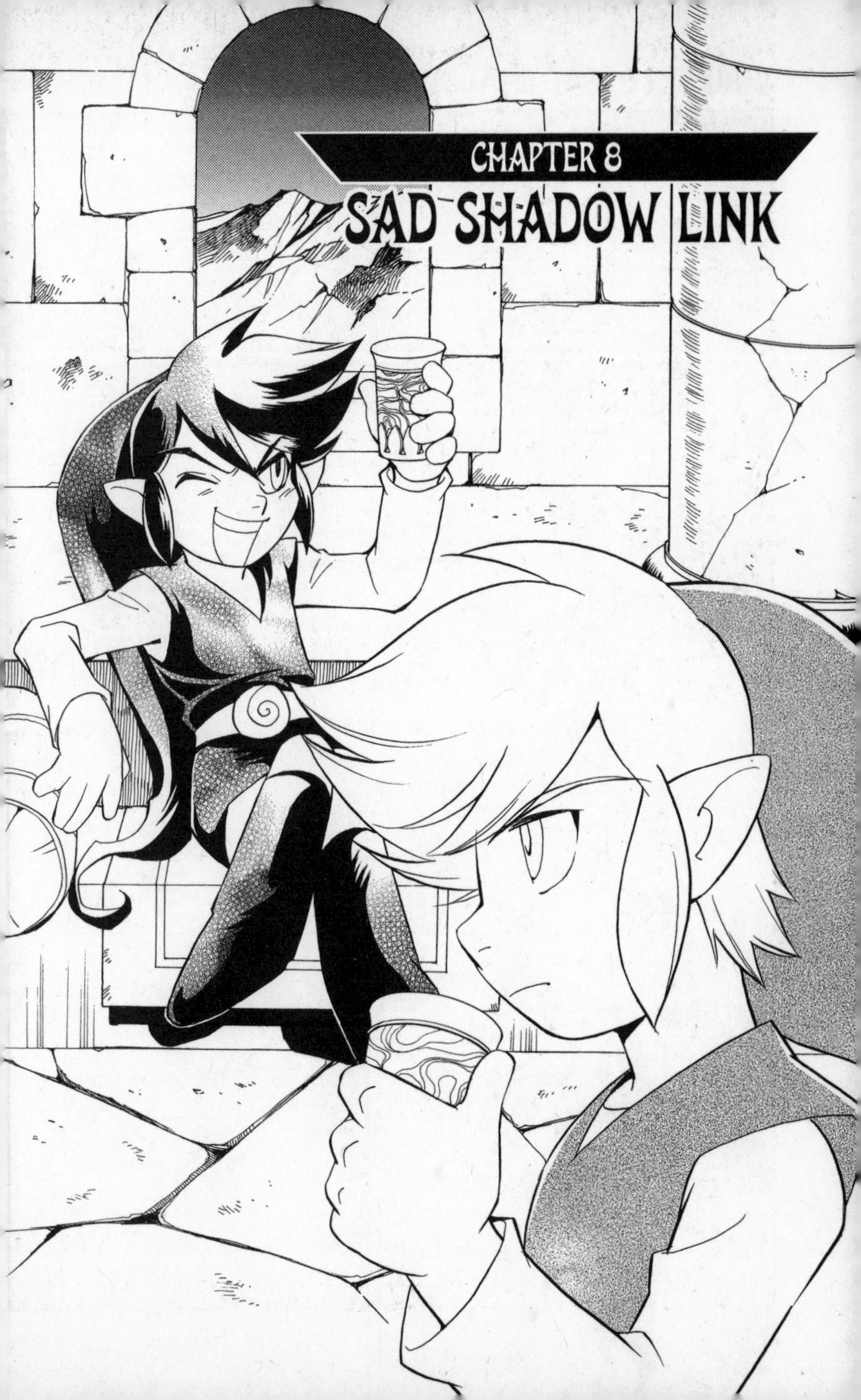
CHAPTER 8
SAD SHADOW LINK

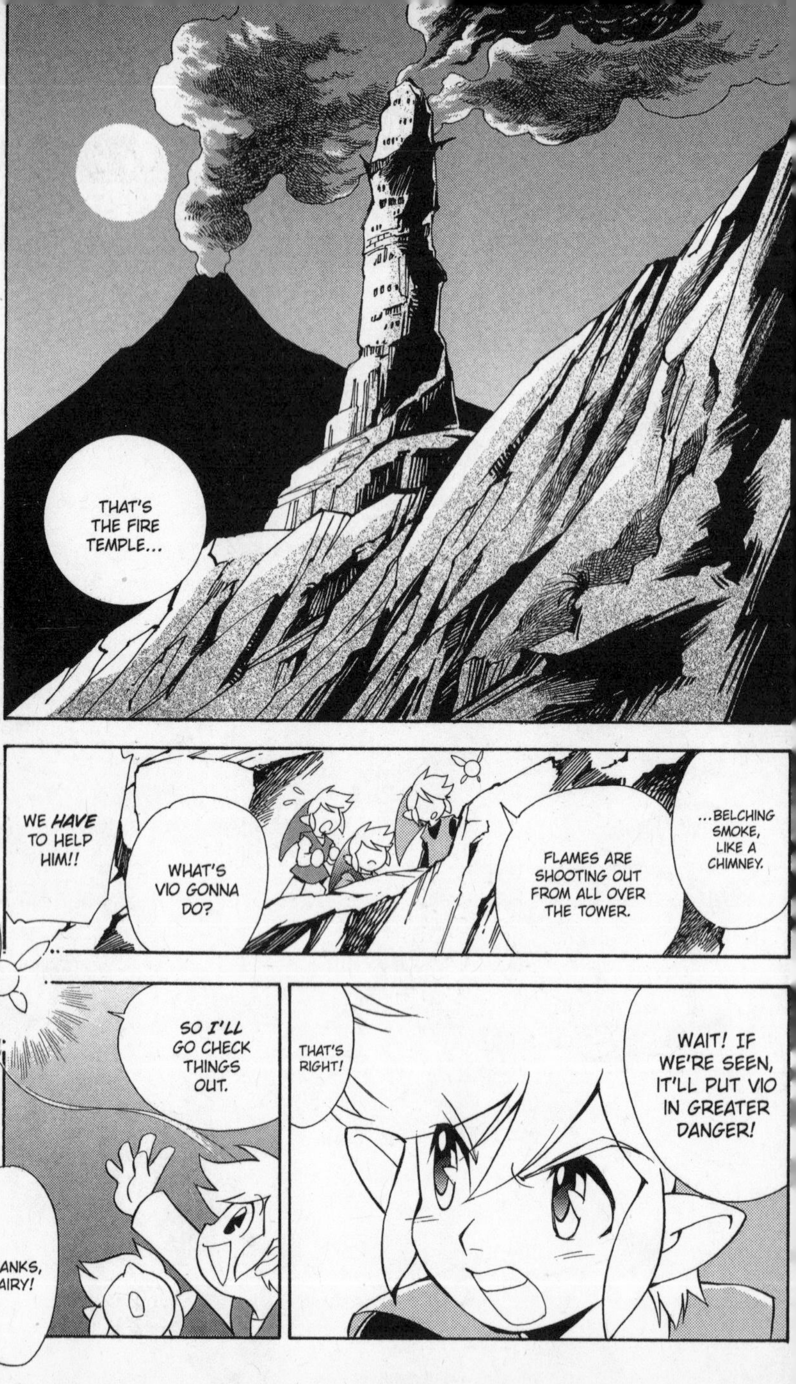
THAT'S THE FIRE TEMPLE...
...BELCHING SMOKE, LIKE A CHIMNEY.
FLAMES ARE SHOOTING OUT FROM ALL OVER THE TOWER.
WHAT'S VIO GONNA DO?
WE *HAVE* TO HELP HIM!!
WAIT! IF WE'RE SEEN, IT'LL PUT VIO IN GREATER DANGER!
THAT'S RIGHT!
SO *I'LL* GO CHECK THINGS OUT.
THANKS, FAIRY!

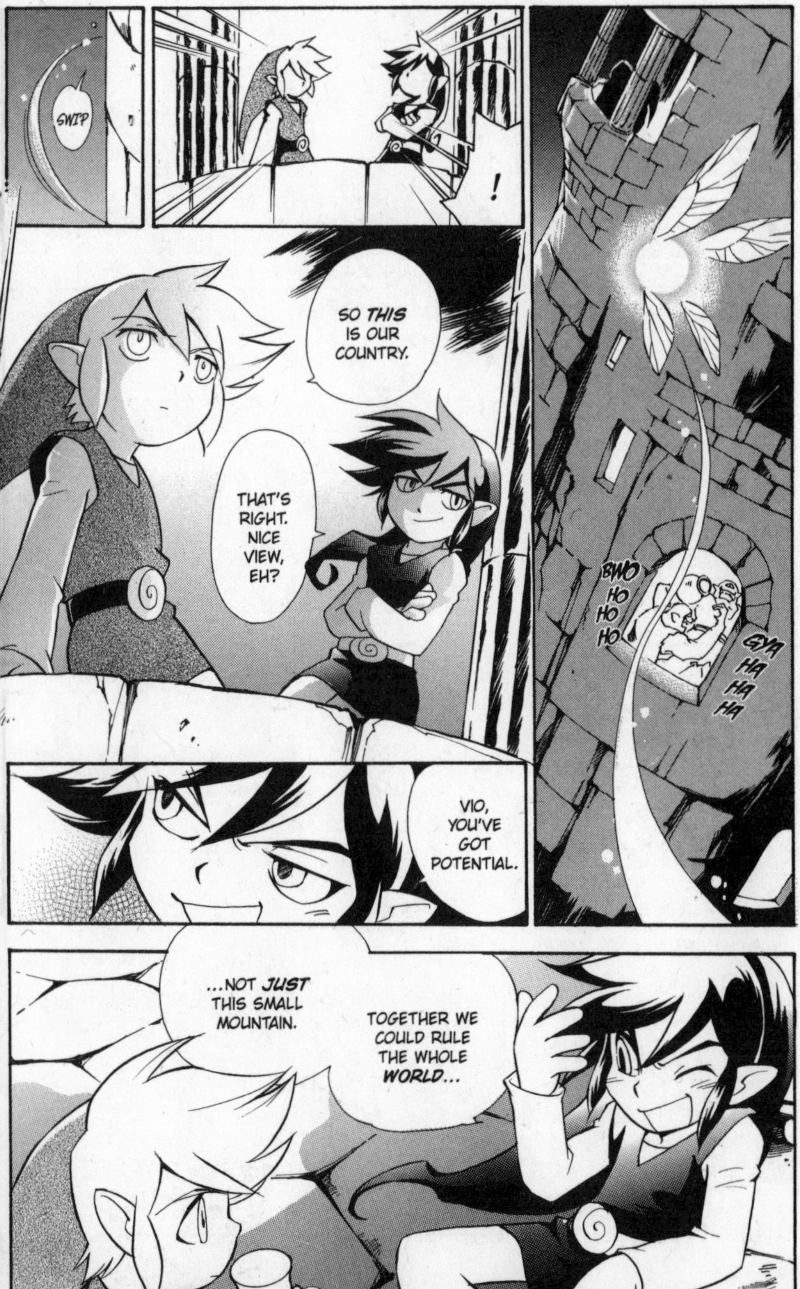
BWO HO HO HO
GYA HA HA HA
!
SWIP
SO *THIS* IS OUR COUNTRY.
THAT'S RIGHT. NICE VIEW, EH?
VIO, YOU'VE GOT POTENTIAL.
TOGETHER WE COULD RULE THE WHOLE ***WORLD***...
...NOT ***JUST*** THIS SMALL MOUNTAIN.

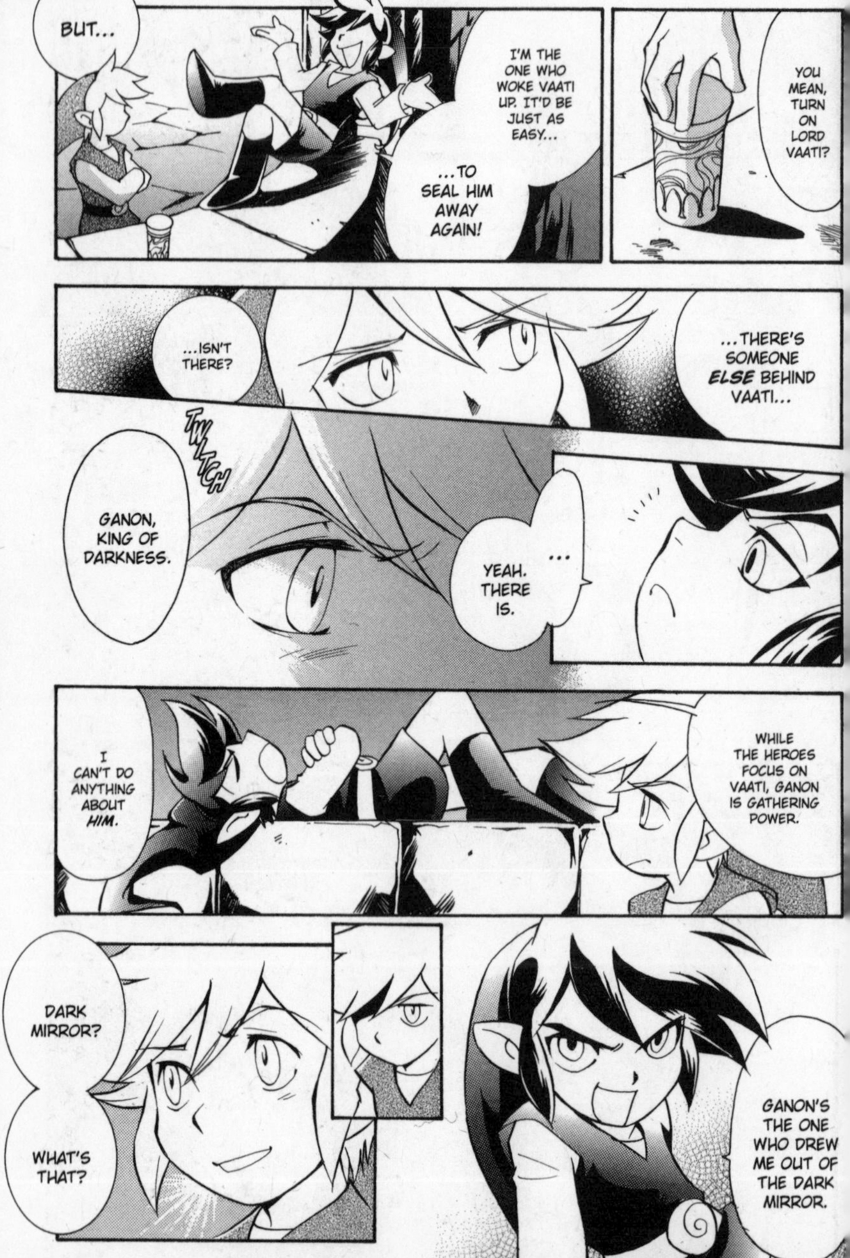
YOU MEAN, TURN ON LORD VAATI?
I'M THE ONE WHO WOKE VAATI UP. IT'D BE JUST AS EASY...
...TO SEAL HIM AWAY AGAIN!
BUT...
...THERE'S SOMEONE ELSE BEHIND VAATI...
...ISN'T THERE?
...
YEAH. THERE IS.
TWITCH
GANON, KING OF DARKNESS.
WHILE THE HEROES FOCUS ON VAATI, GANON IS GATHERING POWER.
I CAN'T DO ANYTHING ABOUT HIM.
GANON'S THE ONE WHO DREW ME OUT OF THE DARK MIRROR.
DARK MIRROR?
WHAT'S THAT?

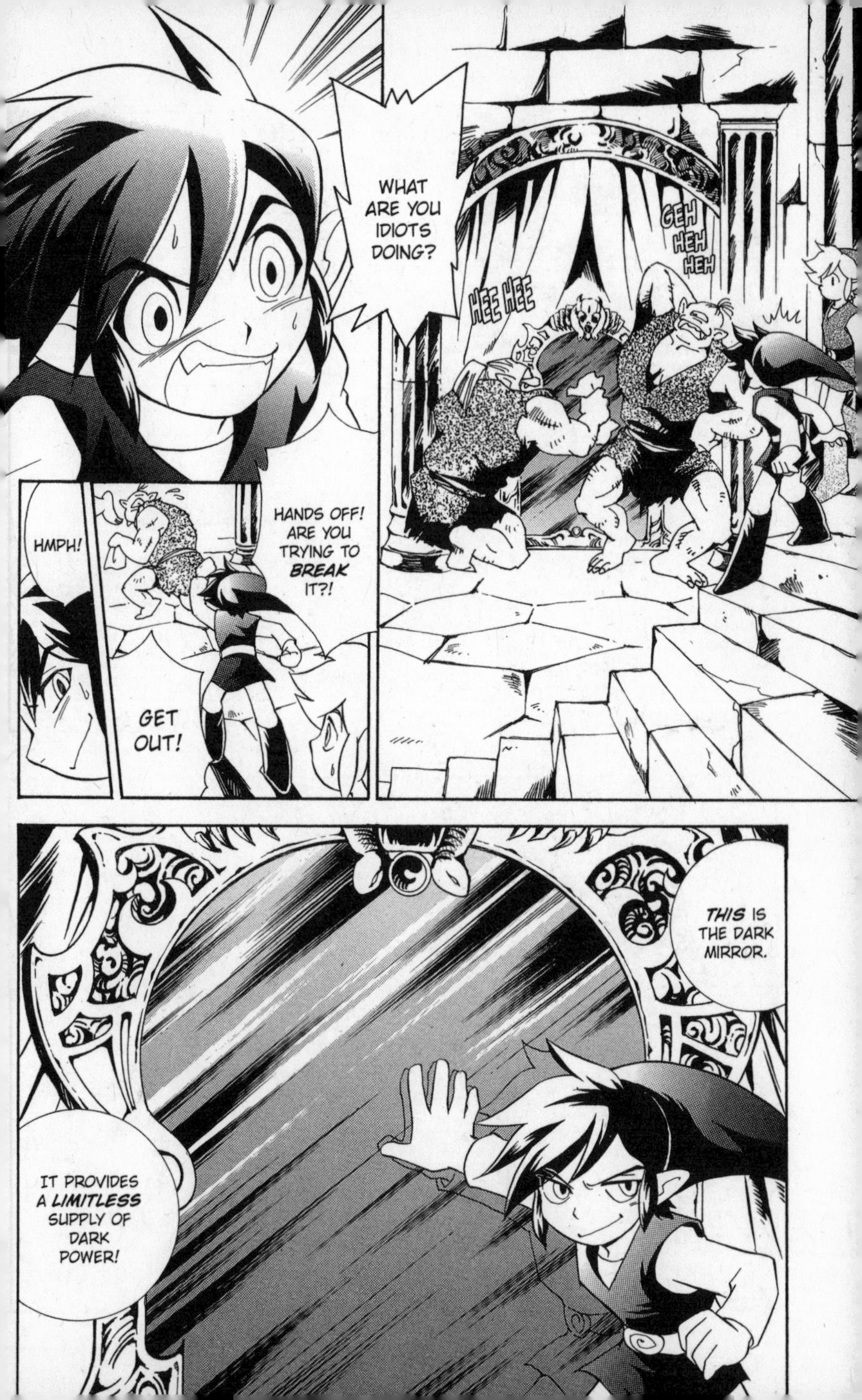
GEH HEH HEH
HEE HEE
WHAT ARE YOU IDIOTS DOING?
HANDS OFF! ARE YOU TRYING TO ***BREAK*** IT?!
GET OUT!
HMPH!
THIS IS THE DARK MIRROR.
IT PROVIDES A ***LIMITLESS*** SUPPLY OF DARK POWER!

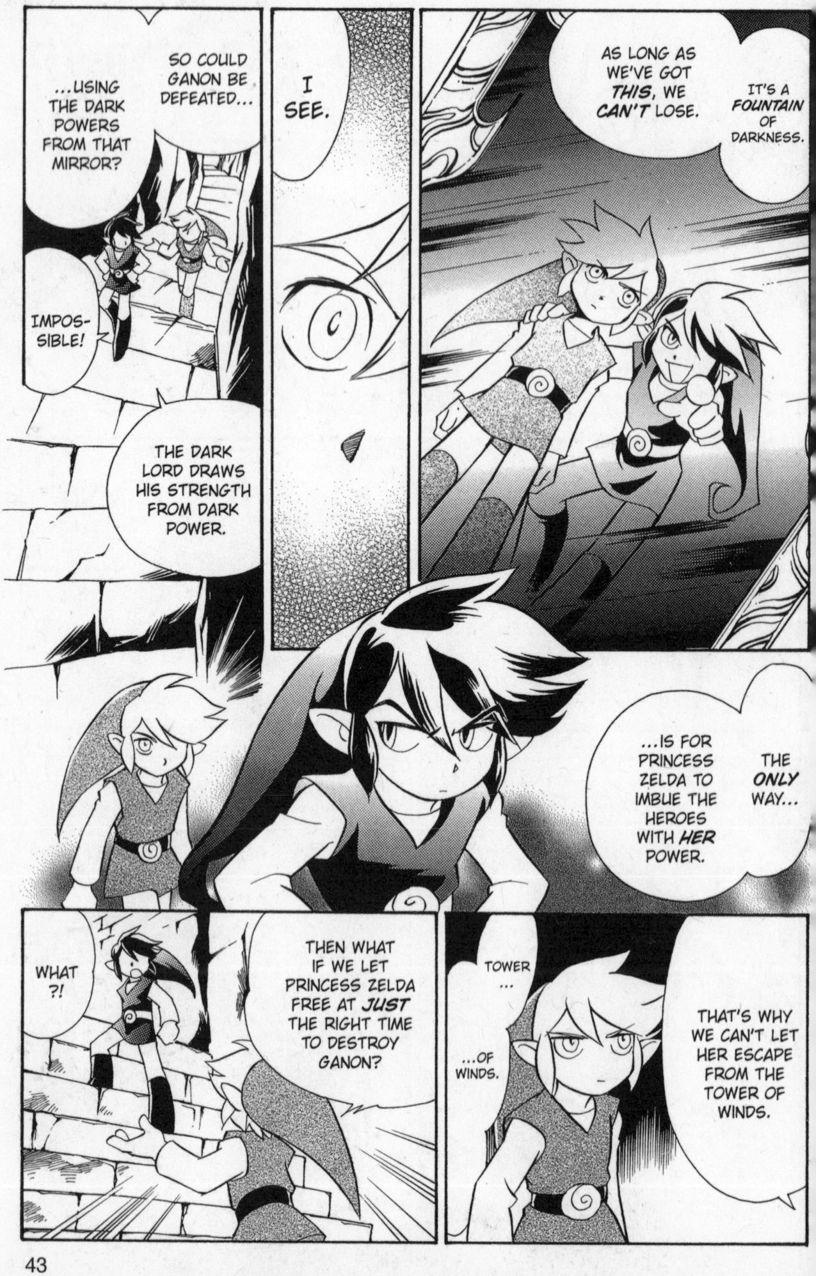
IT'S A FOUNTAIN OF DARKNESS.
AS LONG AS WE'VE GOT THIS, WE CAN'T LOSE.
I SEE.
SO COULD GANON BE DEFEATED...
...USING THE DARK POWERS FROM THAT MIRROR?
IMPOSSIBLE!
THE DARK LORD DRAWS HIS STRENGTH FROM DARK POWER.
THE ONLY WAY...
...IS FOR PRINCESS ZELDA TO IMBUE THE HEROES WITH HER POWER.
THAT'S WHY WE CAN'T LET HER ESCAPE FROM THE TOWER OF WINDS.
TOWER ...
...OF WINDS.
THEN WHAT IF WE LET PRINCESS ZELDA FREE AT JUST THE RIGHT TIME TO DESTROY GANON?
WHAT?!

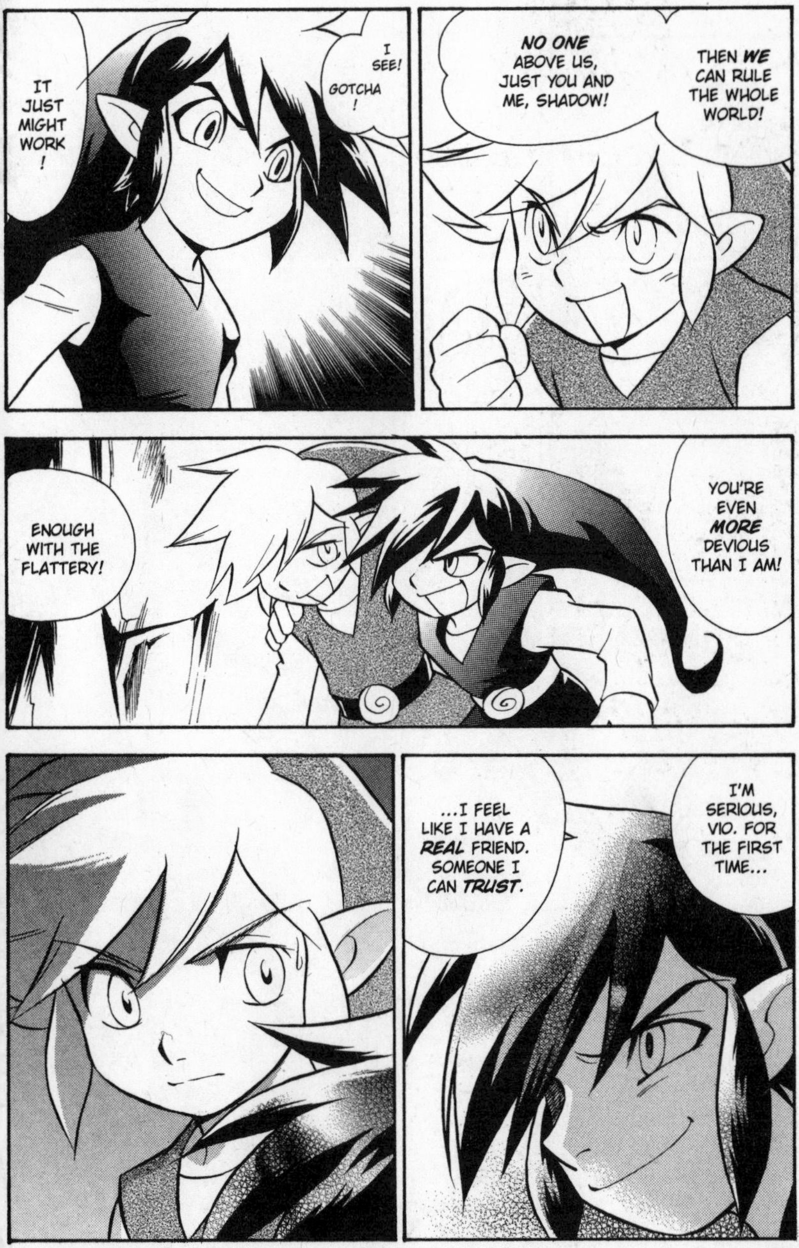
THEN WE CAN RULE THE WHOLE WORLD!
NO ONE ABOVE US, JUST YOU AND ME, SHADOW!
I SEE!
GOTCHA!
IT JUST MIGHT WORK!
YOU'RE EVEN MORE DEVIOUS THAN I AM!
ENOUGH WITH THE FLATTERY!
I'M SERIOUS, VIO. FOR THE FIRST TIME...
...I FEEL LIKE I HAVE A REAL FRIEND. SOMEONE I CAN TRUST.

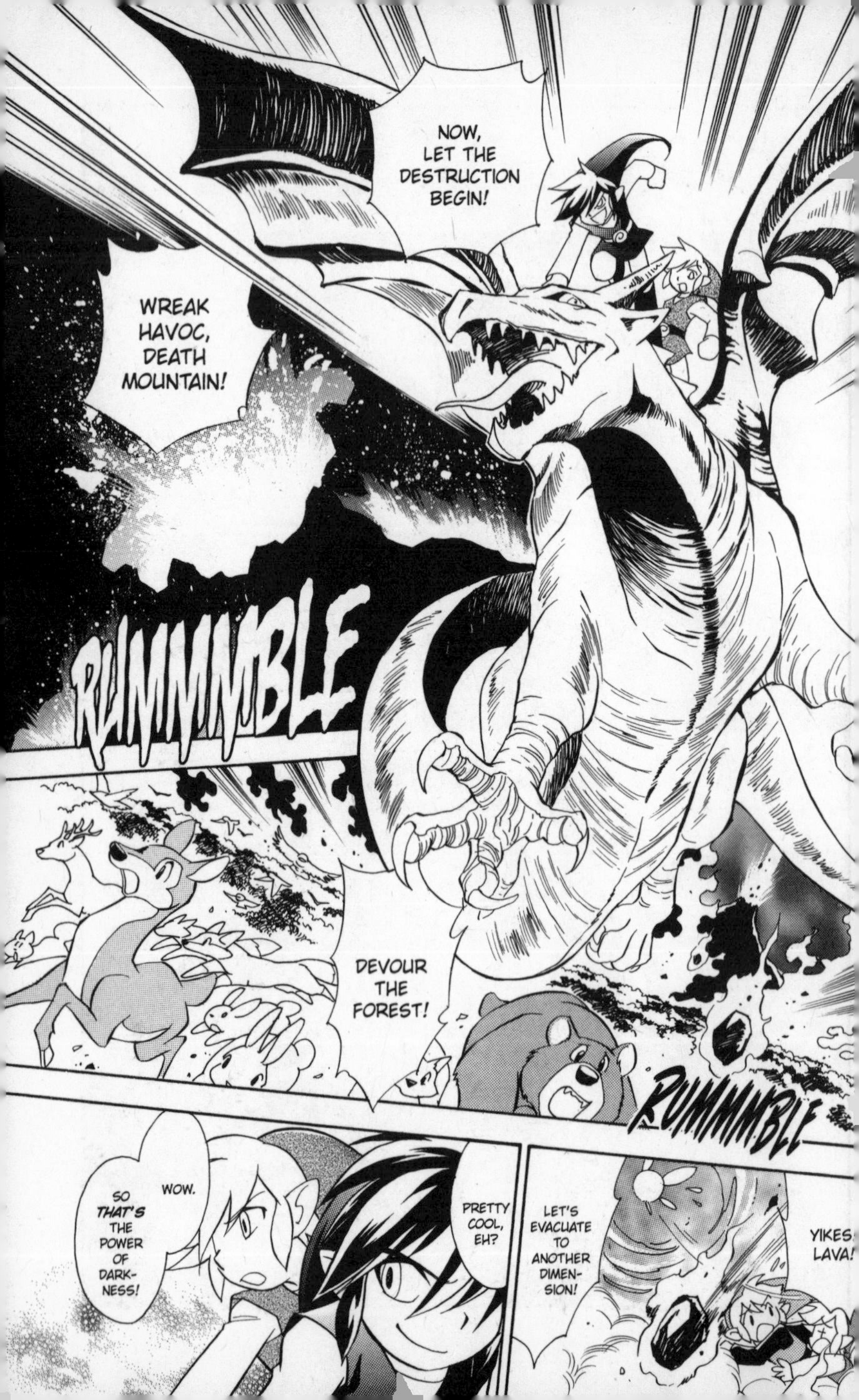
NOW, LET THE DESTRUCTION BEGIN!
WREAK HAVOC, DEATH MOUNTAIN!
RUMMMBLE
DEVOUR THE FOREST!
RUMMMBLE
YIKES! LAVA!
LET'S EVACUATE TO ANOTHER DIMENSION!
PRETTY COOL, EH?
WOW.
SO ***THAT'S*** THE POWER OF DARKNESS!

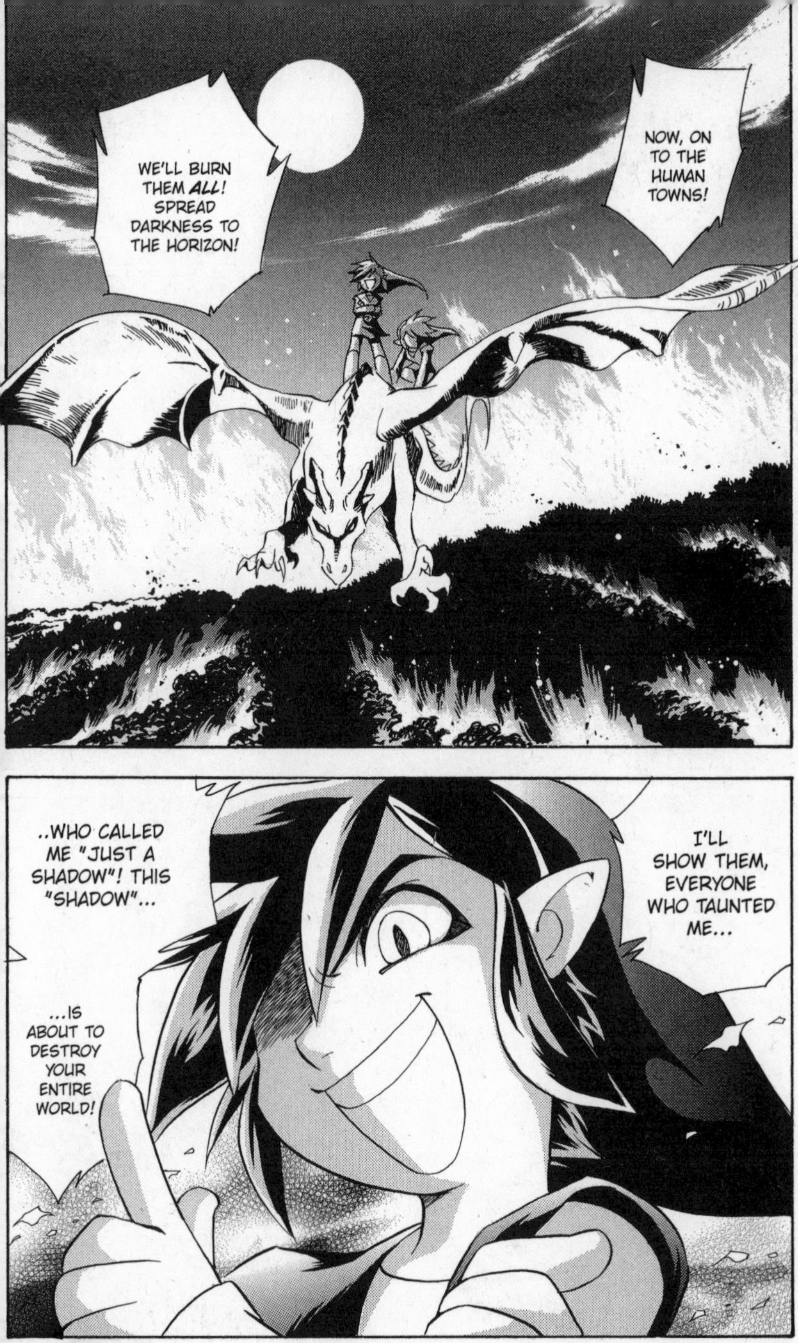
NOW, ON TO THE HUMAN TOWNS!
WE'LL BURN THEM ***ALL***! SPREAD DARKNESS TO THE HORIZON!
I'LL SHOW THEM, EVERYONE WHO TAUNTED ME...
..WHO CALLED ME "JUST A SHADOW"! THIS "SHADOW"...
...IS ABOUT TO DESTROY YOUR ENTIRE WORLD!

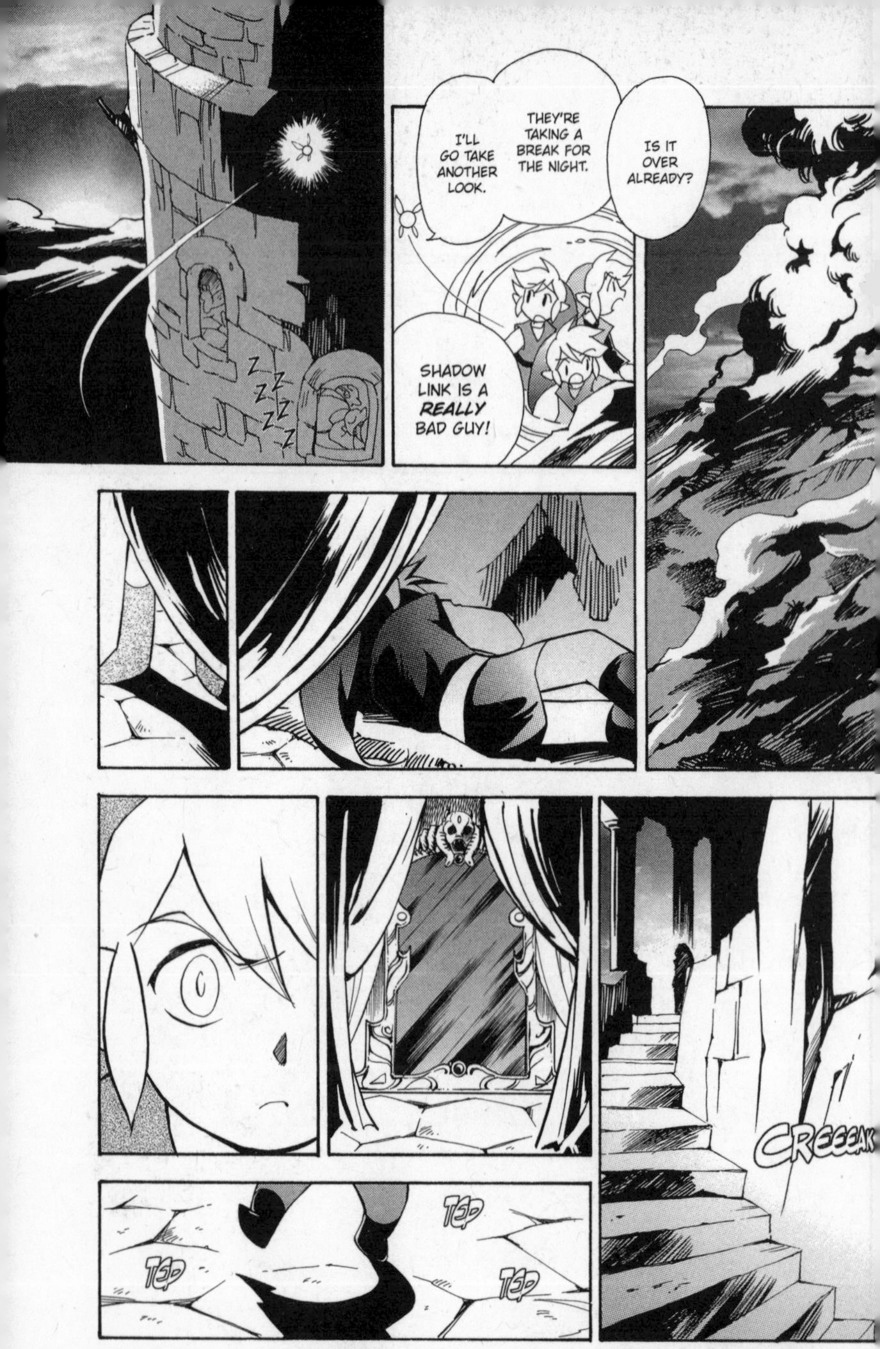

IS IT OVER ALREADY?
THEY'RE TAKING A BREAK FOR THE NIGHT.
I'LL GO TAKE ANOTHER LOOK.
SHADOW LINK IS A *REALLY* BAD GUY!
ZZZZZ
CREEEAK
TEP
TEP
TEP

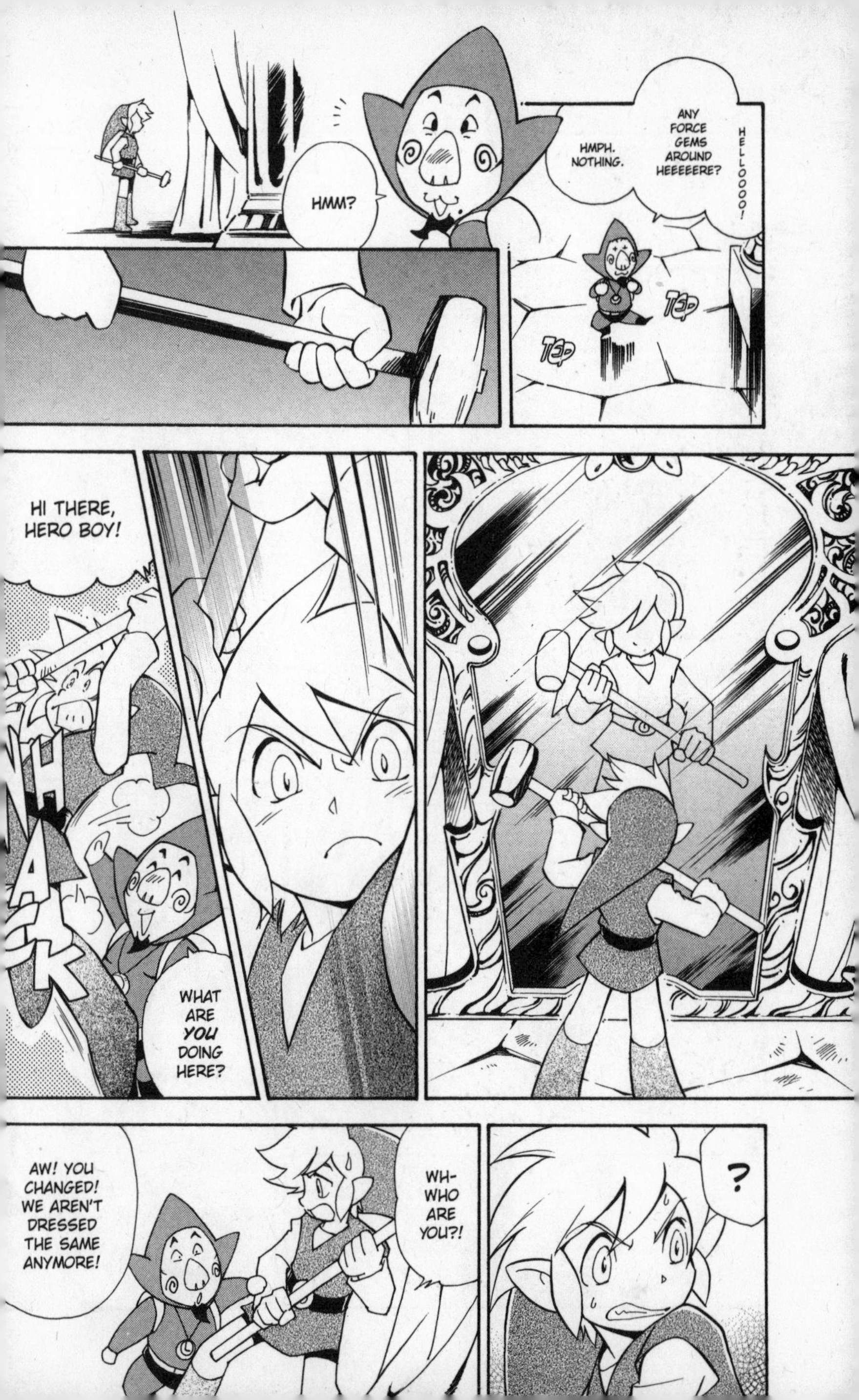
HELLOOOO!
ANY FORCE GEMS AROUND HEEEEERE?
HMPH. NOTHING.
TEP
TEP
HMM?
HI THERE, HERO BOY!
WHAK
WHAT ARE *YOU* DOING HERE?
?
WH- WHO ARE YOU?!
AW! YOU CHANGED! WE AREN'T DRESSED THE SAME ANYMORE!

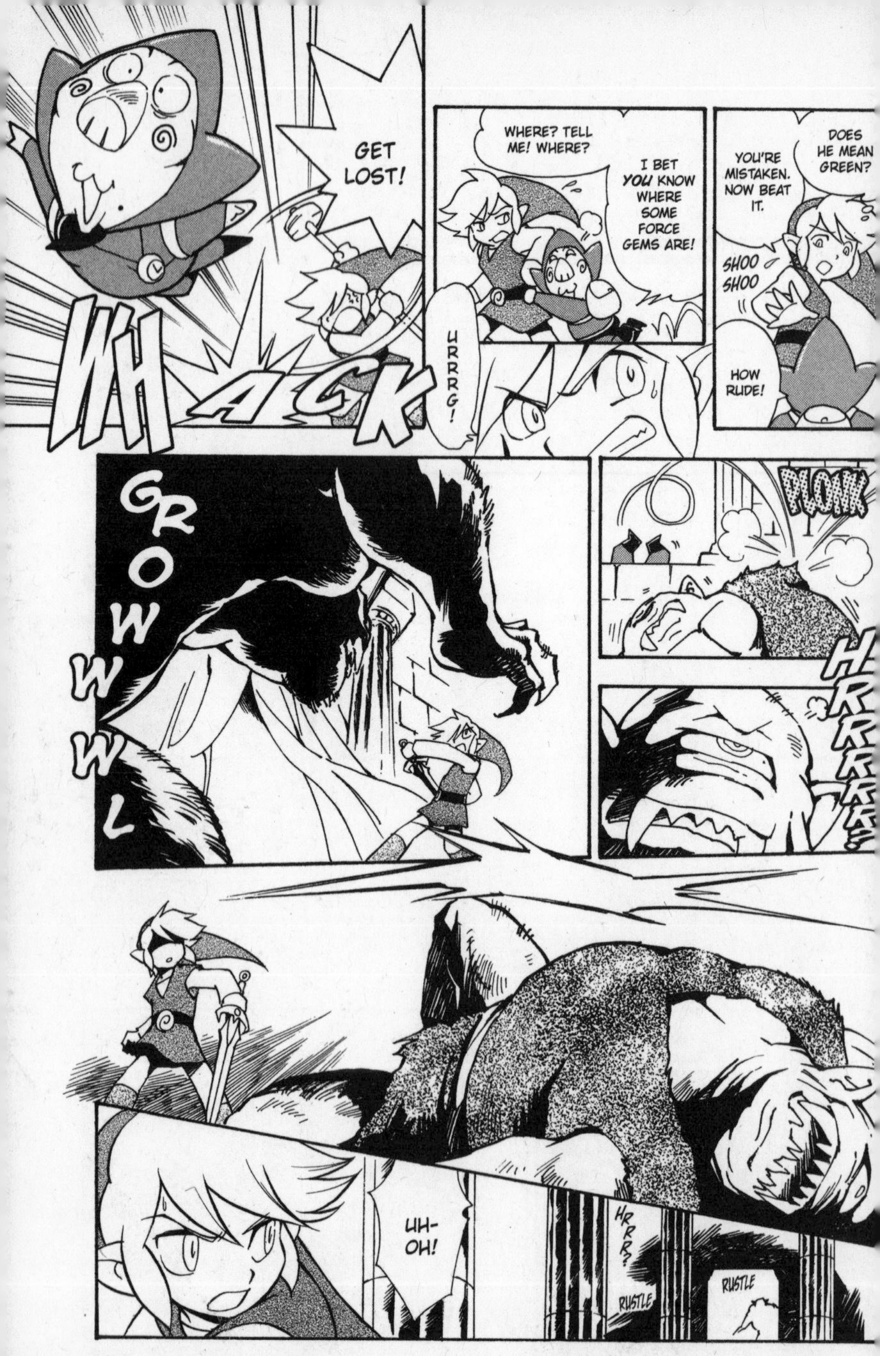
DOES HE MEAN GREEN?
YOU'RE MISTAKEN. NOW BEAT IT.
SHOO SHOO
HOW RUDE!
I BET *YOU* KNOW WHERE SOME FORCE GEMS ARE!
WHERE? TELL ME! WHERE?
URRRG!
GET LOST!
WHACK
PLONK
HRRRRR
GROWWWL
HRRR?
UH-OH!
RUSTLE
RUSTLE

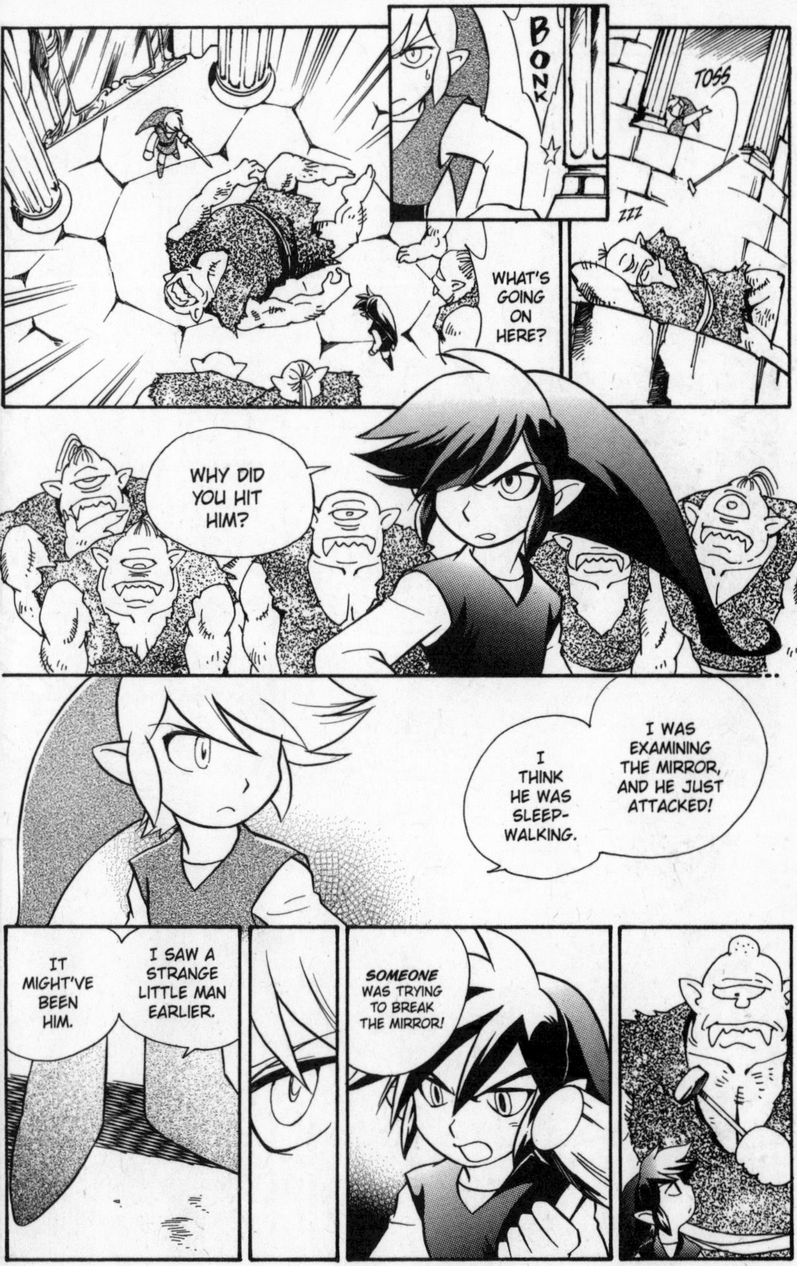
TOSS
ZZZ
BONK
WHAT'S GOING ON HERE?
WHY DID YOU HIT HIM?
I WAS EXAMINING THE MIRROR, AND HE JUST ATTACKED!
I THINK HE WAS SLEEP-WALKING.
SOMEONE WAS TRYING TO BREAK THE MIRROR!
I SAW A STRANGE LITTLE MAN EARLIER.
IT MIGHT'VE BEEN HIM.

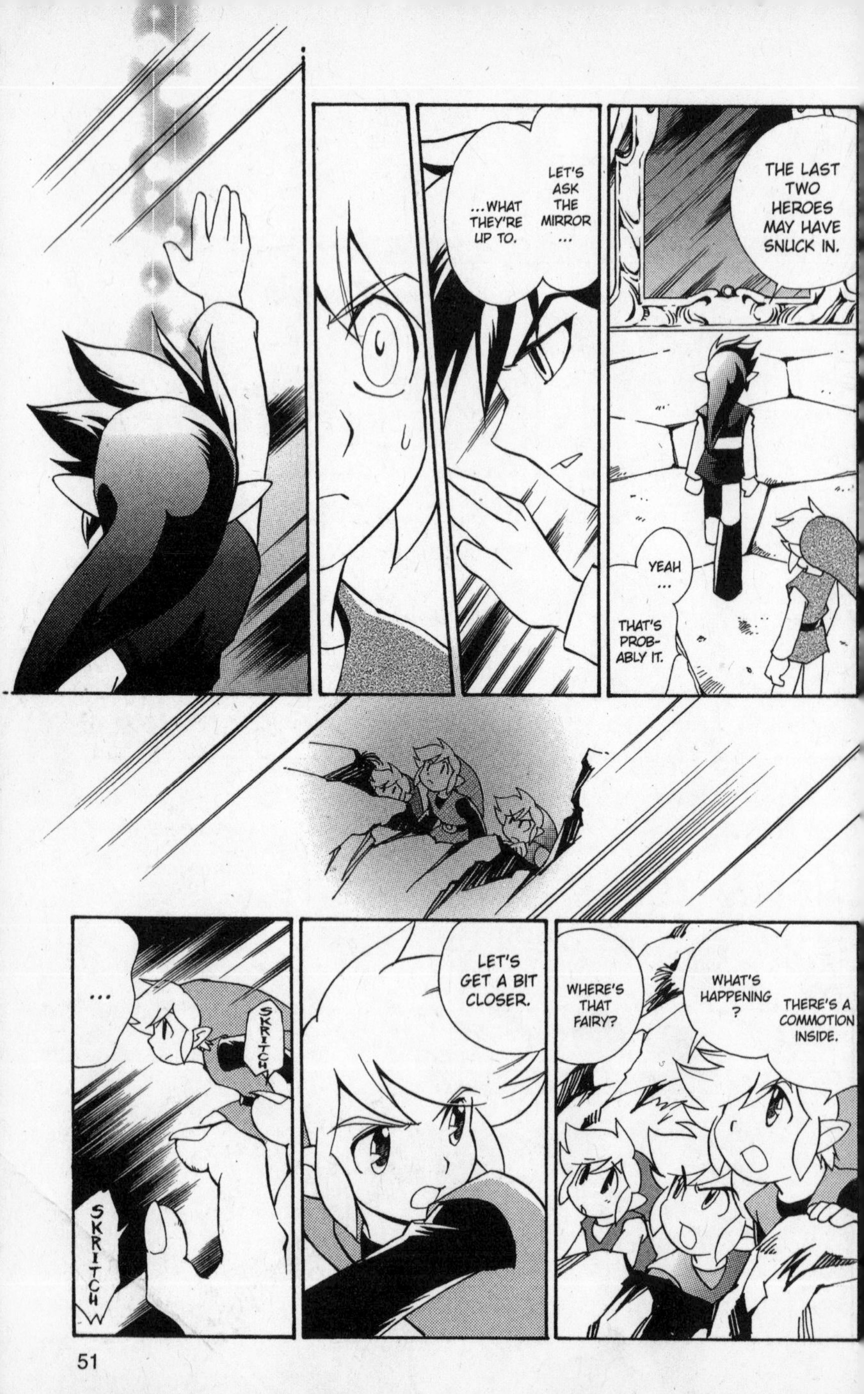
THE LAST TWO HEROES MAY HAVE SNUCK IN.
YEAH...
THAT'S PROBABLY IT.
LET'S ASK THE MIRROR...
...WHAT THEY'RE UP TO.
WHAT'S HAPPENING?
THERE'S A COMMOTION INSIDE.
WHERE'S THAT FAIRY?
LET'S GET A BIT CLOSER.
...
SKRITCH
SKRITCH

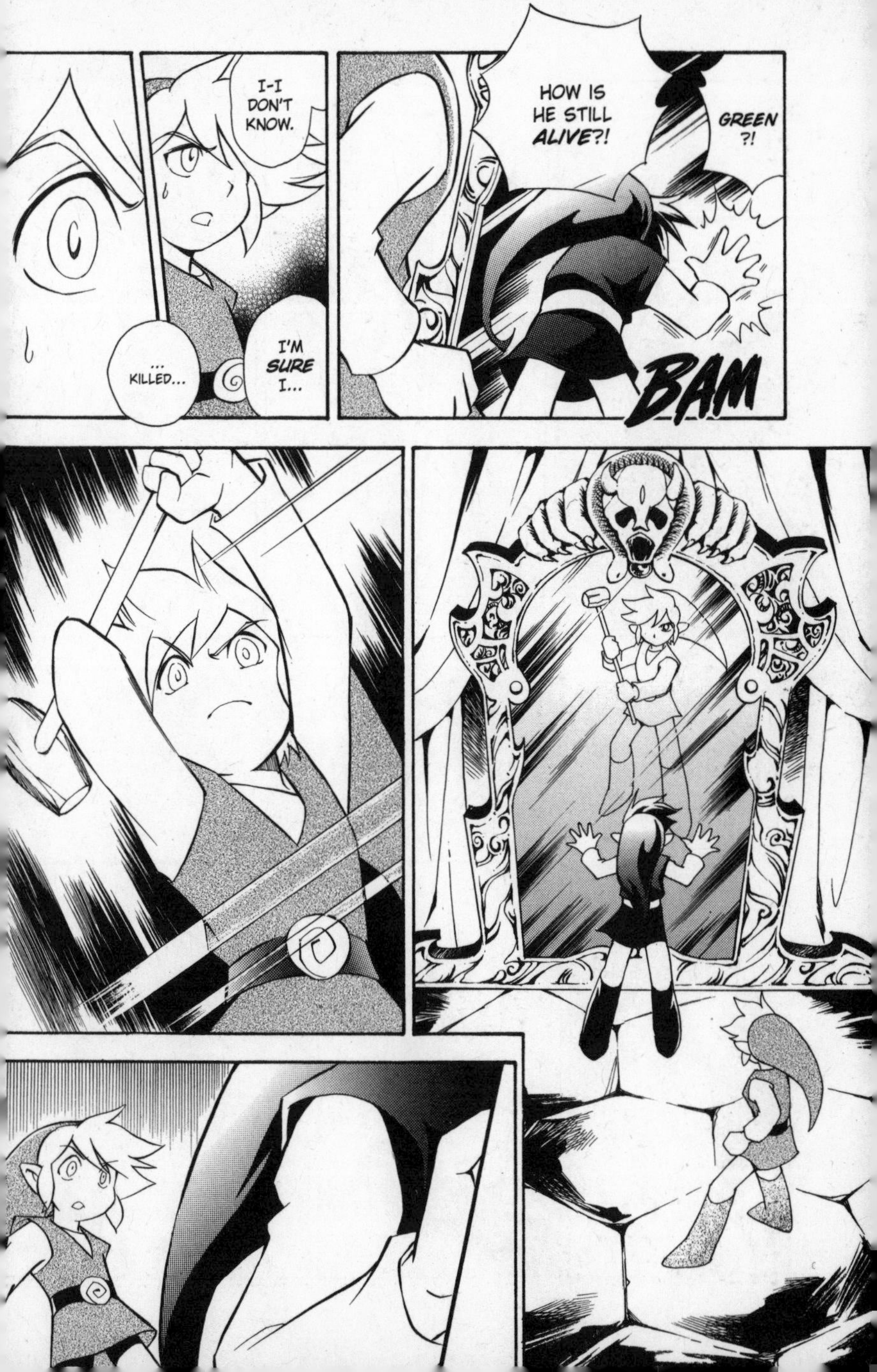
GREEN ?!
HOW IS HE STILL *ALIVE?!*
BAM
I-I DON'T KNOW.
I'M *SURE* I...
...KILLED...

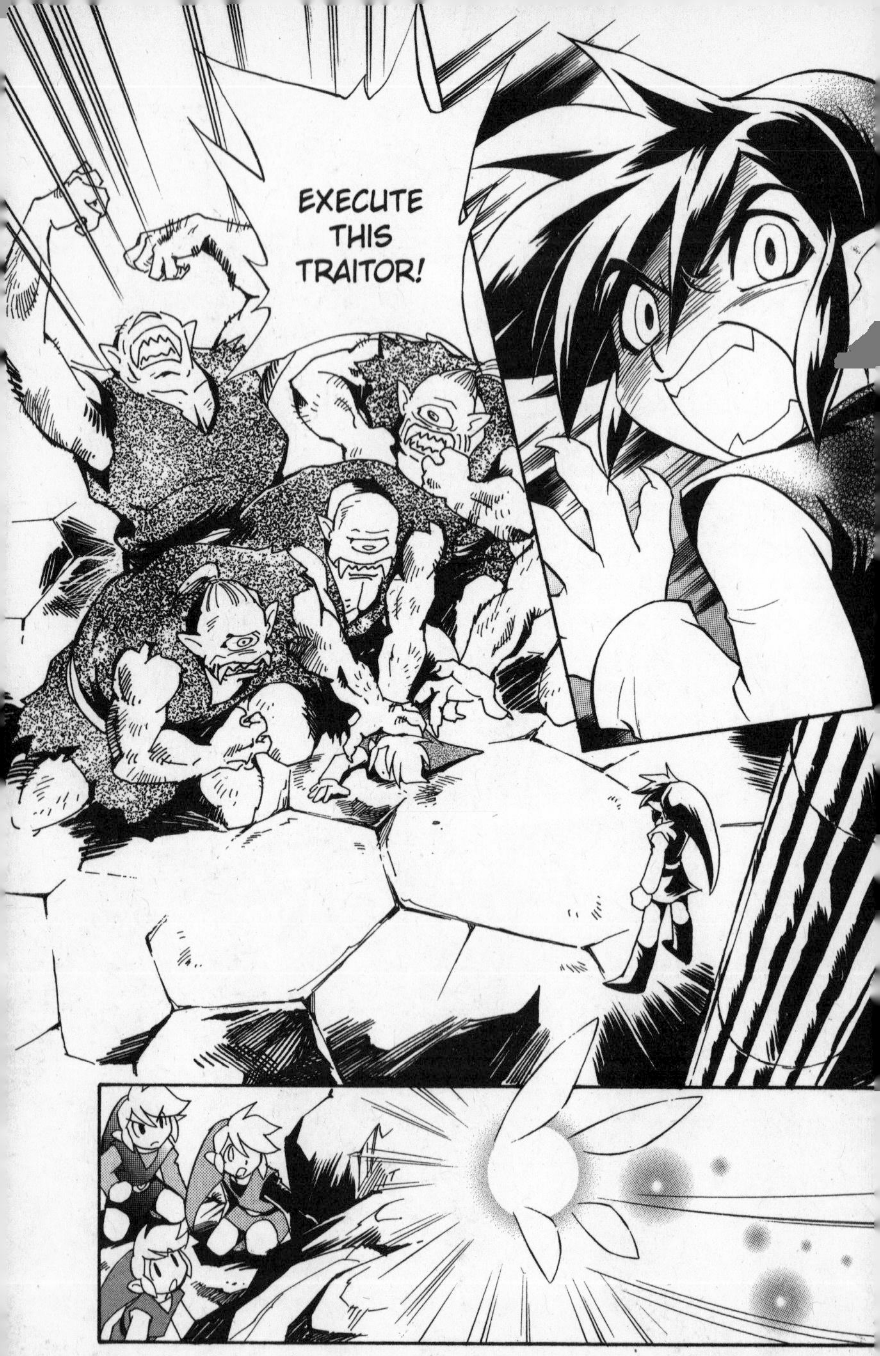
EXECUTE THIS TRAITOR!

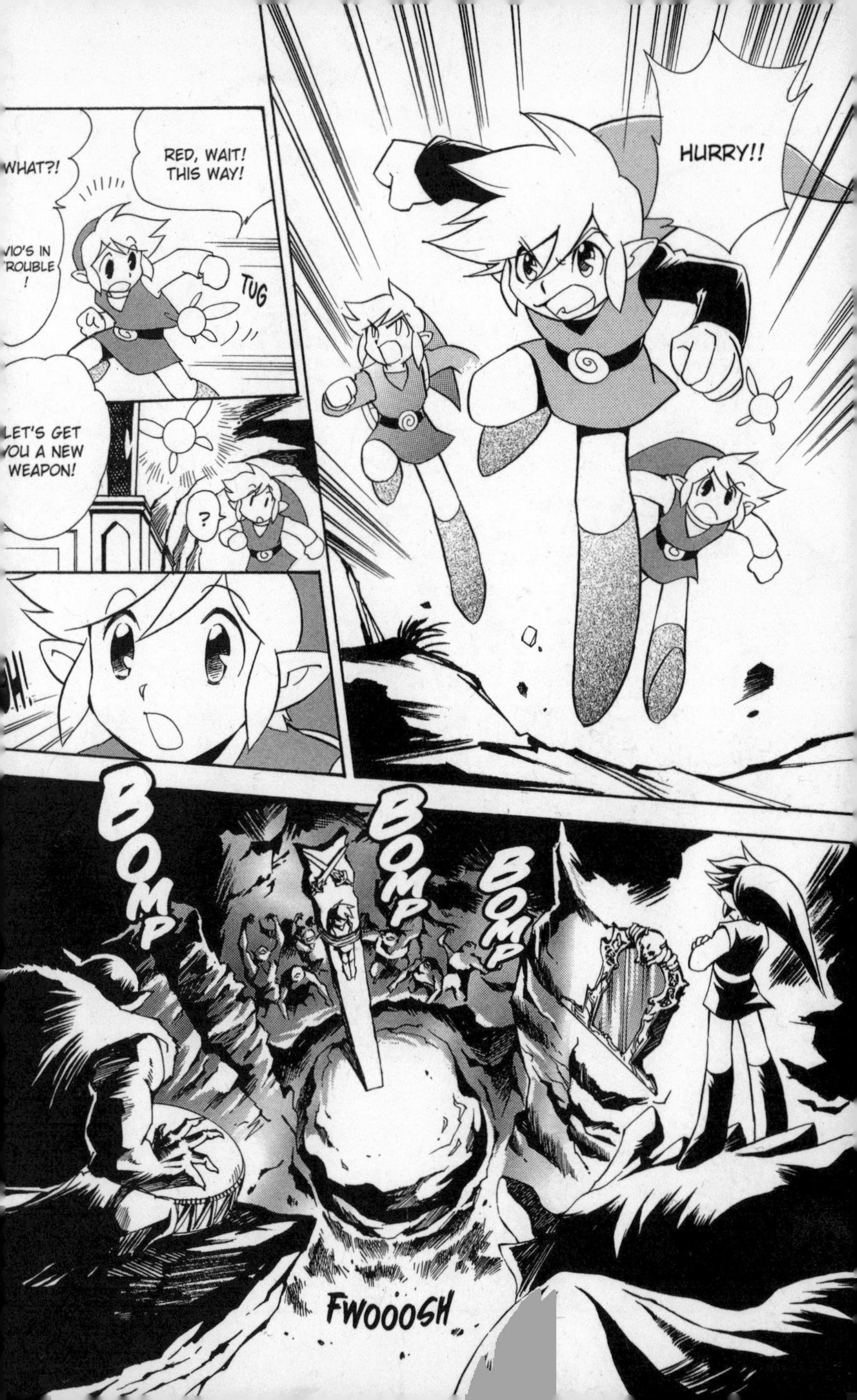
HURRY!!
RED, WAIT! THIS WAY!
WHAT?!
VIO'S IN ROUBLE!
TUG
LET'S GET YOU A NEW WEAPON!
?
BOMP
BOMP
BOMP
FWOOOSH

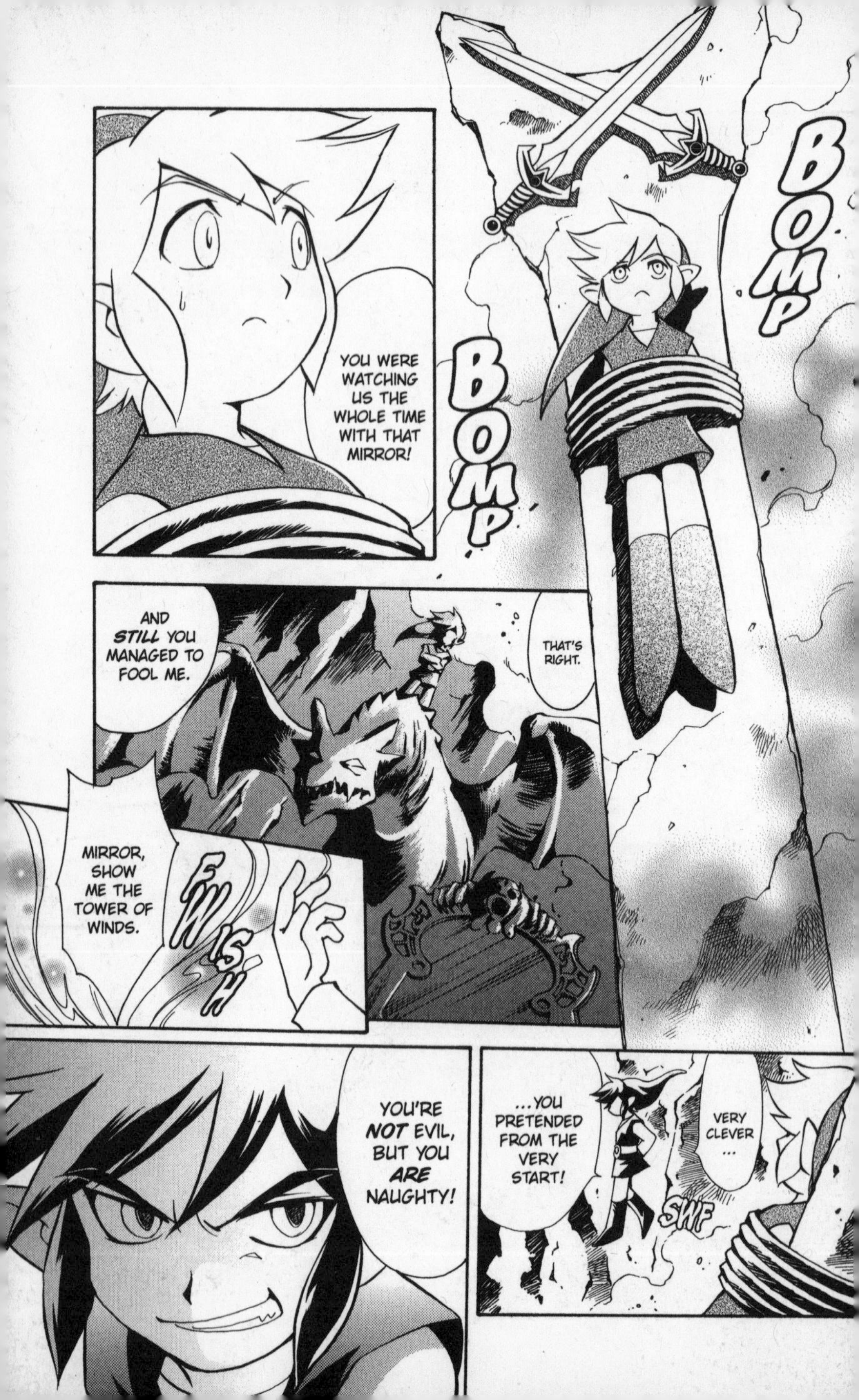
BOMP
BOMP
YOU WERE WATCHING US THE WHOLE TIME WITH THAT MIRROR!
THAT'S RIGHT.
AND *STILL* YOU MANAGED TO FOOL ME.
MIRROR, SHOW ME THE TOWER OF WINDS.
FWISH
VERY CLEVER...
...YOU PRETENDED FROM THE VERY START!
SWF
YOU'RE *NOT* EVIL, BUT YOU *ARE* NAUGHTY!

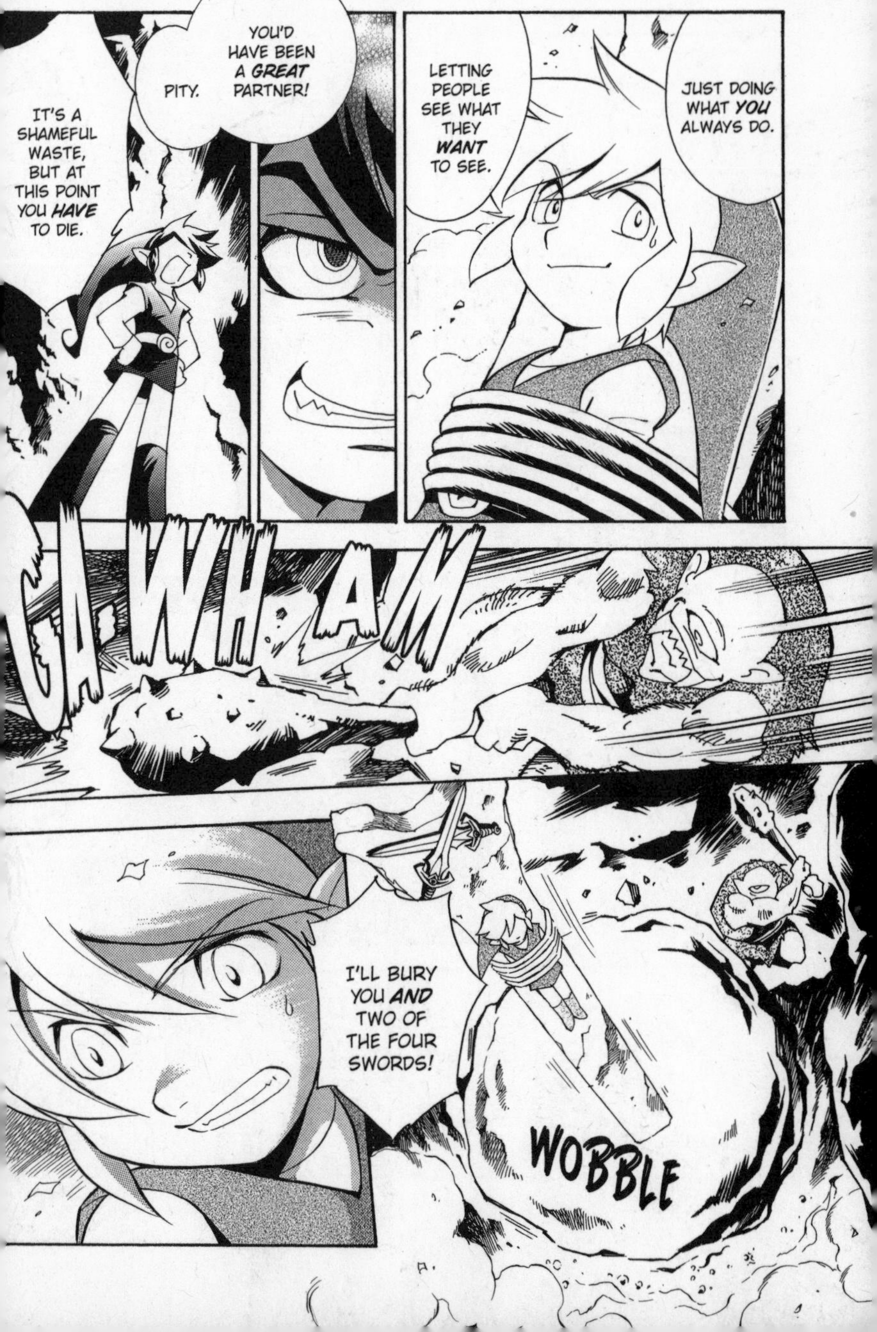
JUST DOING WHAT YOU ALWAYS DO.
LETTING PEOPLE SEE WHAT THEY WANT TO SEE.
YOU'D HAVE BEEN A GREAT PARTNER!
PITY.
IT'S A SHAMEFUL WASTE, BUT AT THIS POINT YOU HAVE TO DIE.
GA-WH-AM
I'LL BURY YOU AND TWO OF THE FOUR SWORDS!
WOBBLE

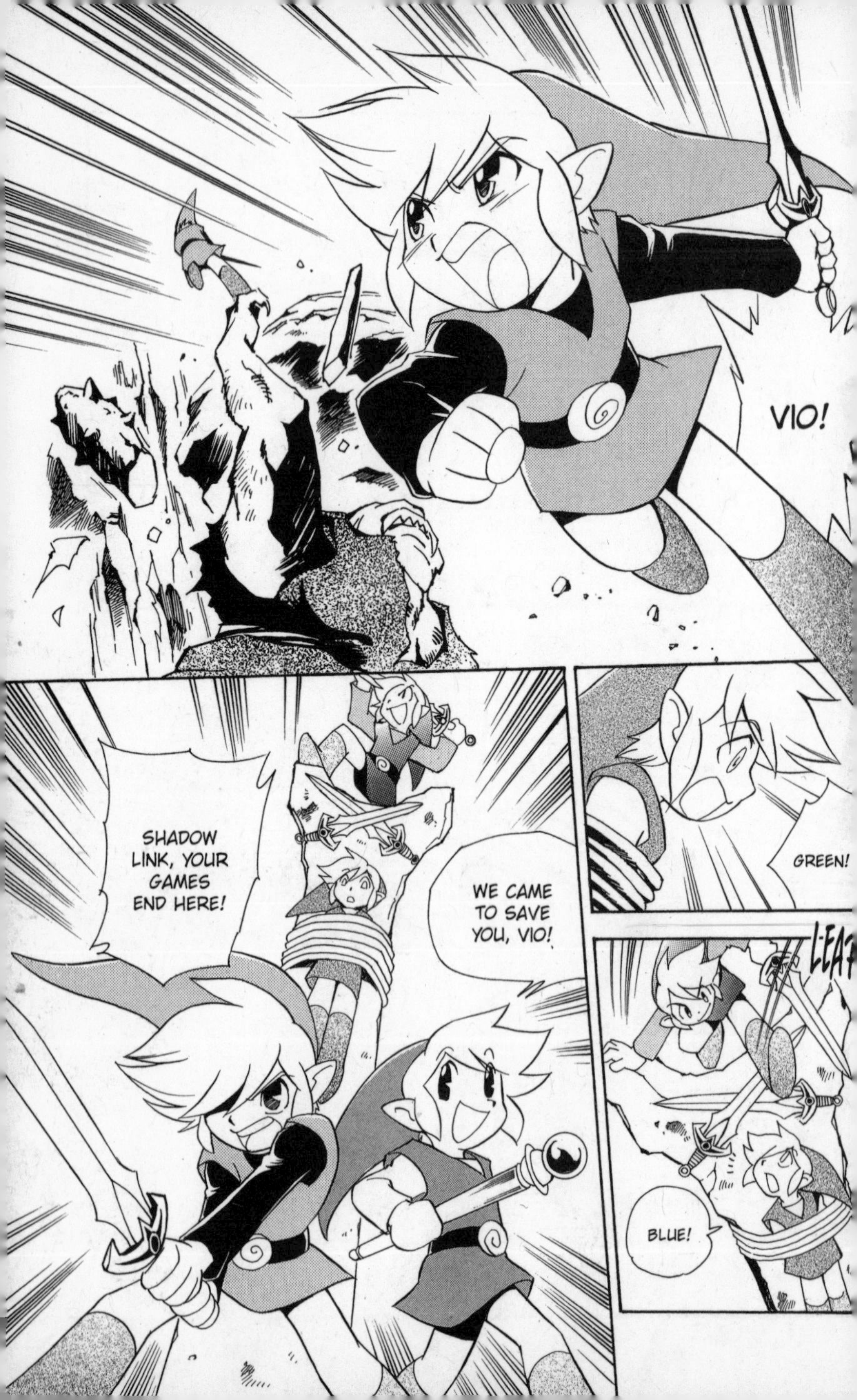
VIO!
GREEN!
BLUE!
WE CAME TO SAVE YOU, VIO!
SHADOW LINK, YOUR GAMES END HERE!

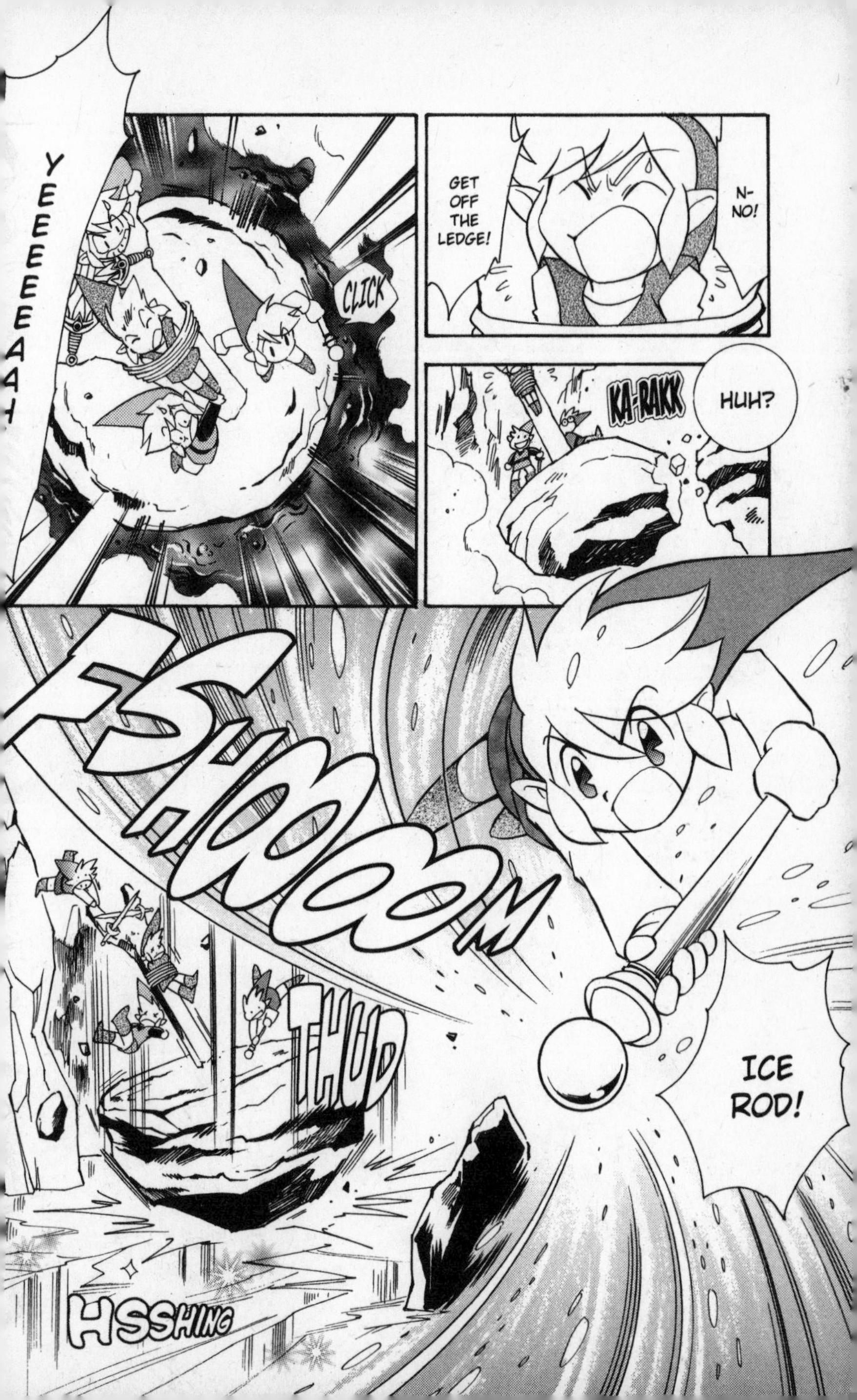
GET OFF THE LEDGE!
N-NO!
KA-RAKK
HUH?
YEEEEEAAH
CLICK
ICE ROD!
FSHOOOM
THUD
HSSHING

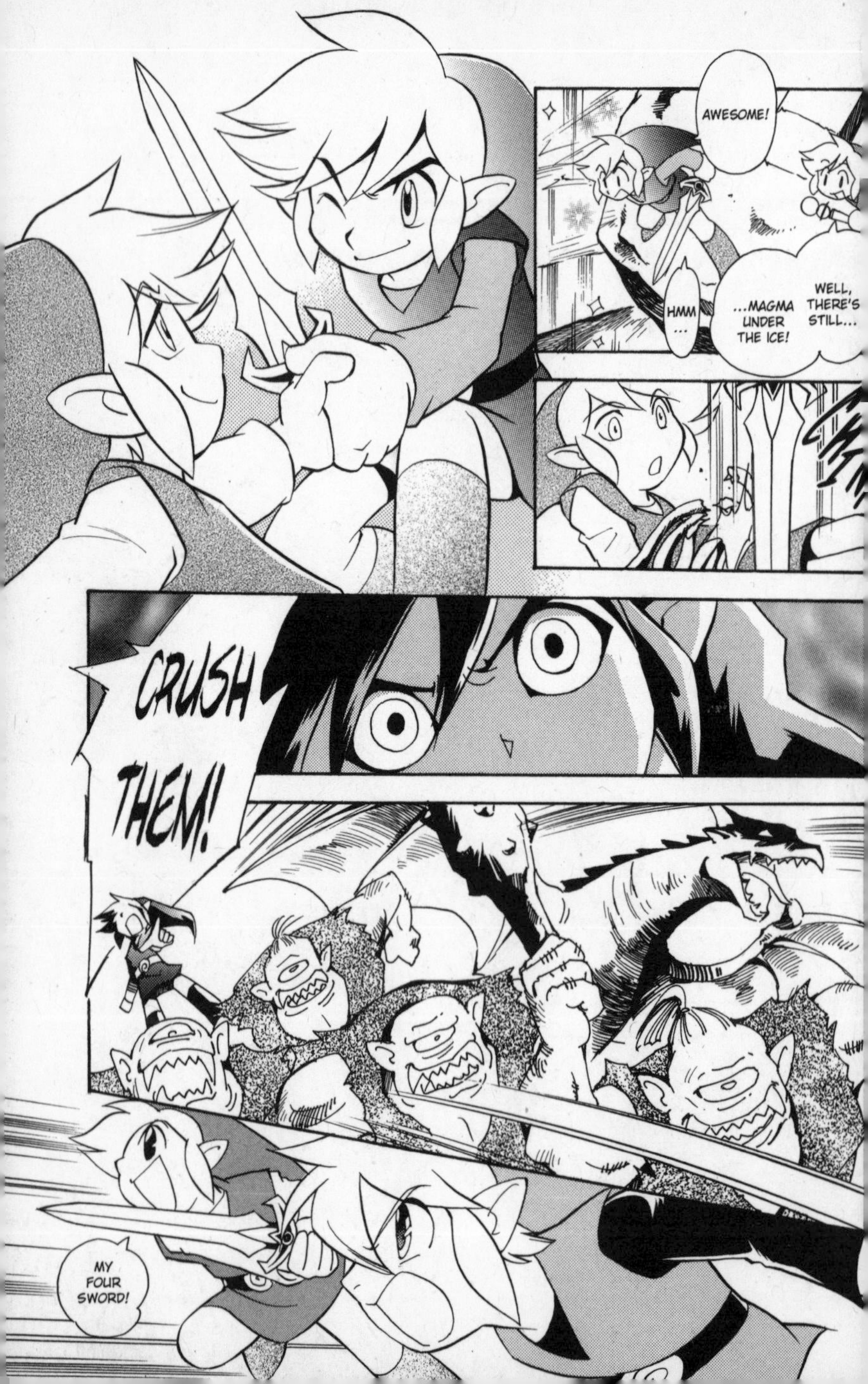
AWESOME!
WELL, THERE'S STILL...
...MAGMA UNDER THE ICE!
HMM...
CRUSH THEM!
MY FOUR SWORD!

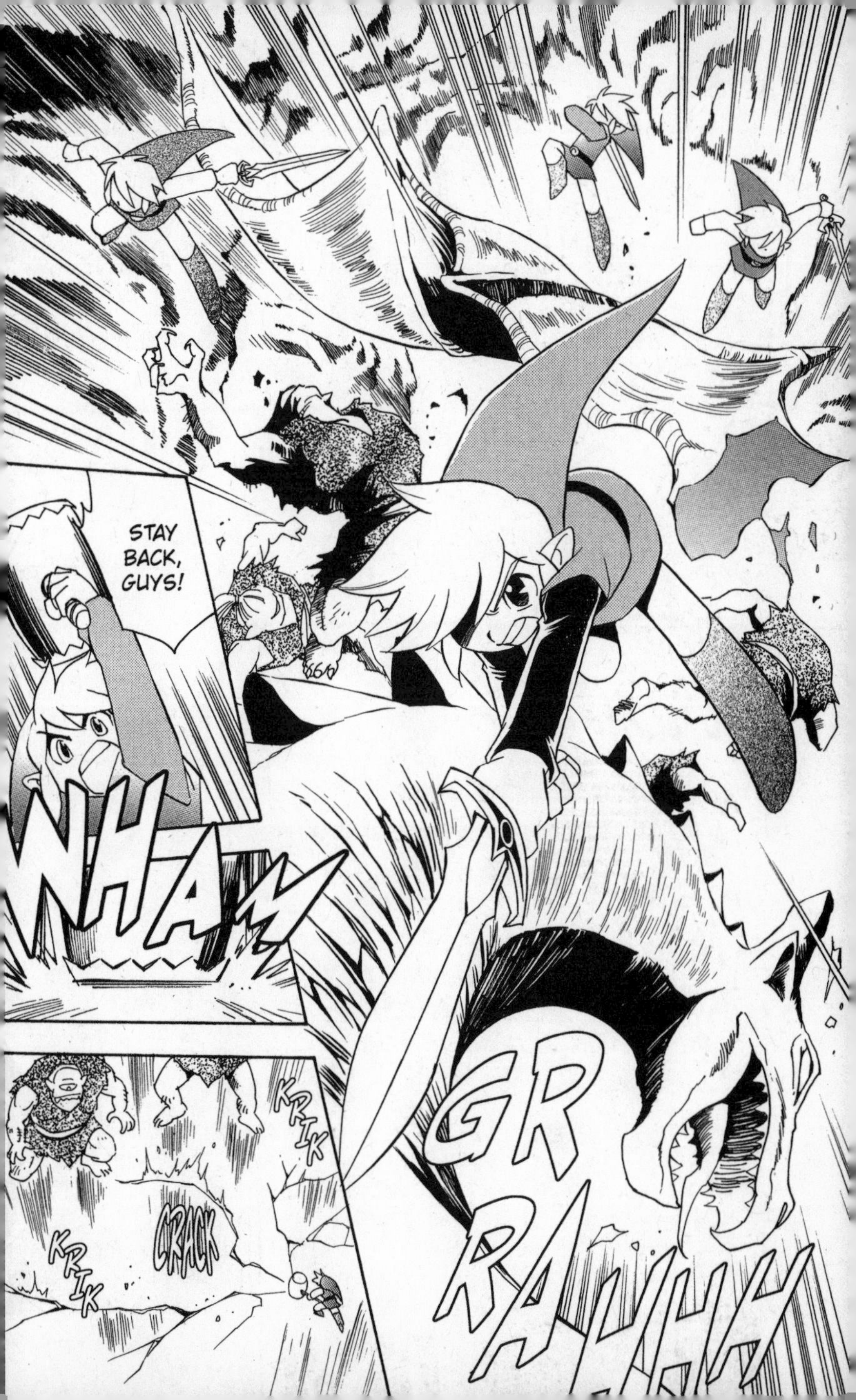
GRRAAHH
STAY BACK, GUYS!
WHAM
KRIK
CRACK
KRIK

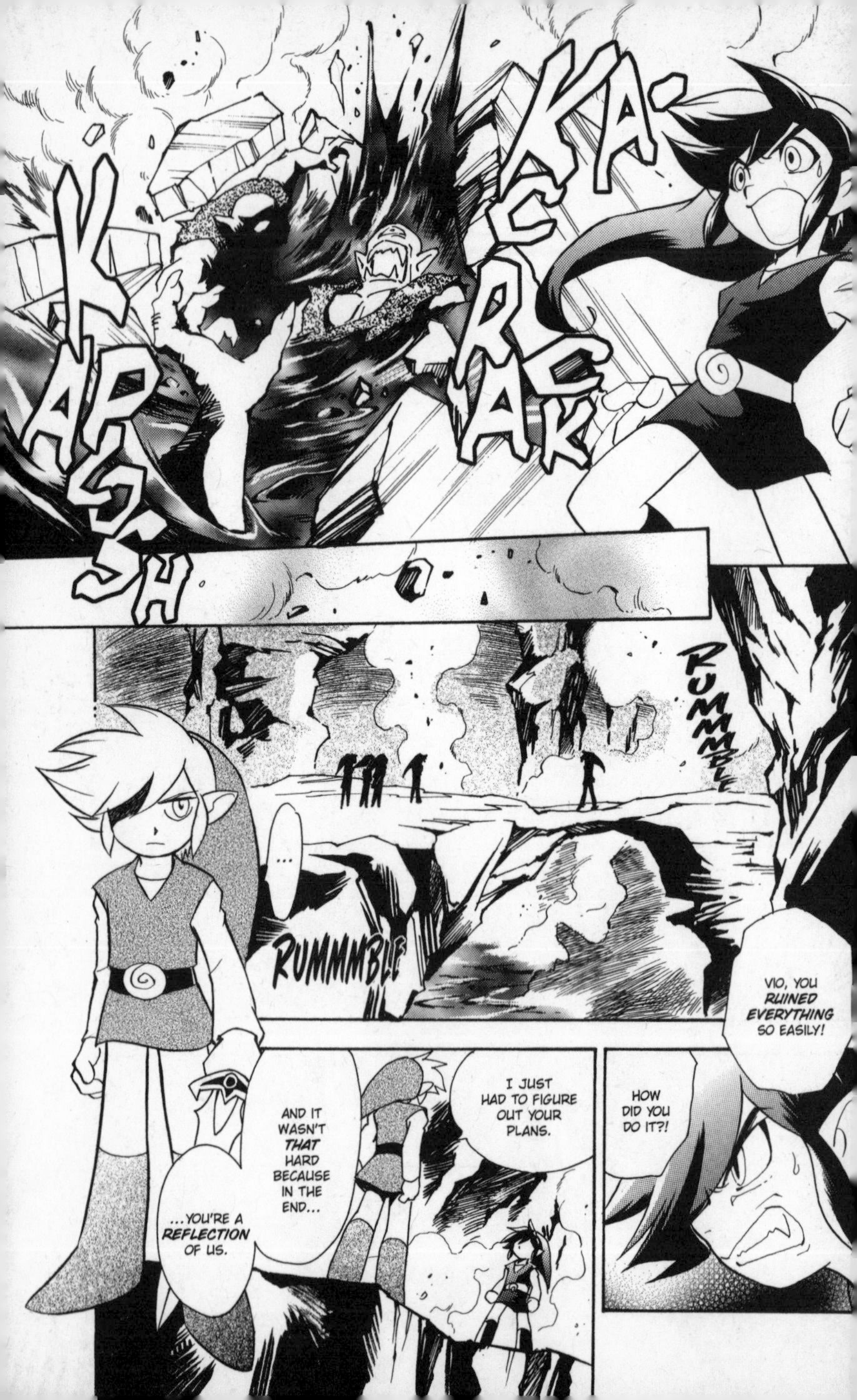
KA-CRACK
KAPSSH
RUMMMBLE
...
RUMMMBLE
VIO, YOU *RUINED EVERYTHING* SO EASILY!
HOW DID YOU DO IT?!
I JUST HAD TO FIGURE OUT YOUR PLANS.
AND IT WASN'T *THAT* HARD BECAUSE IN THE END...
...YOU'RE A *REFLECTION* OF US.

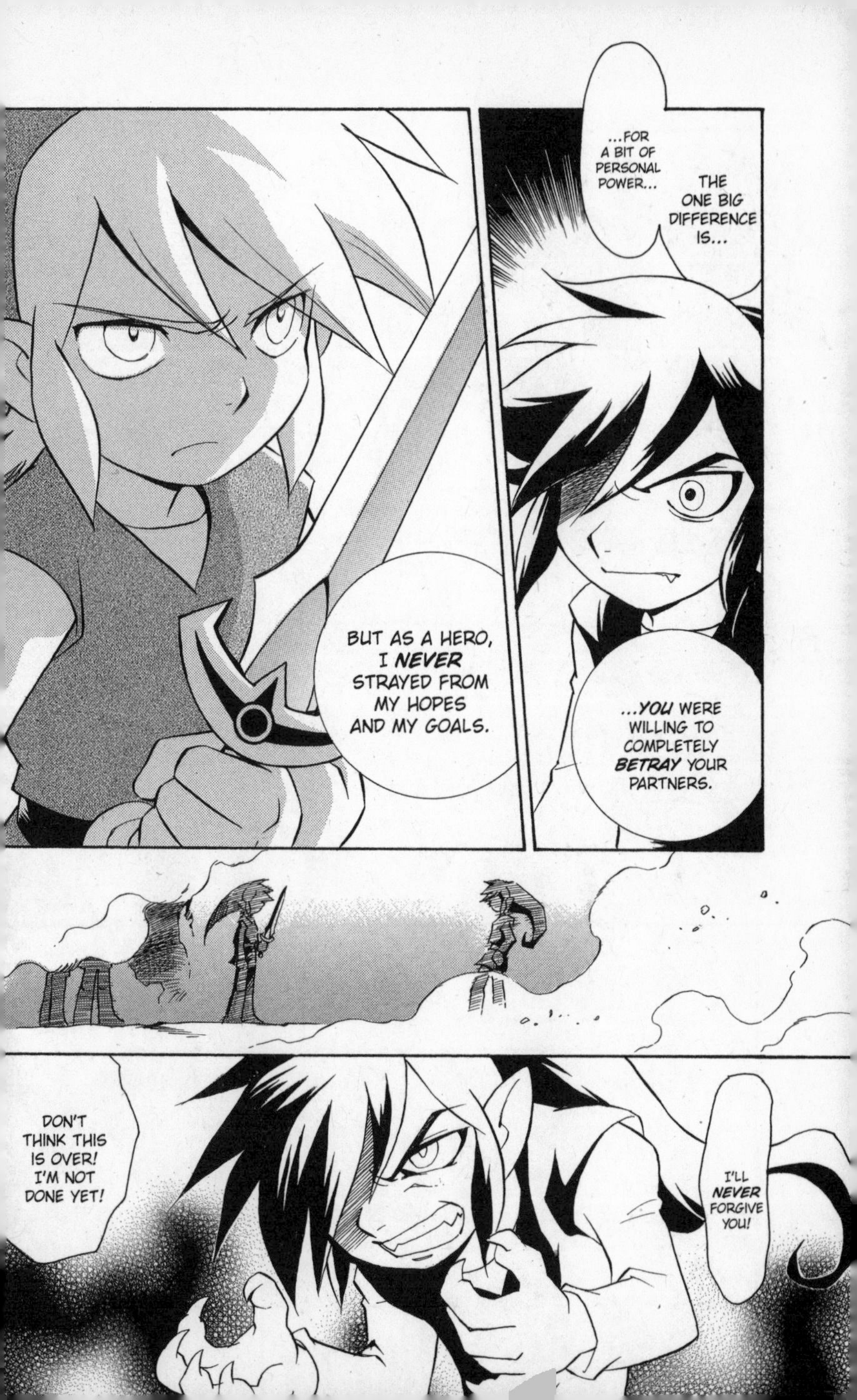
THE ONE BIG DIFFERENCE IS...
...FOR A BIT OF PERSONAL POWER...
...*YOU* WERE WILLING TO COMPLETELY *BETRAY* YOUR PARTNERS.
BUT AS A HERO, I *NEVER* STRAYED FROM MY HOPES AND MY GOALS.
I'LL *NEVER* FORGIVE YOU!
DON'T THINK THIS IS OVER! I'M NOT DONE YET!

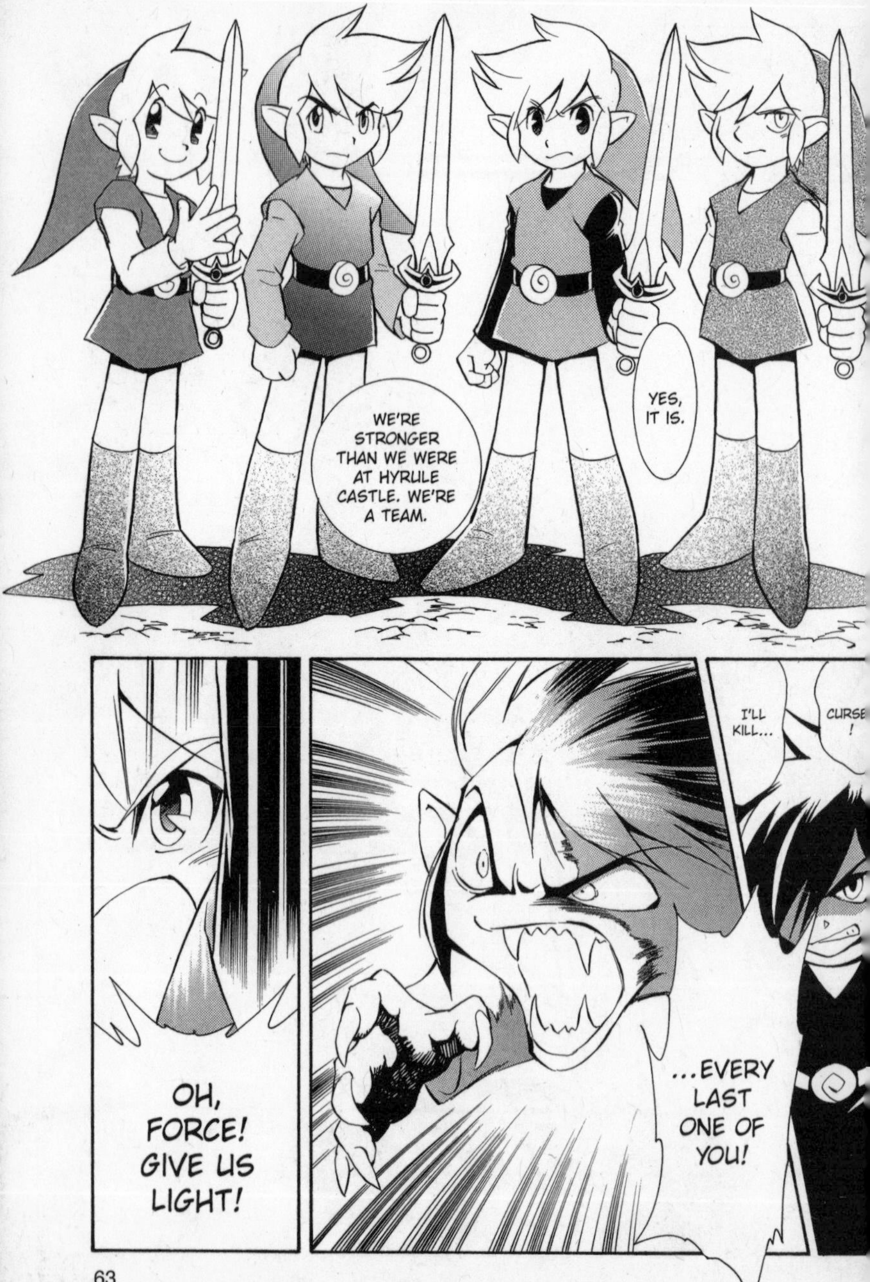
YES, IT IS.
WE'RE STRONGER THAN WE WERE AT HYRULE CASTLE. WE'RE A TEAM.
CURSE!
I'LL KILL...
...EVERY LAST ONE OF YOU!
OH, FORCE! GIVE US LIGHT!

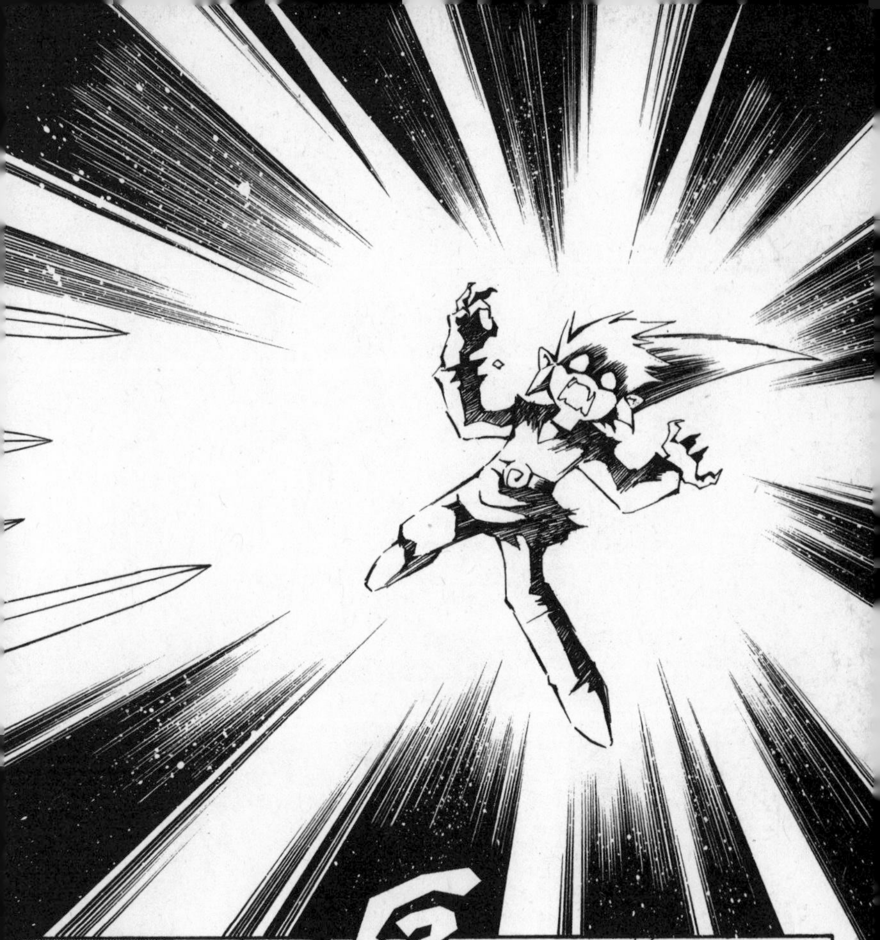
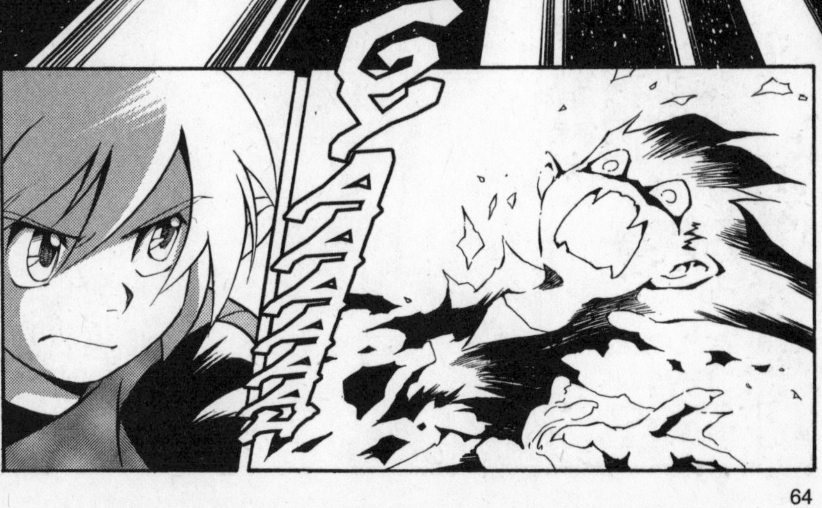

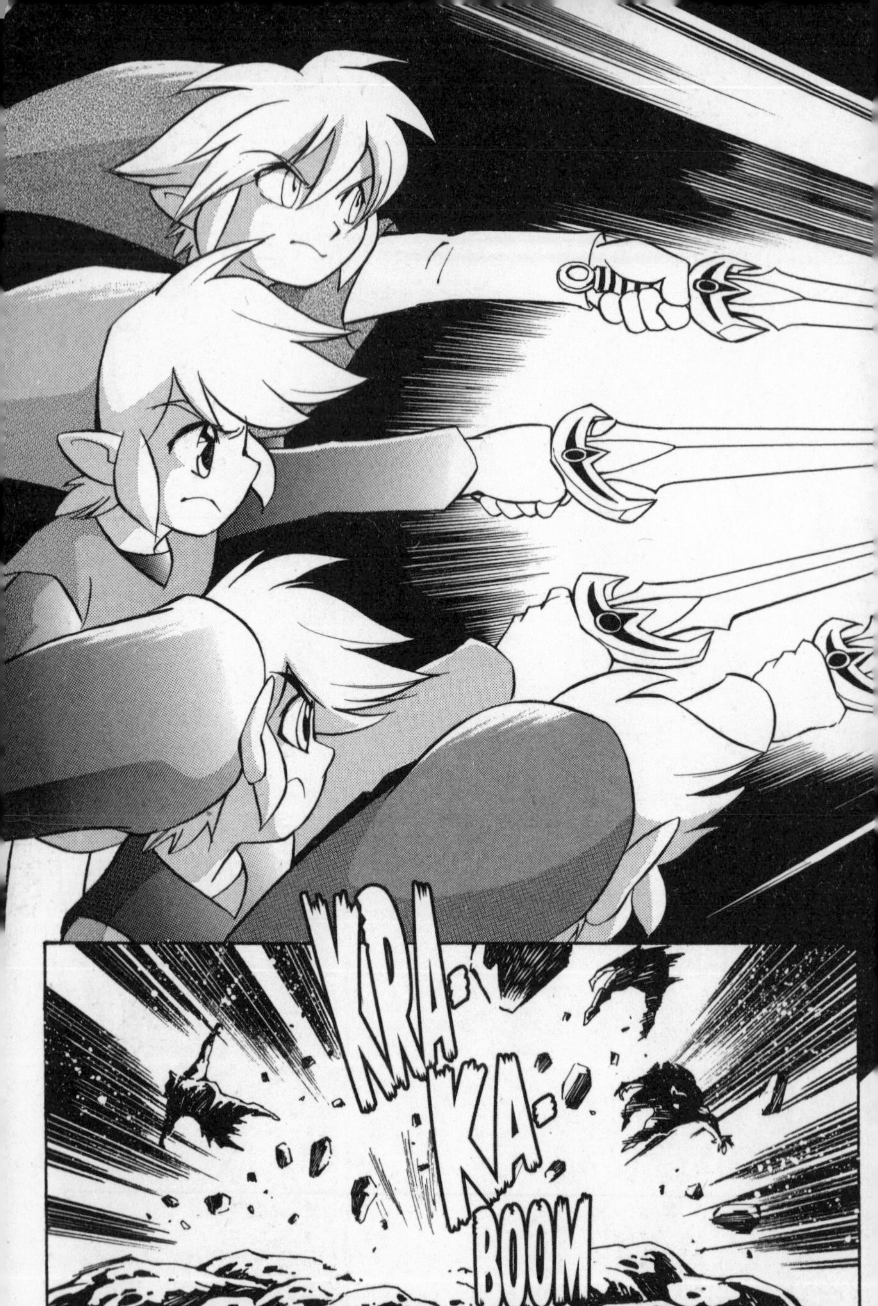
KRA-KA-BOOM

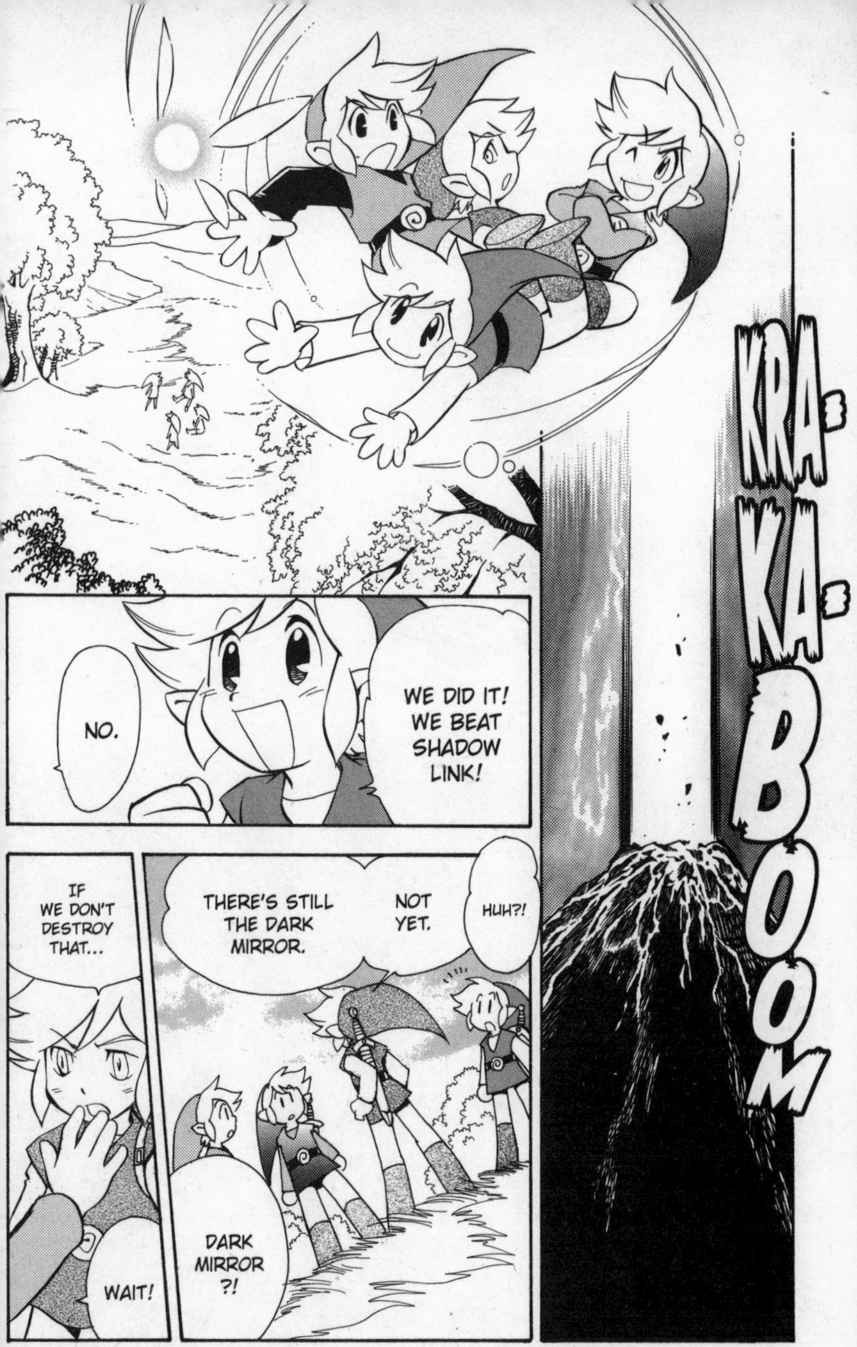
KRA-KA-BOOM
WE DID IT! WE BEAT SHADOW LINK!
NO.
HUH?!
NOT YET.
THERE'S STILL THE DARK MIRROR.
DARK MIRROR?!
IF WE DON'T DESTROY THAT...
WAIT!

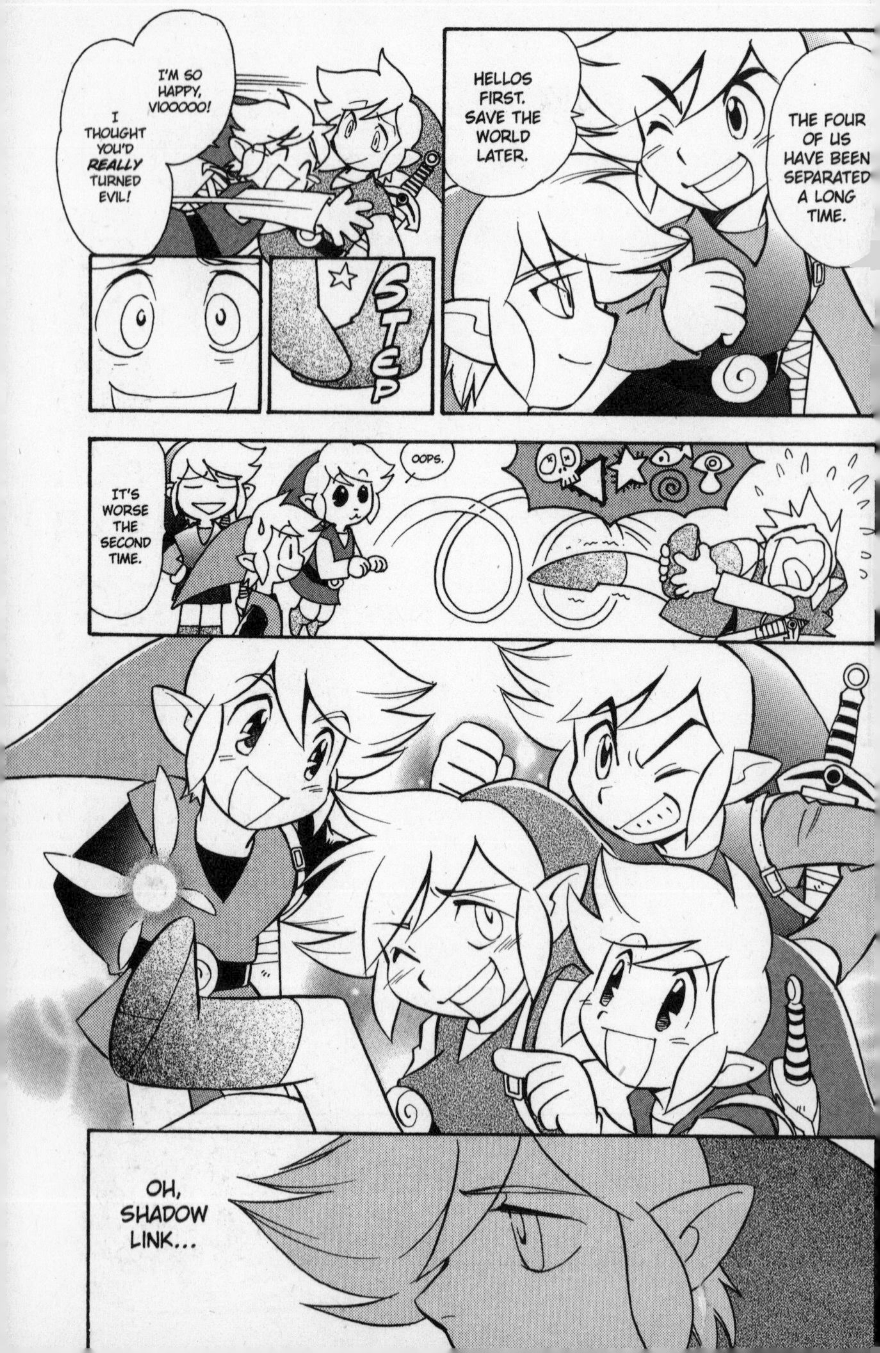
THE FOUR OF US HAVE BEEN SEPARATED A LONG TIME.
HELLOS FIRST. SAVE THE WORLD LATER.
I'M SO HAPPY, VIOOOOO!
I THOUGHT YOU'D *REALLY* TURNED EVIL!
STEP
OOPS.
IT'S WORSE THE SECOND TIME.
OH, SHADOW LINK...

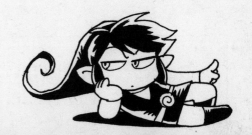

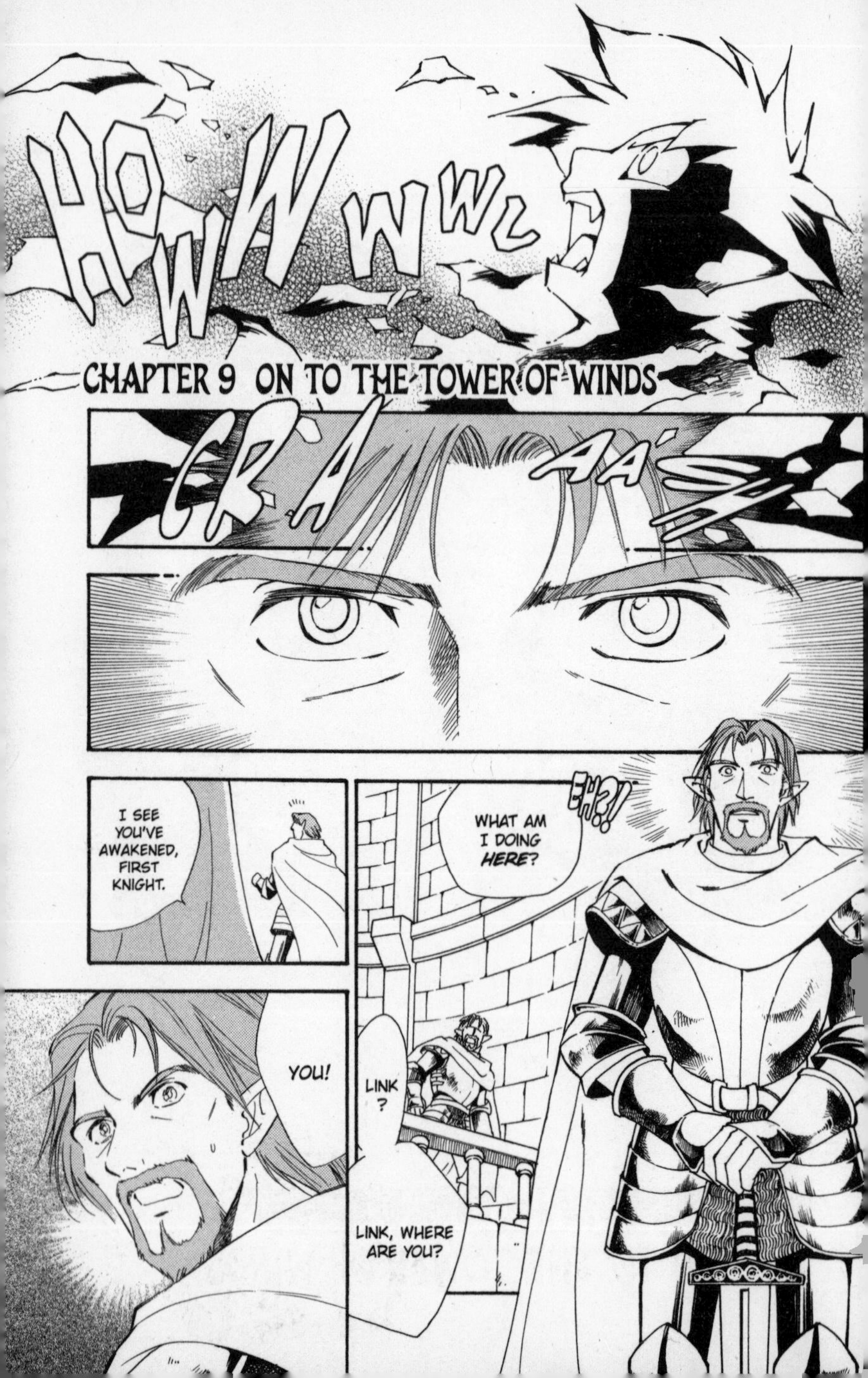
HOWWWWL
CHAPTER 9 ON TO THE TOWER OF WINDS
CRAASH
EH?!
WHAT AM I DOING HERE?
LINK?
LINK, WHERE ARE YOU?
I SEE YOU'VE AWAKENED, FIRST KNIGHT.
YOU!

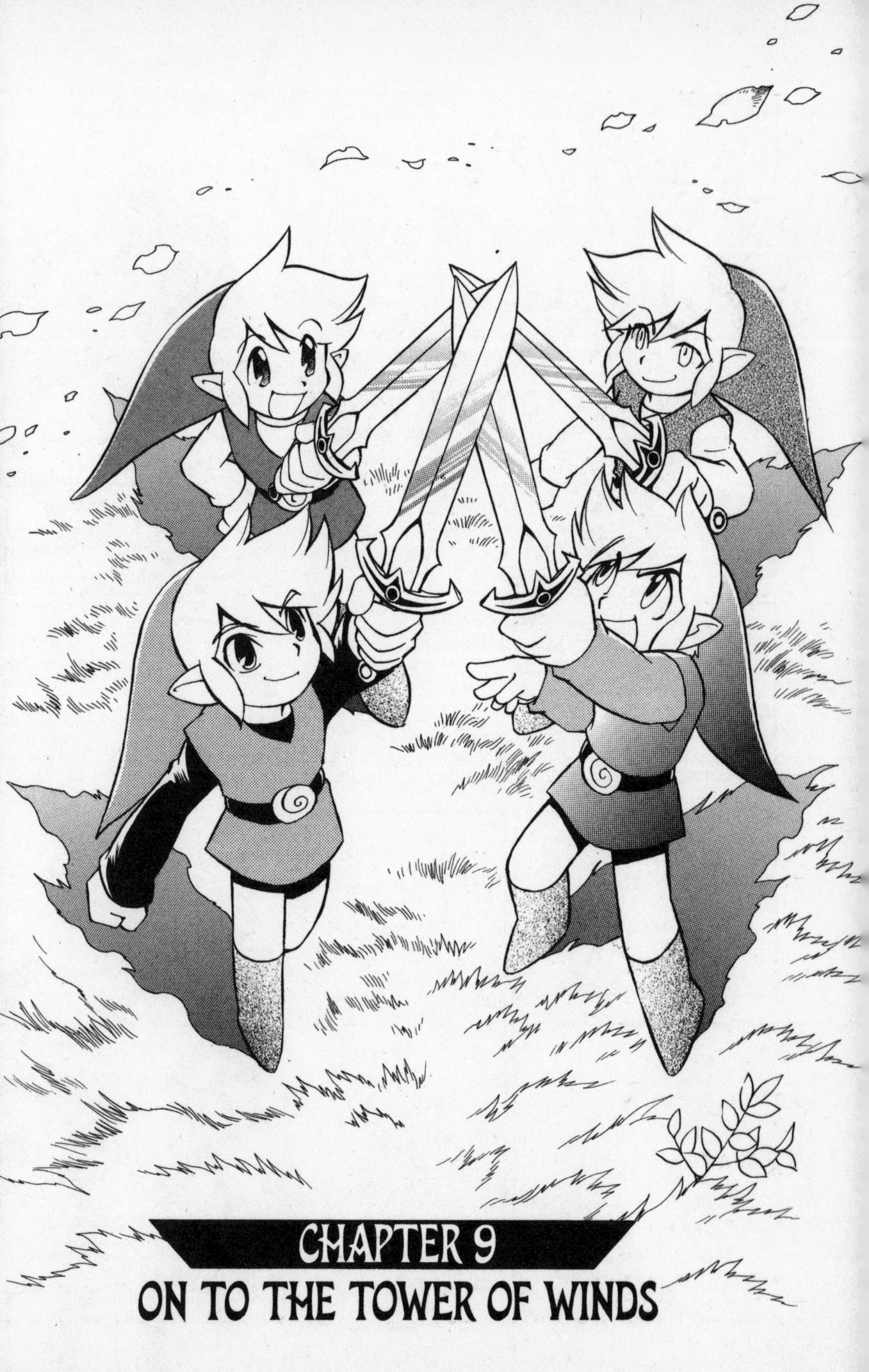

CHAPTER 9

ON TO THE TOWER OF WINDS

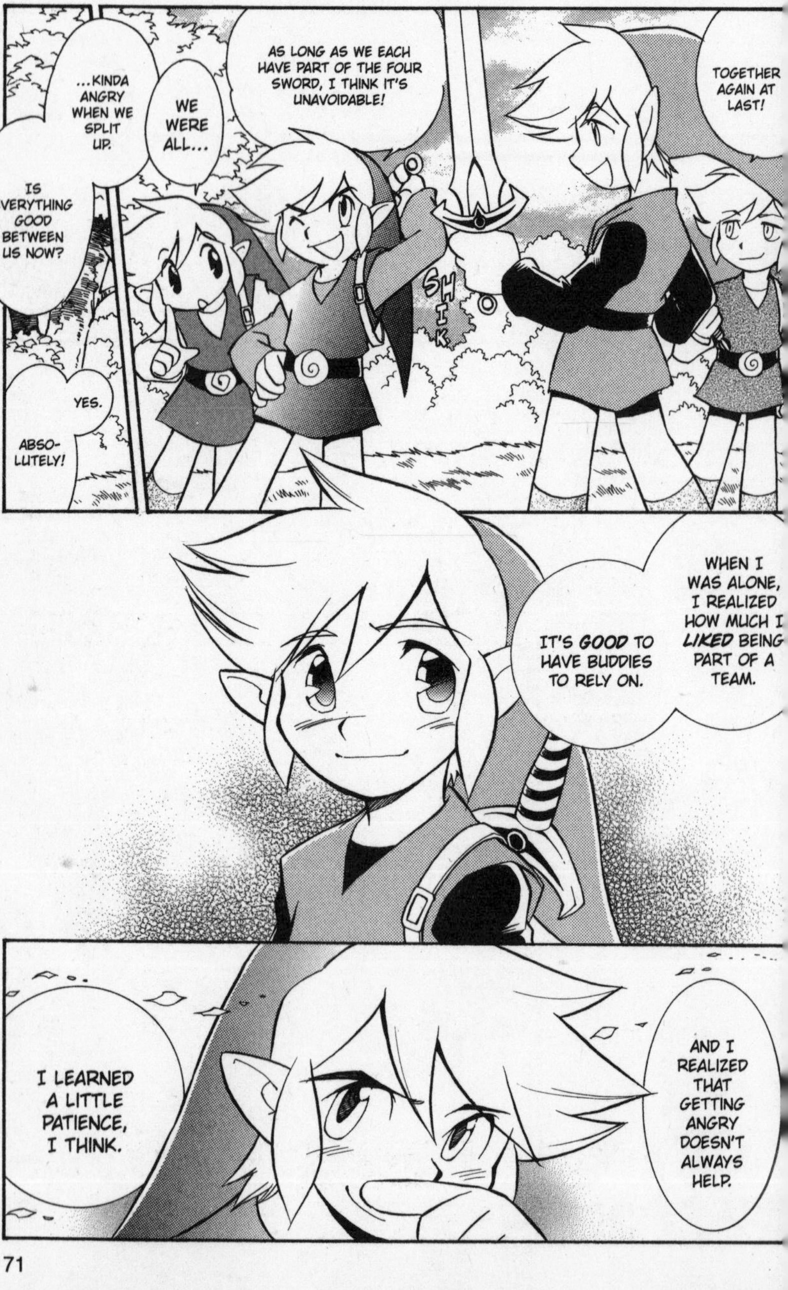
TOGETHER AGAIN AT LAST!
AS LONG AS WE EACH HAVE PART OF THE FOUR SWORD, I THINK IT'S UNAVOIDABLE!
WE WERE ALL...
...KINDA ANGRY WHEN WE SPLIT UP.
SHIK
IS EVERYTHING GOOD BETWEEN US NOW?
YES.
ABSO-LUTELY!
WHEN I WAS ALONE, I REALIZED HOW MUCH I *LIKED* BEING PART OF A TEAM.
IT'S **GOOD** TO HAVE BUDDIES TO RELY ON.
AND I REALIZED THAT GETTING ANGRY DOESN'T ALWAYS HELP.
I LEARNED A LITTLE PATIENCE, I THINK.

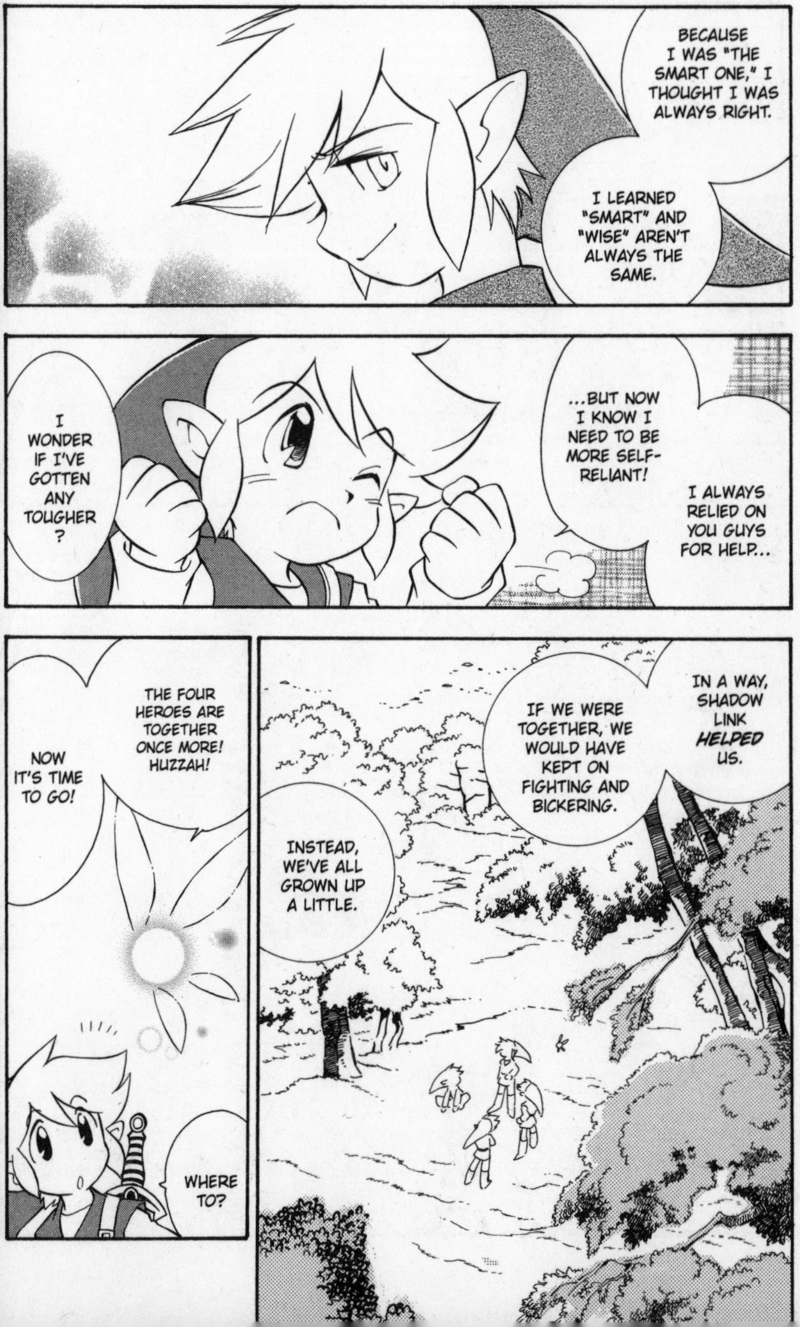
BECAUSE I WAS "THE SMART ONE," I THOUGHT I WAS ALWAYS RIGHT.
I LEARNED "SMART" AND "WISE" AREN'T ALWAYS THE SAME.
I ALWAYS RELIED ON YOU GUYS FOR HELP...
...BUT NOW I KNOW I NEED TO BE MORE SELF-RELIANT!
I WONDER IF I'VE GOTTEN ANY TOUGHER?
IN A WAY, SHADOW LINK ***HELPED*** US.
IF WE WERE TOGETHER, WE WOULD HAVE KEPT ON FIGHTING AND BICKERING.
INSTEAD, WE'VE ALL GROWN UP A LITTLE.
THE FOUR HEROES ARE TOGETHER ONCE MORE! HUZZAH!
NOW IT'S TIME TO GO!
WHERE TO?

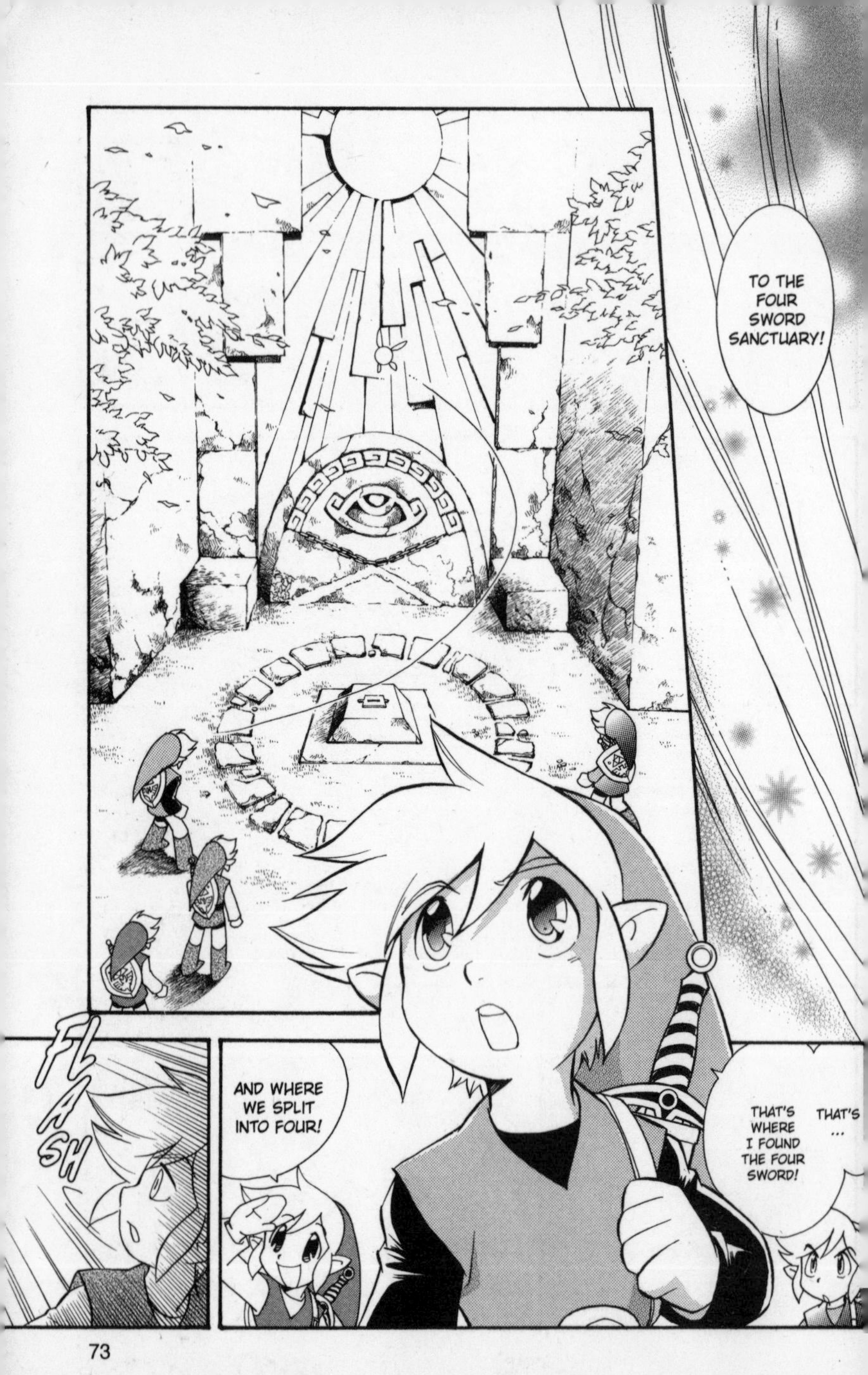
TO THE FOUR SWORD SANCTUARY!
THAT'S ...
THAT'S WHERE I FOUND THE FOUR SWORD!
AND WHERE WE SPLIT INTO FOUR!
FLASH

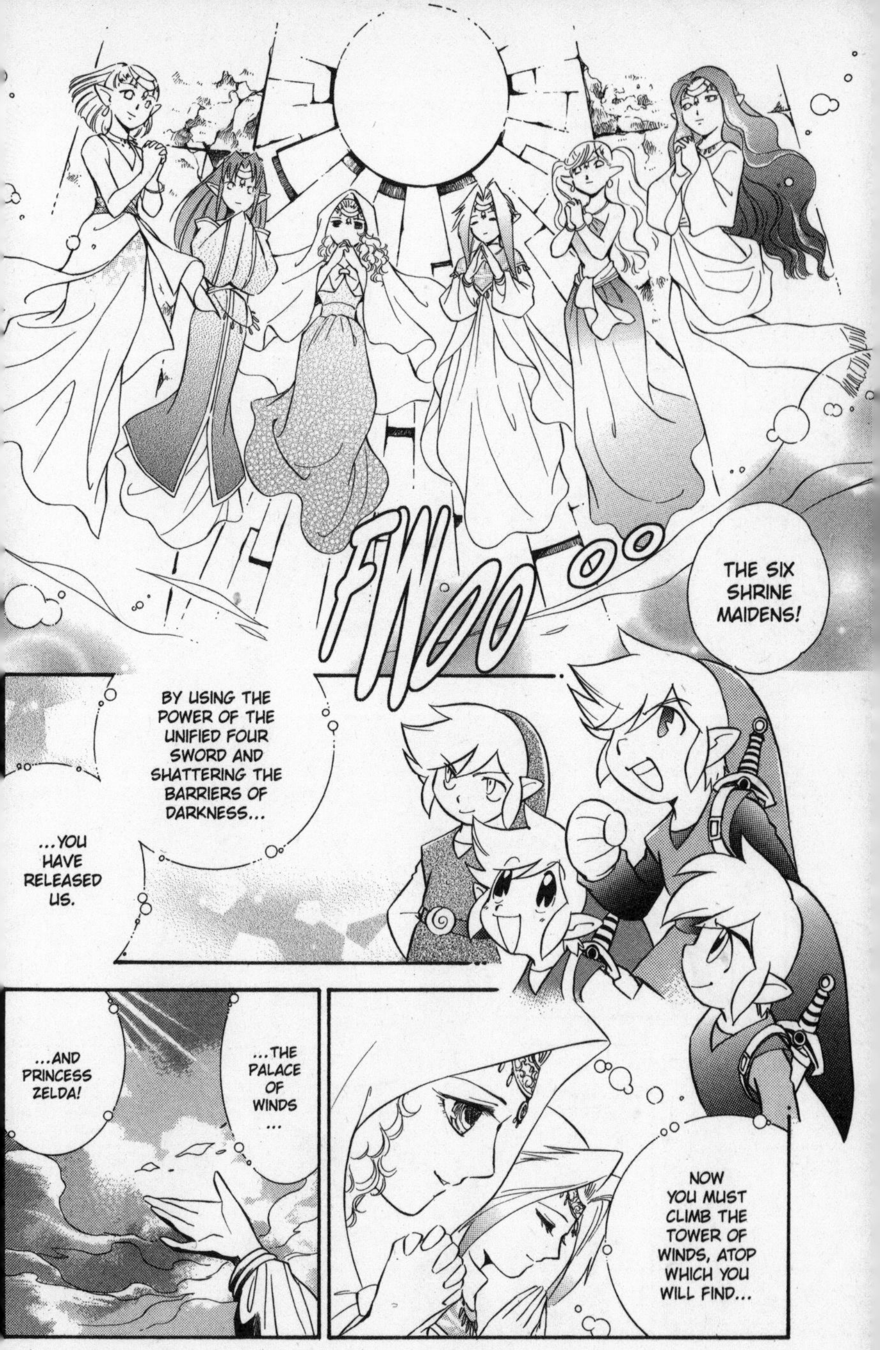
FWOOO
THE SIX SHRINE MAIDENS!
BY USING THE POWER OF THE UNIFIED FOUR SWORD AND SHATTERING THE BARRIERS OF DARKNESS...
...YOU HAVE RELEASED US.
NOW YOU MUST CLIMB THE TOWER OF WINDS, ATOP WHICH YOU WILL FIND...
...THE PALACE OF WINDS...
...AND PRINCESS ZELDA!

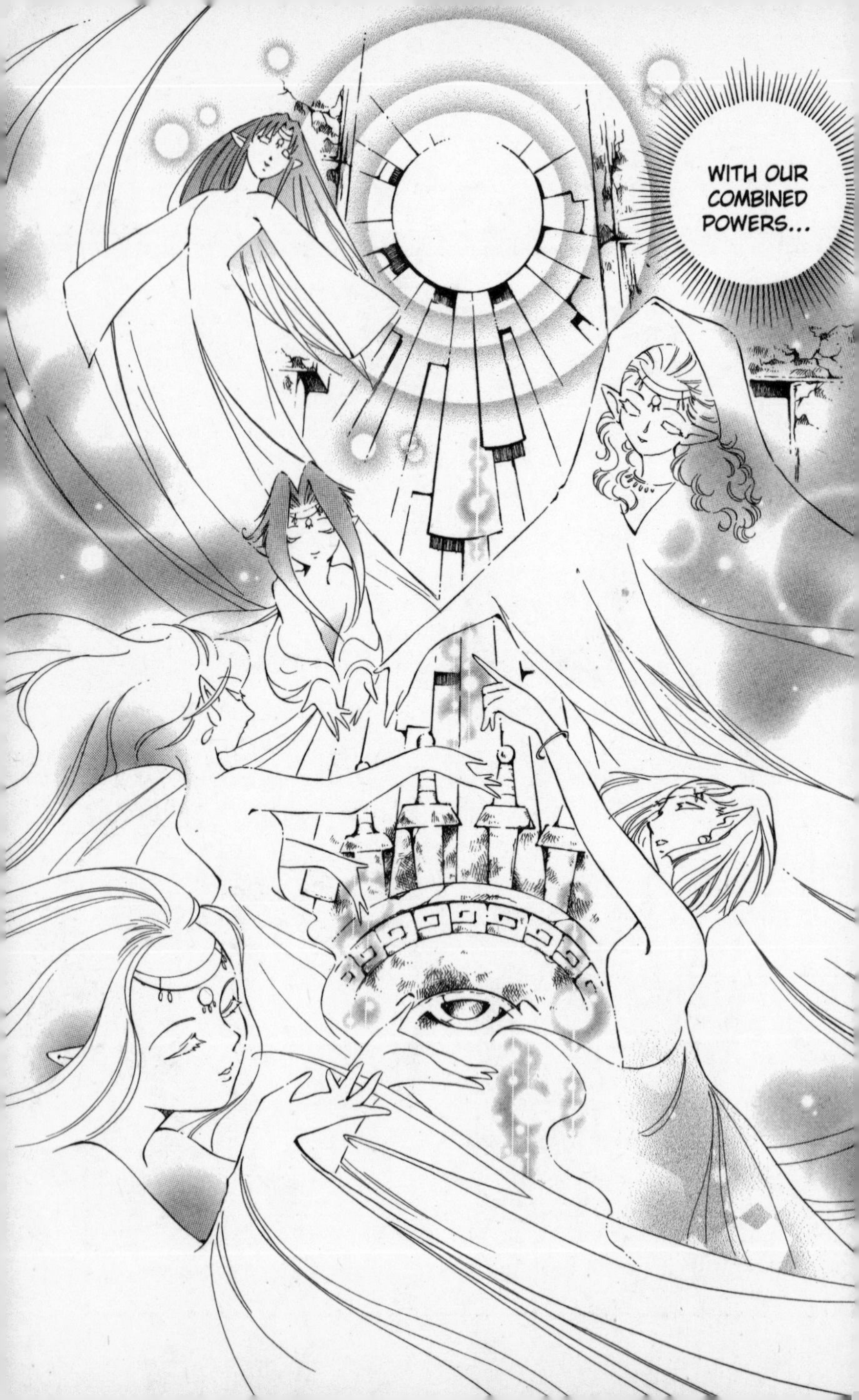
WITH OUR COMBINED POWERS...

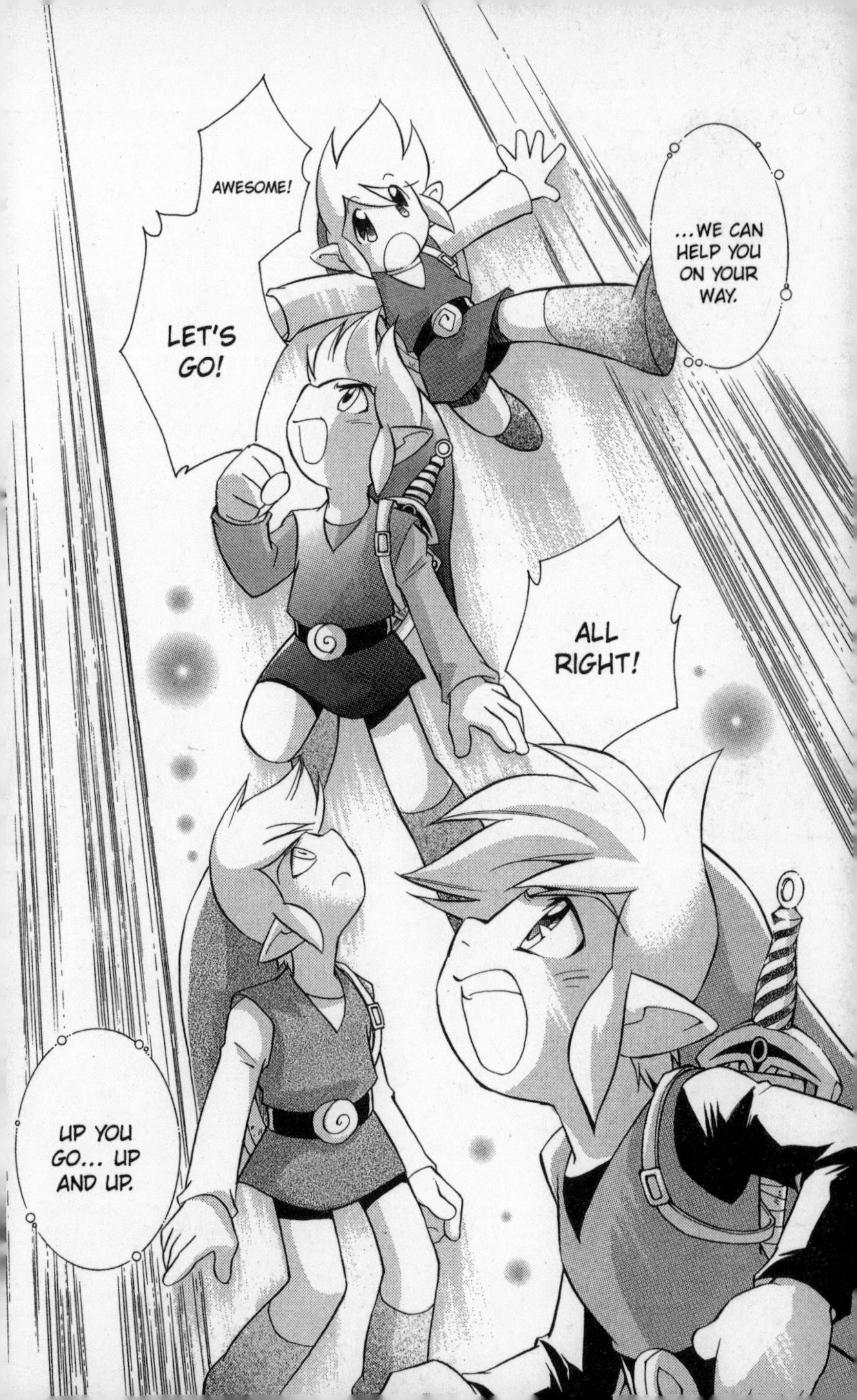
...WE CAN HELP YOU ON YOUR WAY.
AWESOME!
LET'S GO!
ALL RIGHT!
UP YOU GO... UP AND UP.

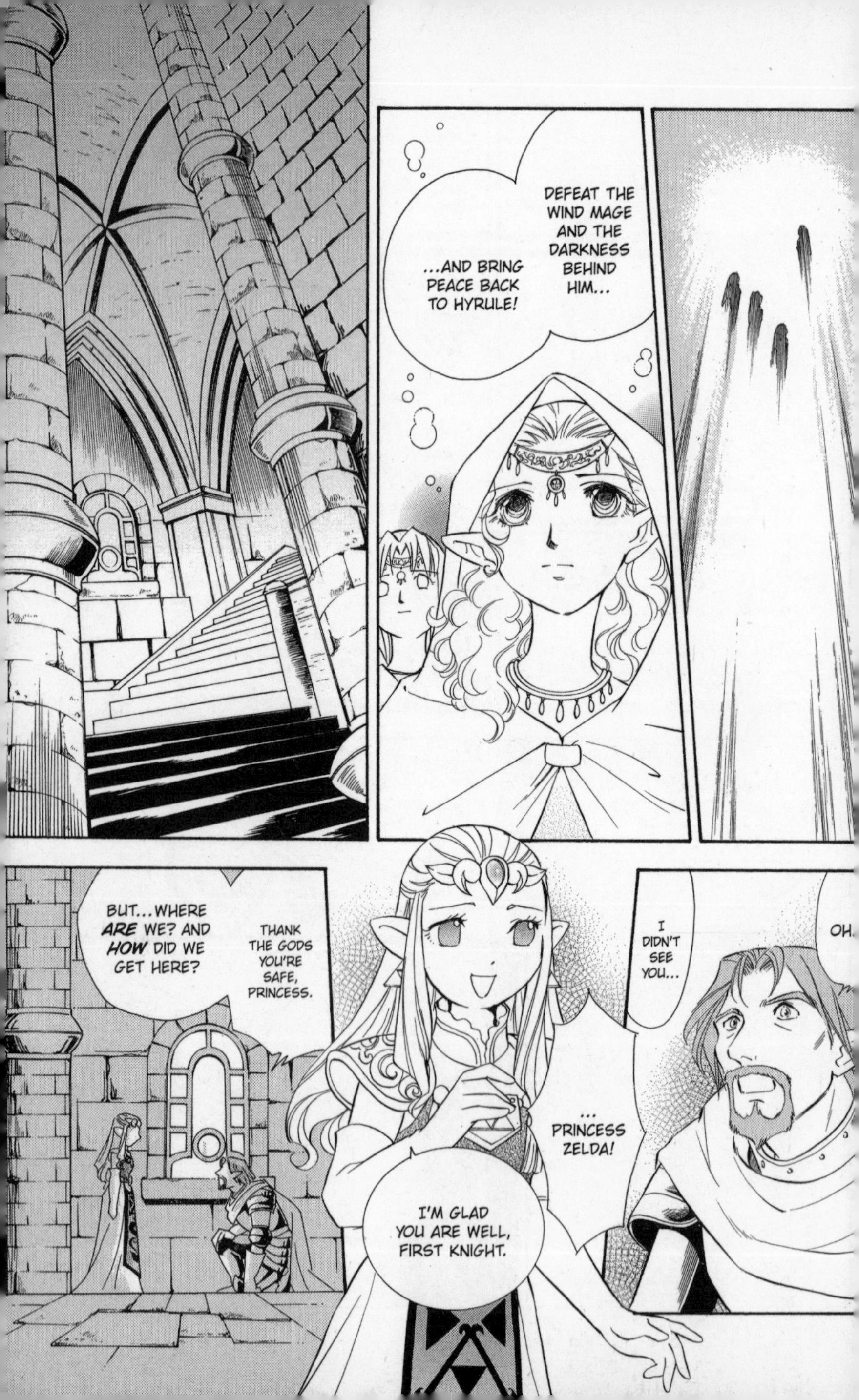
DEFEAT THE WIND MAGE AND THE DARKNESS BEHIND HIM...
...AND BRING PEACE BACK TO HYRULE!
OH.
I DIDN'T SEE YOU...
...PRINCESS ZELDA!
I'M GLAD YOU ARE WELL, FIRST KNIGHT.
THANK THE GODS YOU'RE SAFE, PRINCESS.
BUT...WHERE *ARE* WE? AND *HOW* DID WE GET HERE?

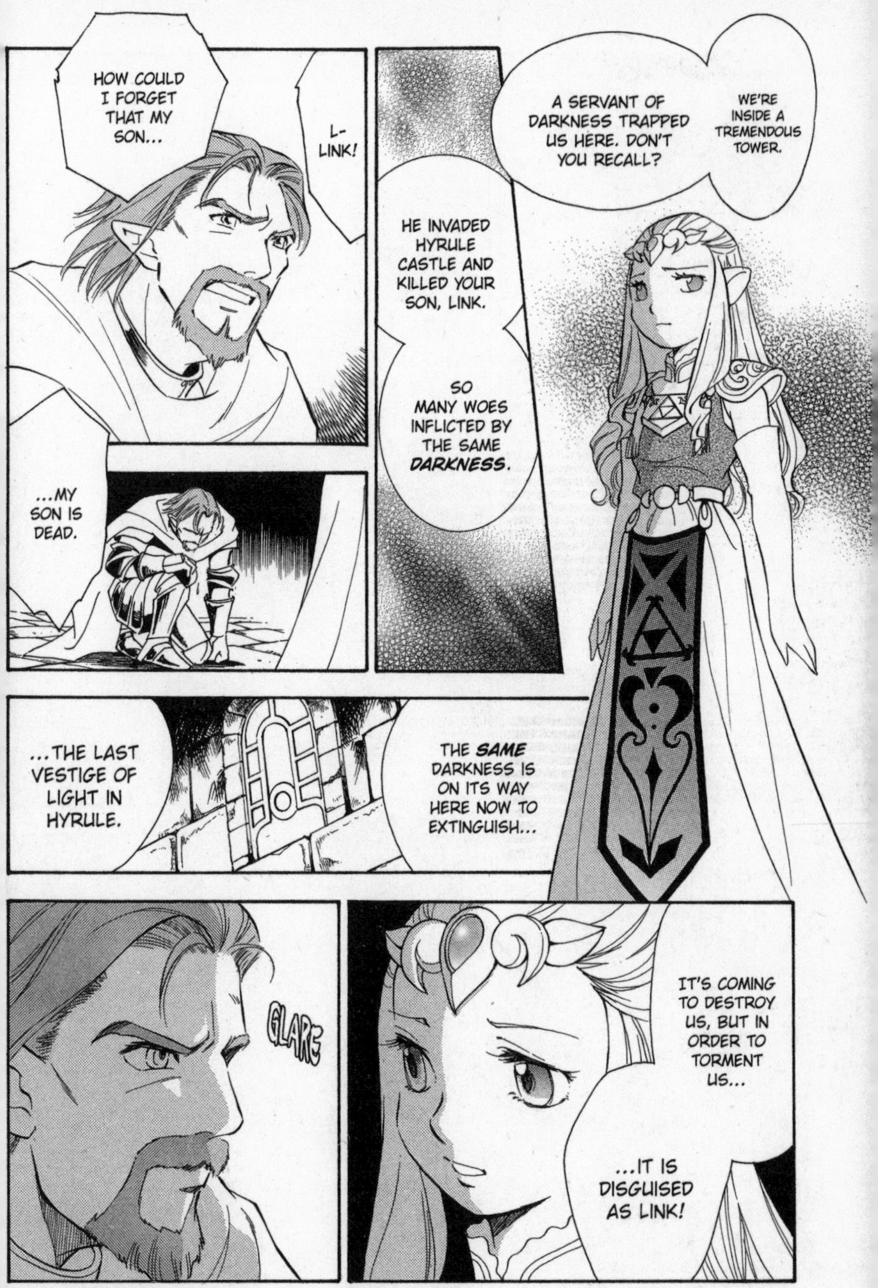
WE'RE INSIDE A TREMENDOUS TOWER.
A SERVANT OF DARKNESS TRAPPED US HERE. DON'T YOU RECALL?
HE INVADED HYRULE CASTLE AND KILLED YOUR SON, LINK.
SO MANY WOES INFLICTED BY THE SAME *DARKNESS*.
L- LINK!
HOW COULD I FORGET THAT MY SON...
...MY SON IS DEAD.
THE *SAME* DARKNESS IS ON ITS WAY HERE NOW TO EXTINGUISH...
...THE LAST VESTIGE OF LIGHT IN HYRULE.
IT'S COMING TO DESTROY US, BUT IN ORDER TO TORMENT US...
...IT IS DISGUISED AS LINK!
GLARE

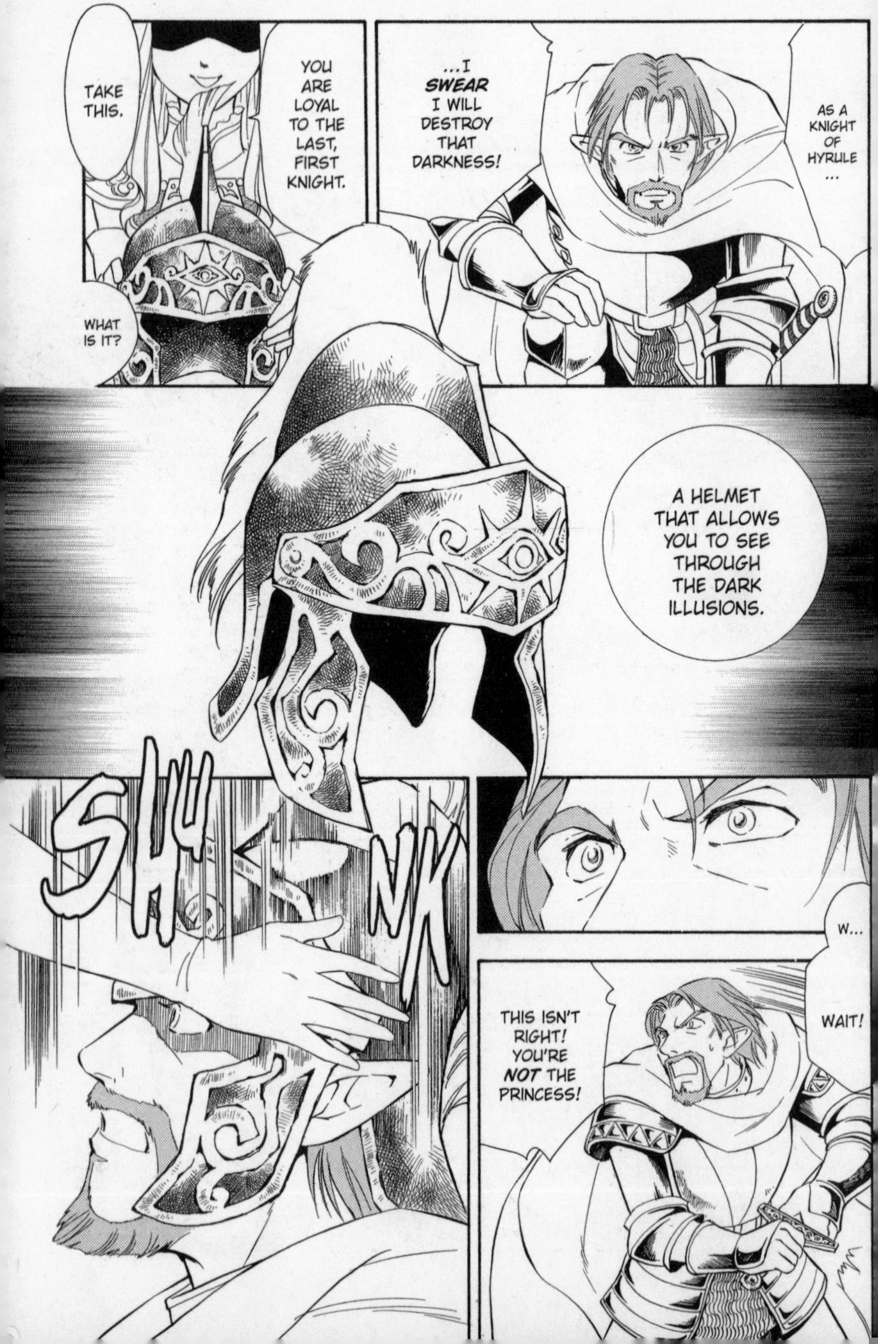
AS A KNIGHT OF HYRULE ...
...I **SWEAR** I WILL DESTROY THAT DARKNESS!
YOU ARE LOYAL TO THE LAST, FIRST KNIGHT.
TAKE THIS.
WHAT IS IT?
A HELMET THAT ALLOWS YOU TO SEE THROUGH THE DARK ILLUSIONS.
W...
WAIT!
THIS ISN'T RIGHT! YOU'RE **NOT** THE PRINCESS!
SHUNK

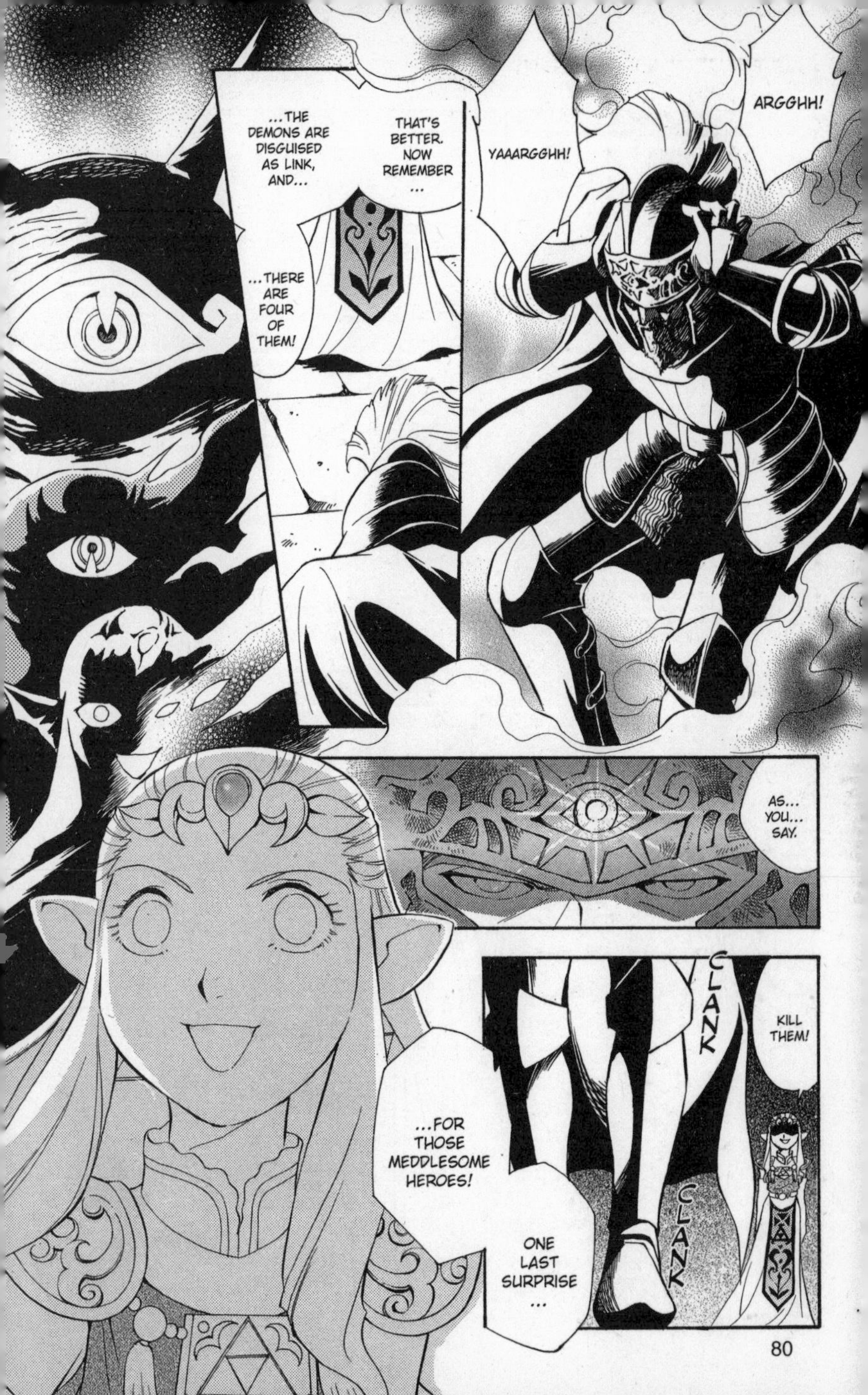
ARGGHH!
YAAARGGHH!
THAT'S BETTER. NOW REMEMBER ...
...THE DEMONS ARE DISGUISED AS LINK, AND...
...THERE ARE FOUR OF THEM!
AS... YOU... SAY.
KILL THEM!
CLANK
CLANK
ONE LAST SURPRISE ...
...FOR THOSE MEDDLESOME HEROES!

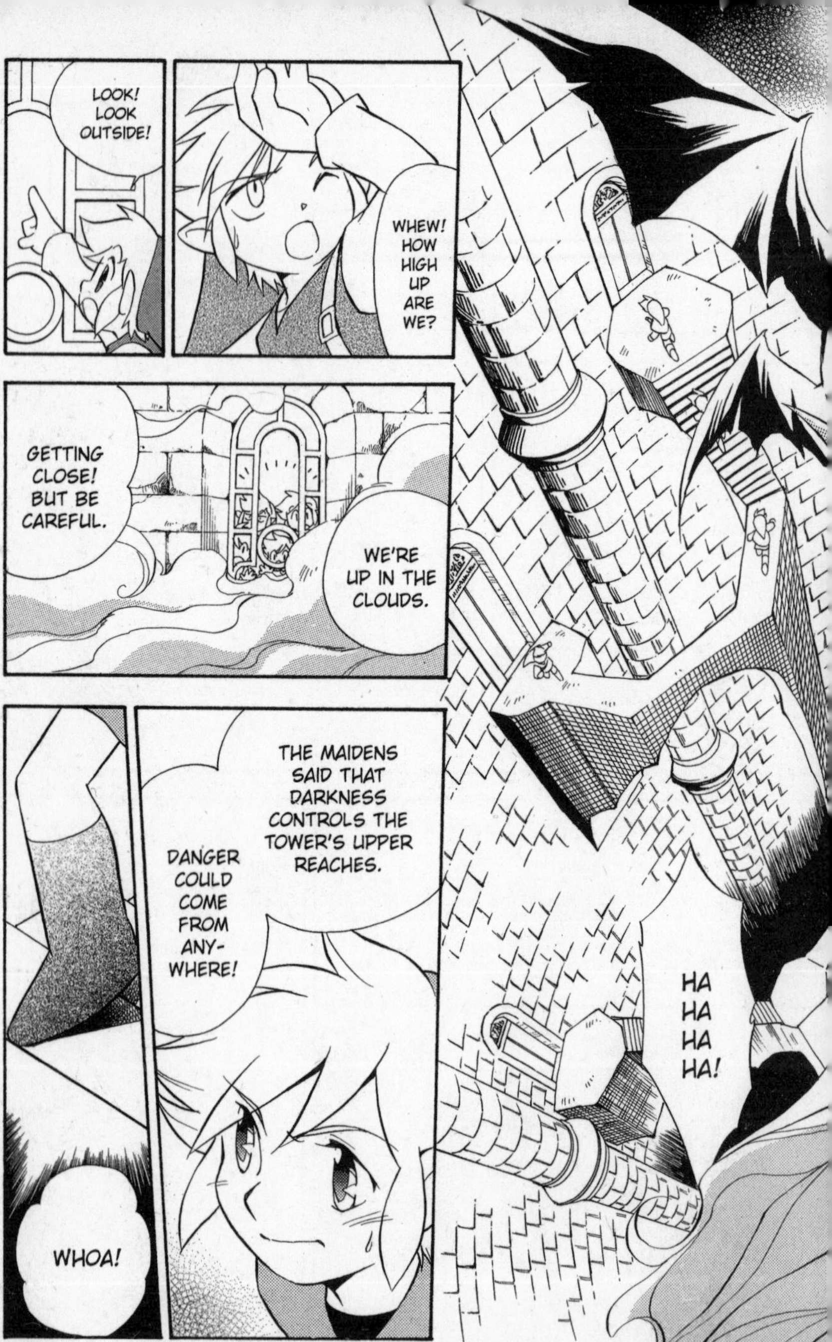
HA HA HA HA!
WHEW! HOW HIGH UP ARE WE?
LOOK! LOOK OUTSIDE!
WE'RE UP IN THE CLOUDS.
GETTING CLOSE! BUT BE CAREFUL.
THE MAIDENS SAID THAT DARKNESS CONTROLS THE TOWER'S UPPER REACHES.
DANGER COULD COME FROM ANY-WHERE!
WHOA!

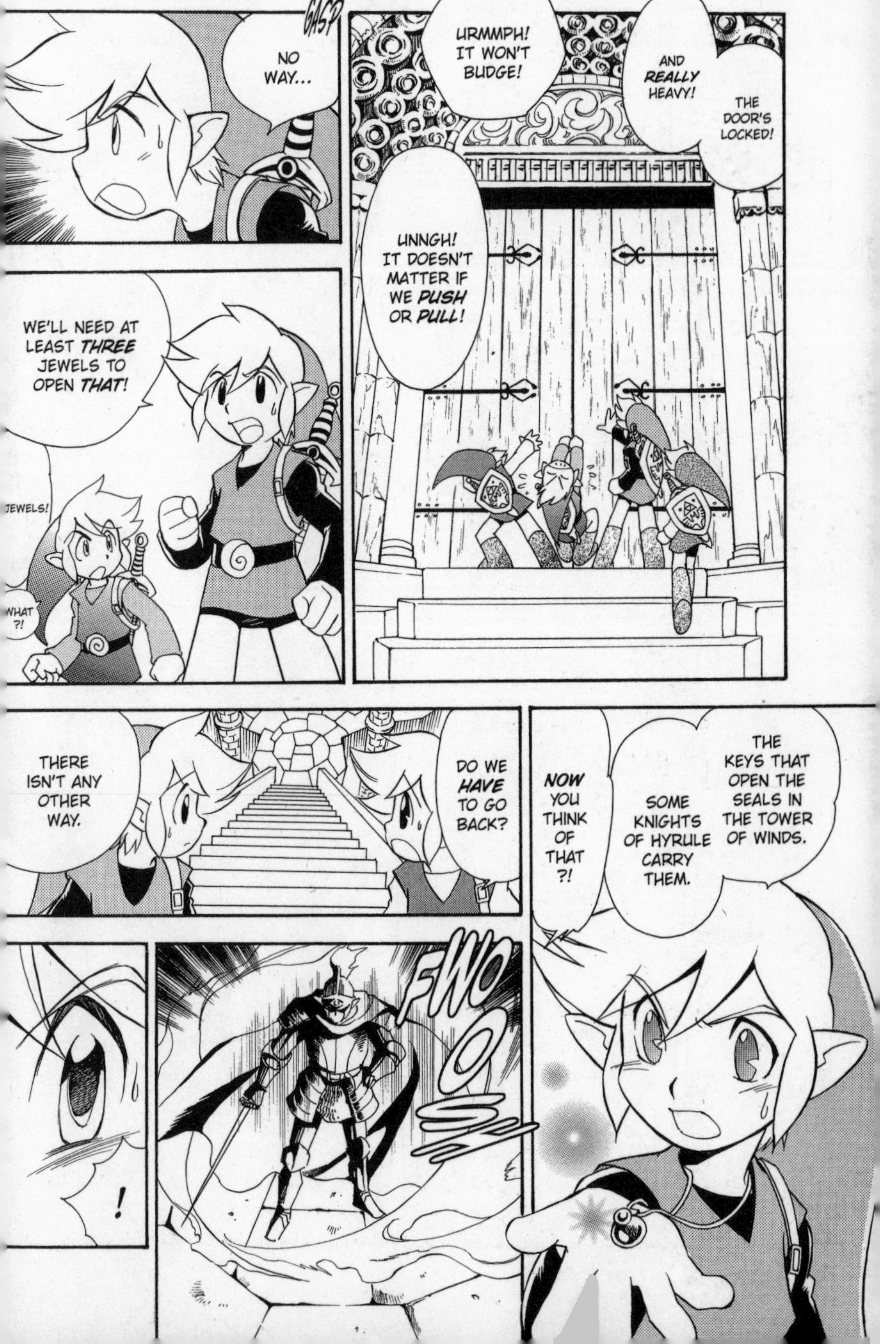
THE DOOR'S LOCKED!
AND REALLY HEAVY!
URMMPH! IT WON'T BUDGE!
UNNGH! IT DOESN'T MATTER IF WE PUSH OR PULL!
GASP
NO WAY...
WE'LL NEED AT LEAST THREE JEWELS TO OPEN THAT!
JEWELS!
WHAT?!
THE KEYS THAT OPEN THE SEALS IN THE TOWER OF WINDS.
SOME KNIGHTS OF HYRULE CARRY THEM.
NOW YOU THINK OF THAT?!
DO WE HAVE TO GO BACK?
THERE ISN'T ANY OTHER WAY.
FWOOOSH
!

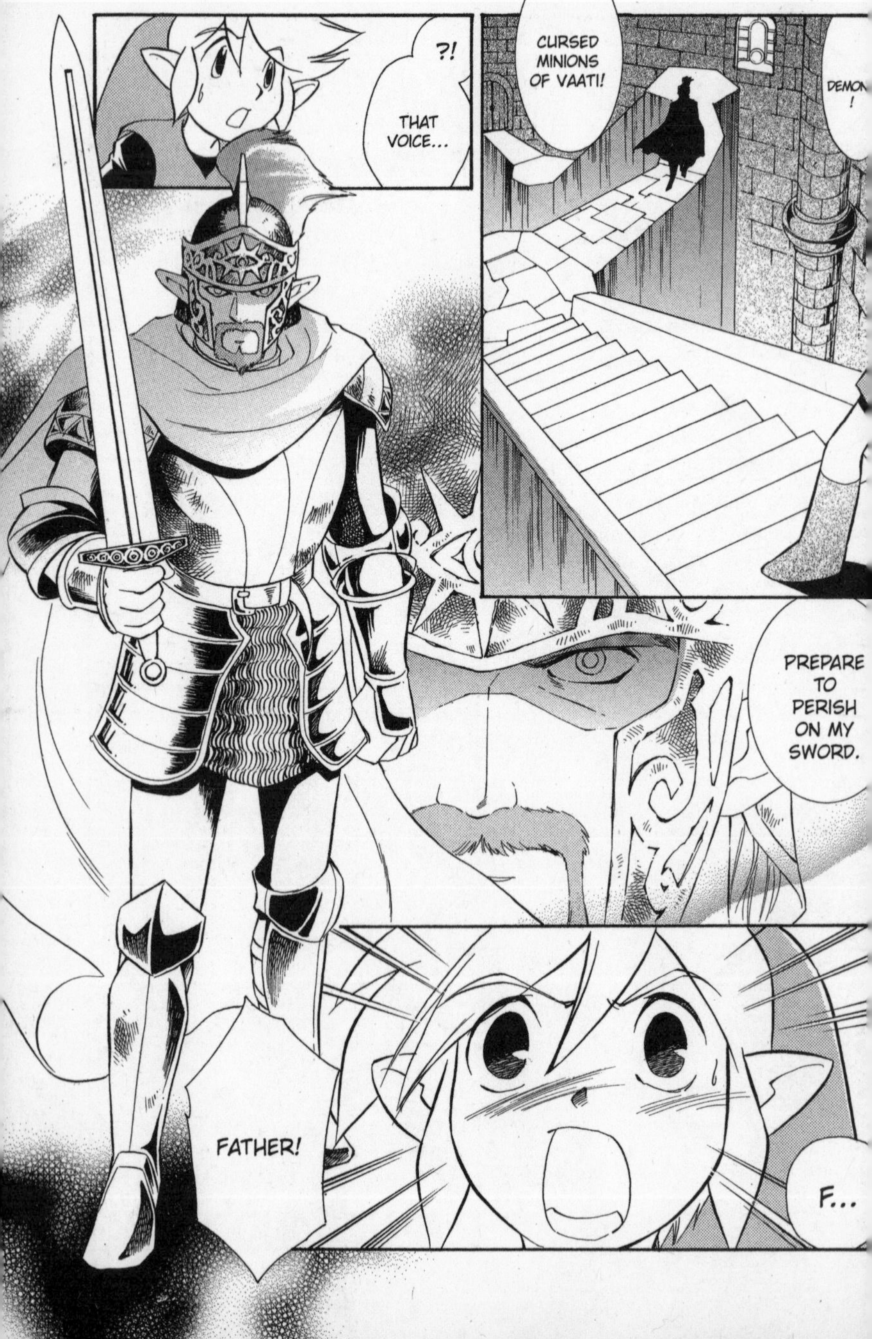
CURSED MINIONS OF VAATI!
DEMON!
?!
THAT VOICE...
PREPARE TO PERISH ON MY SWORD.
F...
FATHER!

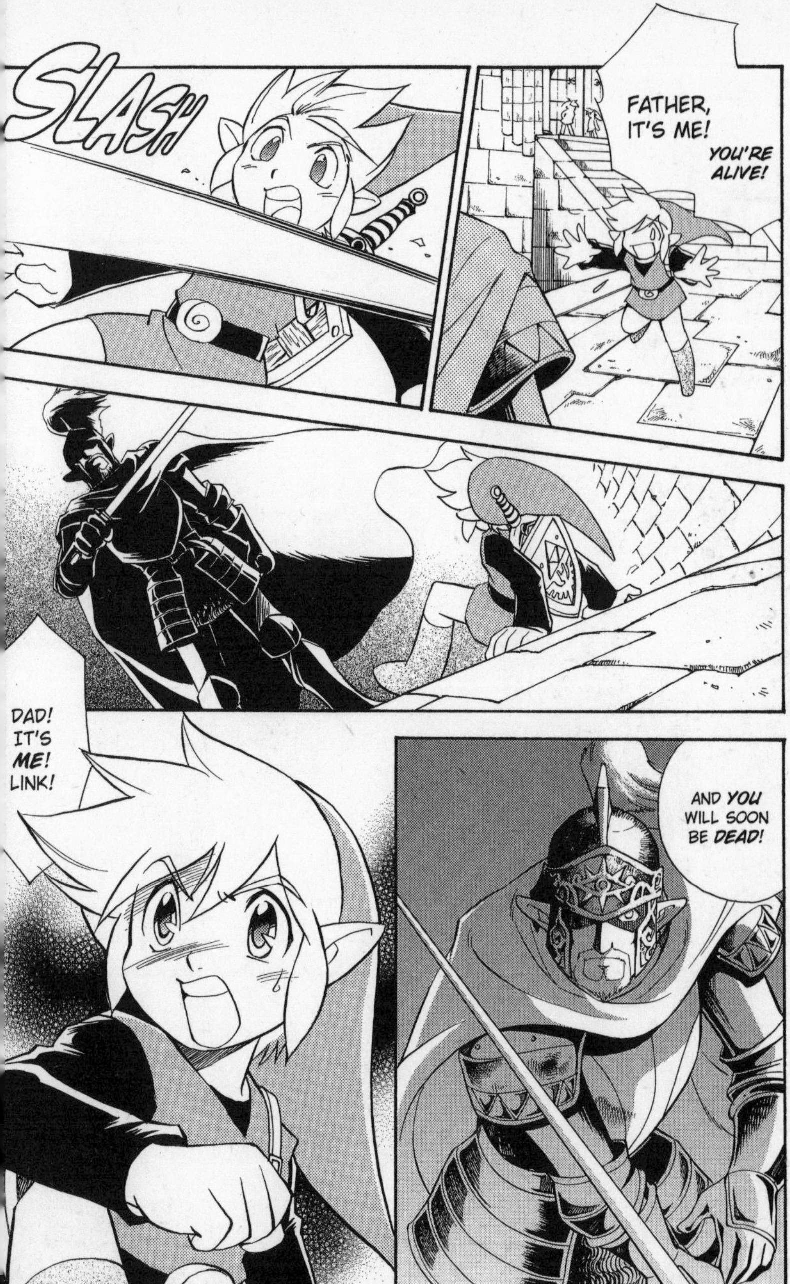
FATHER, IT'S ME!
YOU'RE ALIVE!
SLASH
AND YOU WILL SOON BE DEAD!
DAD! IT'S ME! LINK!

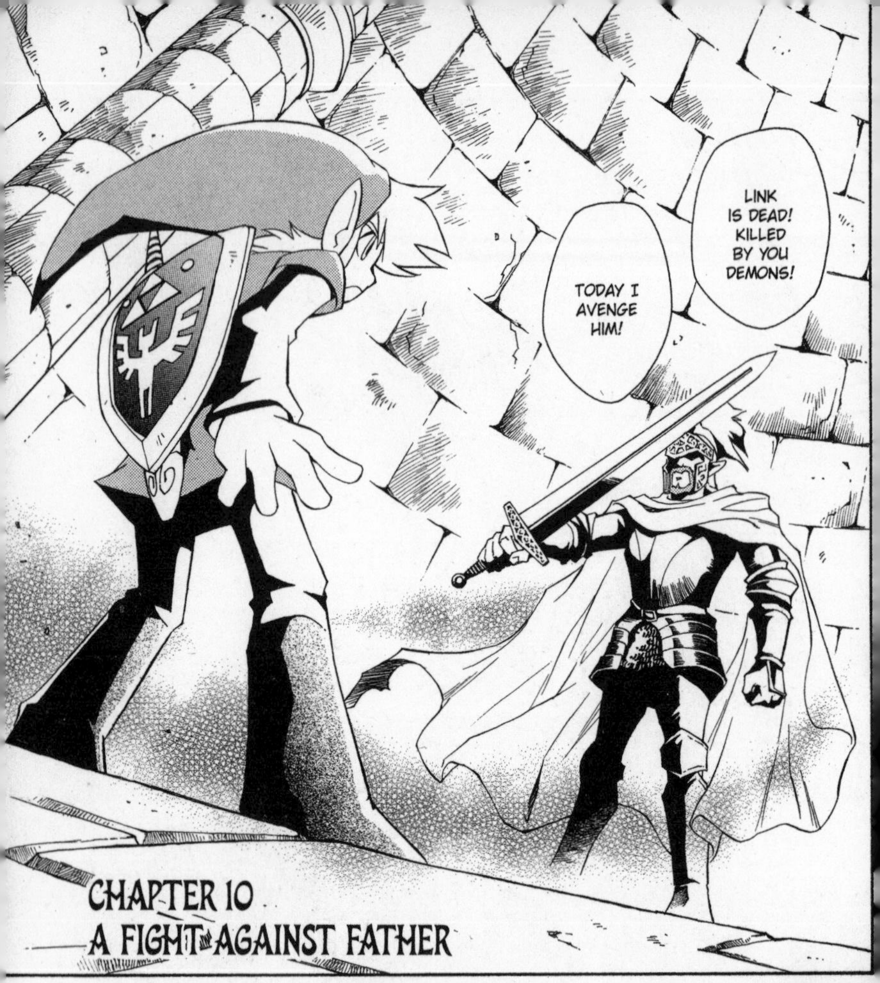
LINK IS DEAD! KILLED BY YOU DEMONS!
TODAY I AVENGE HIM!

CHAPTER 10
A FIGHT AGAINST FATHER

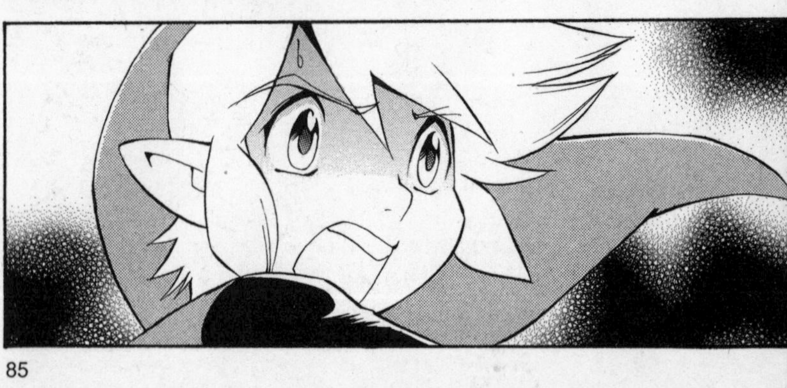

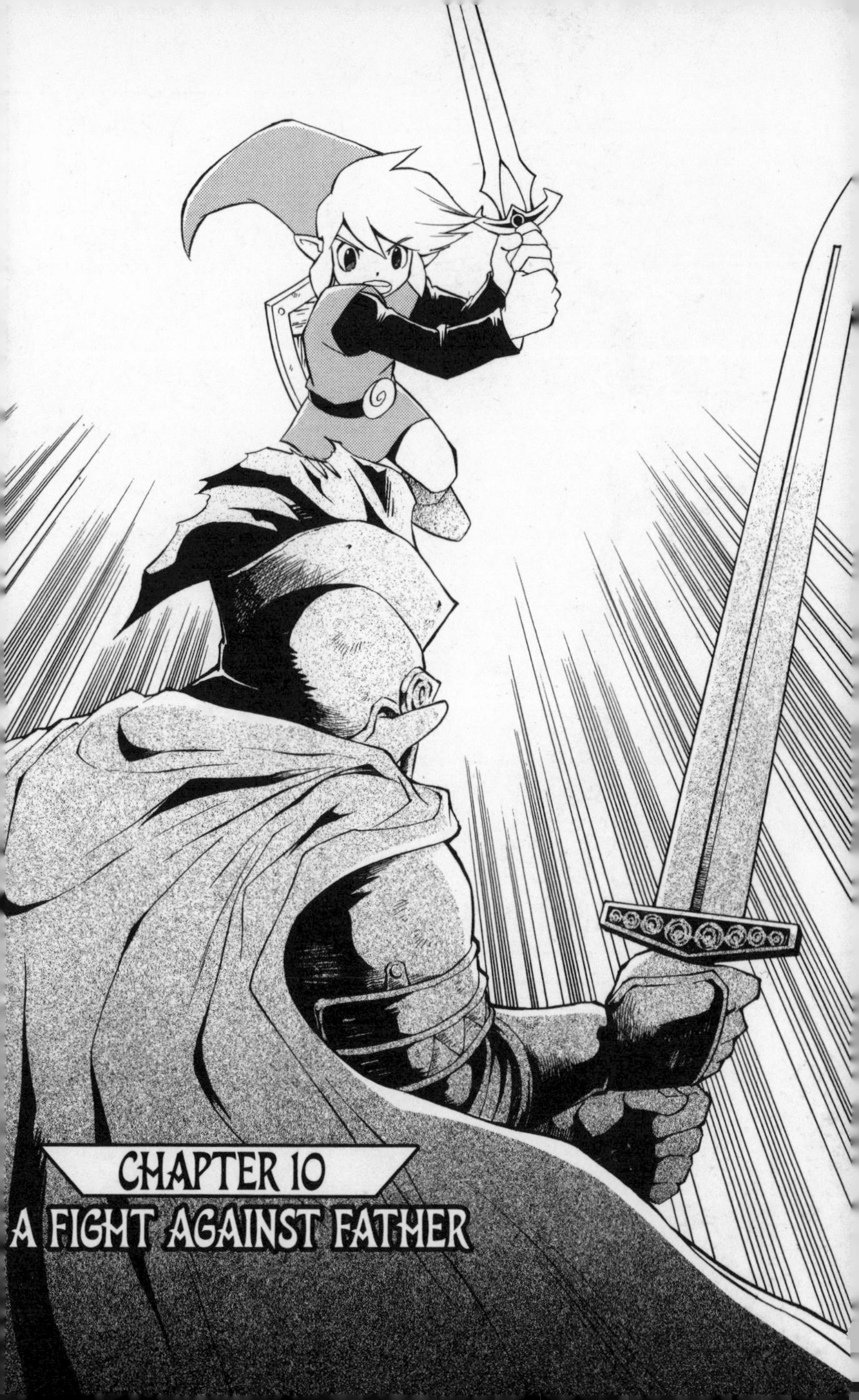
CHAPTER 10
A FIGHT AGAINST FATHER

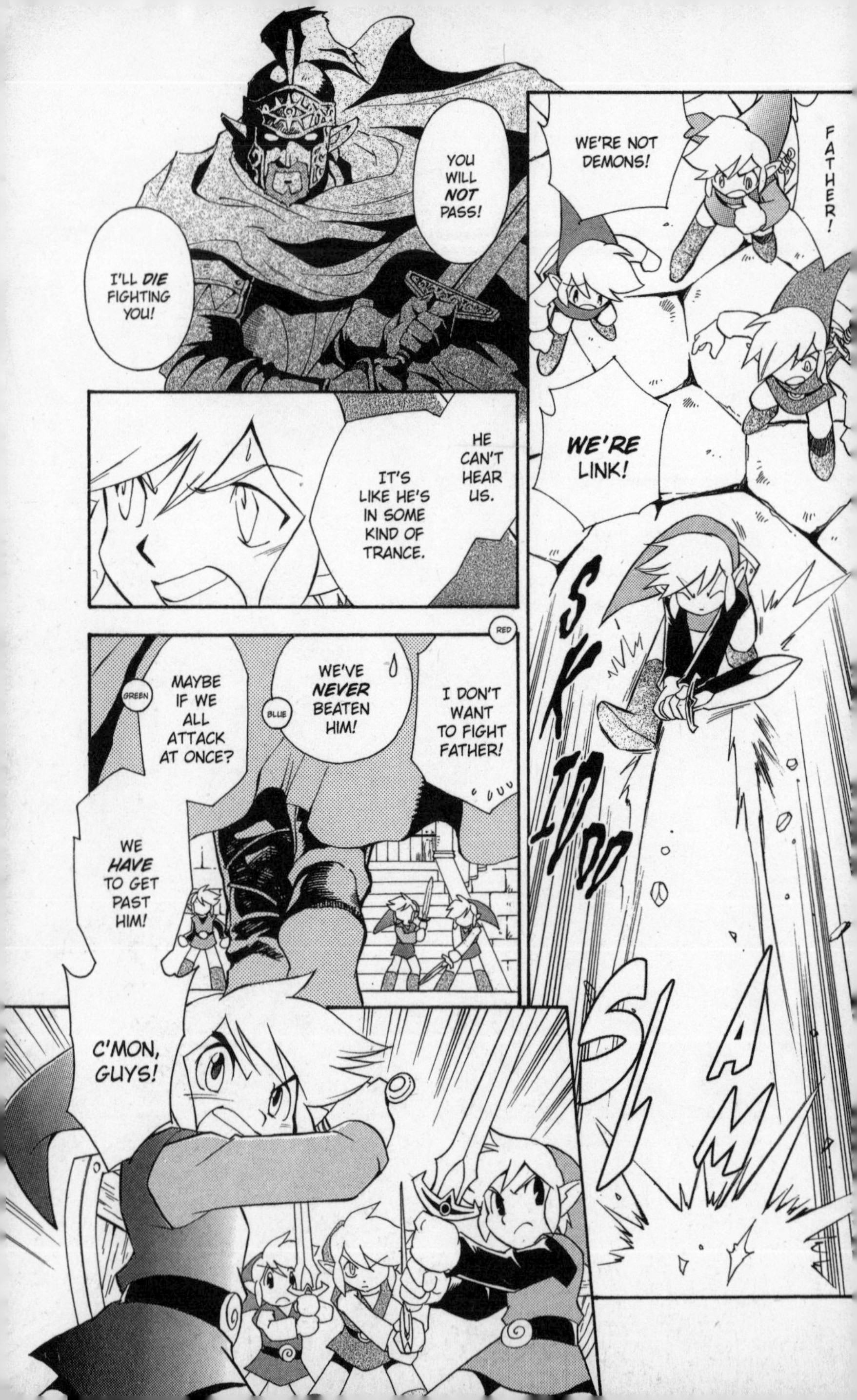
FATHER!
WE'RE NOT DEMONS!
WE'RE LINK!
SKIDOO
SLAM
YOU WILL NOT PASS!
I'LL DIE FIGHTING YOU!
HE CAN'T HEAR US.
IT'S LIKE HE'S IN SOME KIND OF TRANCE.
RED
I DON'T WANT TO FIGHT FATHER!
BLUE
WE'VE NEVER BEATEN HIM!
GREEN
MAYBE IF WE ALL ATTACK AT ONCE?
WE HAVE TO GET PAST HIM!
C'MON, GUYS!

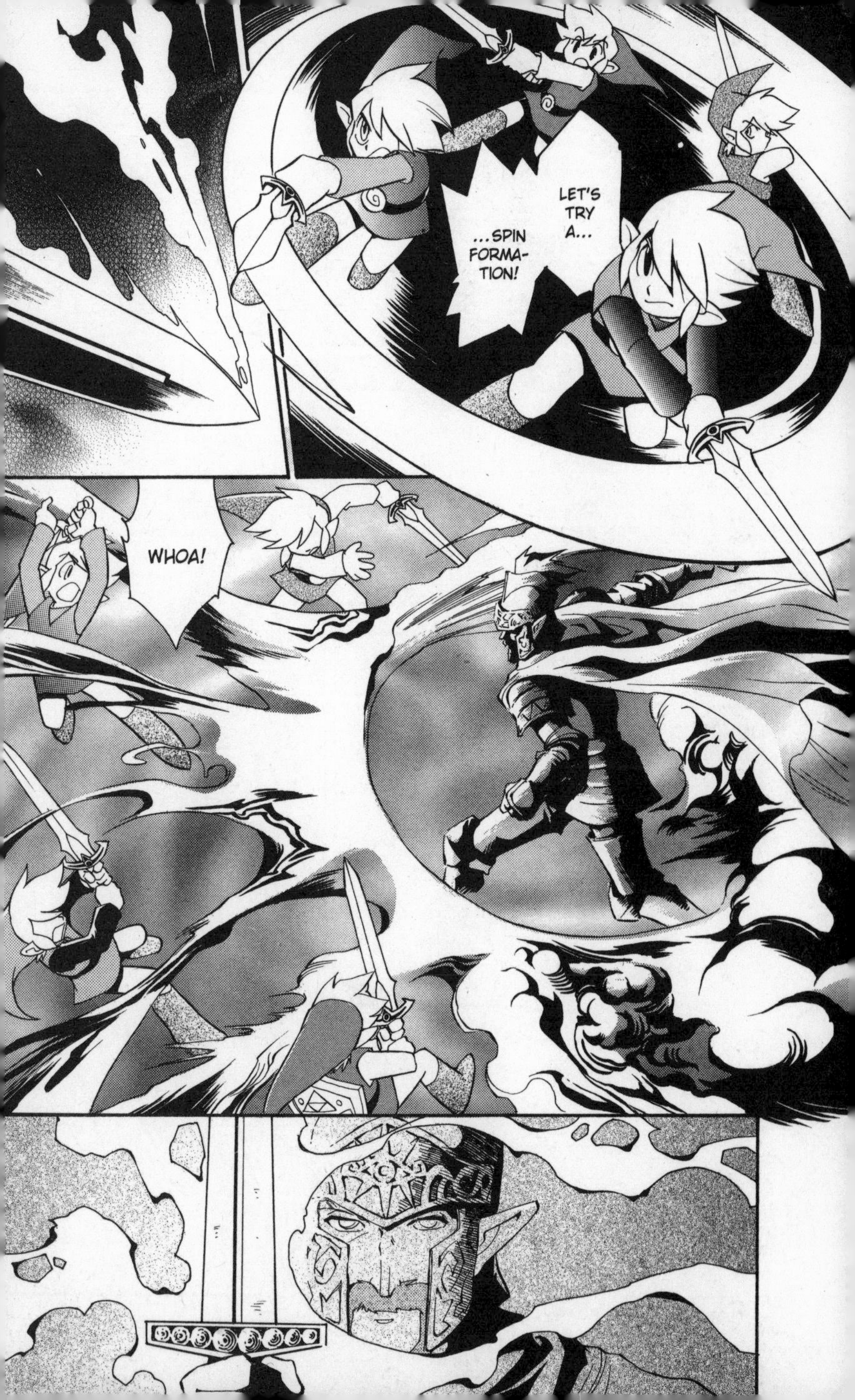
LET'S TRY A...
...SPIN FORMATION!
WHOA!

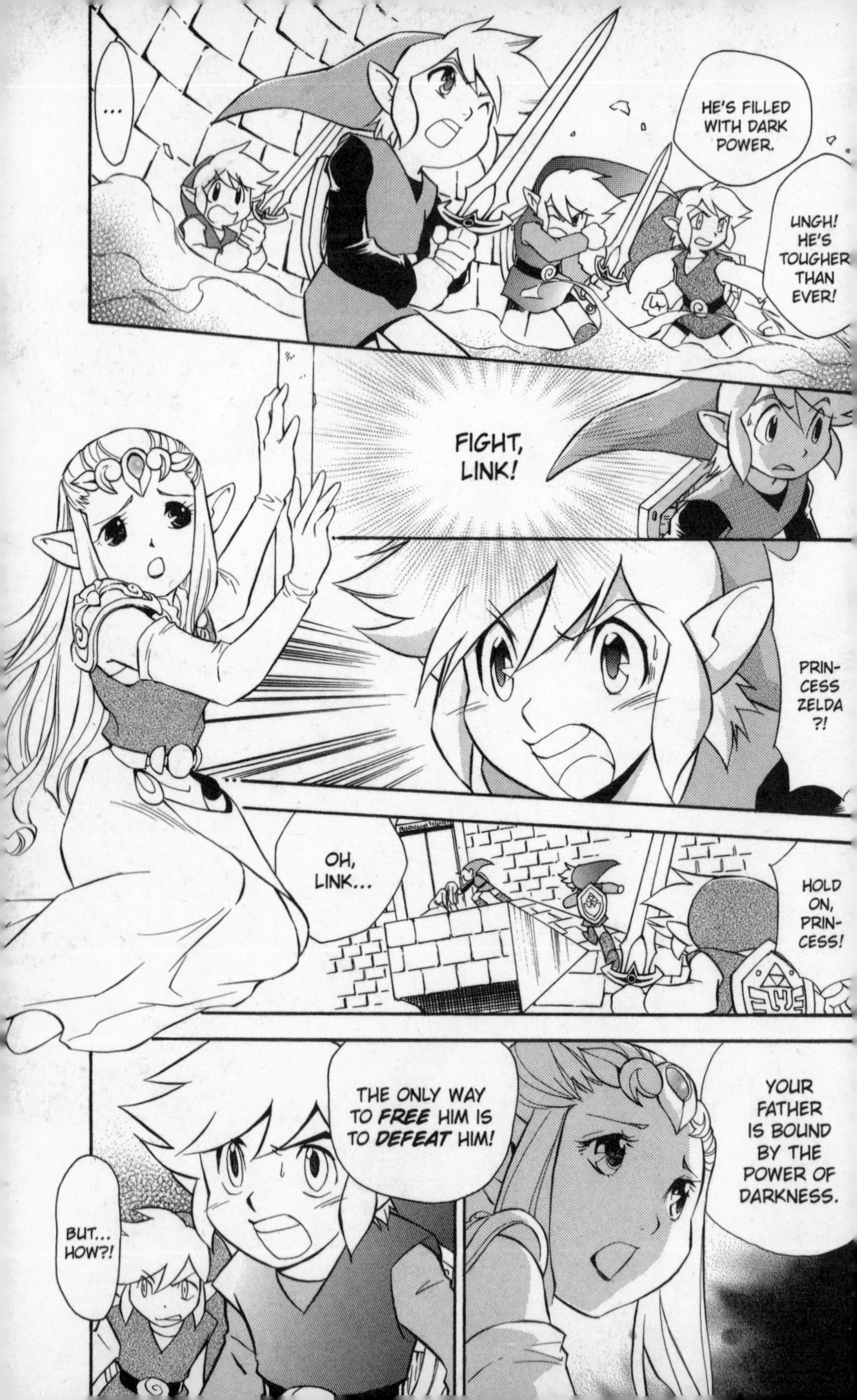
HE'S FILLED WITH DARK POWER.
UNGH! HE'S TOUGHER THAN EVER!
...
FIGHT, LINK!
PRIN-CESS ZELDA ?!
HOLD ON, PRIN-CESS!
OH, LINK...
YOUR FATHER IS BOUND BY THE POWER OF DARKNESS.
THE ONLY WAY TO *FREE* HIM IS TO *DEFEAT* HIM!
BUT... HOW?!

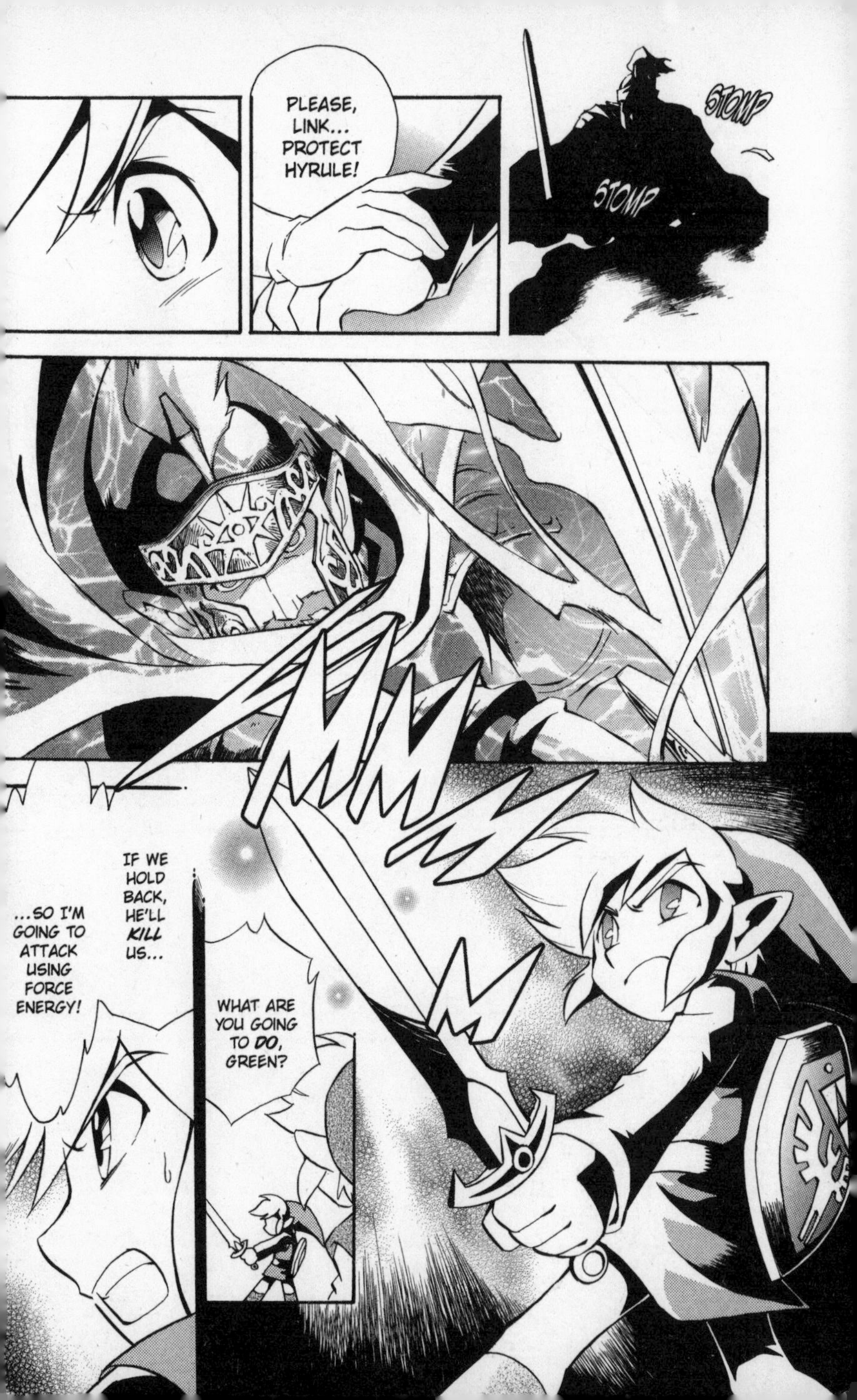
STOMP
STOMP
PLEASE, LINK... PROTECT HYRULE!
WHAT ARE YOU GOING TO DO, GREEN?
IF WE HOLD BACK, HE'LL KILL US...
...SO I'M GOING TO ATTACK USING FORCE ENERGY!

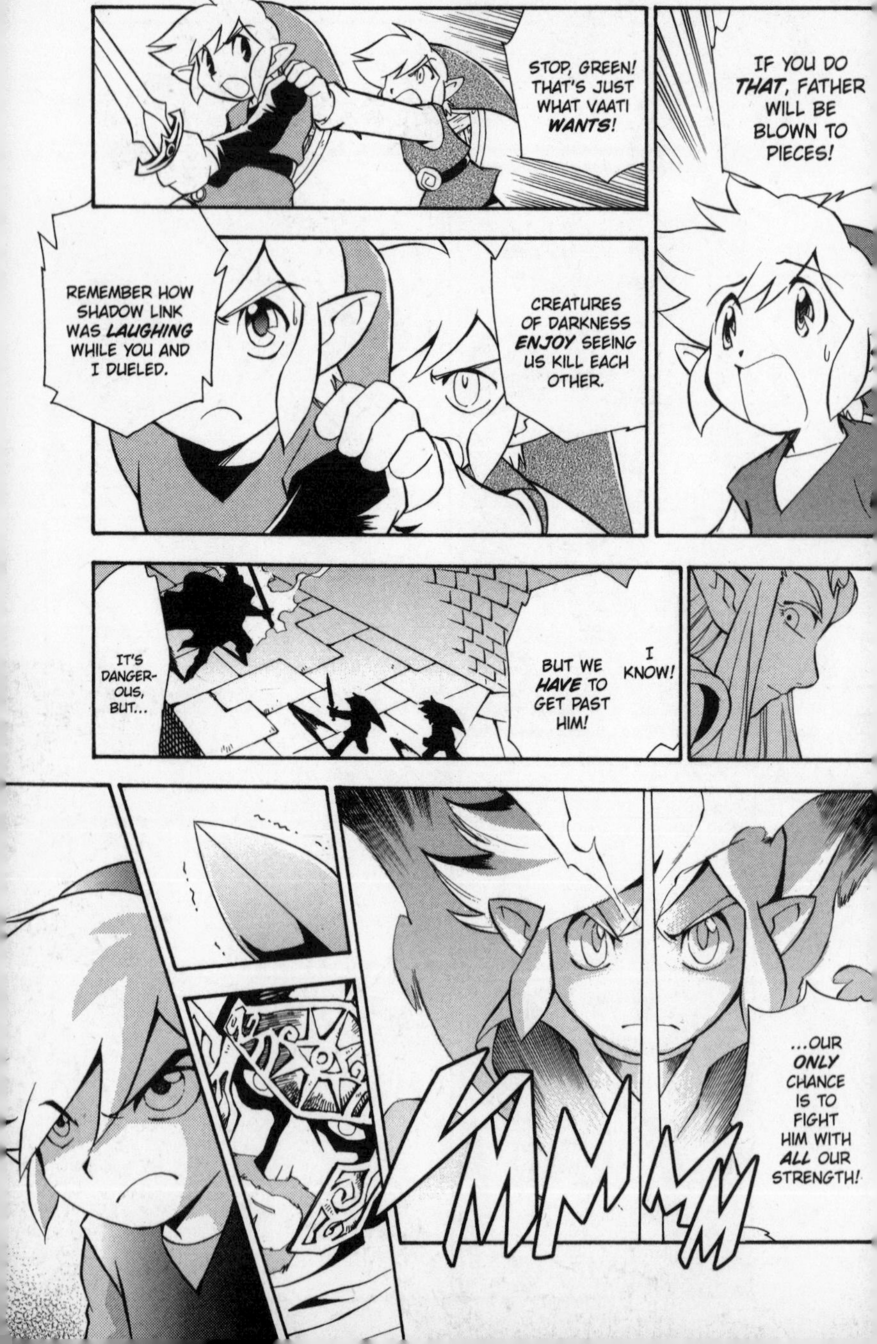
IF YOU DO THAT, FATHER WILL BE BLOWN TO PIECES!
STOP, GREEN! THAT'S JUST WHAT VAATI WANTS!
CREATURES OF DARKNESS ENJOY SEEING US KILL EACH OTHER.
REMEMBER HOW SHADOW LINK WAS LAUGHING WHILE YOU AND I DUELED.
I KNOW!
BUT WE HAVE TO GET PAST HIM!
IT'S DANGER-OUS, BUT...
...OUR ONLY CHANCE IS TO FIGHT HIM WITH ALL OUR STRENGTH!

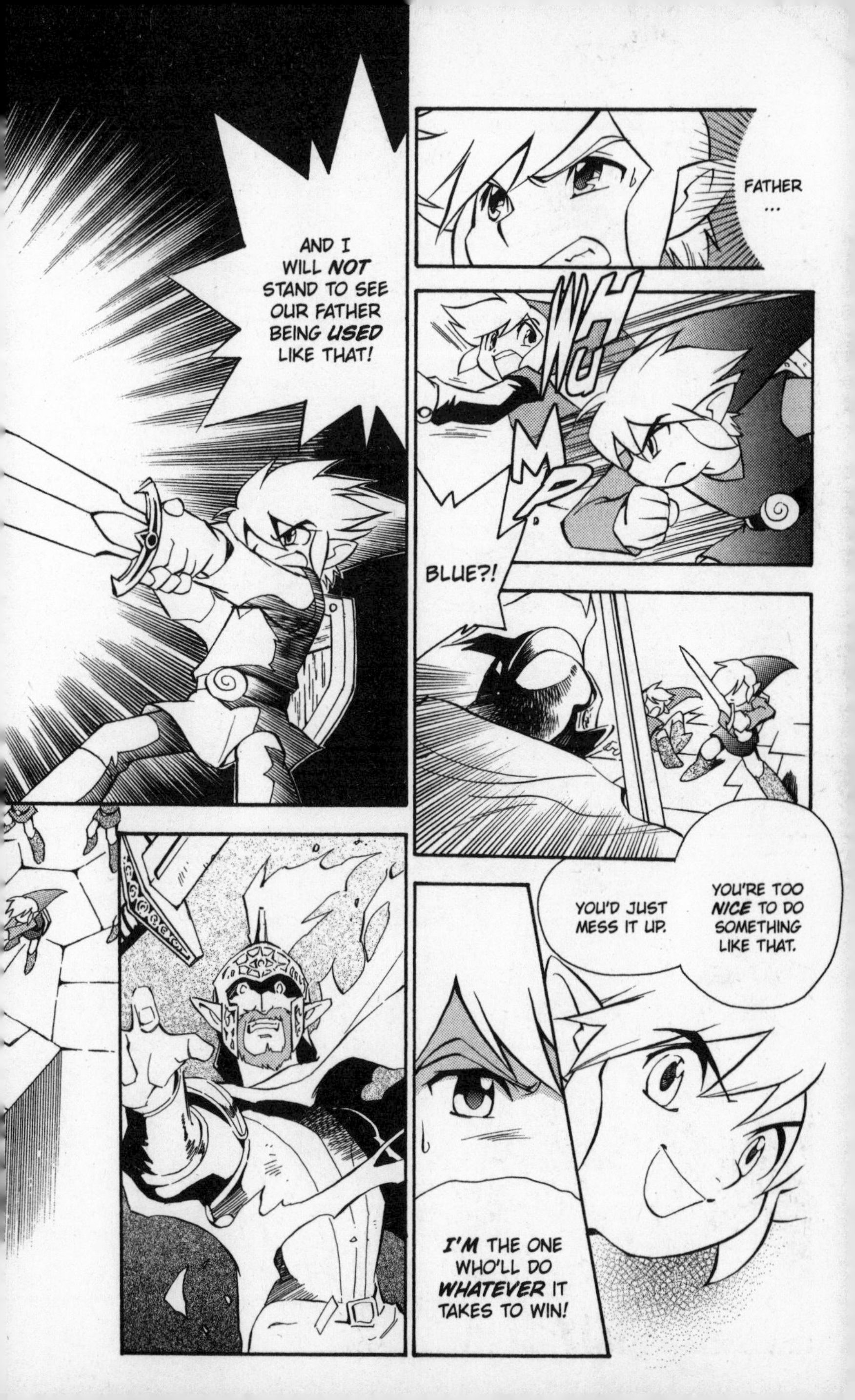
FATHER ...
WHUMP
BLUE?!
AND I WILL **NOT** STAND TO SEE OUR FATHER BEING **USED** LIKE THAT!
YOU'RE TOO **NICE** TO DO SOMETHING LIKE THAT.
YOU'D JUST MESS IT UP.
I'M THE ONE WHO'LL DO **WHATEVER** IT TAKES TO WIN!

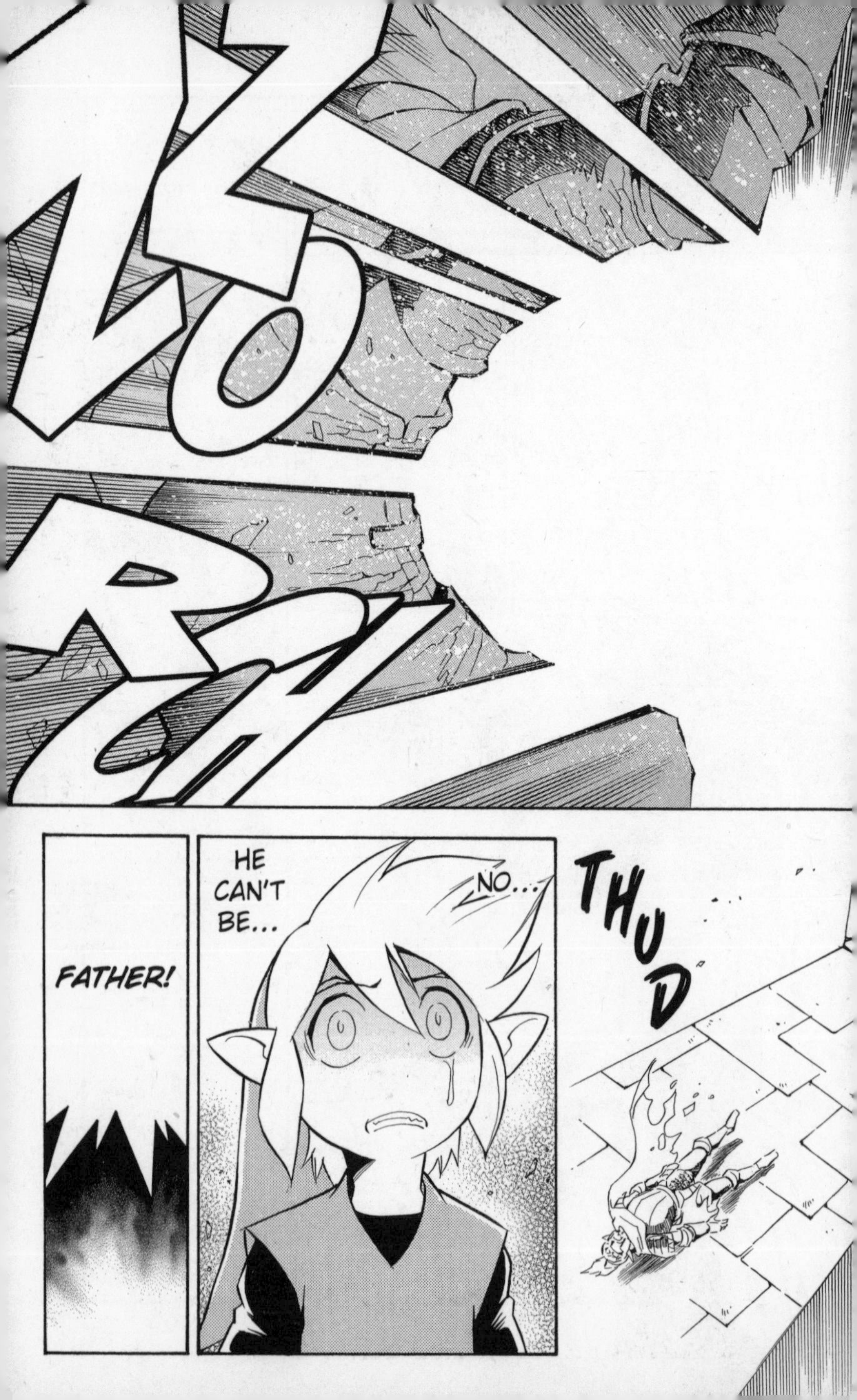
THUD
NO...
HE CAN'T BE...
FATHER!

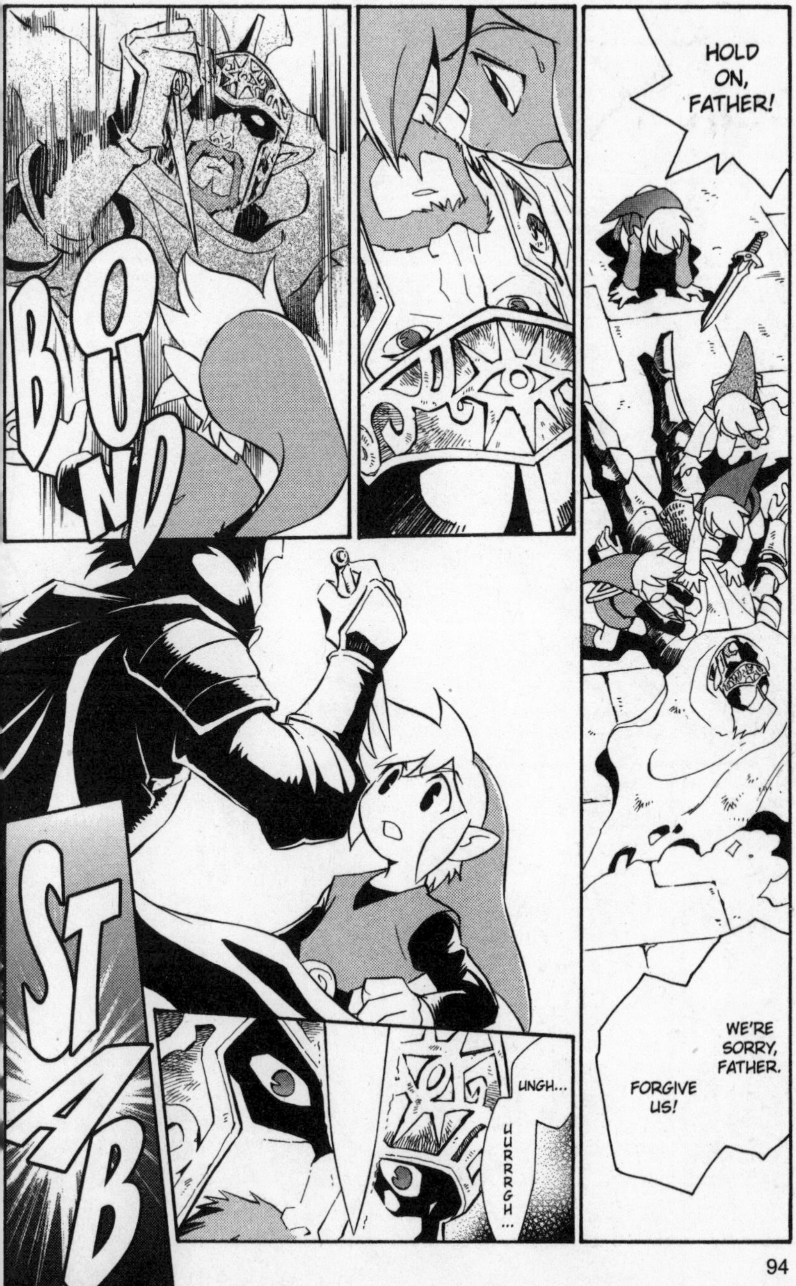
HOLD ON, FATHER!
WE'RE SORRY, FATHER.
FORGIVE US!
BOUND
STAB
UNGH...
UURRRGH...

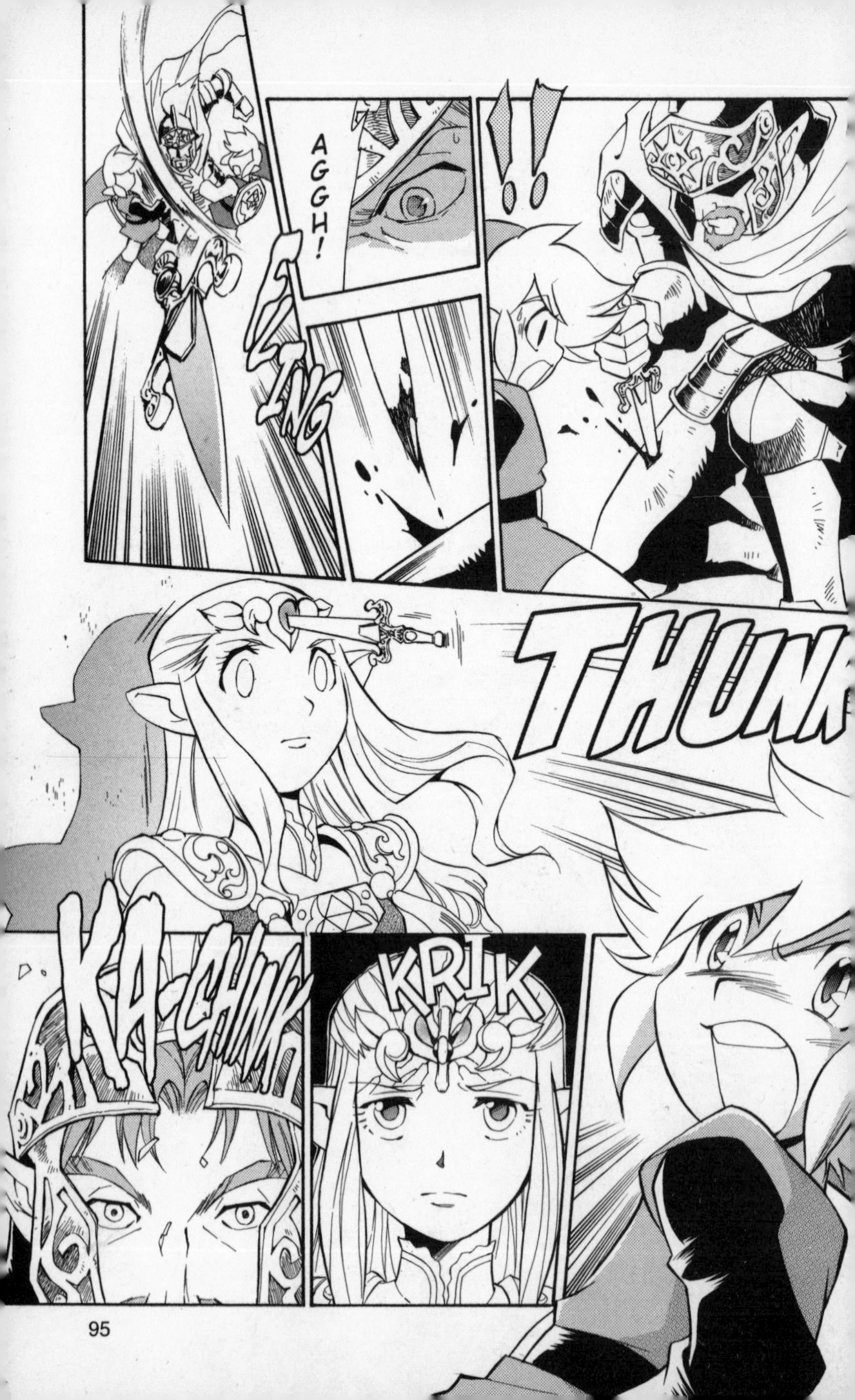
!!
AGGH!
ZING
THUN
KRIK
KA-CHINK

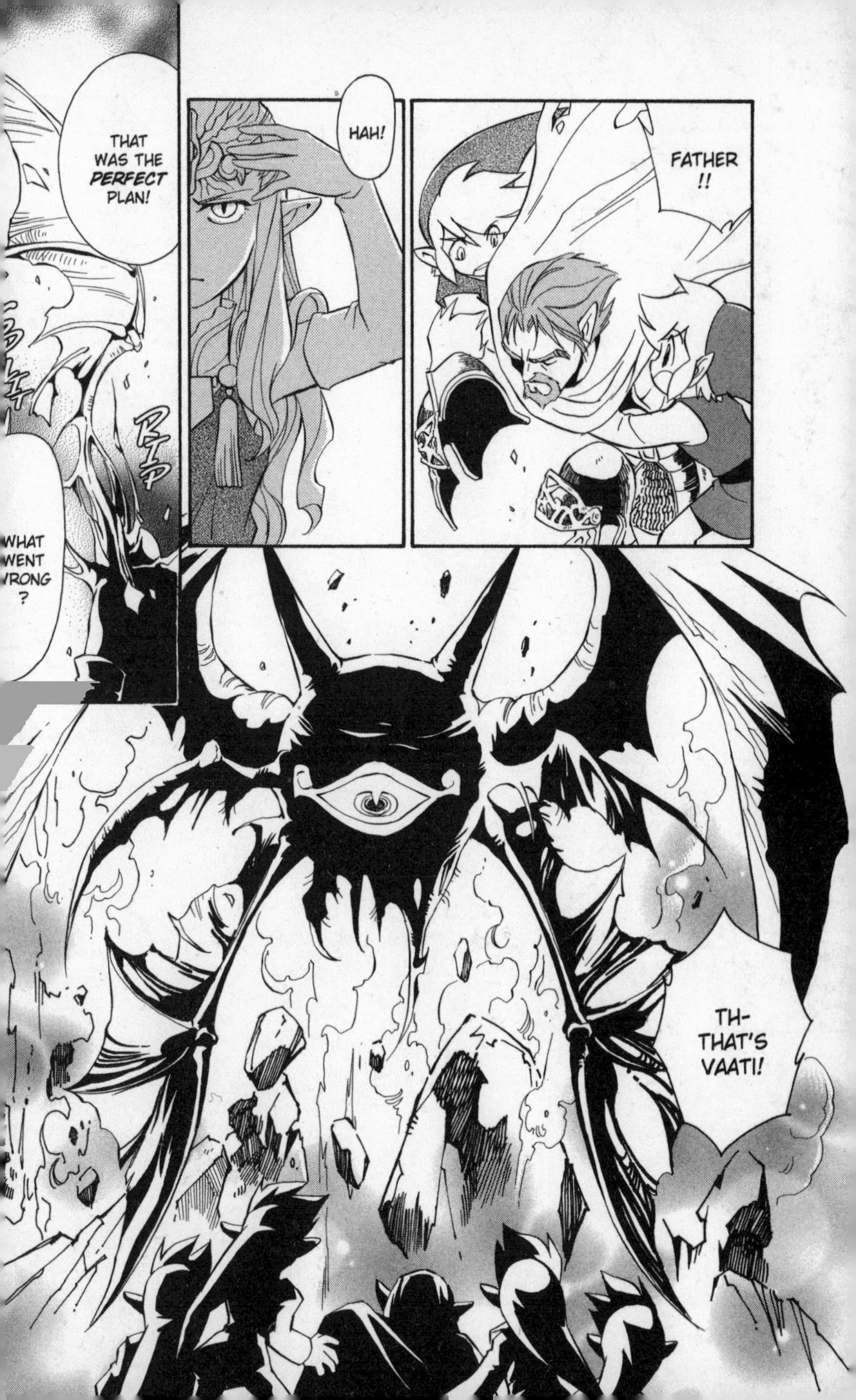
FATHER!!
HAH!
THAT WAS THE PERFECT PLAN!
RIP
WHAT WENT WRONG?
TH-THAT'S VAATI!

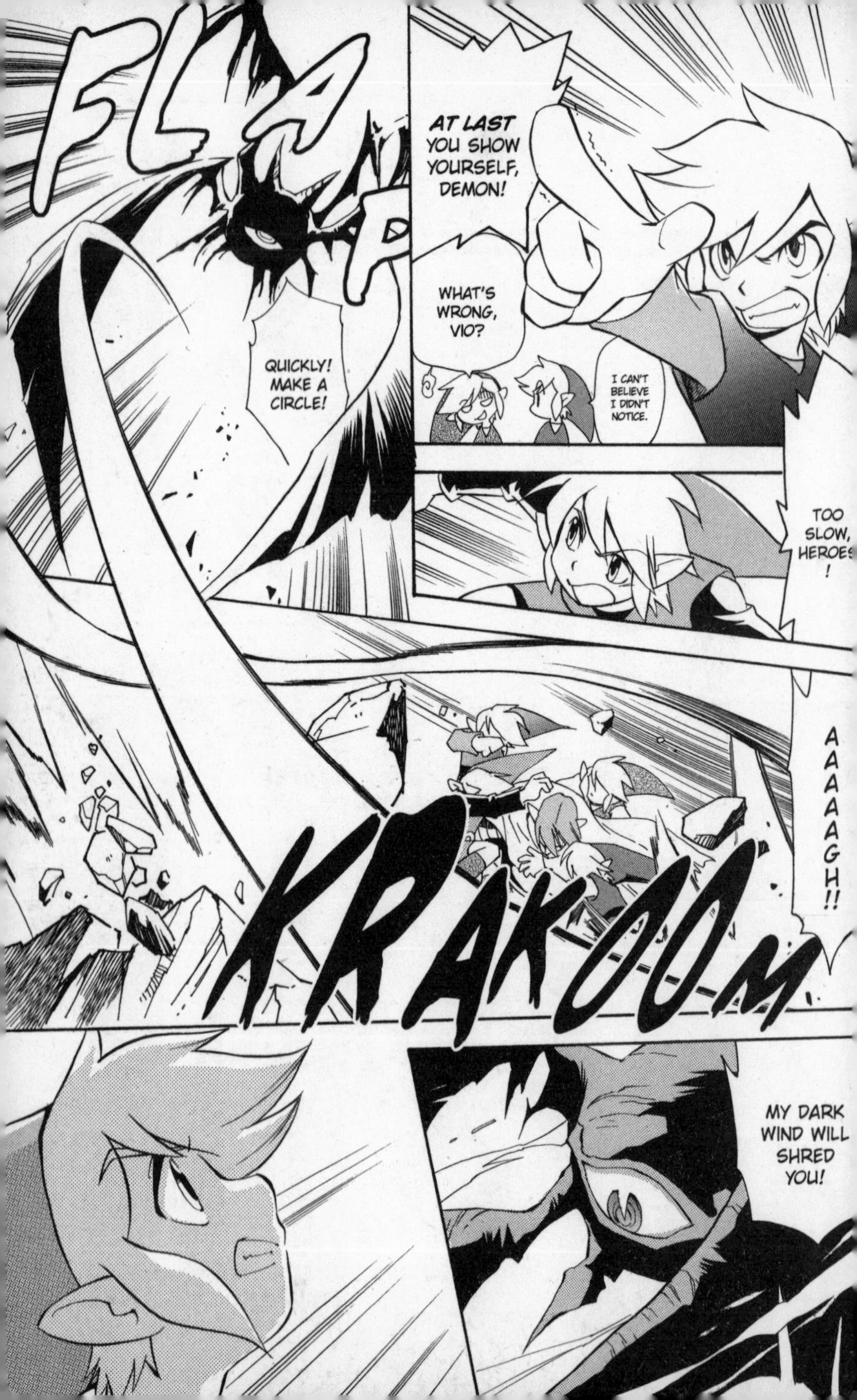
AT LAST YOU SHOW YOURSELF, DEMON!
I CAN'T BELIEVE I DIDN'T NOTICE.
WHAT'S WRONG, VIO?
FLAP
QUICKLY! MAKE A CIRCLE!
TOO SLOW, HEROES!
AAAAAAGH!!
KRAKOOM
MY DARK WIND WILL SHRED YOU!

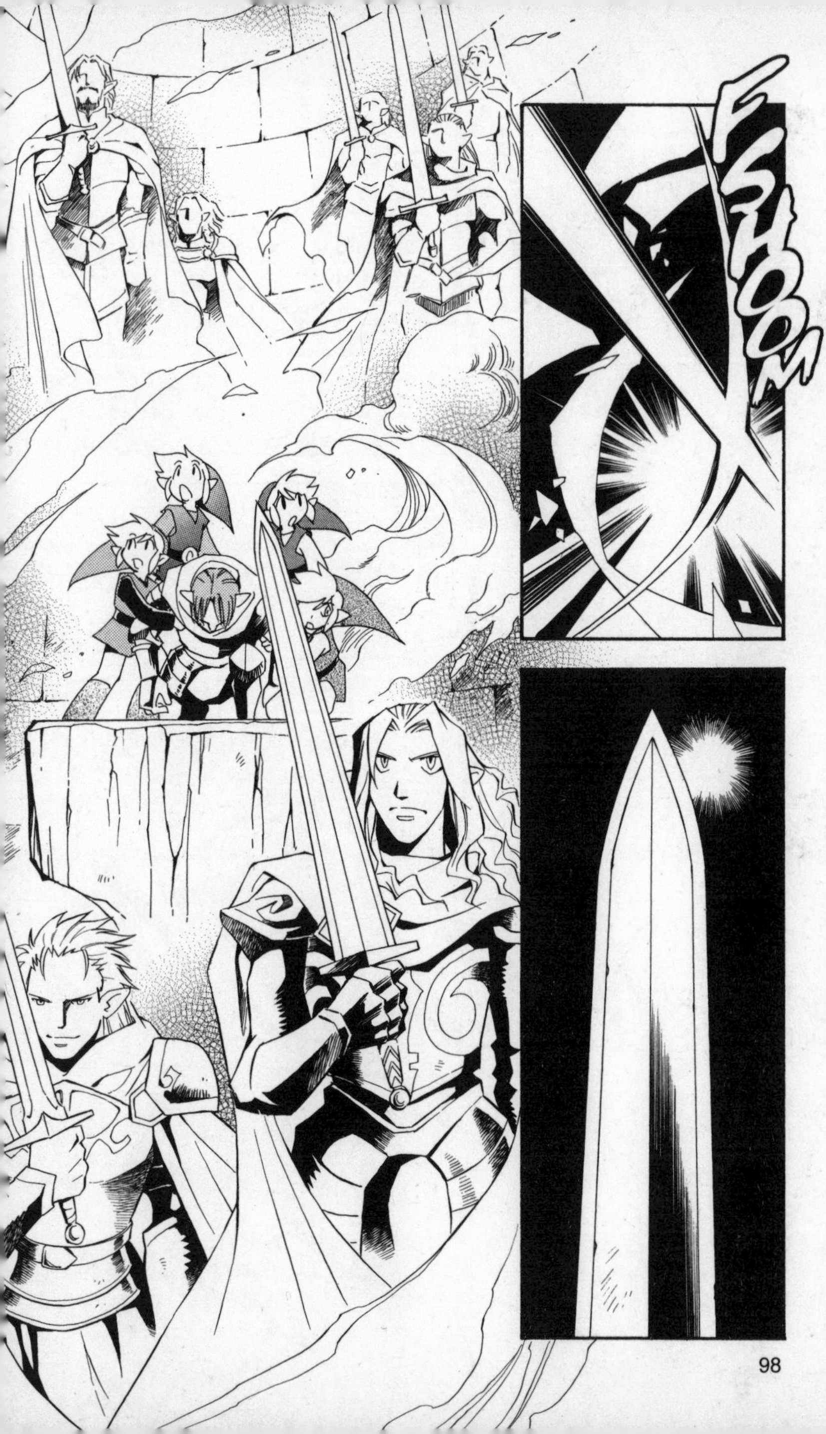
FSHOOM

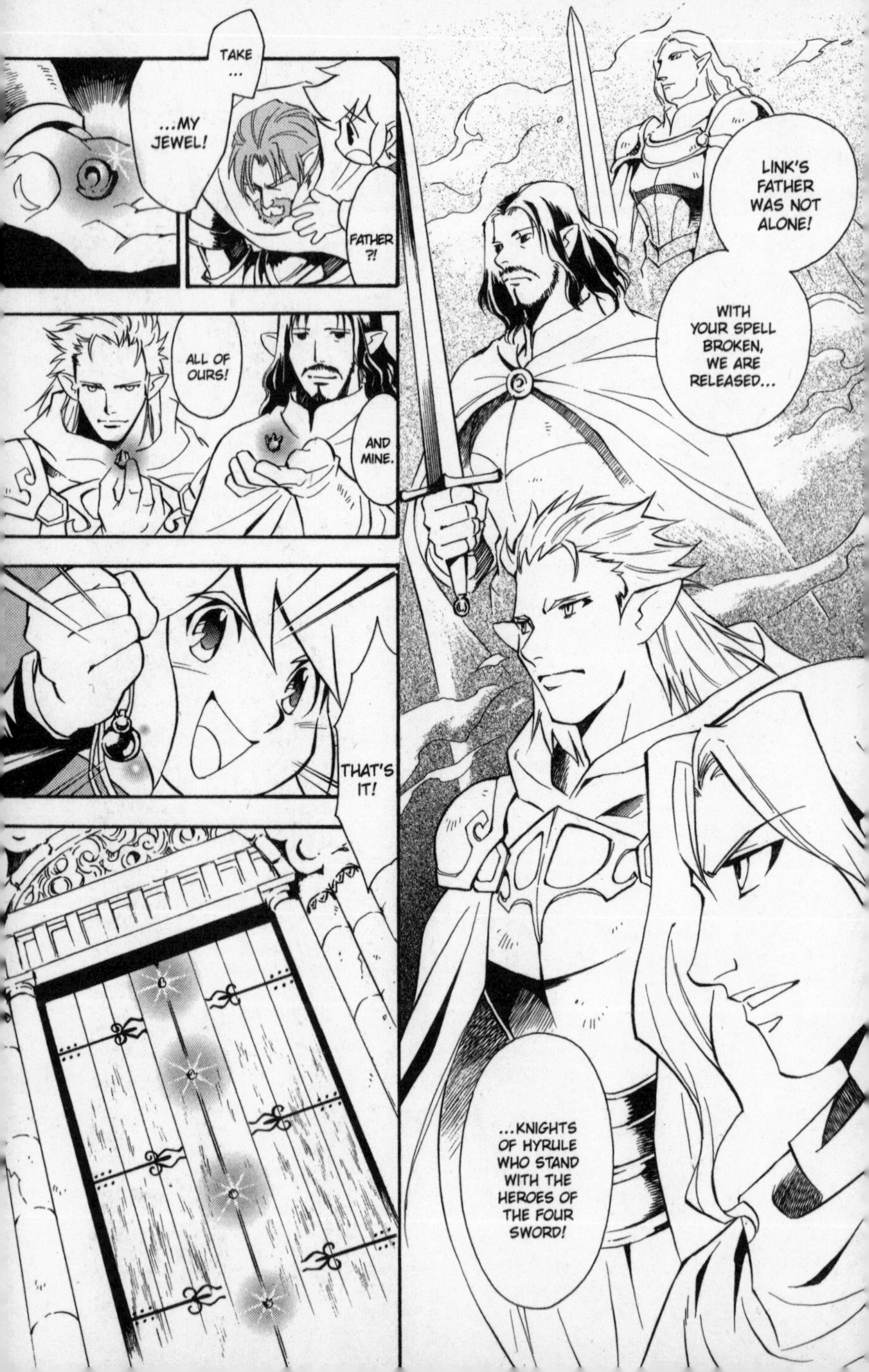
LINK'S FATHER WAS NOT ALONE!
WITH YOUR SPELL BROKEN, WE ARE RELEASED...
...KNIGHTS OF HYRULE WHO STAND WITH THE HEROES OF THE FOUR SWORD!
TAKE ...
...MY JEWEL!
FATHER ?!
ALL OF OURS!
AND MINE.
THAT'S IT!

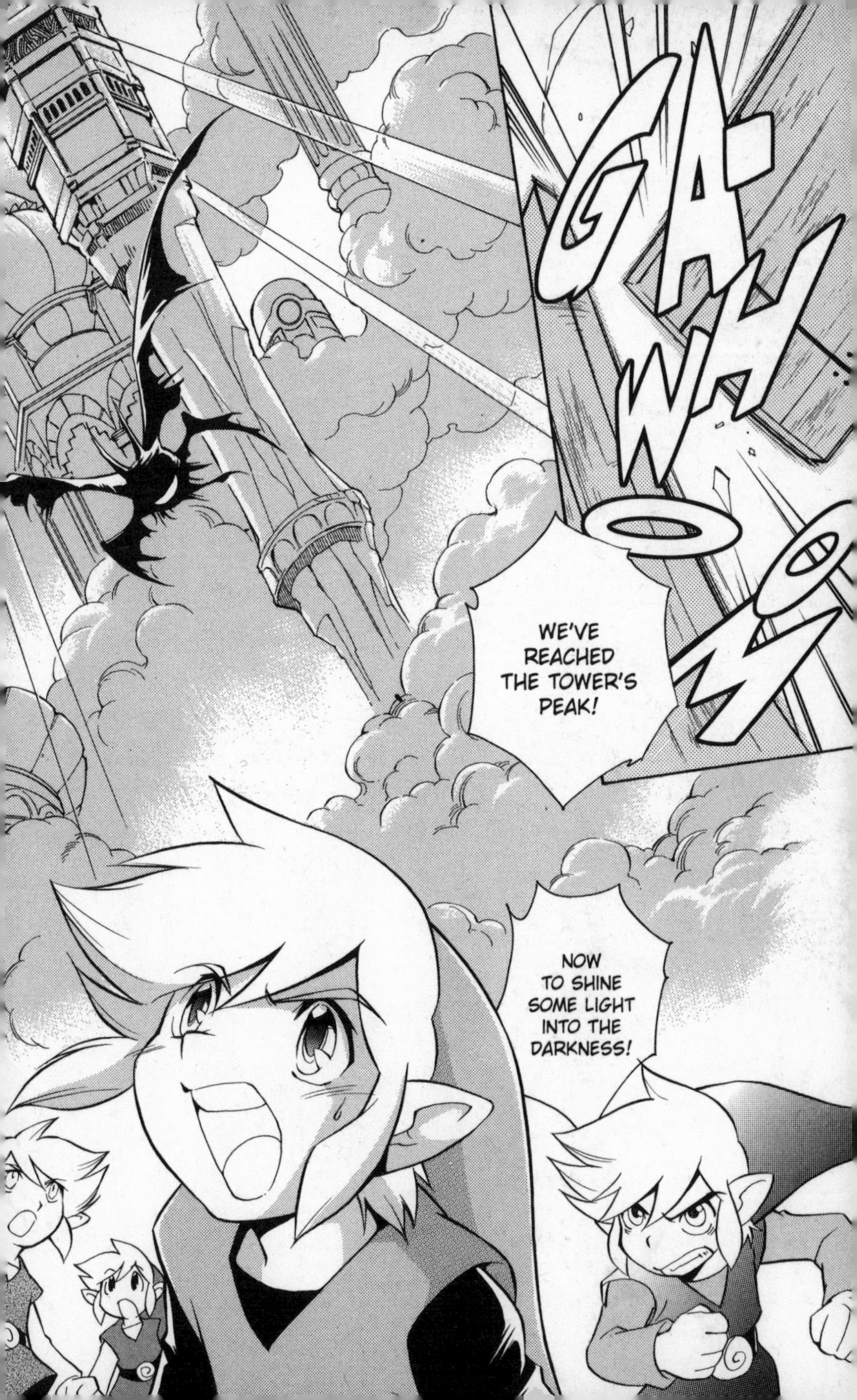
GA-WHOOM
WE'VE REACHED THE TOWER'S PEAK!
NOW TO SHINE SOME LIGHT INTO THE DARKNESS!

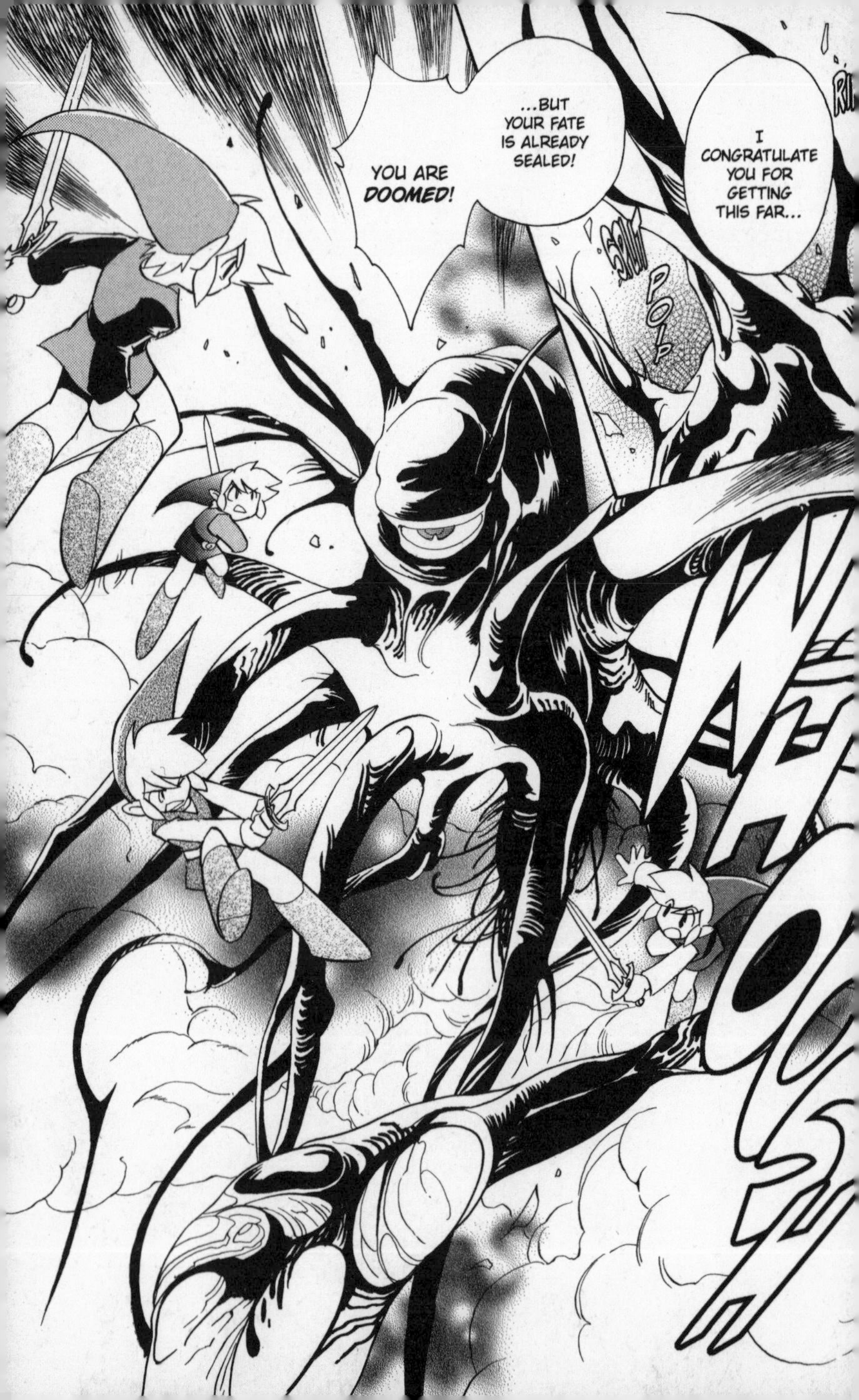
I CONGRATULATE YOU FOR GETTING THIS FAR...
...BUT YOUR FATE IS ALREADY SEALED!
YOU ARE *DOOMED!*
POP
WHOOSH

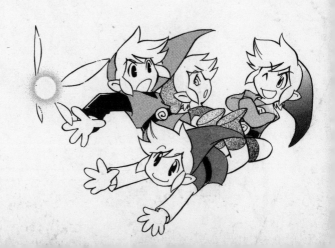

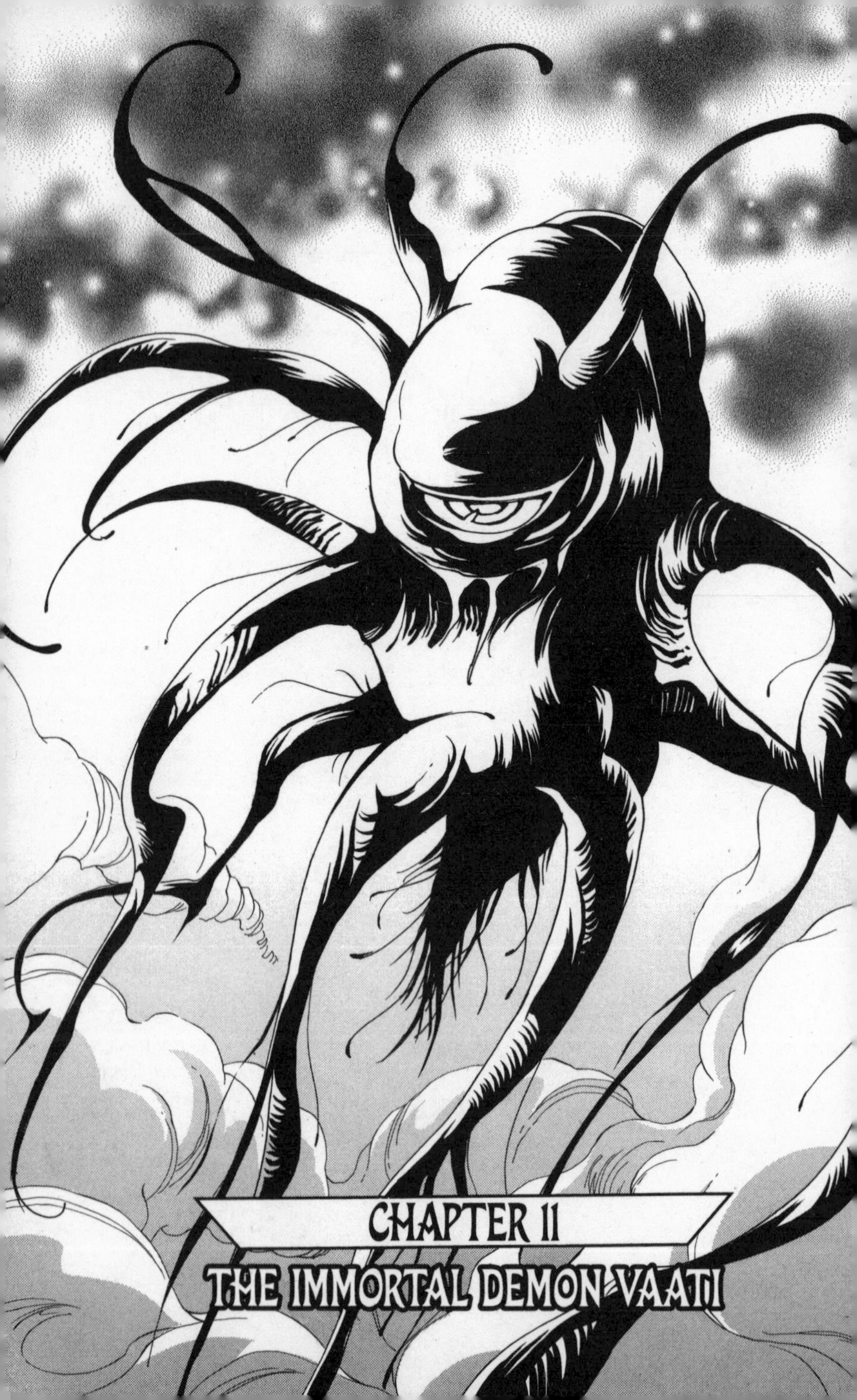
CHAPTER 11
THE IMMORTAL DEMON VAATI

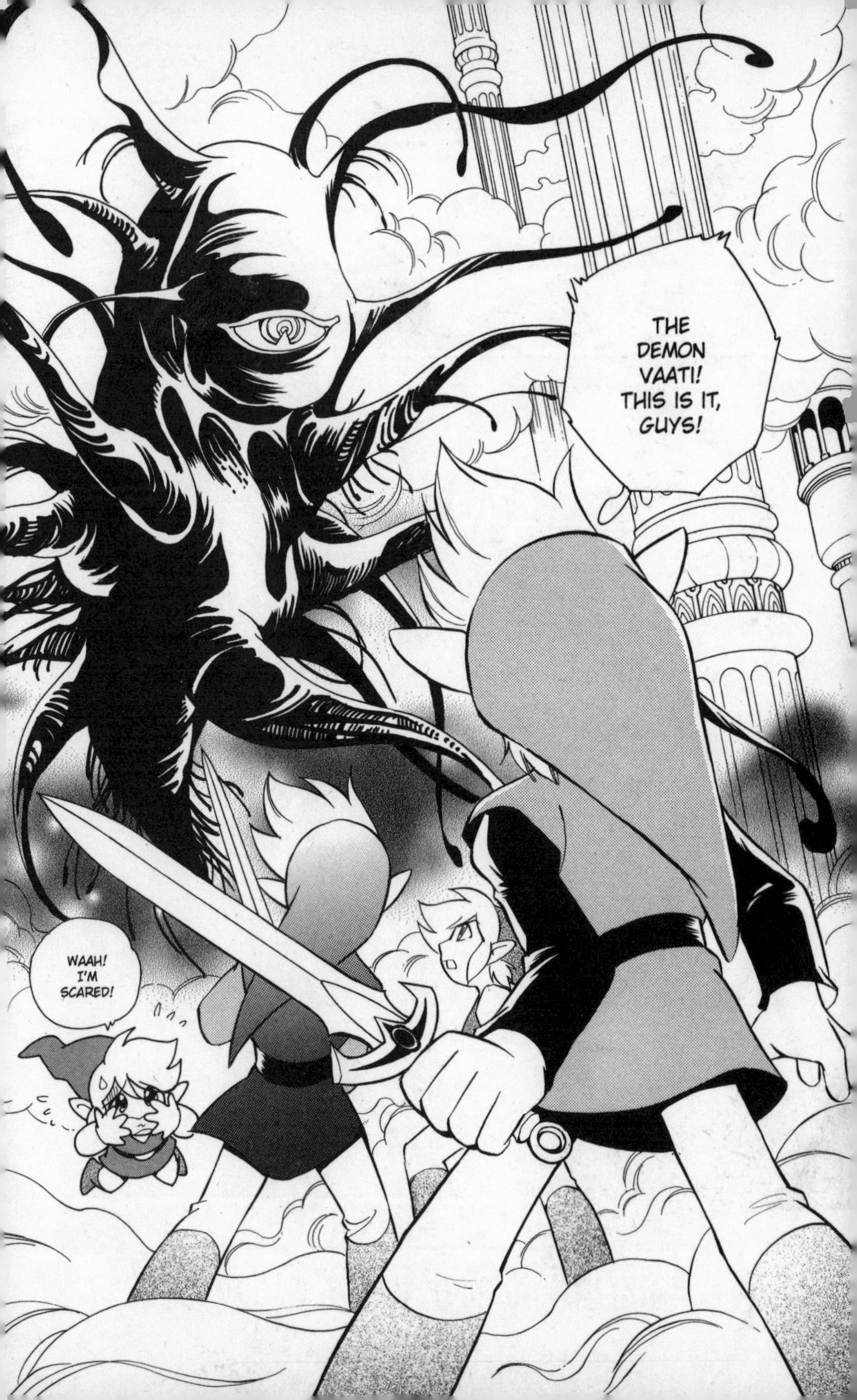
THE DEMON VAATI! THIS IS IT, GUYS!
WAAH! I'M SCARED!

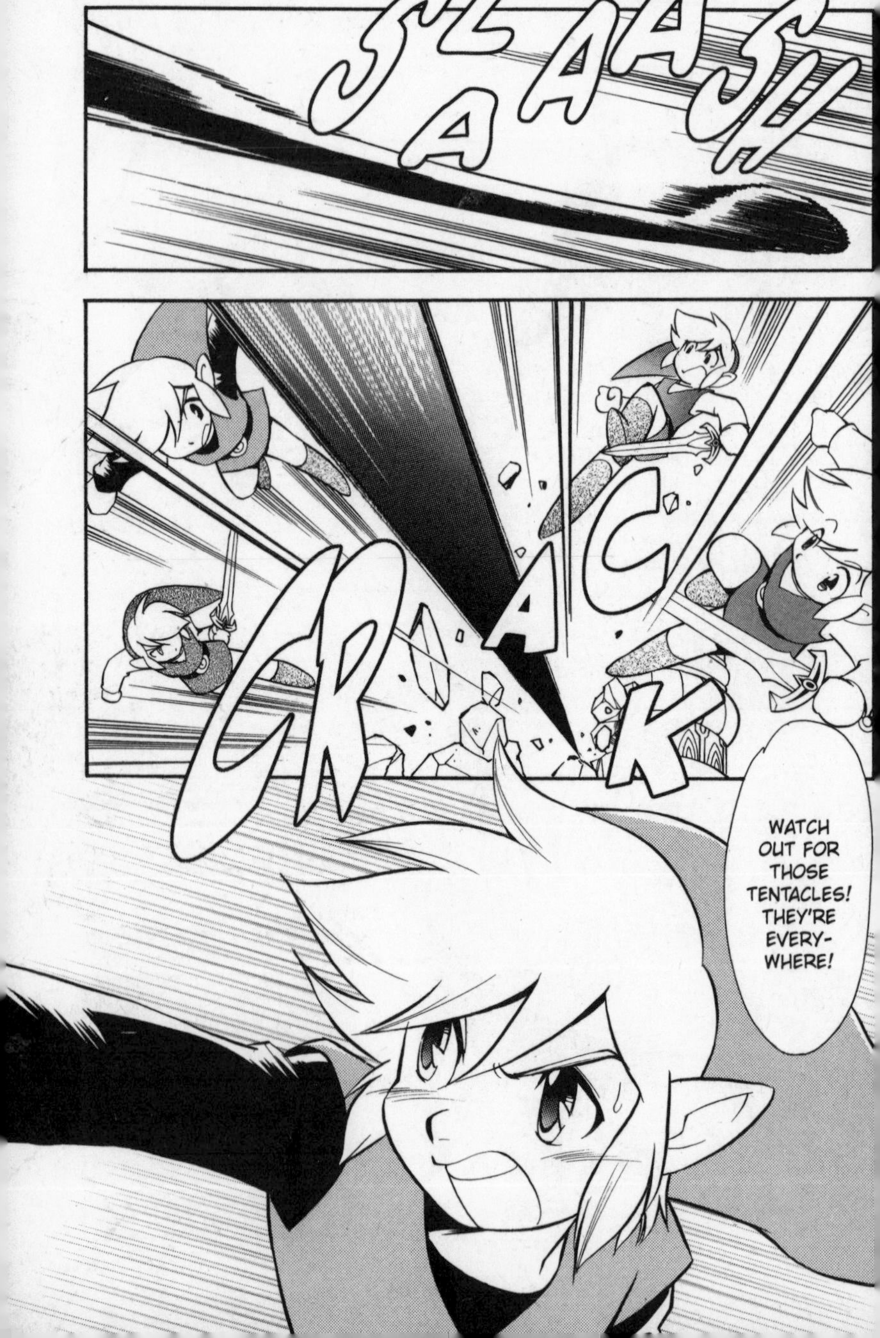
SLAAASH
CRACK
WATCH OUT FOR THOSE TENTACLES! THEY'RE EVERY-WHERE!

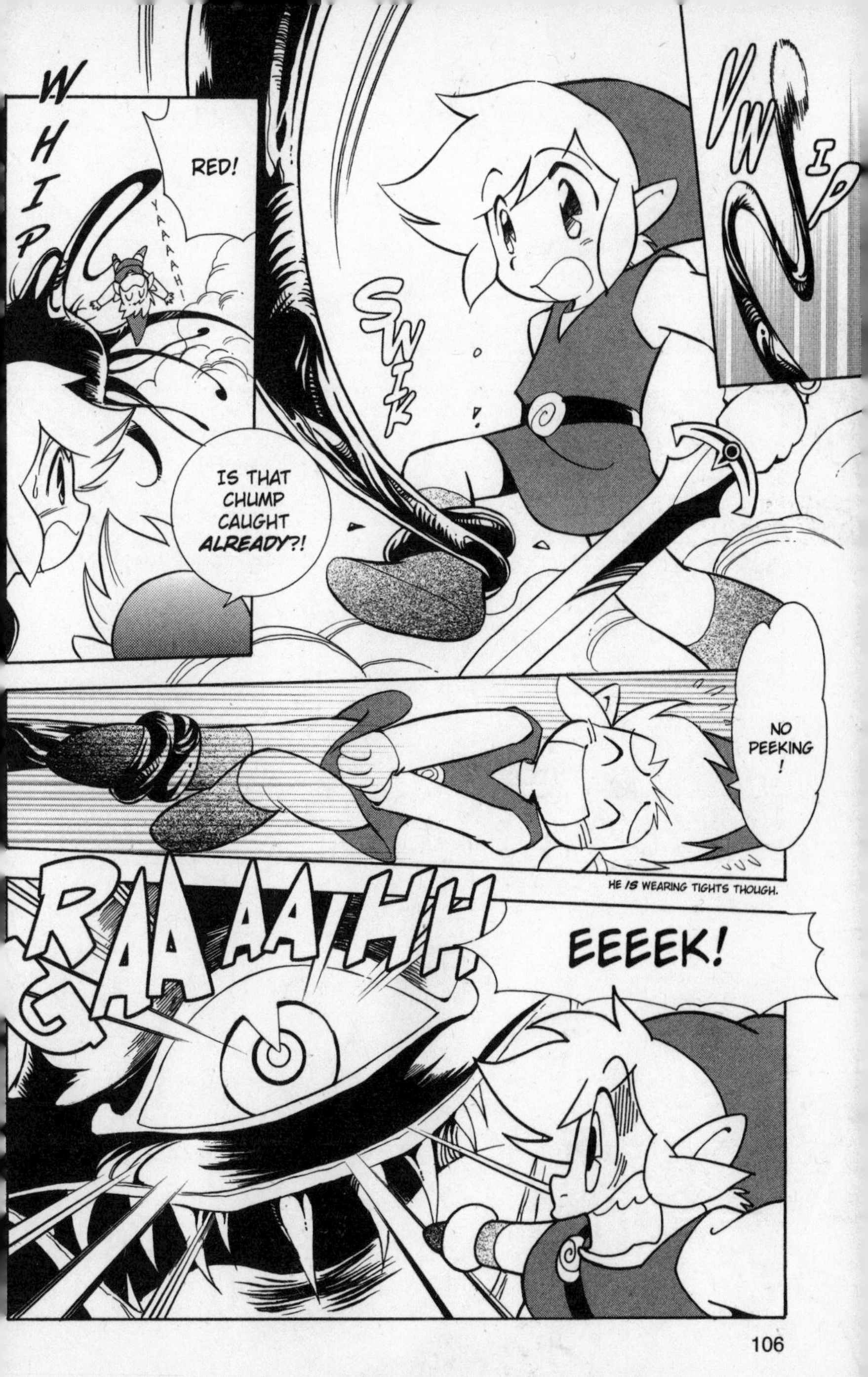
VWIP
SWIK
WHIP
RED!
YAAAAAH!
IS THAT CHUMP CAUGHT ALREADY?!
NO PEEKING!
HE IS WEARING TIGHTS THOUGH.
EEEEK!
RAAAHH

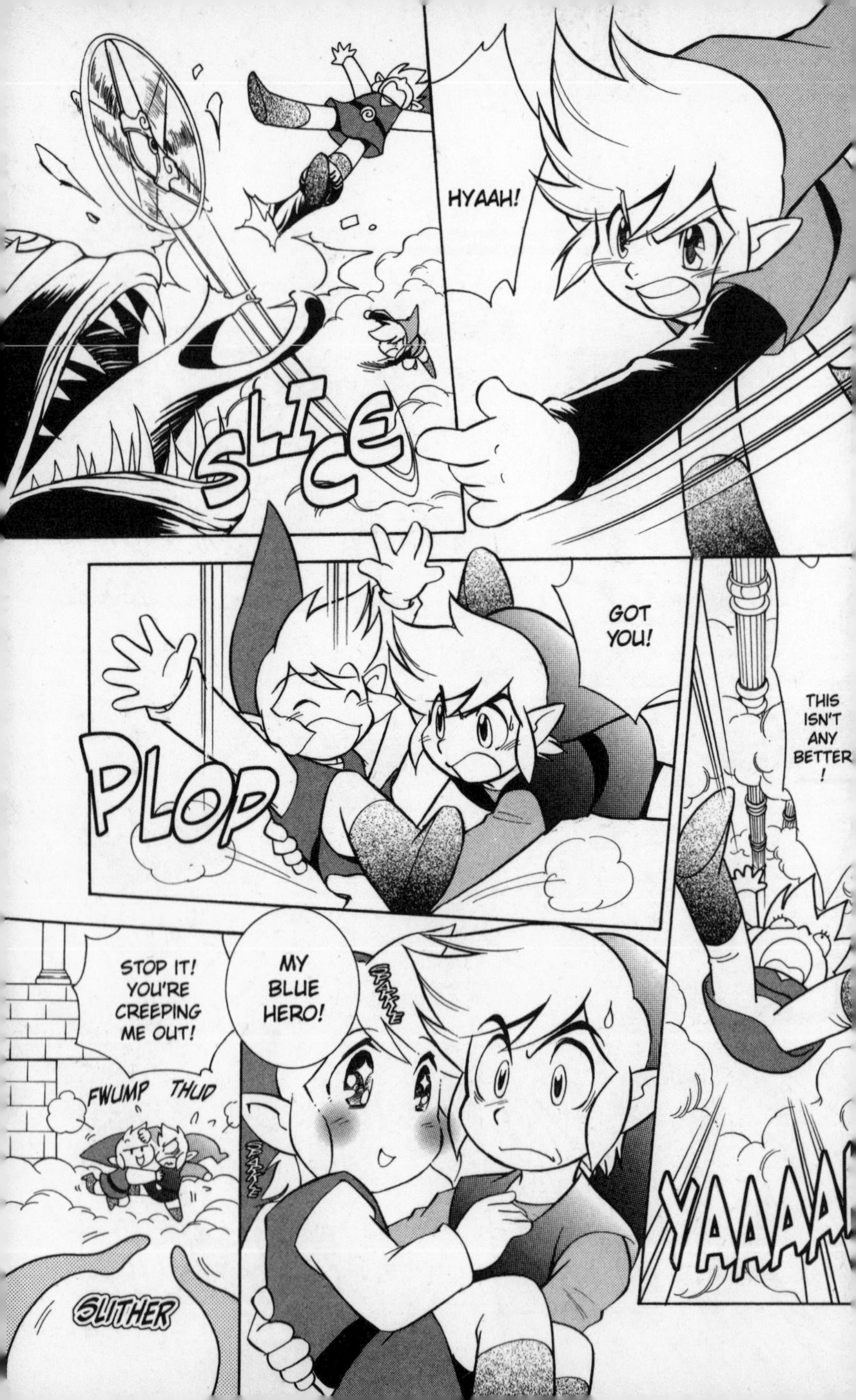
HYAAH!
SLICE
THIS ISN'T ANY BETTER!
YAAAA
GOT YOU!
PLOP
MY BLUE HERO!
STOP IT! YOU'RE CREEPING ME OUT!
FWUMP
THUD
SLITHER

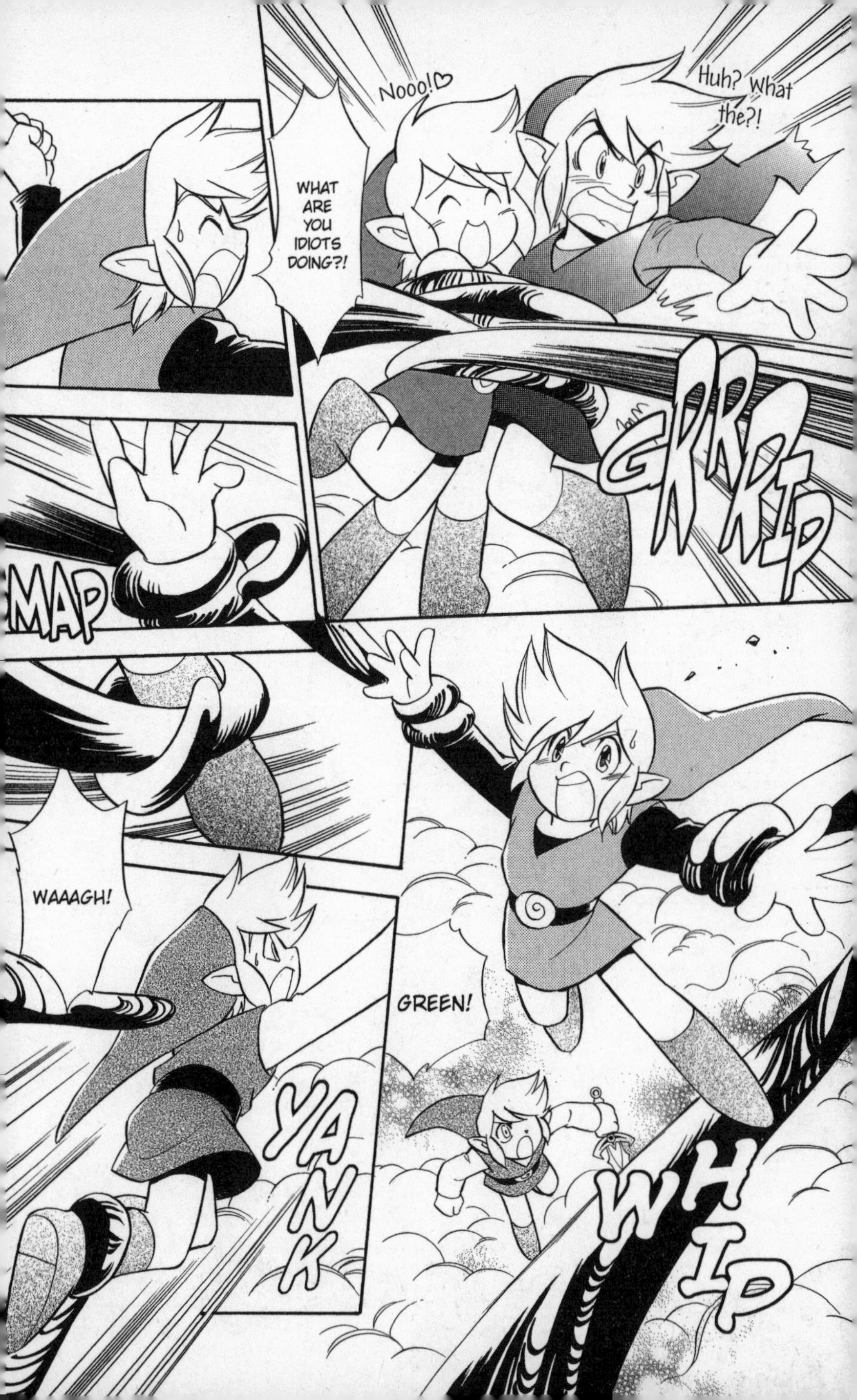
Huh? What the?!
Nooo!♡
WHAT ARE YOU IDIOTS DOING?!
MAP
GREEN!
WHIP
WAAAGH!
YANK

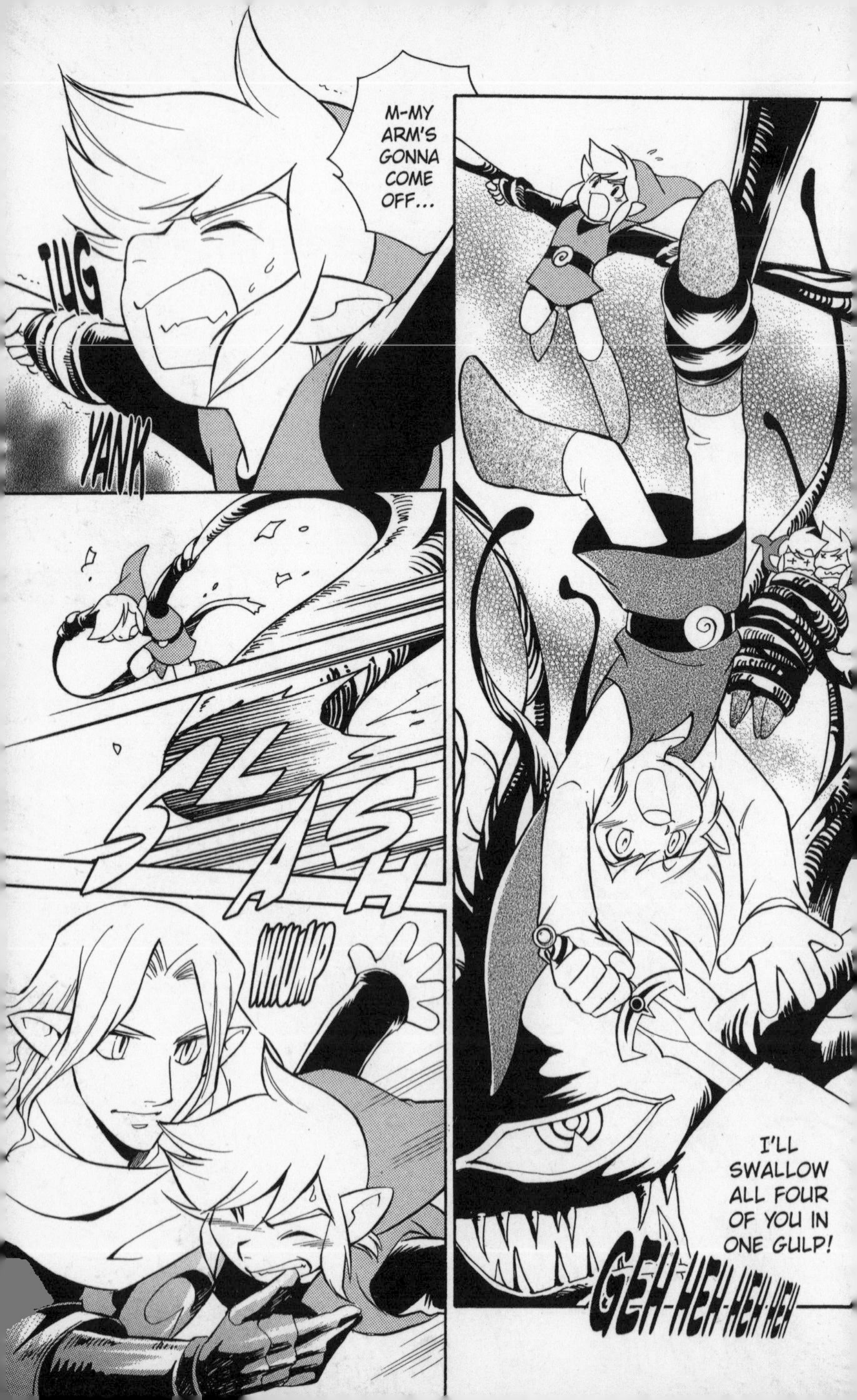
I'LL SWALLOW ALL FOUR OF YOU IN ONE GULP!
GEH-HEH-HEH-HEH
M-MY ARM'S GONNA COME OFF...
TUG
YANK
SLASH
WHUMP

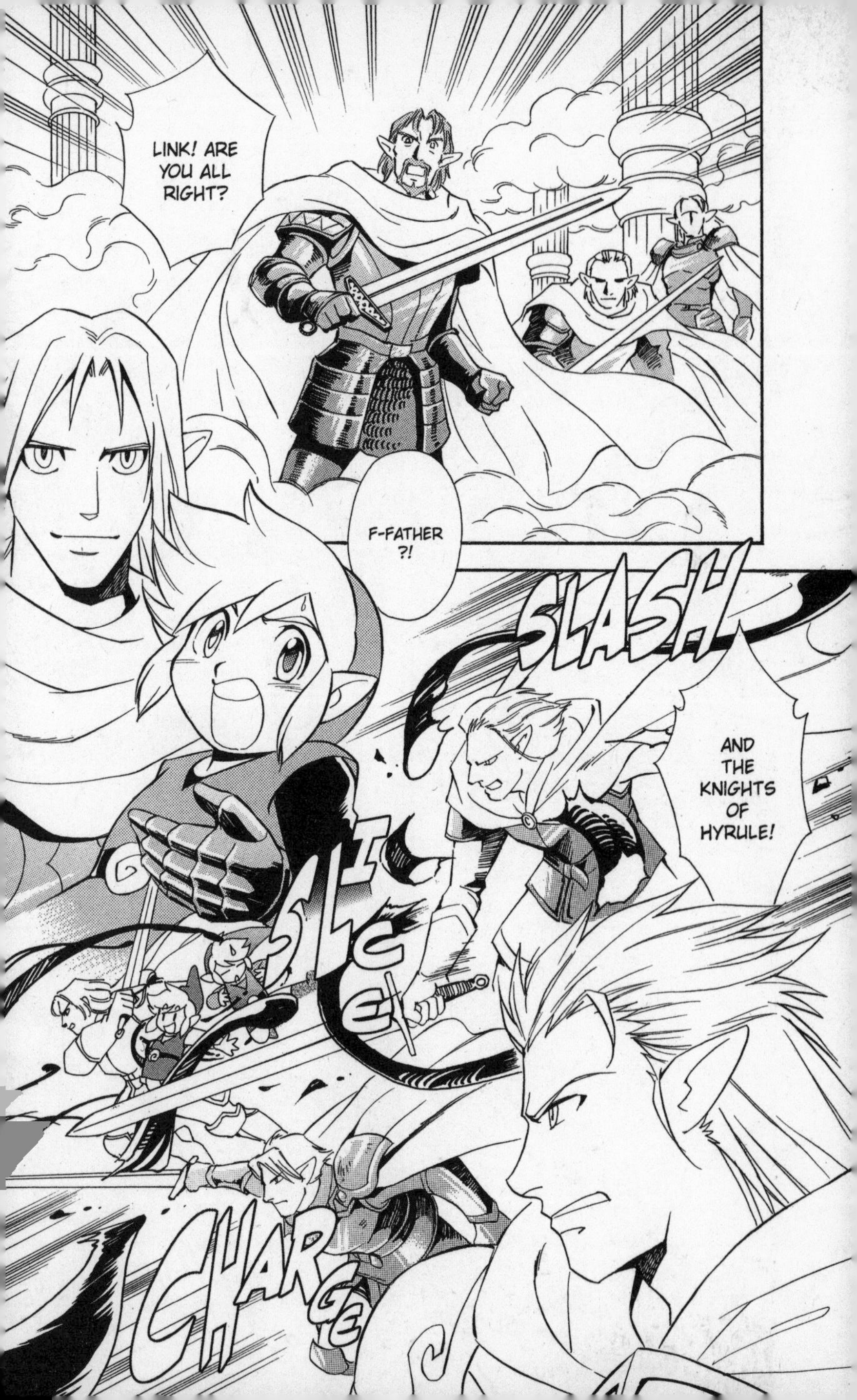
LINK! ARE YOU ALL RIGHT?
F-FATHER ?!
SLASH
AND THE KNIGHTS OF HYRULE!
SLICE
CHARGE

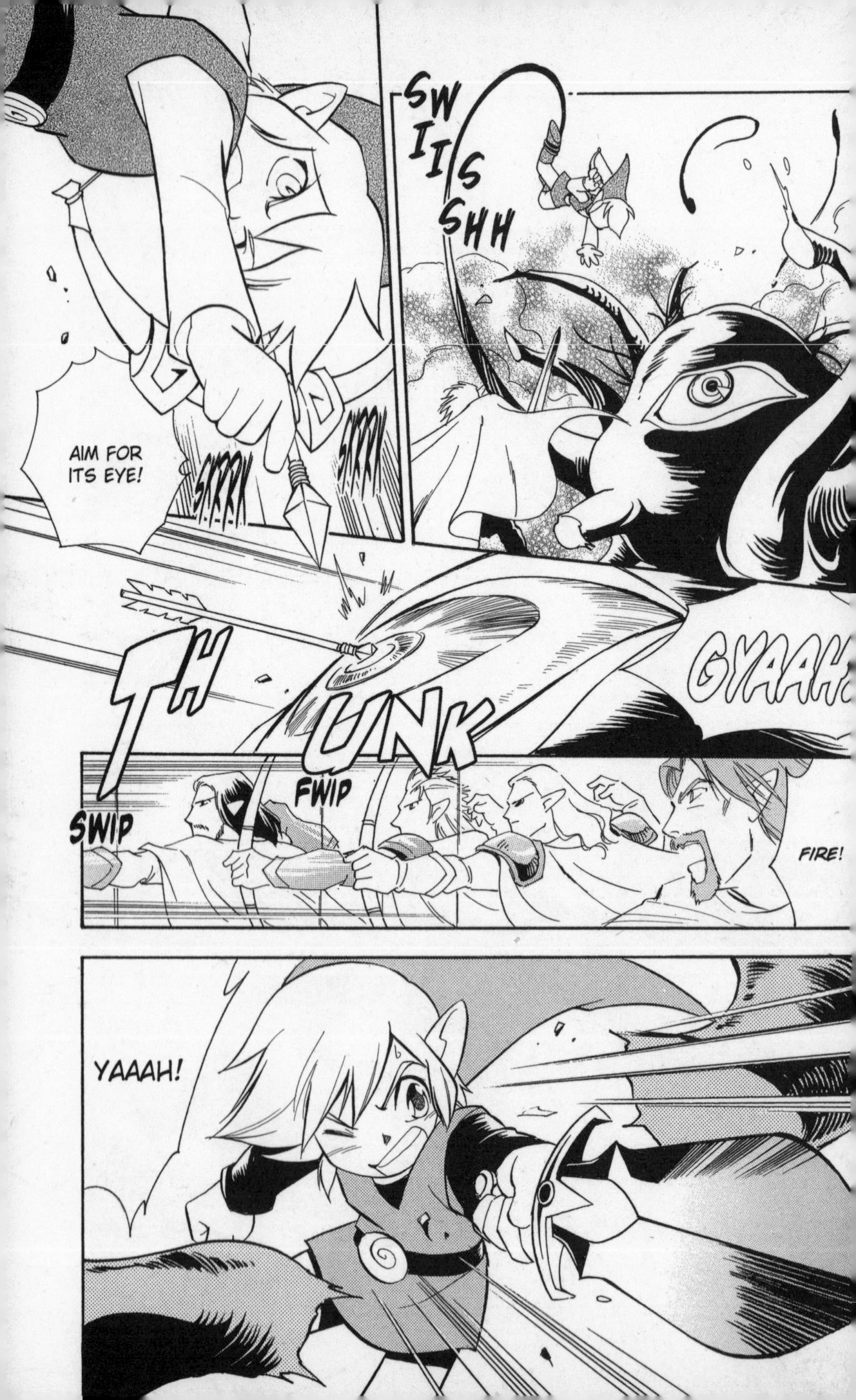

SWIISSHH
AIM FOR ITS EYE!
SKRRK
SKRRK
GYAAH
THUNK
FIRE!
FWIP
SWIP
YAAAH!

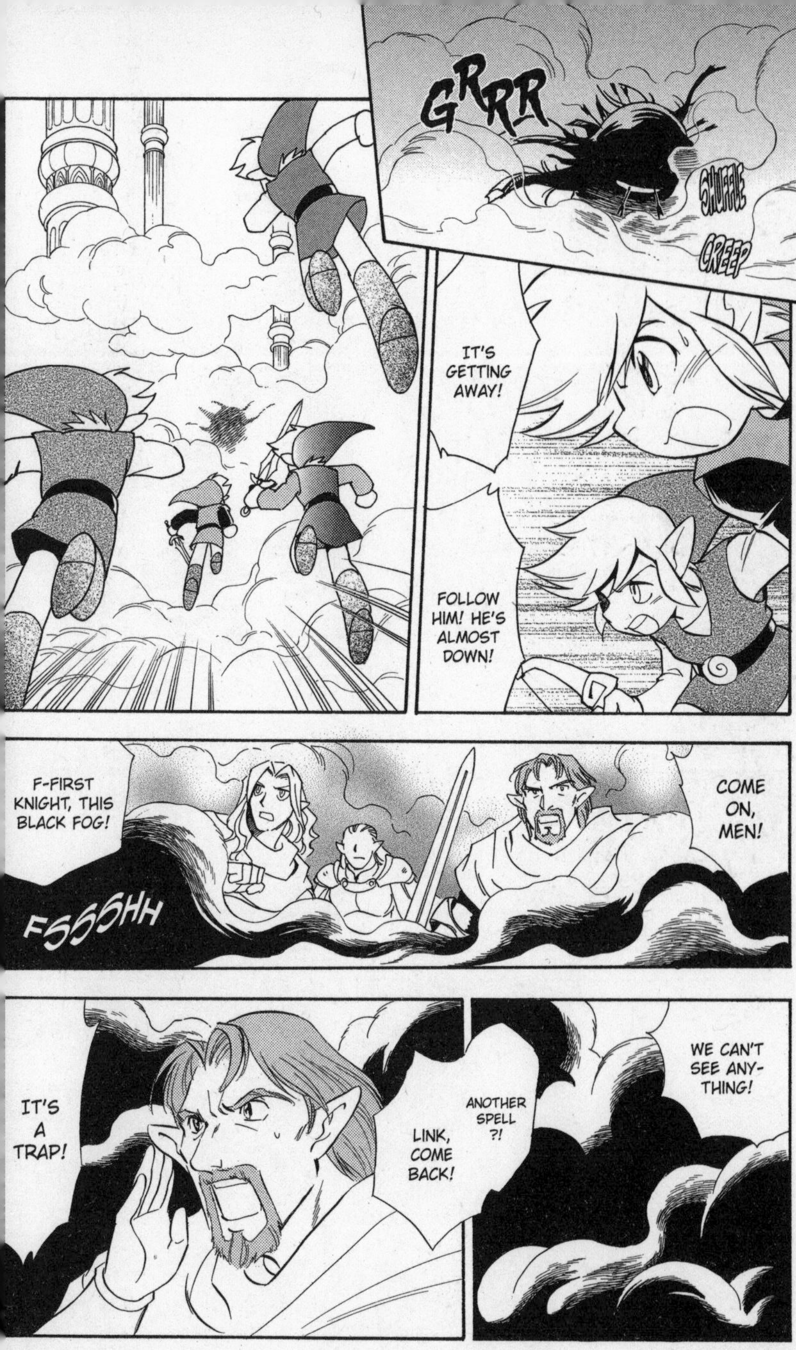
GRRR
SHUFFLE
CREEP
IT'S GETTING AWAY!
FOLLOW HIM! HE'S ALMOST DOWN!
COME ON, MEN!
F-FIRST KNIGHT, THIS BLACK FOG!
FSSSHH
WE CAN'T SEE ANY-THING!
ANOTHER SPELL ?!
LINK, COME BACK!
IT'S A TRAP!

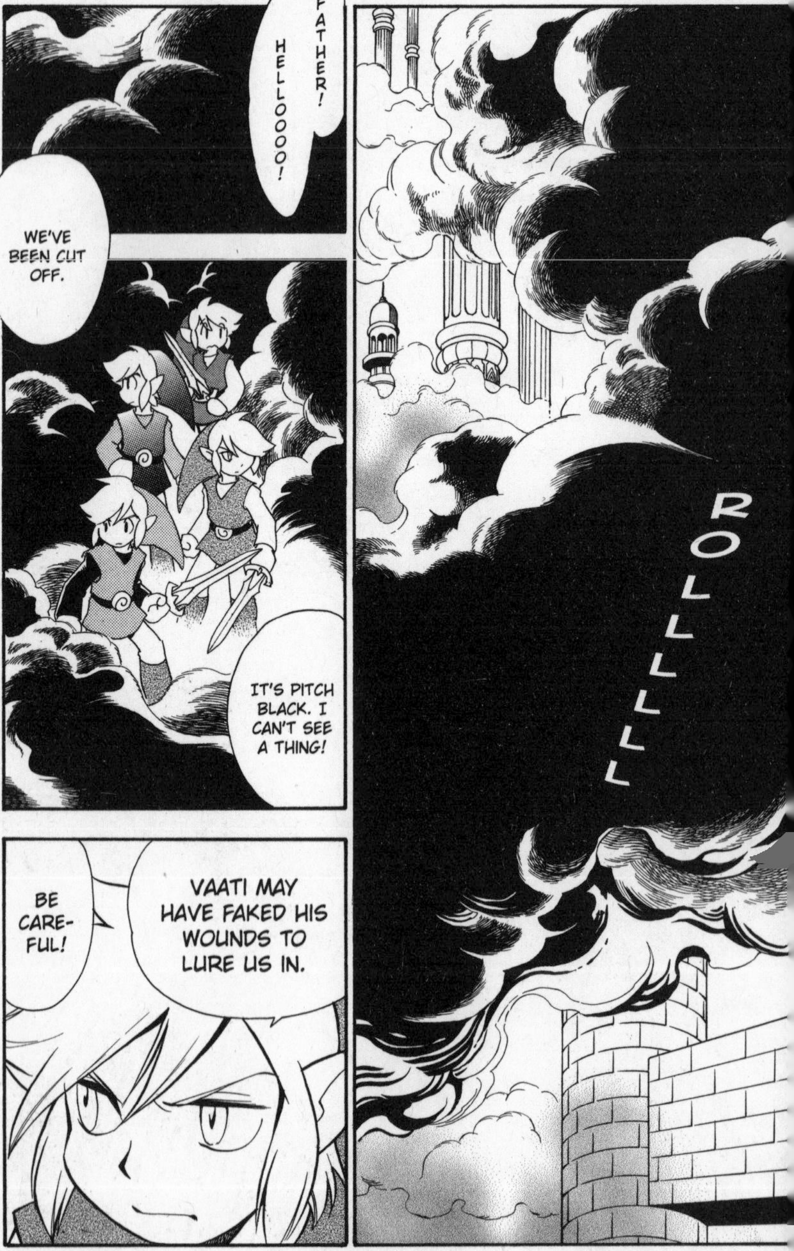
ROLLLLLL
FATHER!
HELLOOOO!
WE'VE BEEN CUT OFF.
IT'S PITCH BLACK. I CAN'T SEE A THING!
VAATI MAY HAVE FAKED HIS WOUNDS TO LURE US IN.
BE CAREFUL!

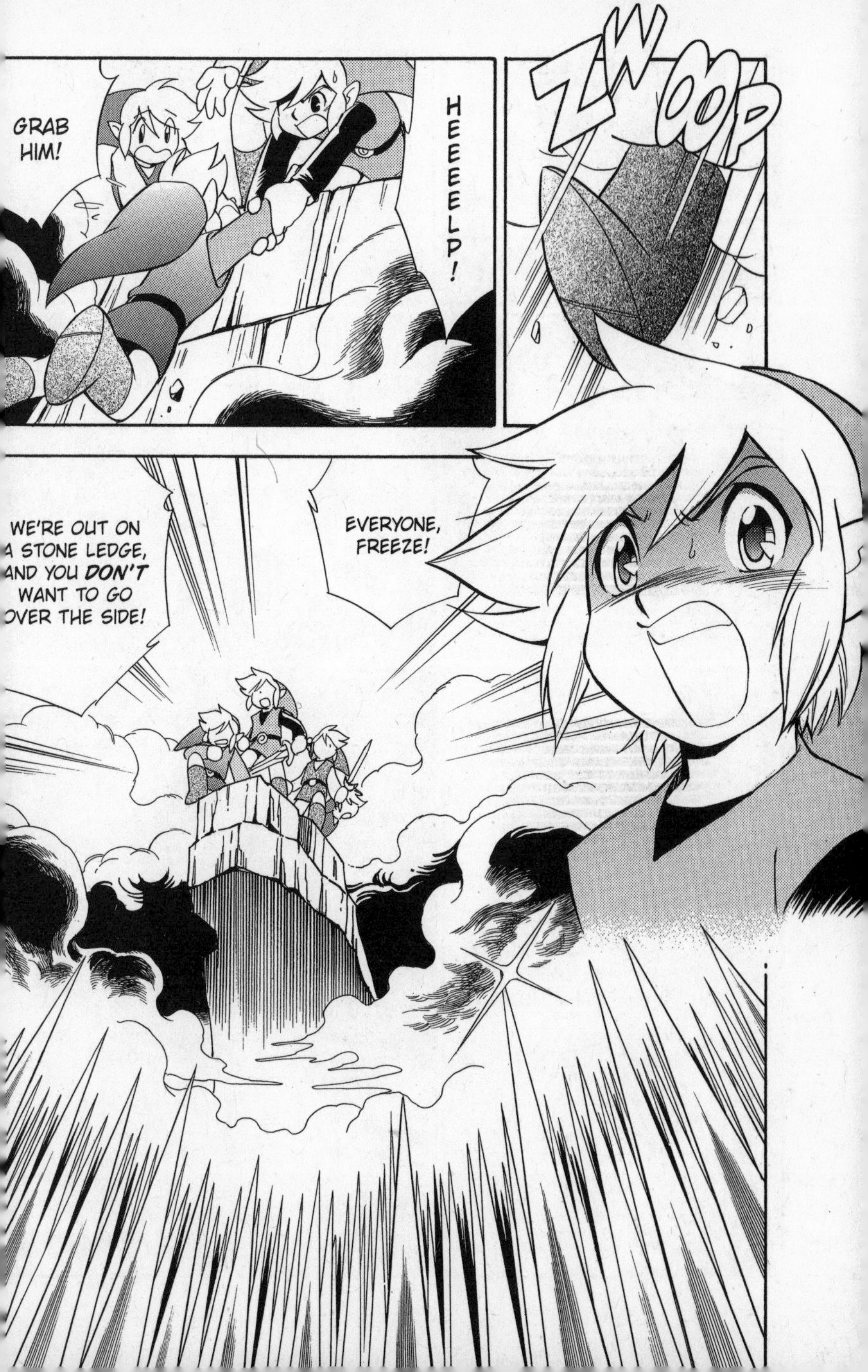
ZWOOP
HEEEEELP!
GRAB HIM!
EVERYONE, FREEZE!
WE'RE OUT ON A STONE LEDGE, AND YOU DON'T WANT TO GO OVER THE SIDE!

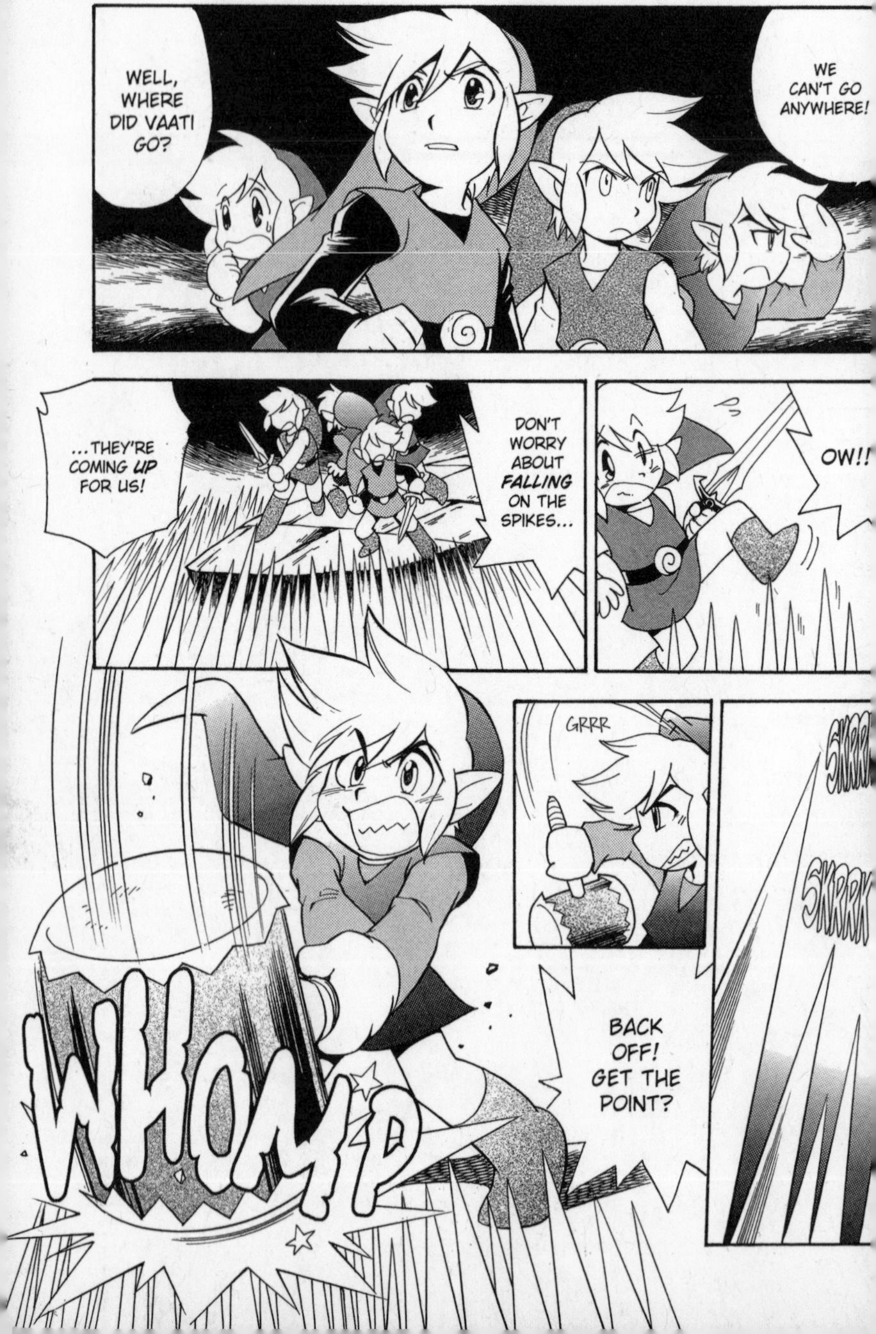
WE CAN'T GO ANYWHERE!
WELL, WHERE DID VAATI GO?
OW!!
DON'T WORRY ABOUT *FALLING* ON THE SPIKES...
...THEY'RE COMING *UP* FOR US!
SKRRK
GRRR
BACK OFF! GET THE POINT?
WHOMP

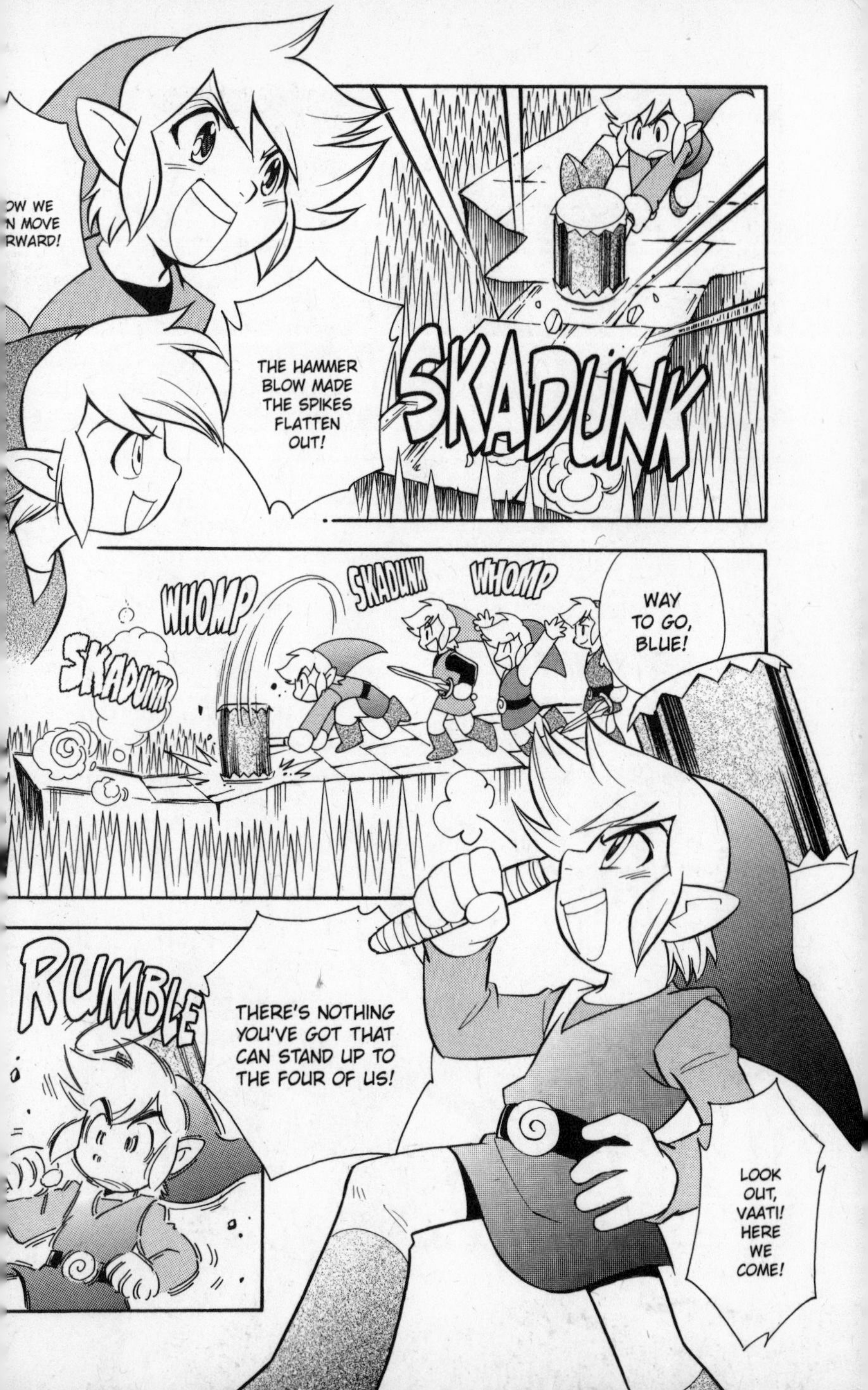
SKADUNK
THE HAMMER BLOW MADE THE SPIKES FLATTEN OUT!
OW WE N MOVE RWARD!
WAY TO GO, BLUE!
WHOMP
SKADUNK
WHOMP
SKADUNK
THERE'S NOTHING YOU'VE GOT THAT CAN STAND UP TO THE FOUR OF US!
LOOK OUT, VAATI! HERE WE COME!
RUMBLE

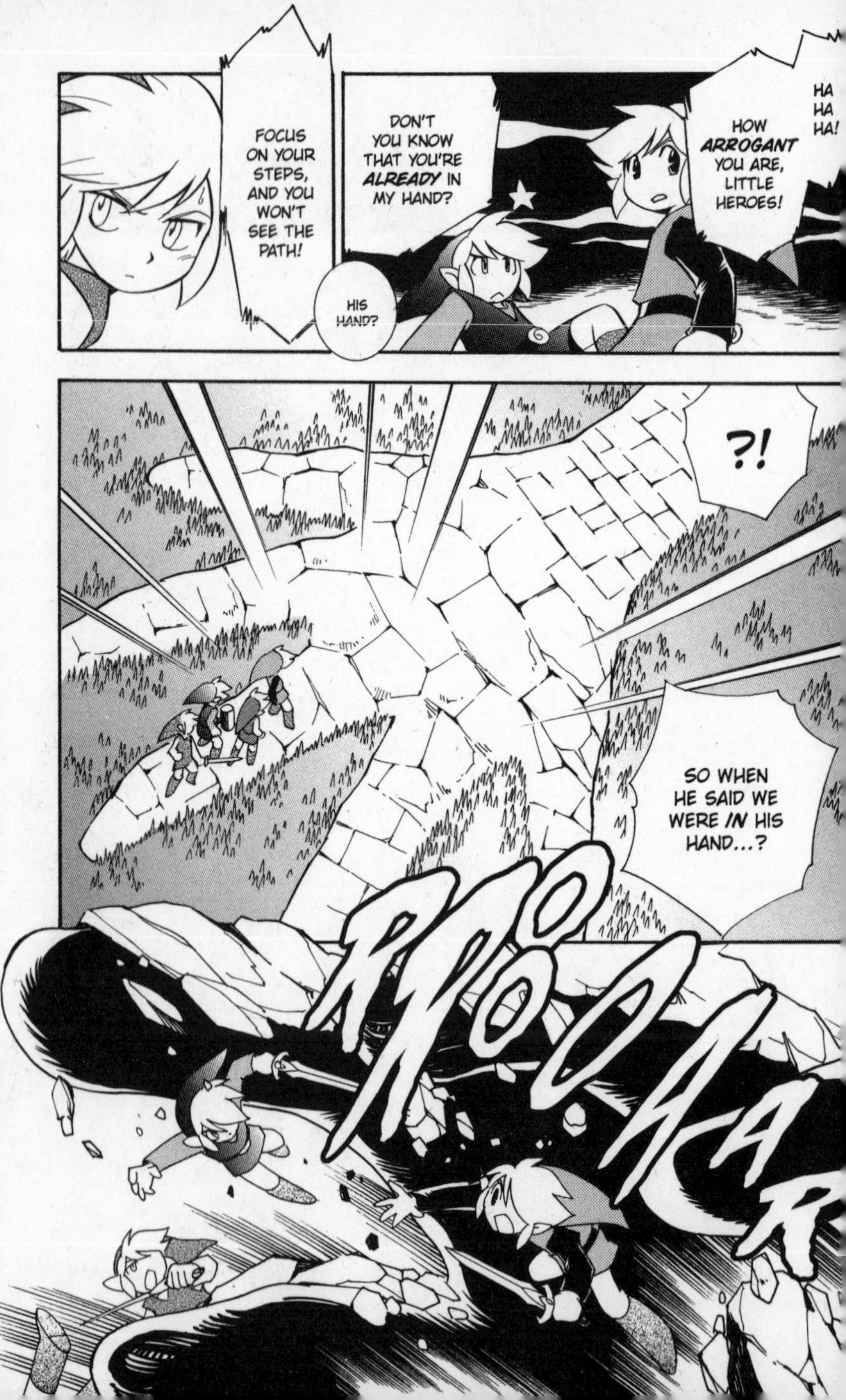
HA HA HA!
HOW ARROGANT YOU ARE, LITTLE HEROES!
DON'T YOU KNOW THAT YOU'RE ALREADY IN MY HAND?
HIS HAND?
FOCUS ON YOUR STEPS, AND YOU WON'T SEE THE PATH!
?!
SO WHEN HE SAID WE WERE IN HIS HAND...?

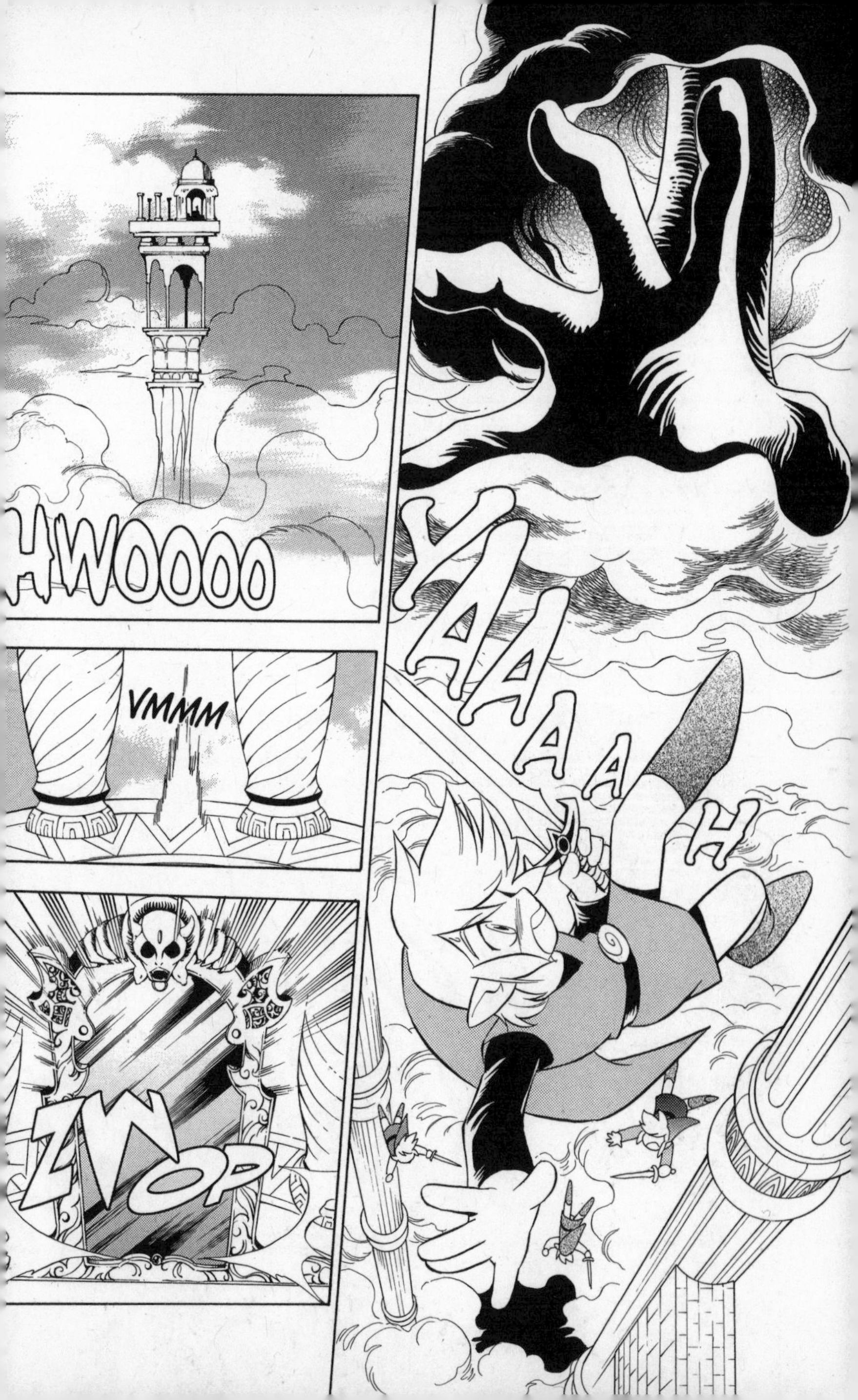
YAAAAAAH
HWOOOO
VMMM
ZWOP

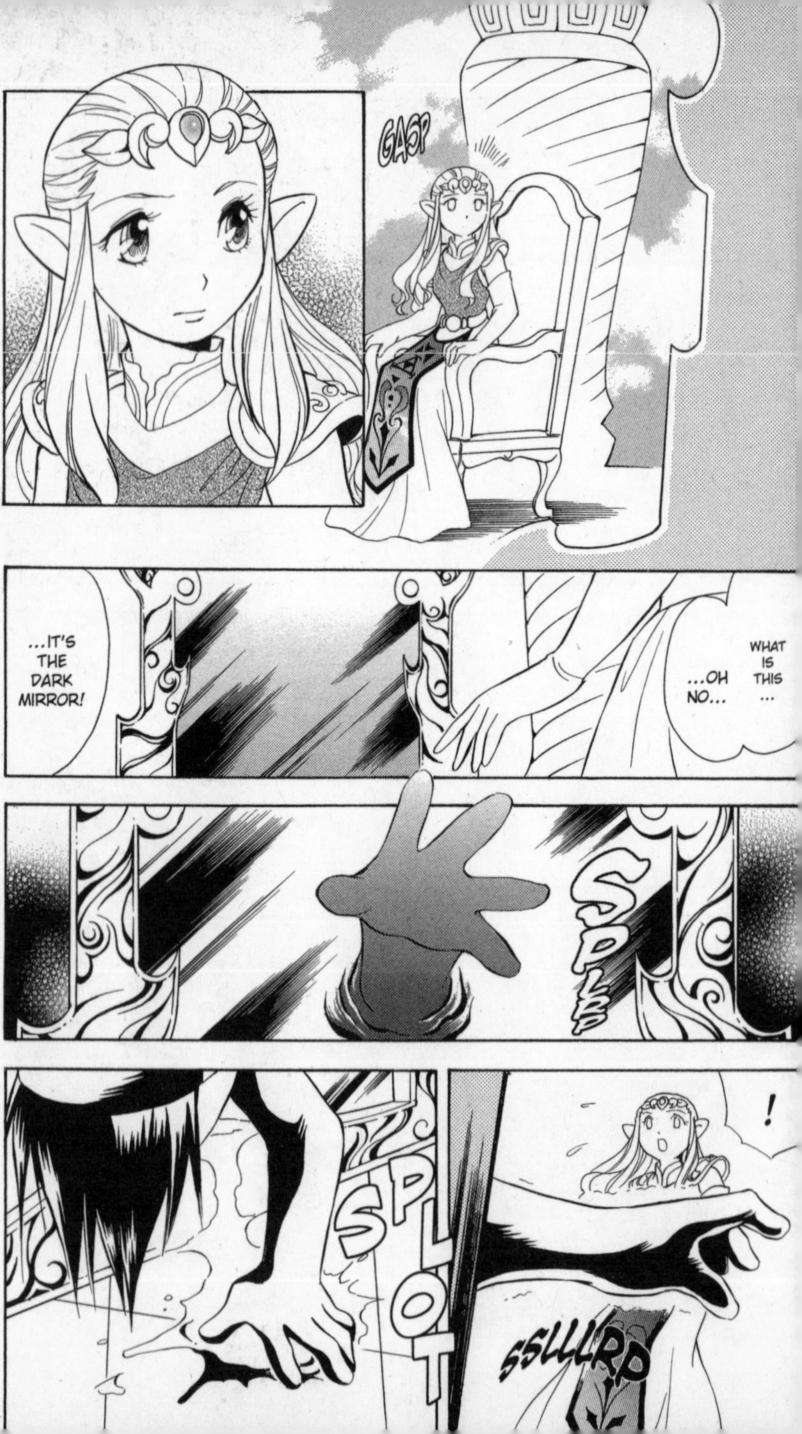
GASP
WHAT IS THIS ...
...OH NO...
...IT'S THE DARK MIRROR!
!
SSLLLRP
SPLOT

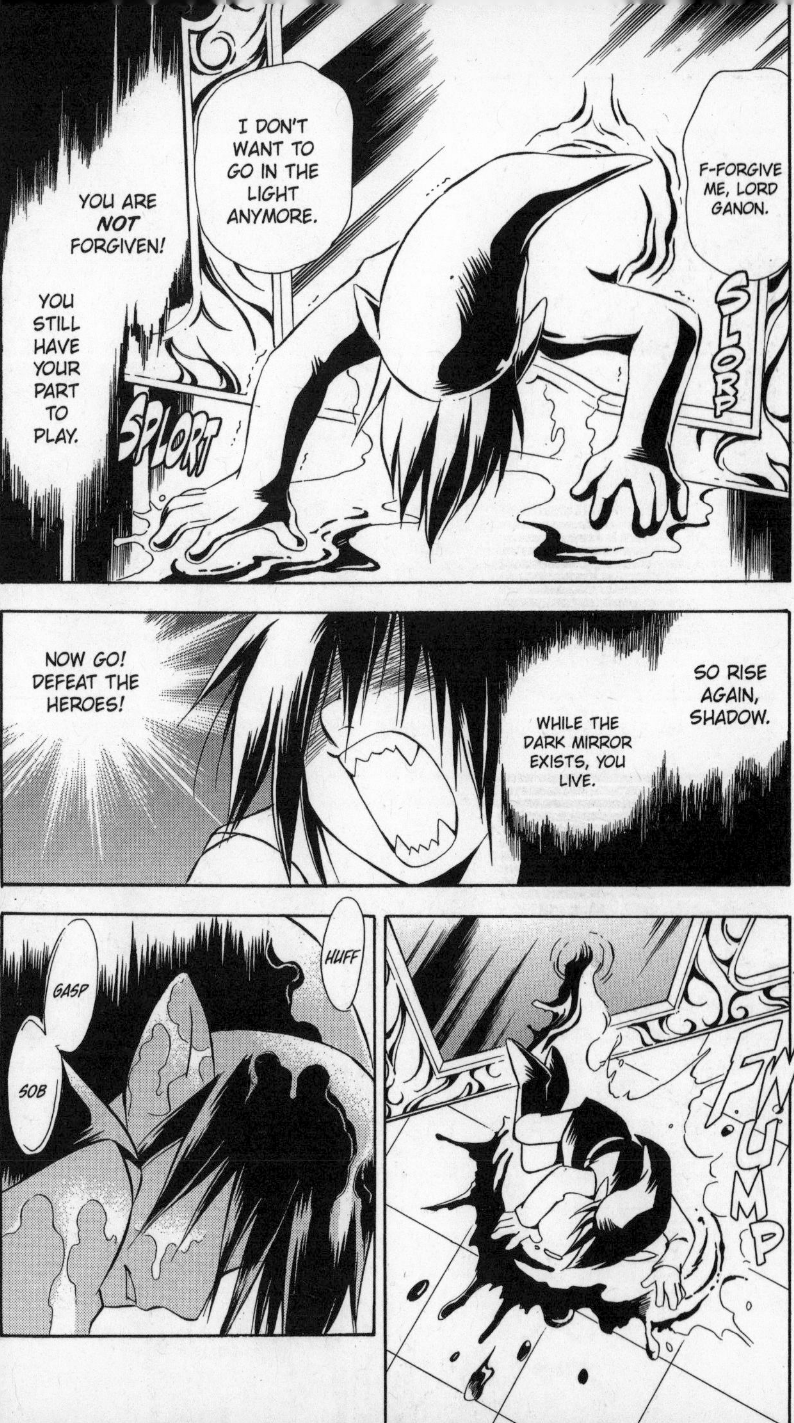
F-FORGIVE ME, LORD GANON.
SLORP
I DON'T WANT TO GO IN THE LIGHT ANYMORE.
YOU ARE *NOT* FORGIVEN!
YOU STILL HAVE YOUR PART TO PLAY.
SPLORT
SO RISE AGAIN, SHADOW.
WHILE THE DARK MIRROR EXISTS, YOU LIVE.
NOW GO! DEFEAT THE HEROES!
FWUMP
HUFF
GASP
SOB

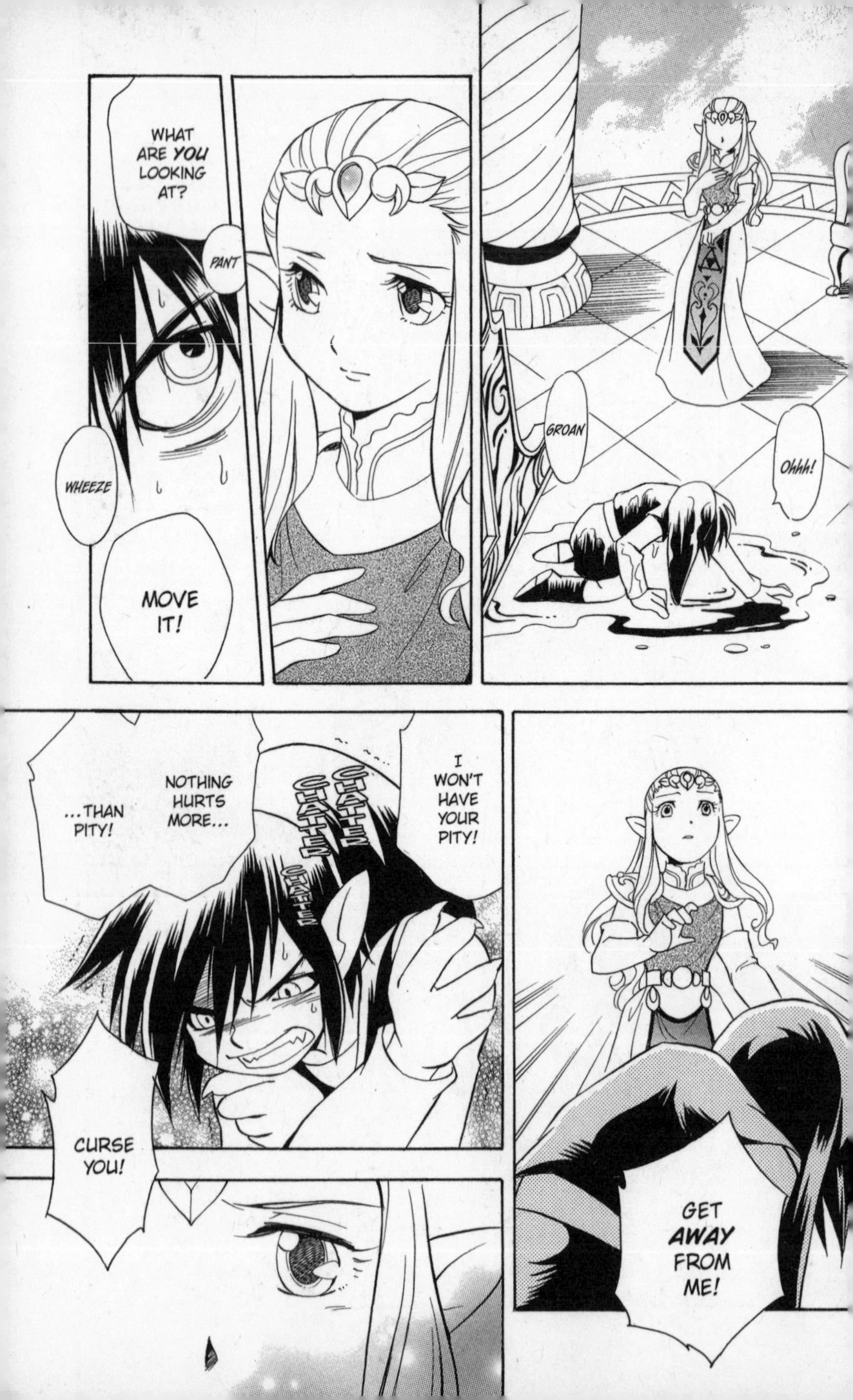
Ohhh!
GROAN
WHAT ARE YOU LOOKING AT?
PANT
WHEEZE
MOVE IT!
GET AWAY FROM ME!
I WON'T HAVE YOUR PITY!
CHATTER
CHATTER
CHATTER
NOTHING HURTS MORE...
...THAN PITY!
CURSE YOU!

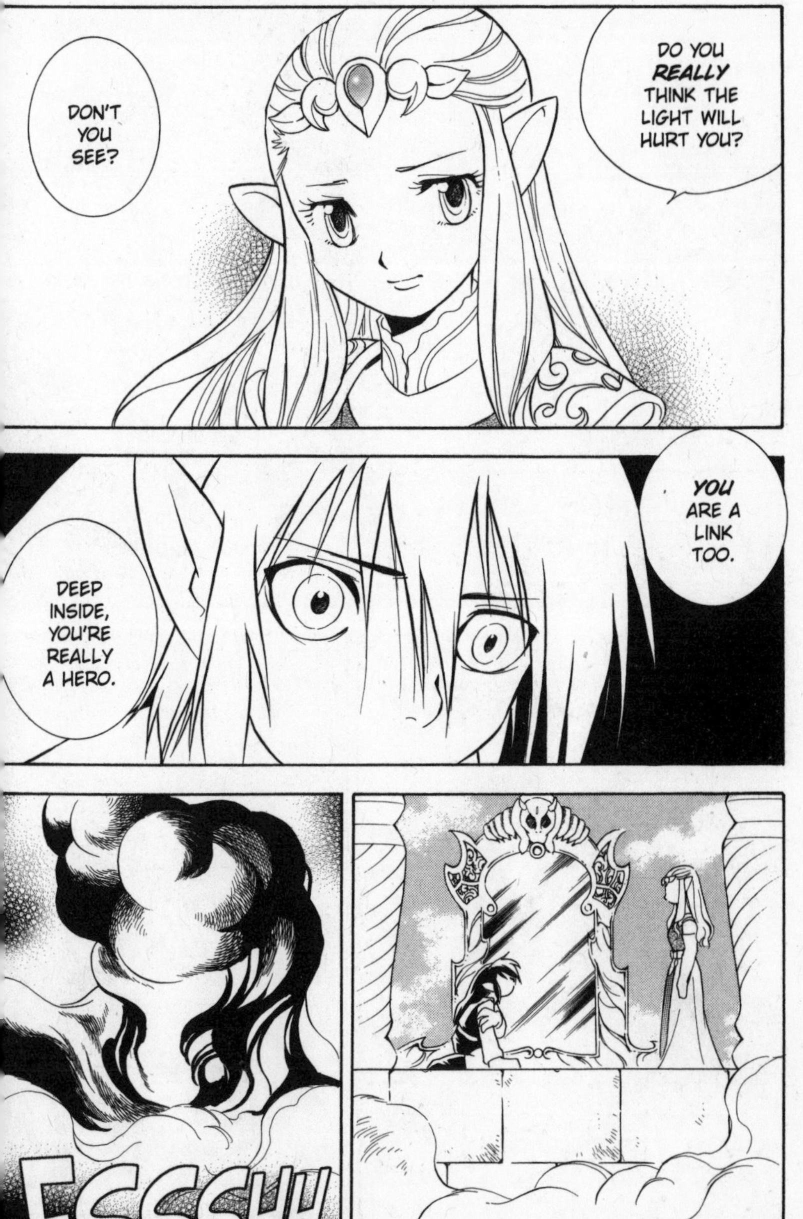
DO YOU REALLY THINK THE LIGHT WILL HURT YOU?
DON'T YOU SEE?
YOU ARE A LINK TOO.
DEEP INSIDE, YOU'RE REALLY A HERO.
FSSSHH

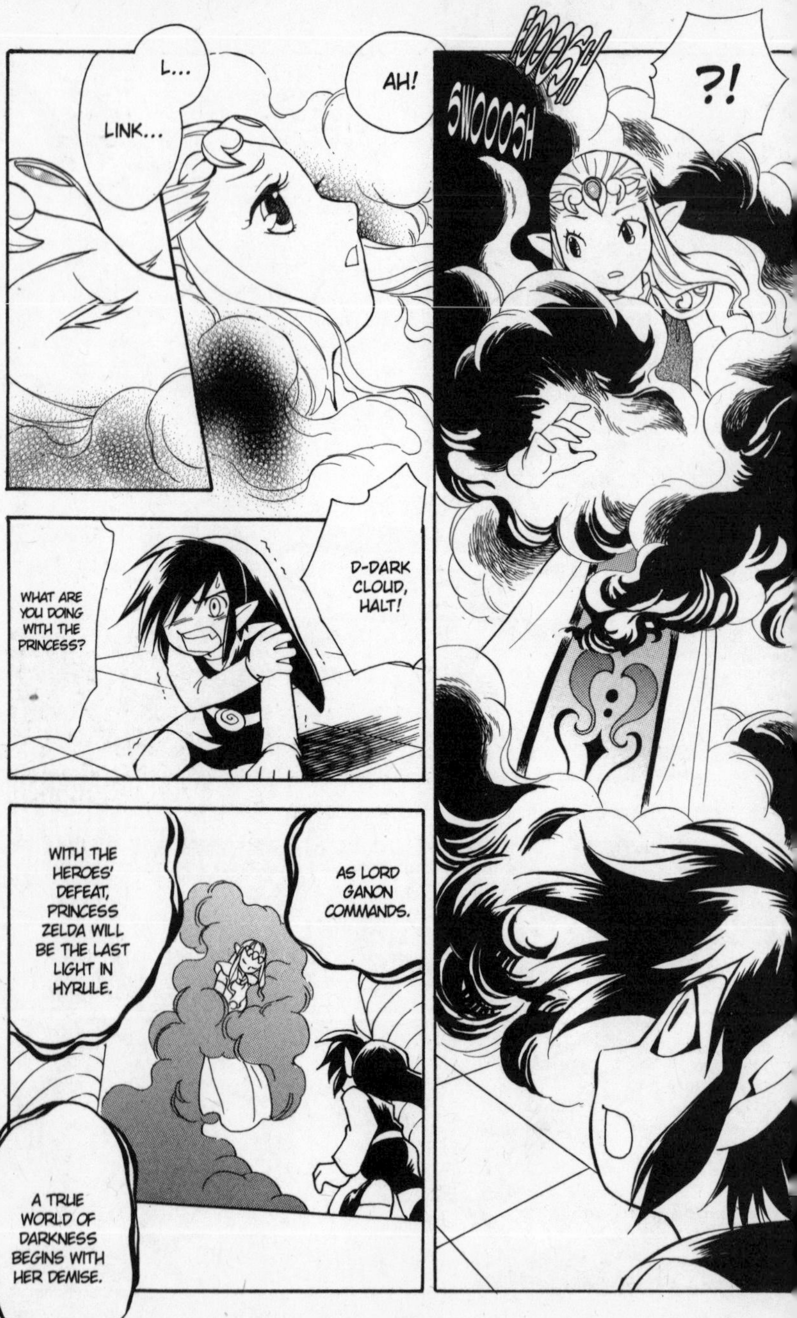
?!
FOOOSH
SWOOOSH
AH!
L...
LINK...
D-DARK CLOUD, HALT!
WHAT ARE YOU DOING WITH THE PRINCESS?
AS LORD GANON COMMANDS.
WITH THE HEROES' DEFEAT, PRINCESS ZELDA WILL BE THE LAST LIGHT IN HYRULE.
A TRUE WORLD OF DARKNESS BEGINS WITH HER DEMISE.

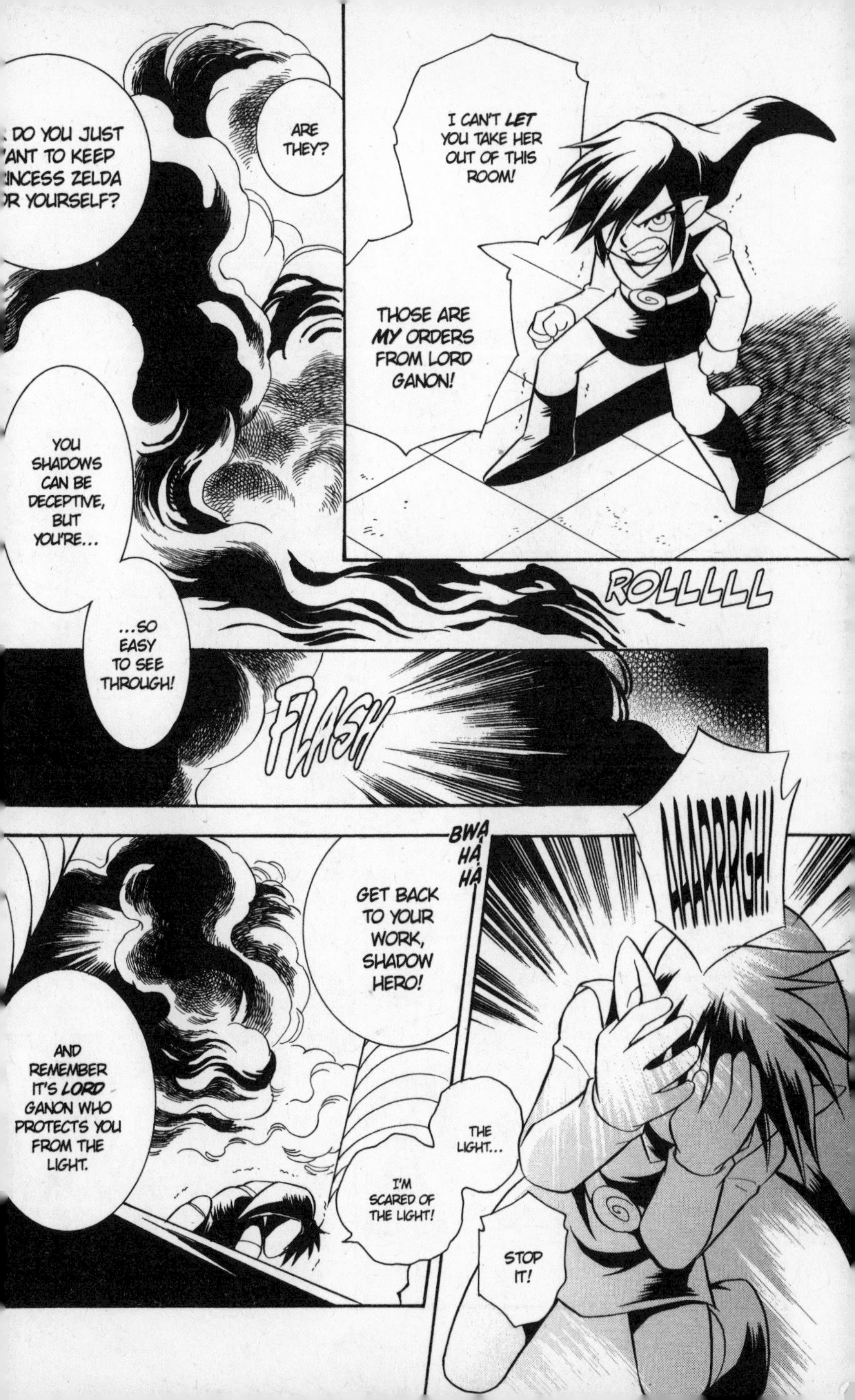
I CAN'T *LET* YOU TAKE HER OUT OF THIS ROOM!
THOSE ARE *MY* ORDERS FROM LORD GANON!
ARE THEY?
DO YOU JUST ANT TO KEEP INCESS ZELDA R YOURSELF?
YOU SHADOWS CAN BE DECEPTIVE, BUT YOU'RE...
ROLLLLL
...SO EASY TO SEE THROUGH!
FLASH
AAARRRGH!
BWA HA HA
GET BACK TO YOUR WORK, SHADOW HERO!
AND REMEMBER IT'S *LORD* GANON WHO PROTECTS YOU FROM THE LIGHT.
THE LIGHT...
I'M SCARED OF THE LIGHT!
STOP IT!

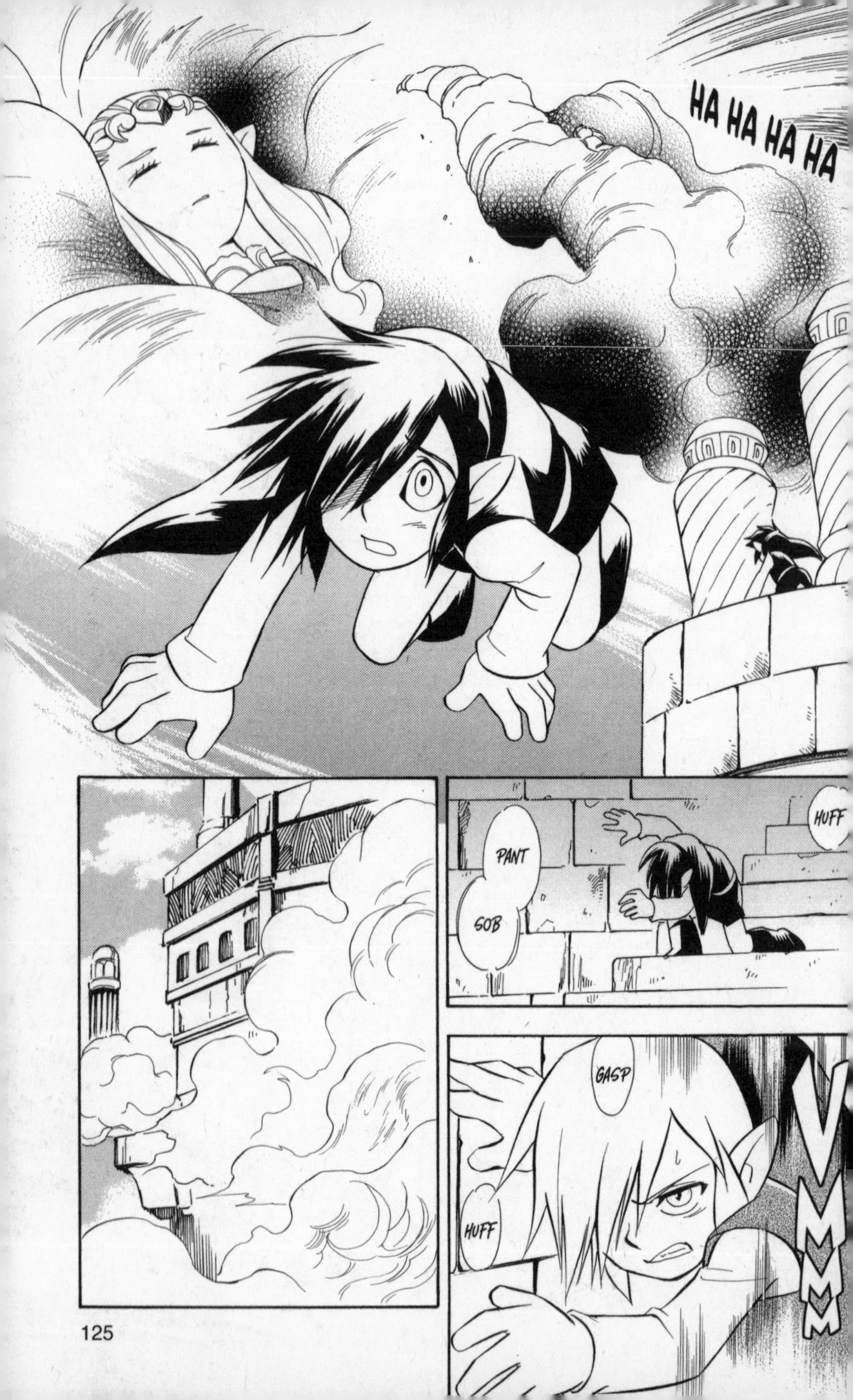
HA HA HA HA
HUFF
PANT
SOB
VMMMMM
GASP
HUFF

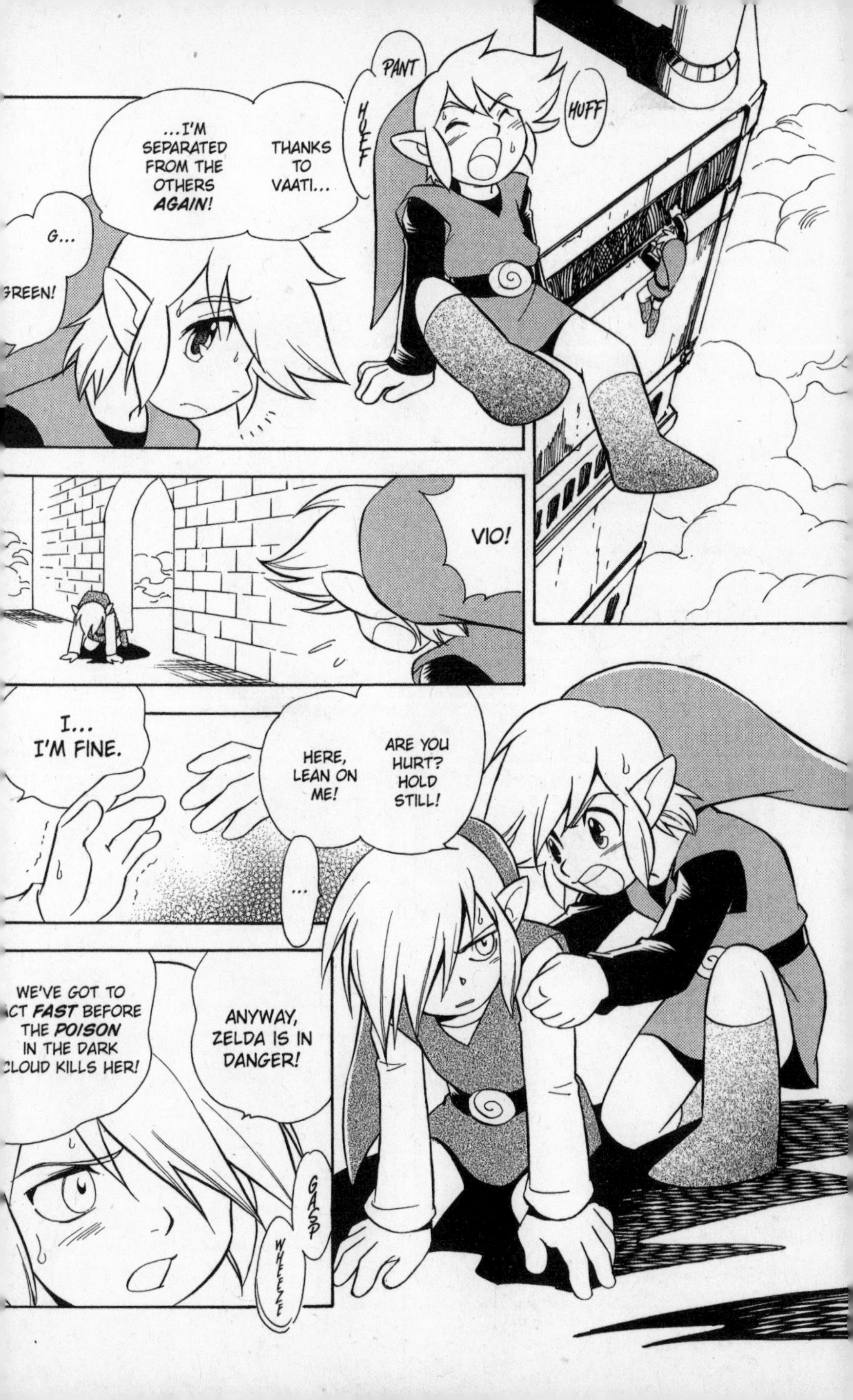
PANT
HUFF
HUFF
THANKS TO VAATI...
...I'M SEPARATED FROM THE OTHERS AGAIN!
G...
GREEN!
VIO!
ARE YOU HURT? HOLD STILL!
HERE, LEAN ON ME!
...
I... I'M FINE.
ANYWAY, ZELDA IS IN DANGER!
WE'VE GOT TO CT FAST BEFORE THE POISON IN THE DARK LOUD KILLS HER!
GASP
WHEEZE

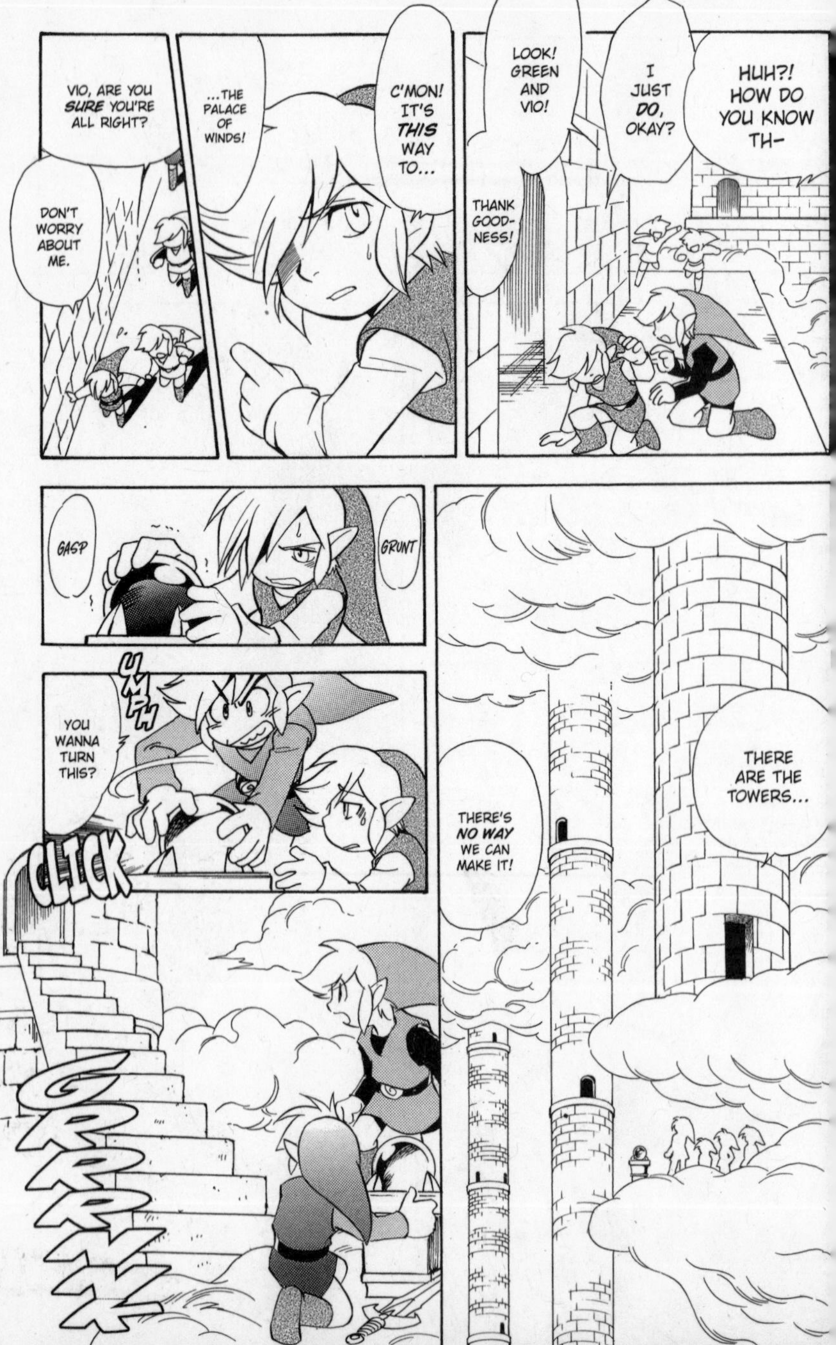
HUH?! HOW DO YOU KNOW TH-
I JUST DO, OKAY?
LOOK! GREEN AND VIO!
THANK GOODNESS!
C'MON! IT'S THIS WAY TO...
...THE PALACE OF WINDS!
VIO, ARE YOU SURE YOU'RE ALL RIGHT?
DON'T WORRY ABOUT ME.
THERE ARE THE TOWERS...
THERE'S NO WAY WE CAN MAKE IT!
GRUNT
GASP
UMPH
YOU WANNA TURN THIS?
CLICK
GRRRNK

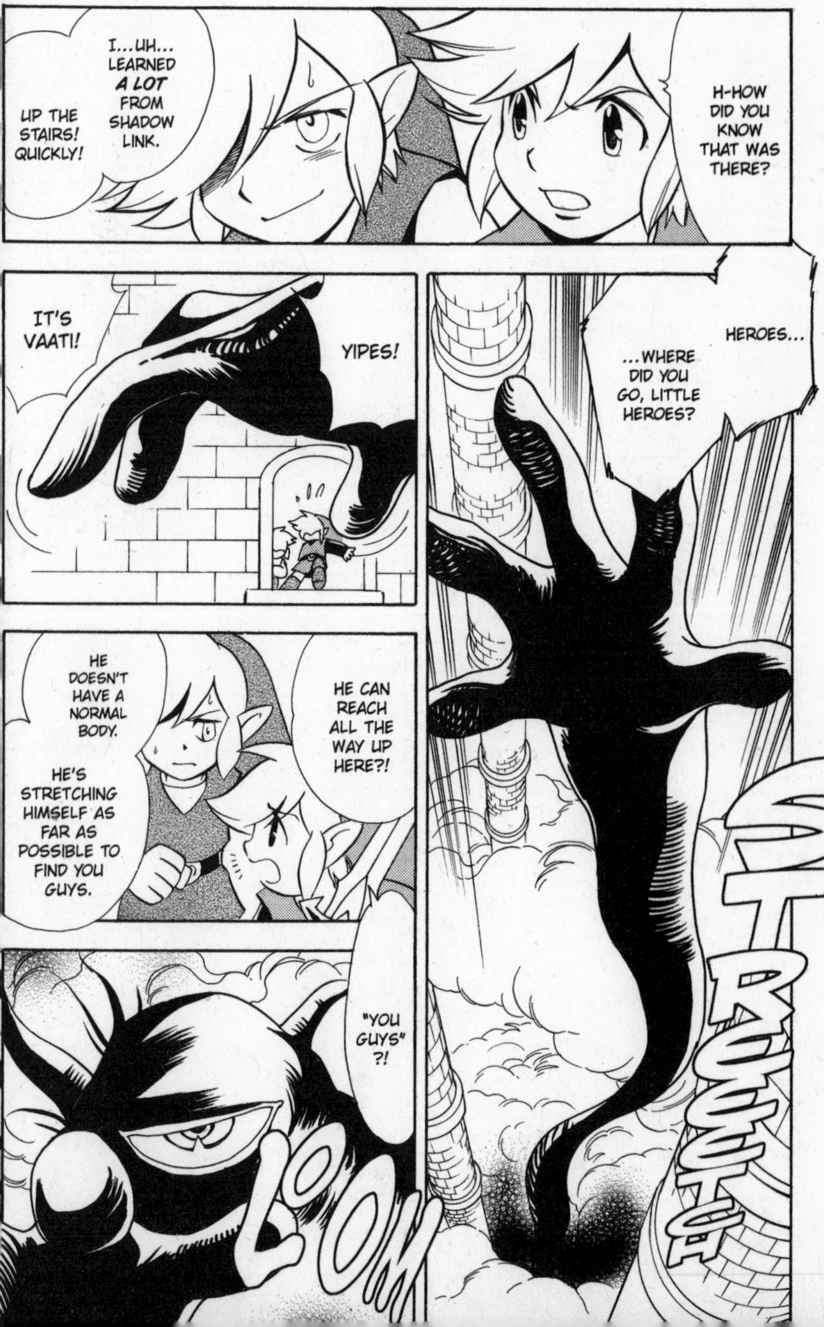
H-HOW DID YOU KNOW THAT WAS THERE?
I...UH... LEARNED A LOT FROM SHADOW LINK.
UP THE STAIRS! QUICKLY!
HEROES...
...WHERE DID YOU GO, LITTLE HEROES?
STREEEETCH
YIPES!
IT'S VAATI!
HE CAN REACH ALL THE WAY UP HERE?!
HE DOESN'T HAVE A NORMAL BODY.
HE'S STRETCHING HIMSELF AS FAR AS POSSIBLE TO FIND YOU GUYS.
"YOU GUYS"?!
LOOM

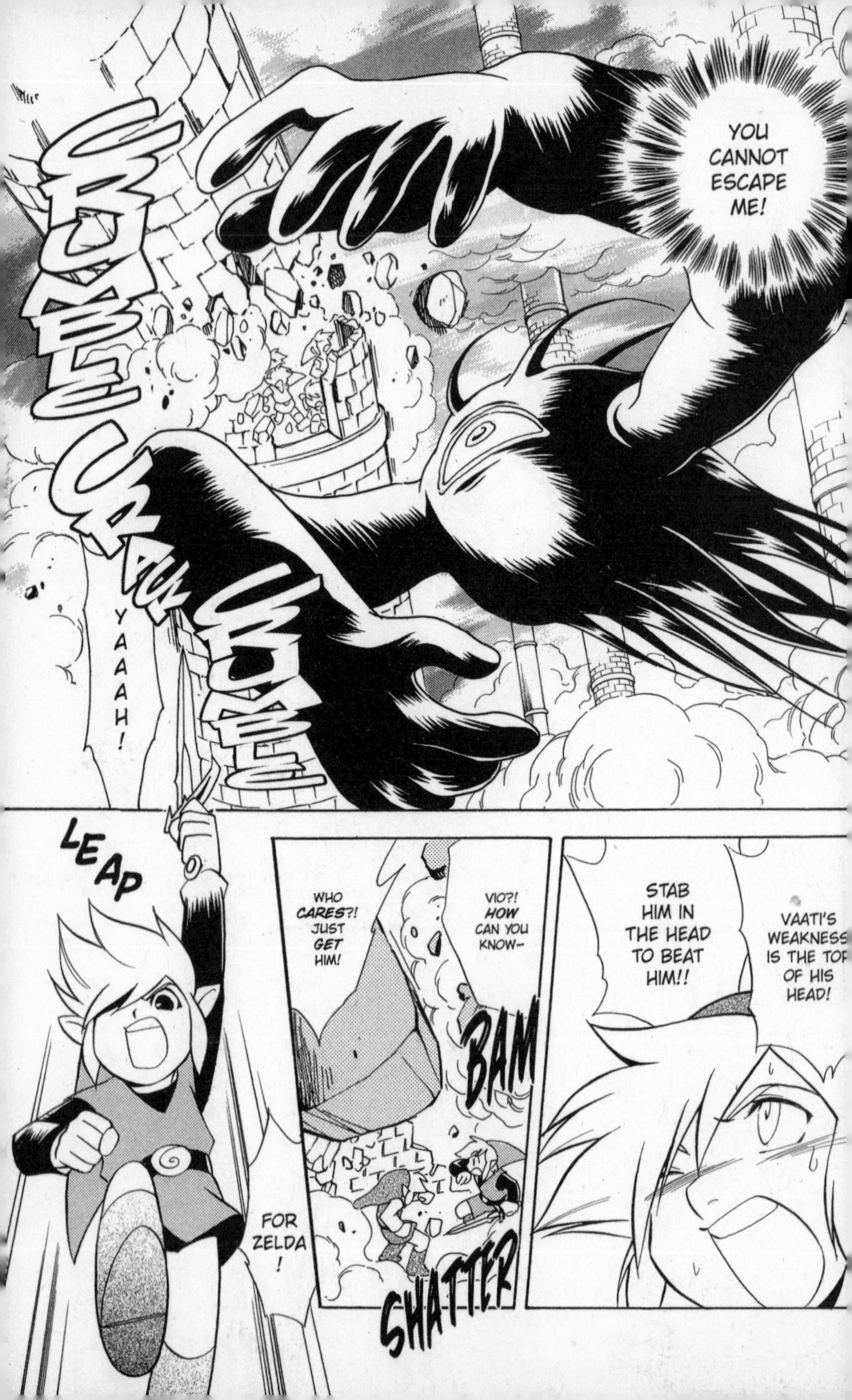
YOU CANNOT ESCAPE ME!
YAAAAH!
VAATI'S WEAKNESS IS THE TOP OF HIS HEAD!
STAB HIM IN THE HEAD TO BEAT HIM!!
VIO?! HOW CAN YOU KNOW–
WHO CARES?! JUST GET HIM!
BAM
SHATTER
LEAP
FOR ZELDA!

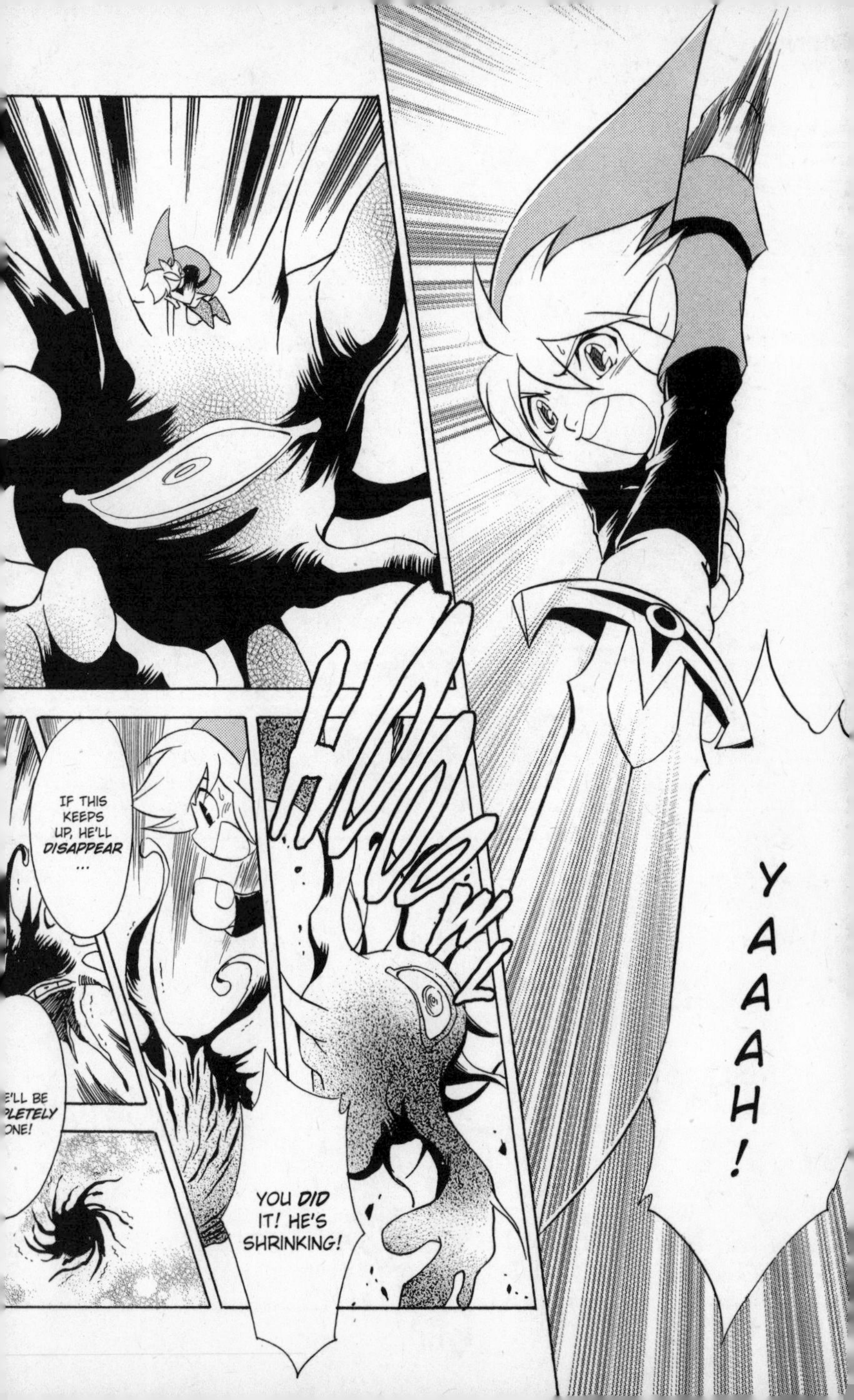
YAAAH!
HOOOWL!
YOU DID IT! HE'S SHRINKING!
IF THIS KEEPS UP, HE'LL DISAPPEAR...
E'LL BE PLETELY ONE!

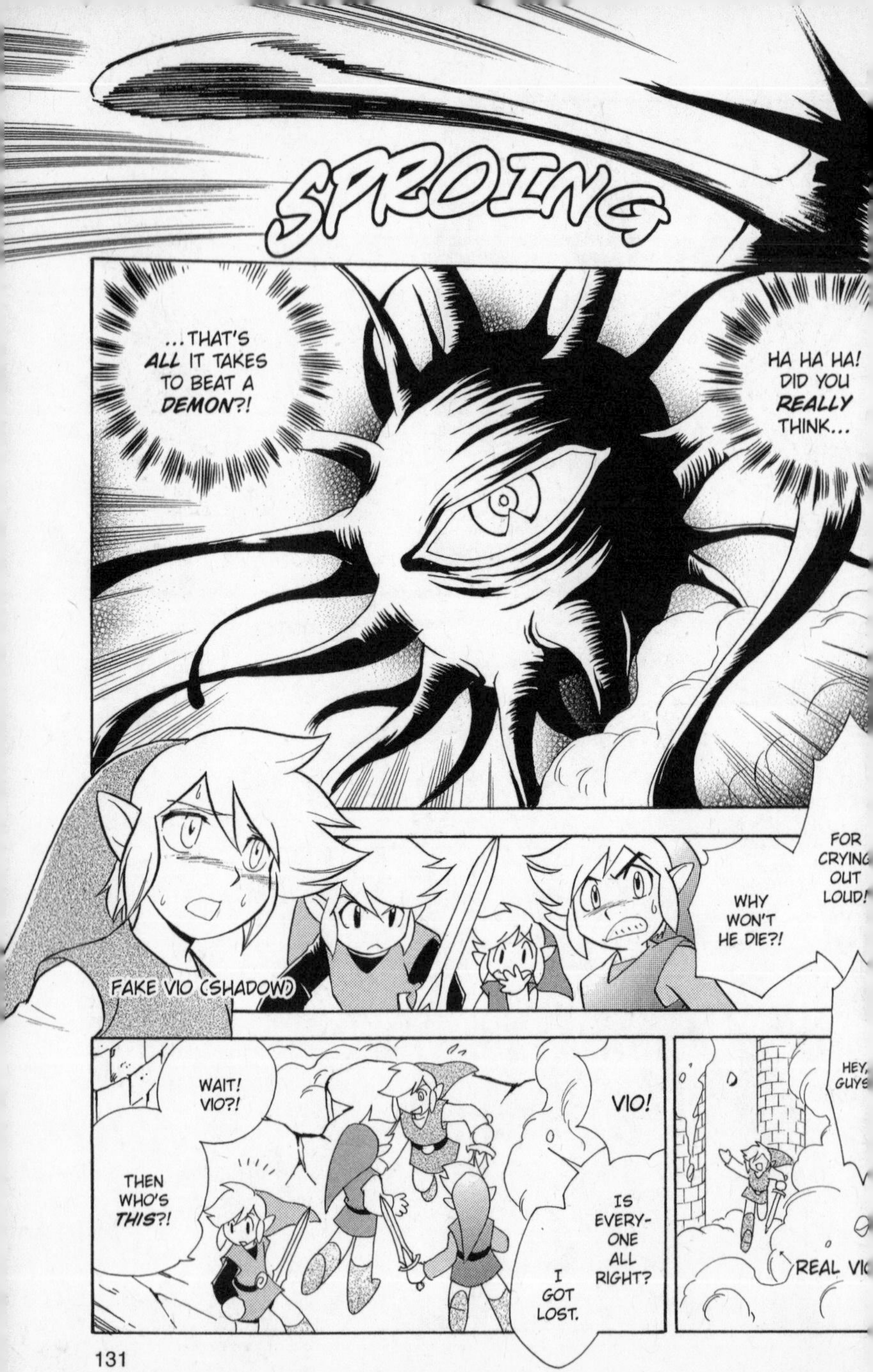
SPROING
HA HA HA! DID YOU *REALLY* THINK...
...THAT'S *ALL* IT TAKES TO BEAT A *DEMON*?!
FOR CRYING OUT LOUD!
WHY WON'T HE DIE?!
FAKE VIO (SHADOW)
HEY, GUYS
REAL VI
VIO!
IS EVERY-ONE ALL RIGHT?
I GOT LOST.
WAIT! VIO?!
THEN WHO'S *THIS*?!

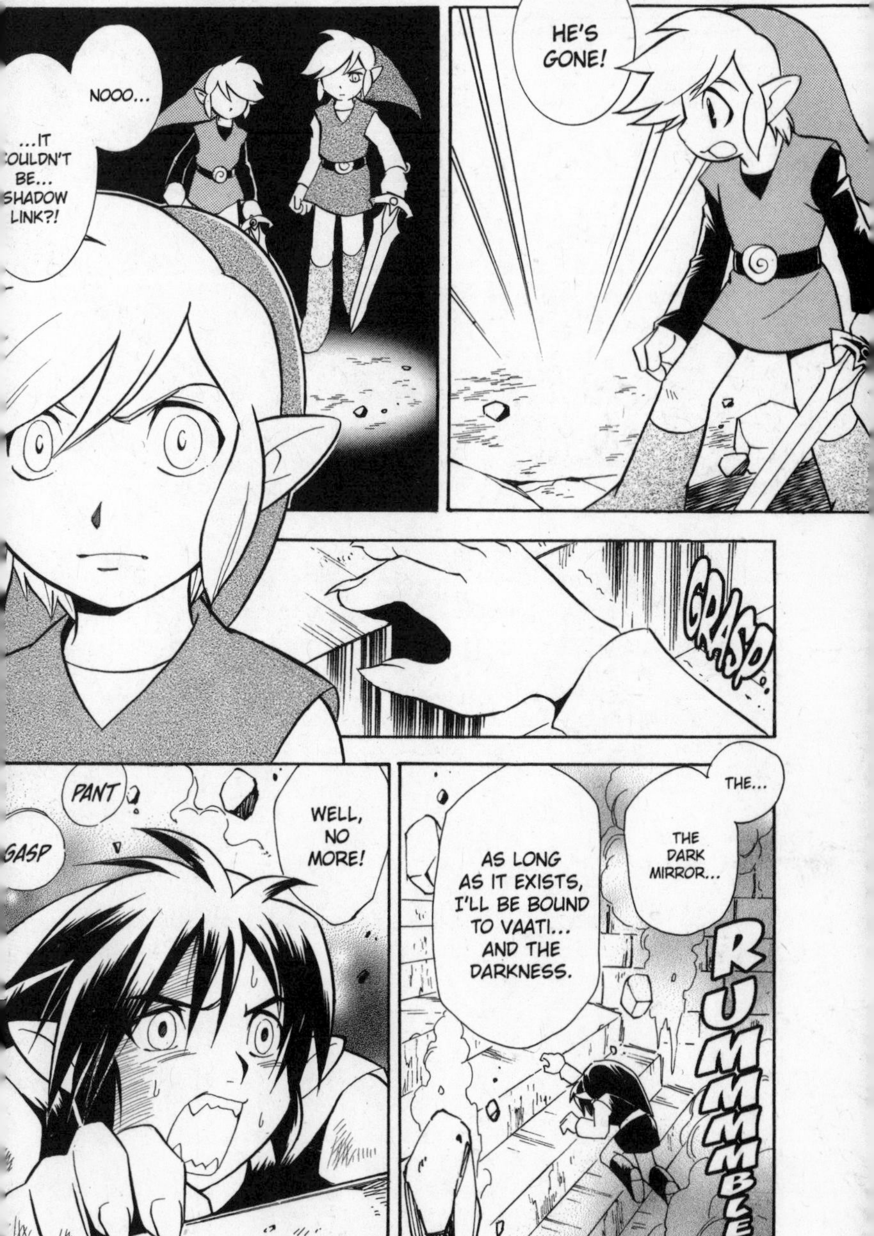
HE'S GONE!
NOOO...
...IT COULDN'T BE... SHADOW LINK?!
GRASP
THE...
THE DARK MIRROR...
AS LONG AS IT EXISTS, I'LL BE BOUND TO VAATI... AND THE DARKNESS.
RUMMMMBLE
WELL, NO MORE!
PANT
GASP

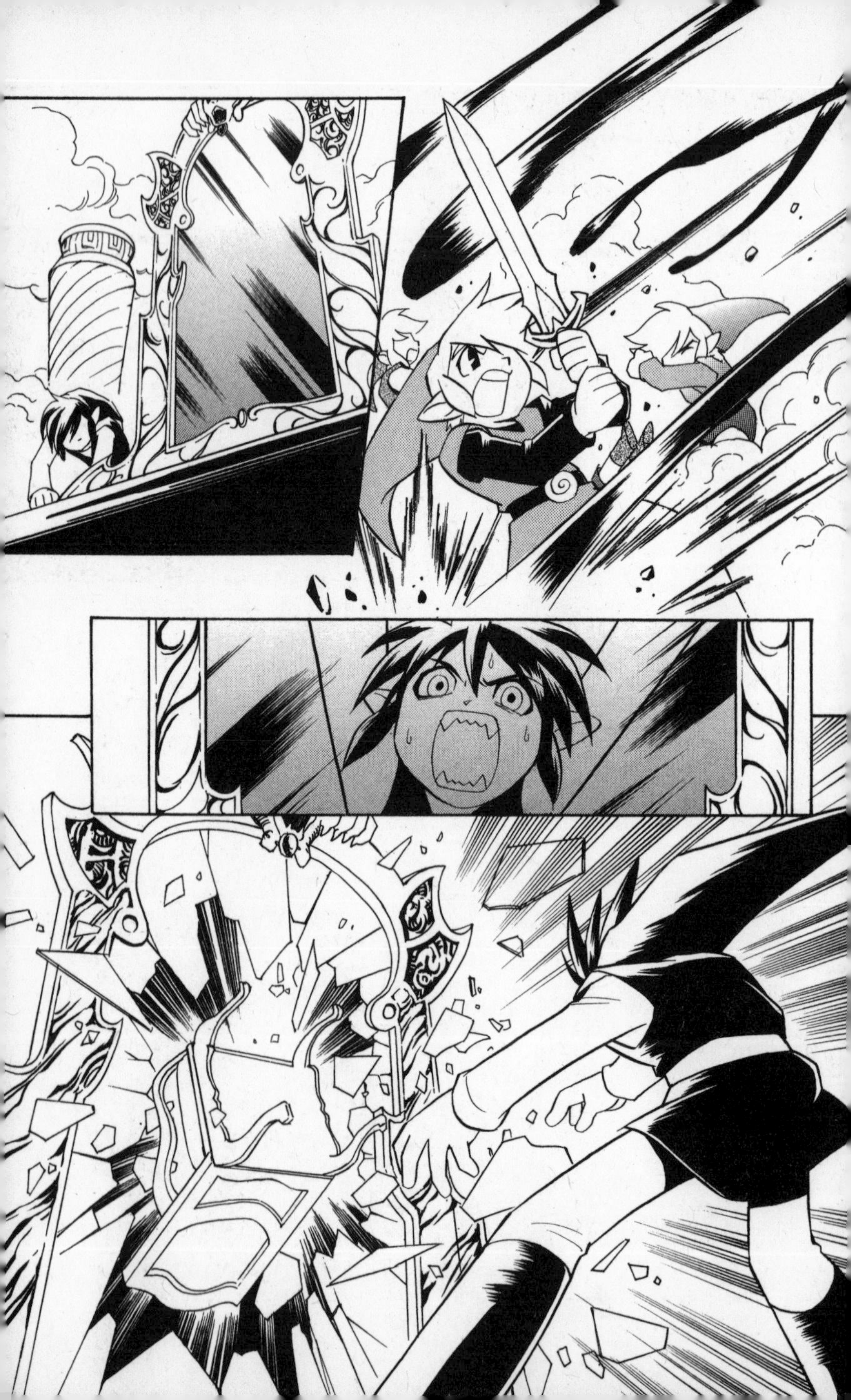

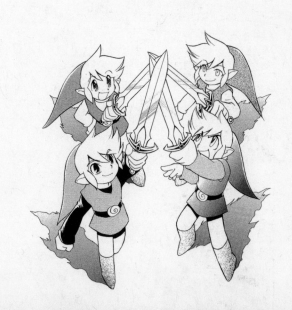

CHAPTER 12 THE FOUR SWORD FOREVER!

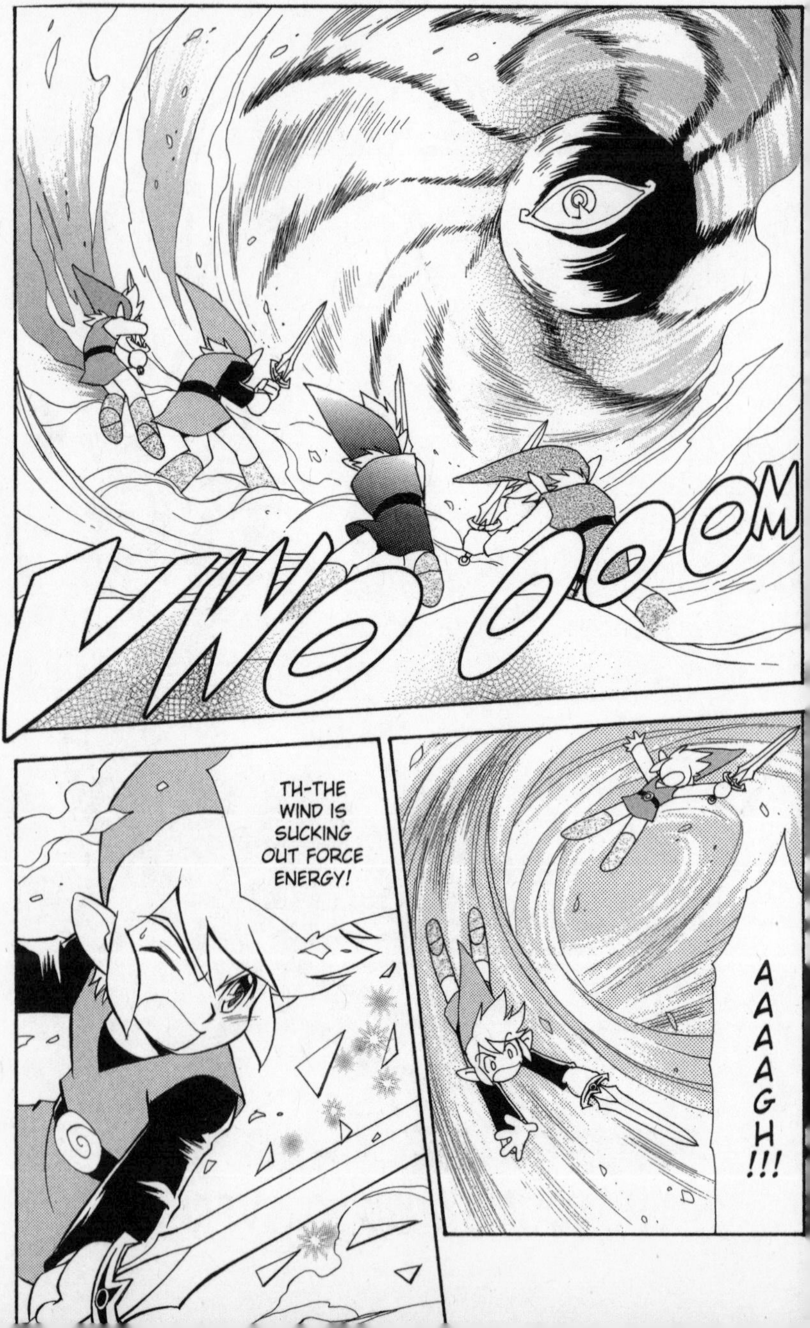
VWOOOOOM
AAAAAGH!!!
TH-THE WIND IS SUCKING OUT FORCE ENERGY!

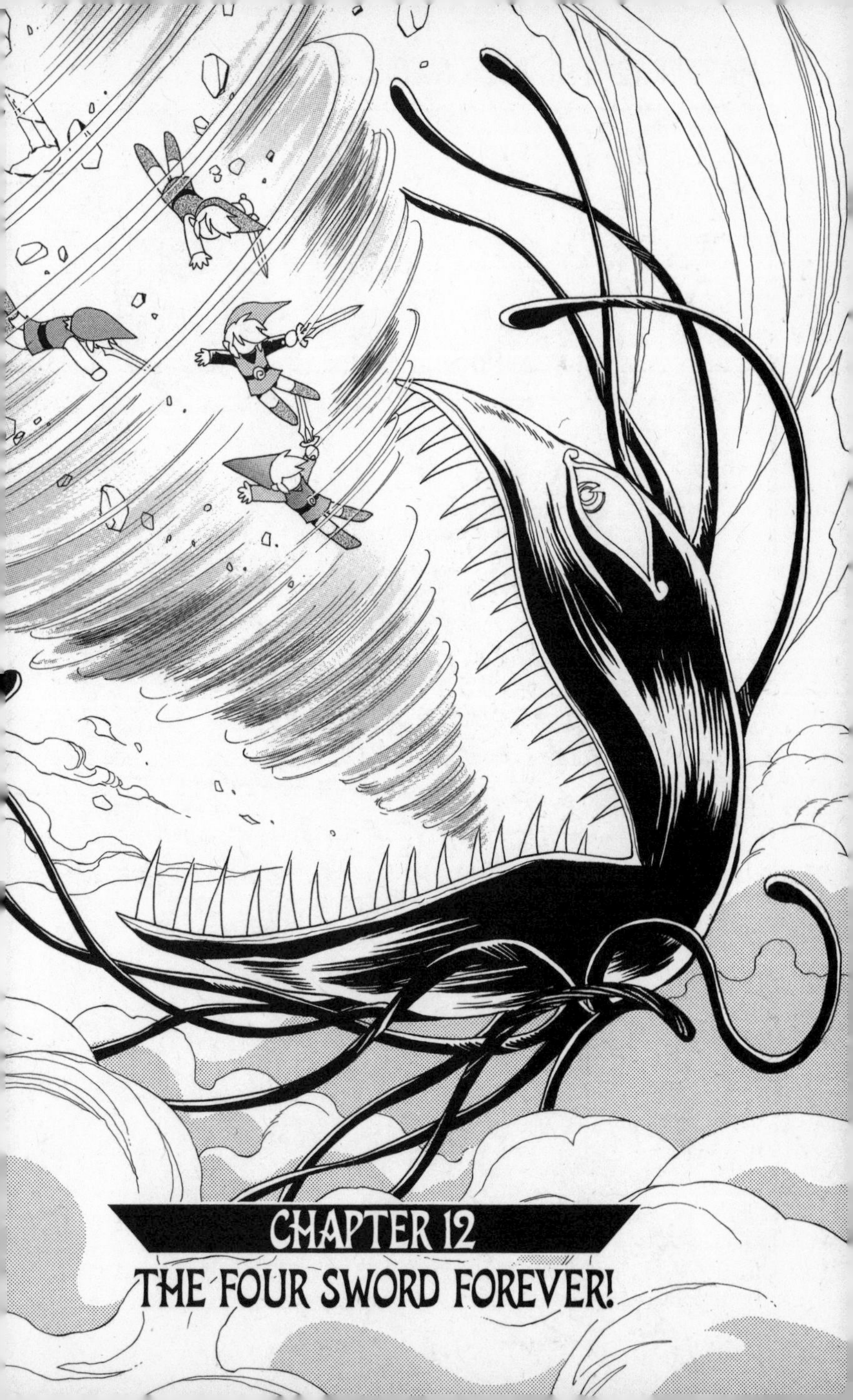
CHAPTER 12
THE FOUR SWORD FOREVER!

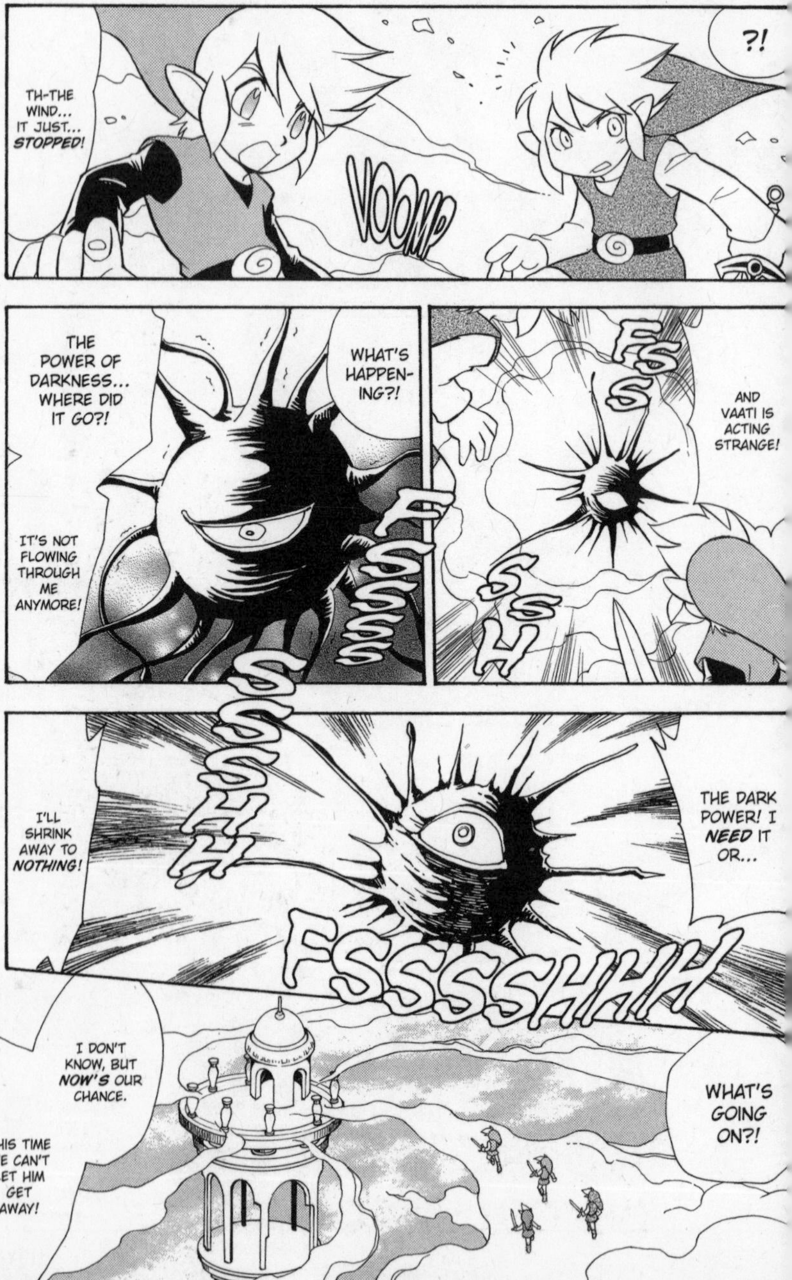
?!
VOOMP
TH-THE WIND... IT JUST... *STOPPED!*
FSS
AND VAATI IS ACTING STRANGE!
SSH
WHAT'S HAPPEN-ING?!
THE POWER OF DARKNESS... WHERE DID IT *GO?!*
FSSSSS
IT'S NOT FLOWING THROUGH ME ANYMORE!
THE DARK POWER! I *NEED* IT OR...
SSSHHH
I'LL SHRINK AWAY TO *NOTHING!*
FSSSSHHH
WHAT'S GOING ON?!
I DON'T KNOW, BUT *NOW'S* OUR CHANCE.
THIS TIME WE CAN'T LET HIM GET AWAY!

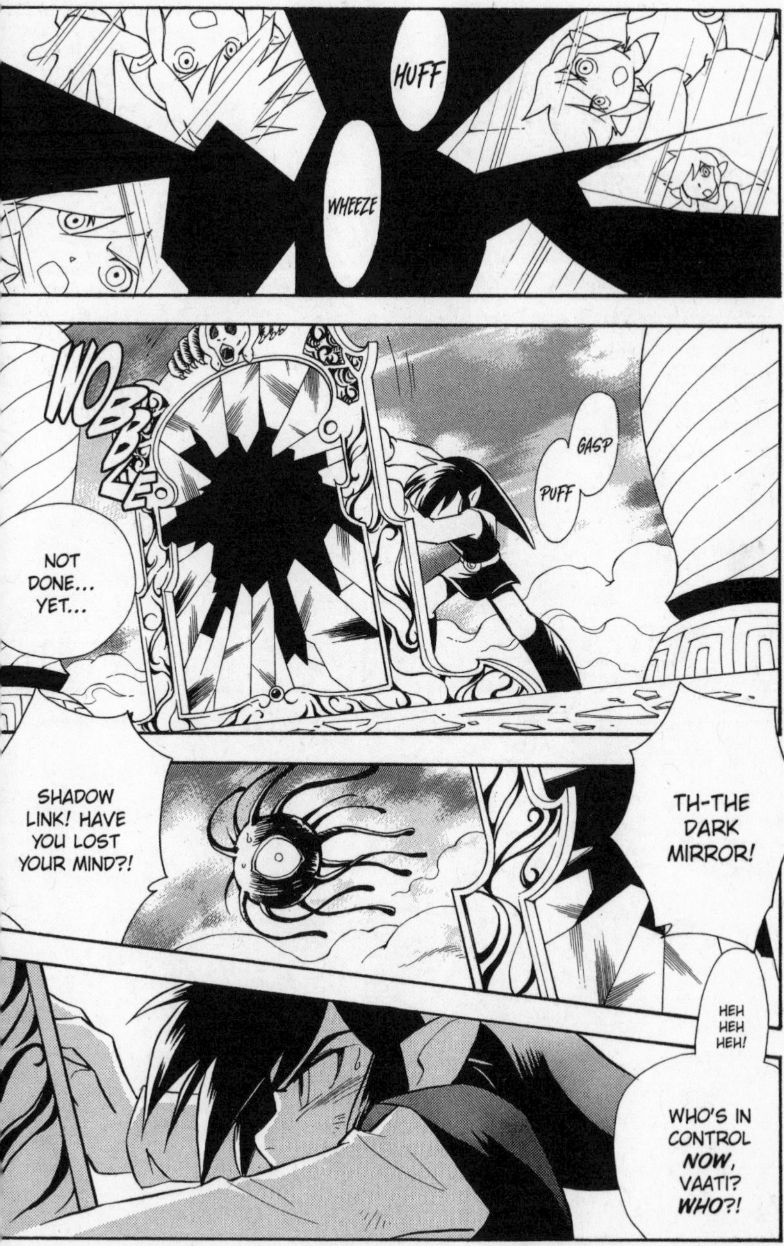
HUFF
WHEEZE
GASP
PUFF
WOBBLE
NOT DONE... YET...
TH-THE DARK MIRROR!
SHADOW LINK! HAVE YOU LOST YOUR MIND?!
HEH HEH HEH!
WHO'S IN CONTROL *NOW*, VAATI? *WHO*?!

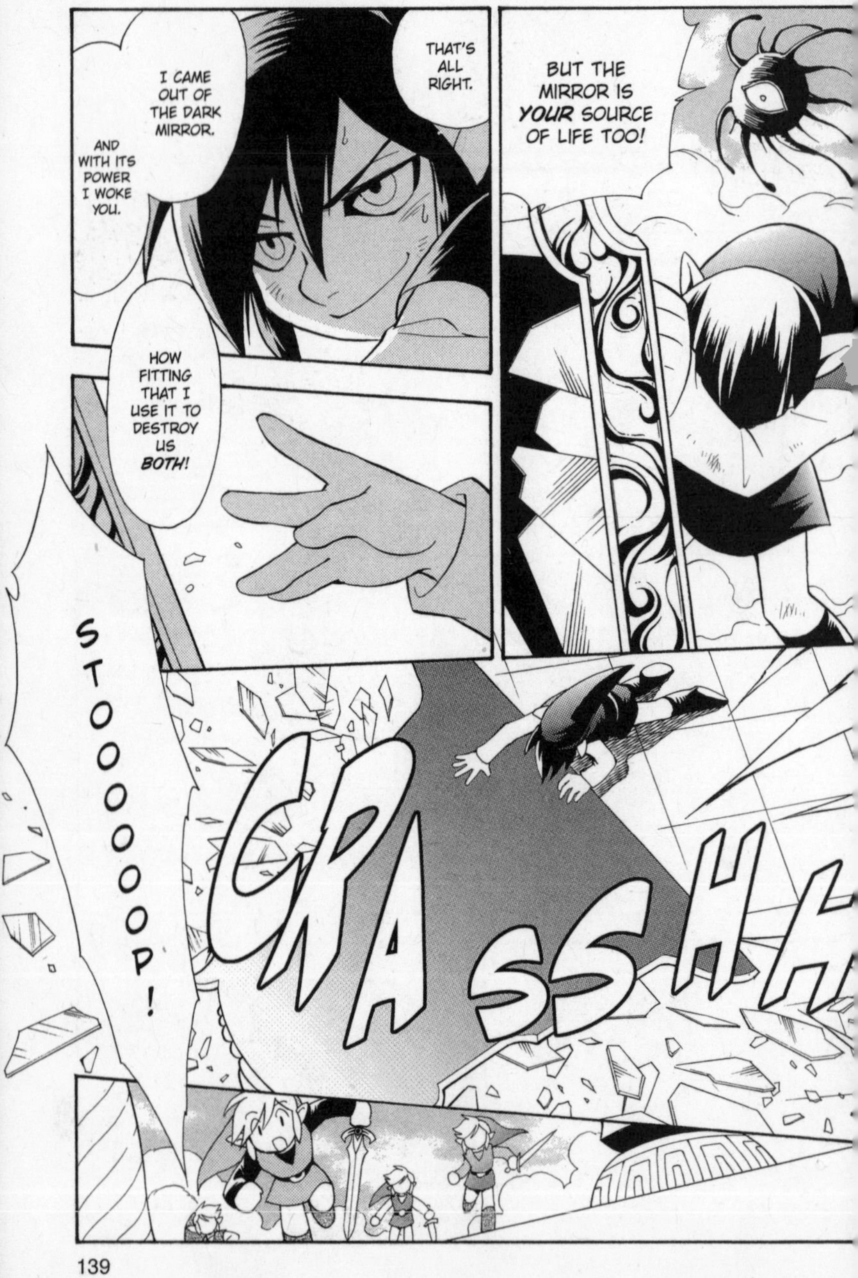
BUT THE MIRROR IS ***YOUR*** SOURCE OF LIFE TOO!
THAT'S ALL RIGHT.
I CAME OUT OF THE DARK MIRROR.
AND WITH ITS POWER I WOKE YOU.
HOW FITTING THAT I USE IT TO DESTROY US ***BOTH!***
CRASSHH
STOOOOOOOP!

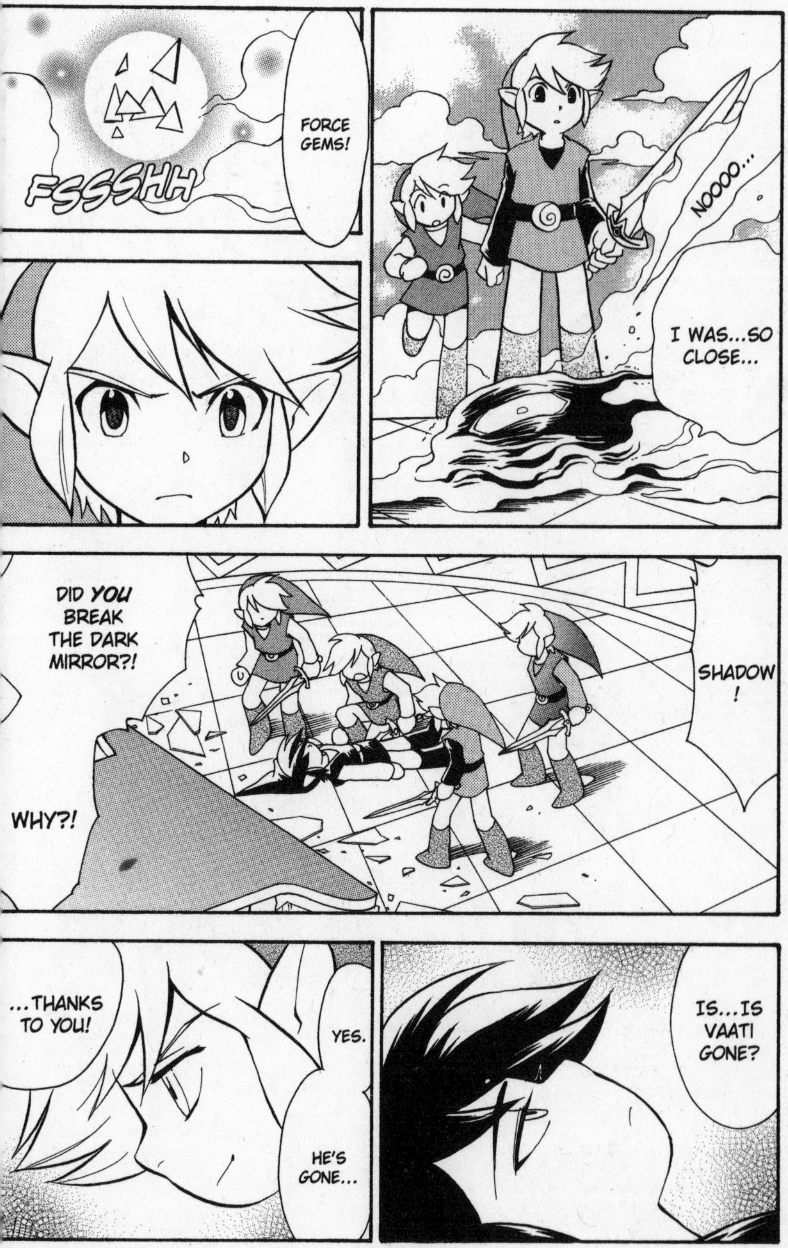
NOOOO...
I WAS...SO CLOSE...
FORCE GEMS!
FSSSHH
SHADOW!
DID YOU BREAK THE DARK MIRROR?!
WHY?!
IS...IS VAATI GONE?
YES.
HE'S GONE...
...THANKS TO YOU!

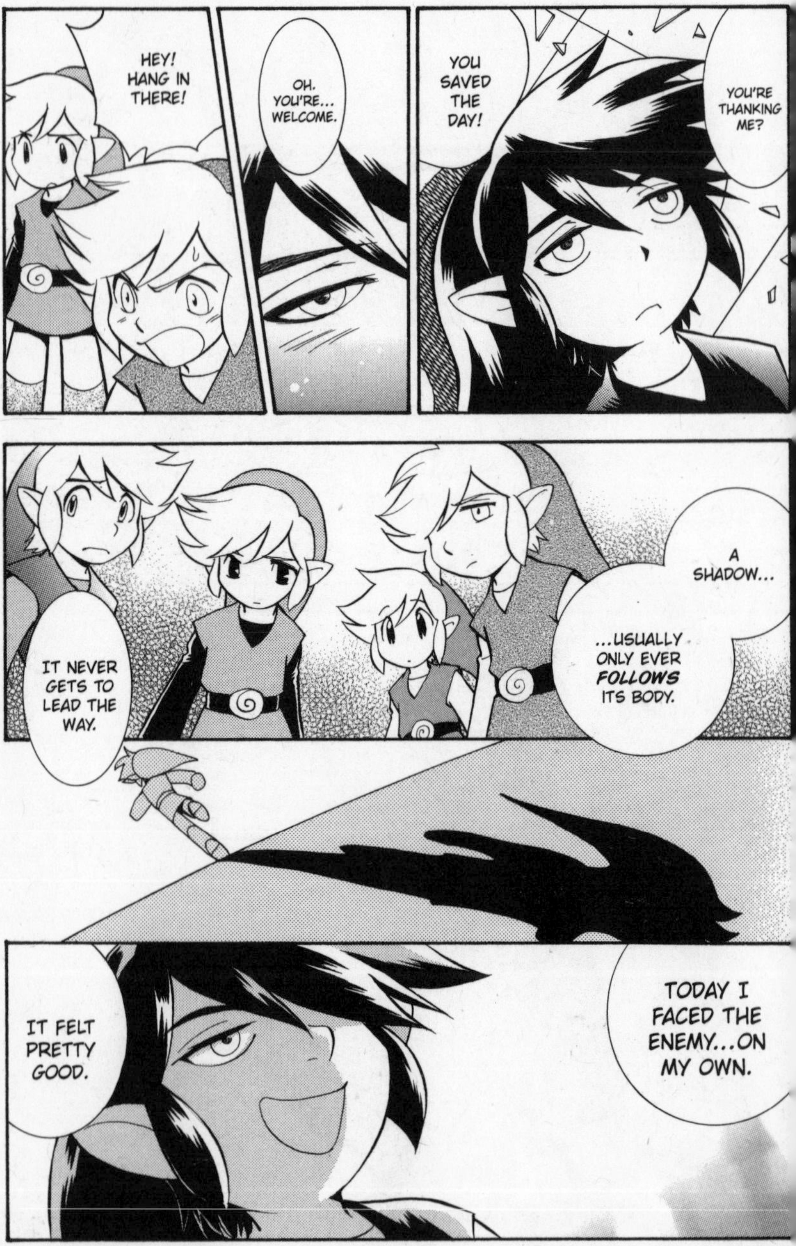
YOU'RE THANKING ME?
YOU SAVED THE DAY!
OH. YOU'RE... WELCOME.
HEY! HANG IN THERE!
A SHADOW...
...USUALLY ONLY EVER FOLLOWS ITS BODY.
IT NEVER GETS TO LEAD THE WAY.
TODAY I FACED THE ENEMY...ON MY OWN.
IT FELT PRETTY GOOD.

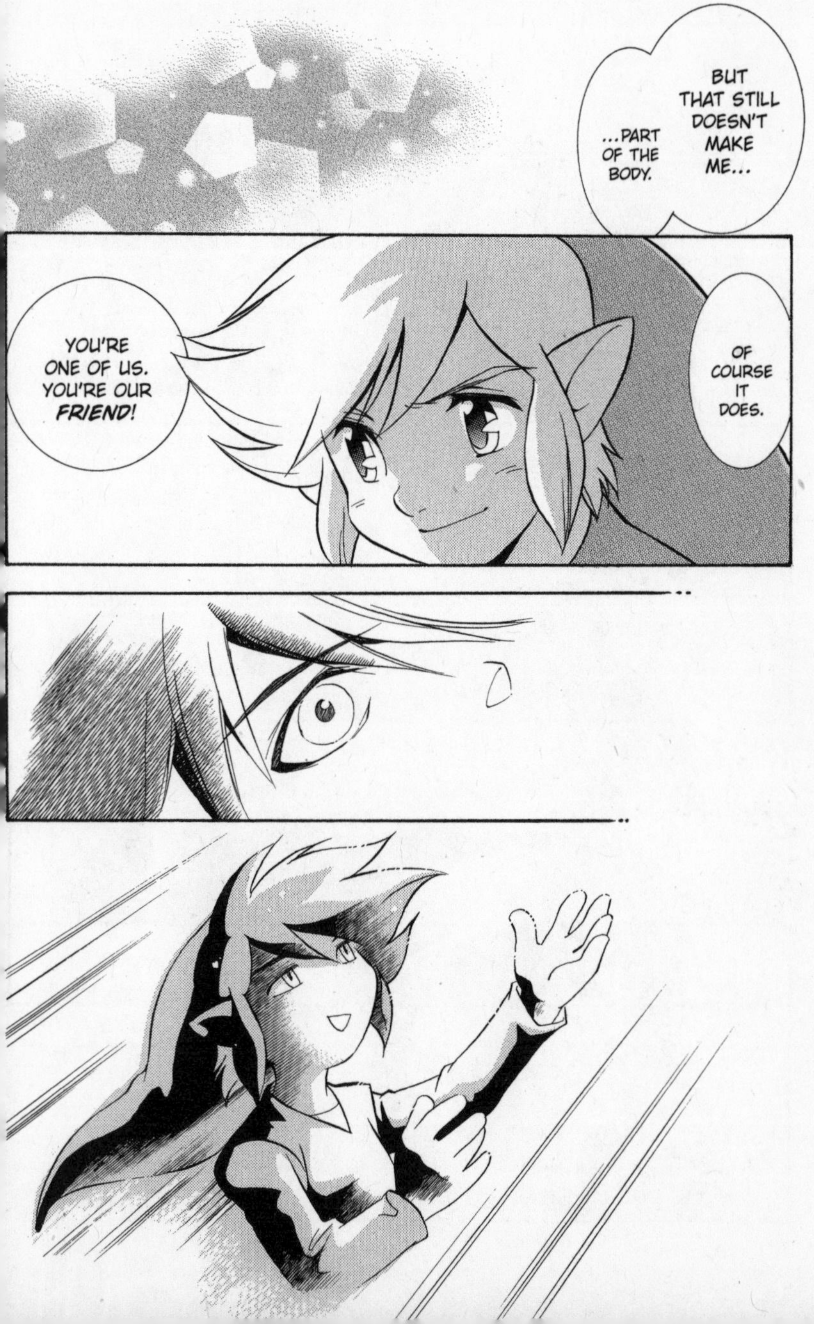

BUT THAT STILL DOESN'T MAKE ME...
...PART OF THE BODY.
OF COURSE IT DOES.
YOU'RE ONE OF US. YOU'RE OUR *FRIEND*!

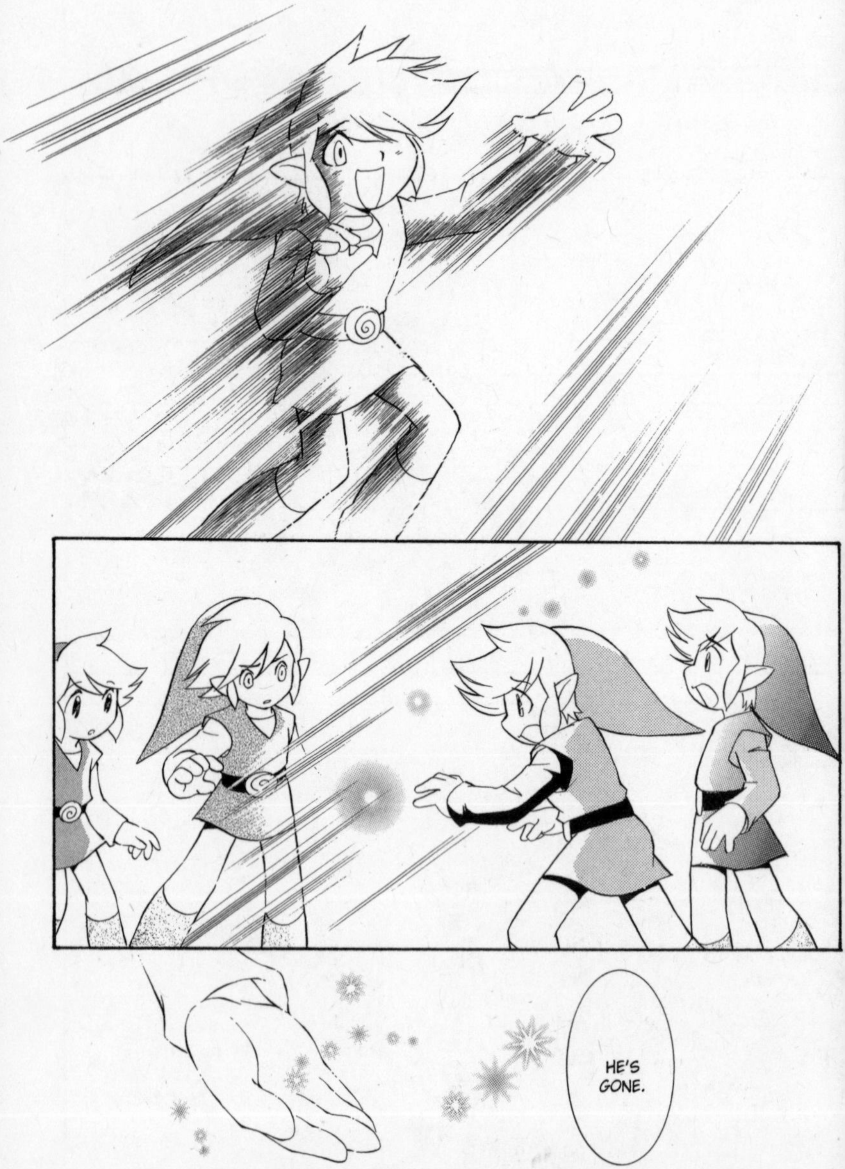
HE'S GONE.

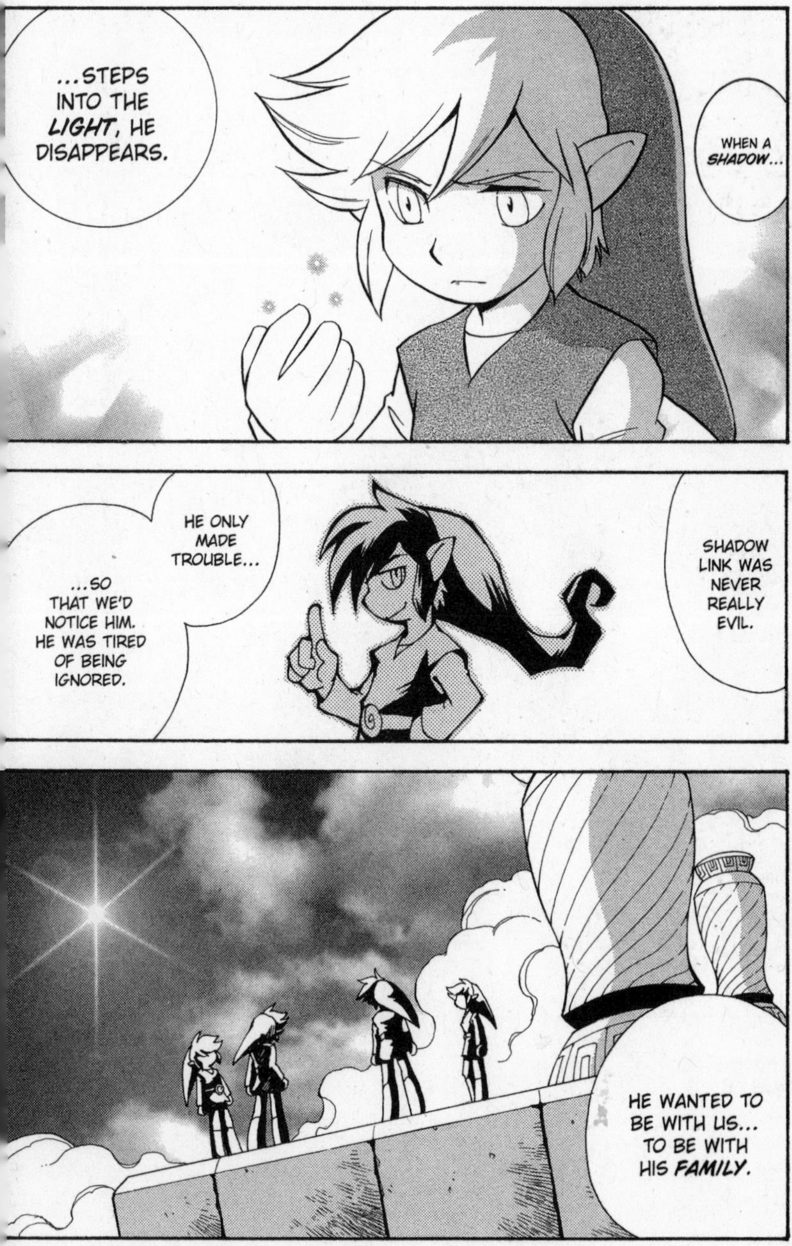
WHEN A SHADOW...
...STEPS INTO THE LIGHT, HE DISAPPEARS.
SHADOW LINK WAS NEVER REALLY EVIL.
HE ONLY MADE TROUBLE...
...SO THAT WE'D NOTICE HIM. HE WAS TIRED OF BEING IGNORED.
HE WANTED TO BE WITH US... TO BE WITH HIS FAMILY.

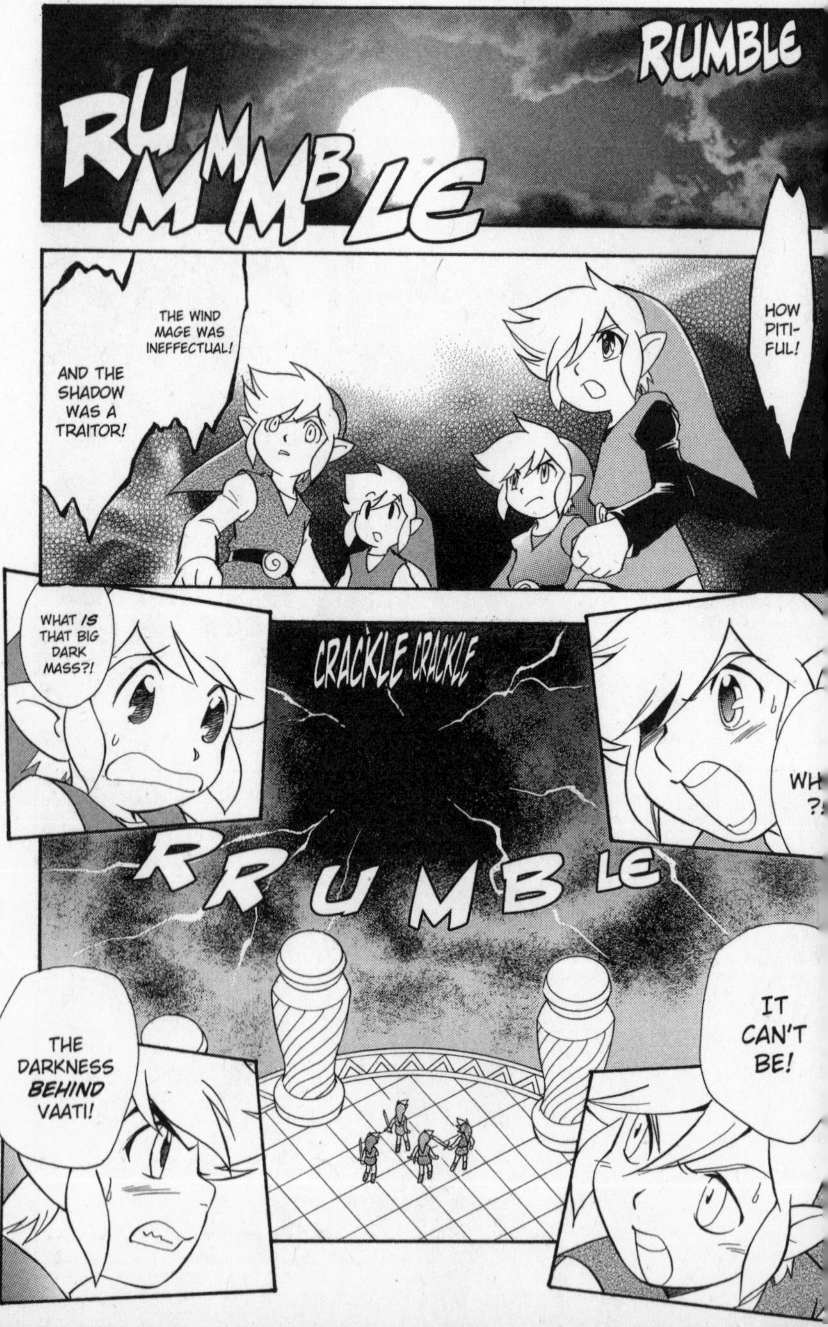
RUMBLE
RUMMMMBLE
HOW PITIFUL!
THE WIND MAGE WAS INEFFECTUAL!
AND THE SHADOW WAS A TRAITOR!
WH ?!
CRACKLE CRACKLE
WHAT *IS* THAT BIG DARK MASS?!
RRUMBLE
IT CAN'T BE!
THE DARKNESS *BEHIND* VAATI!

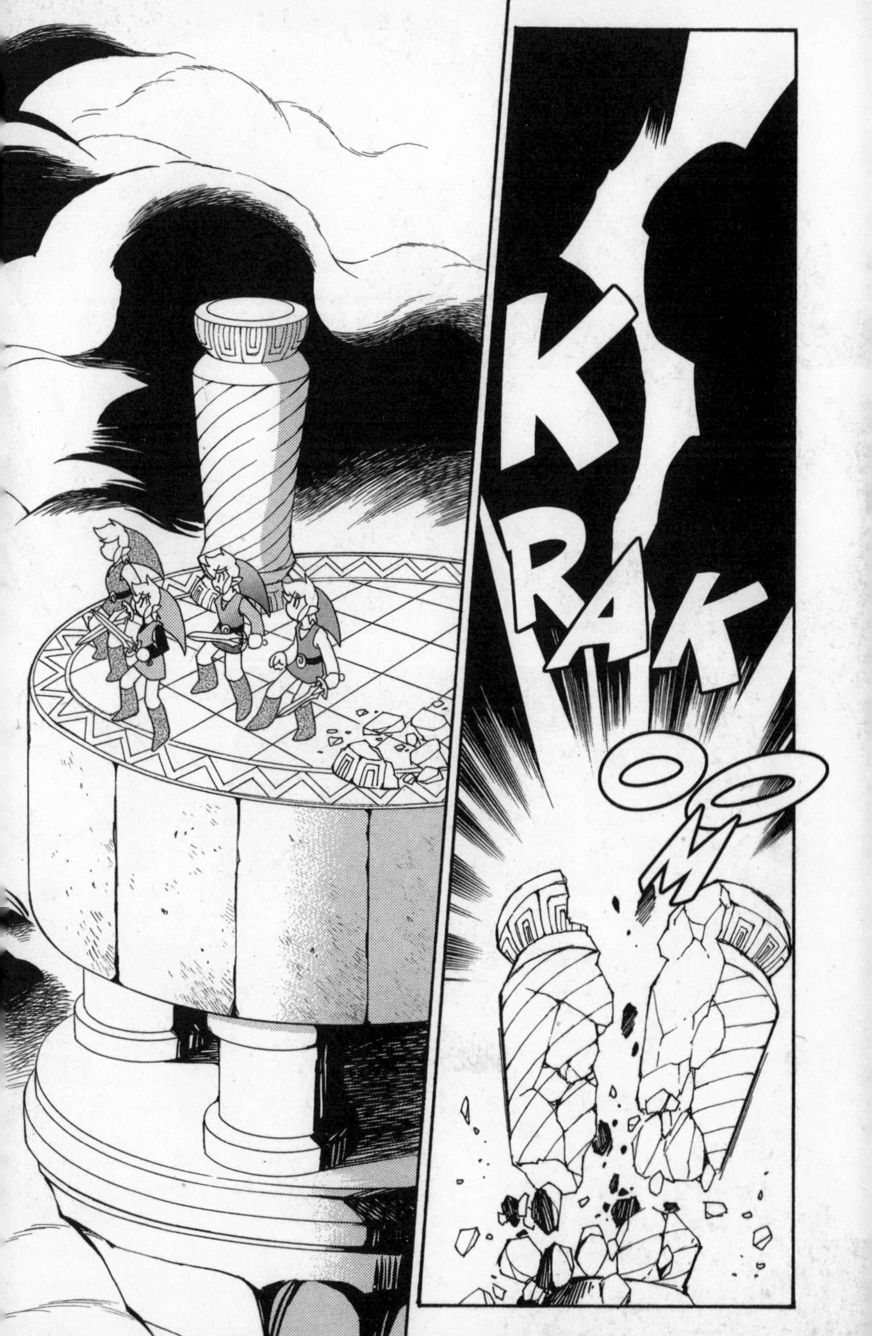
KRAK
OOM

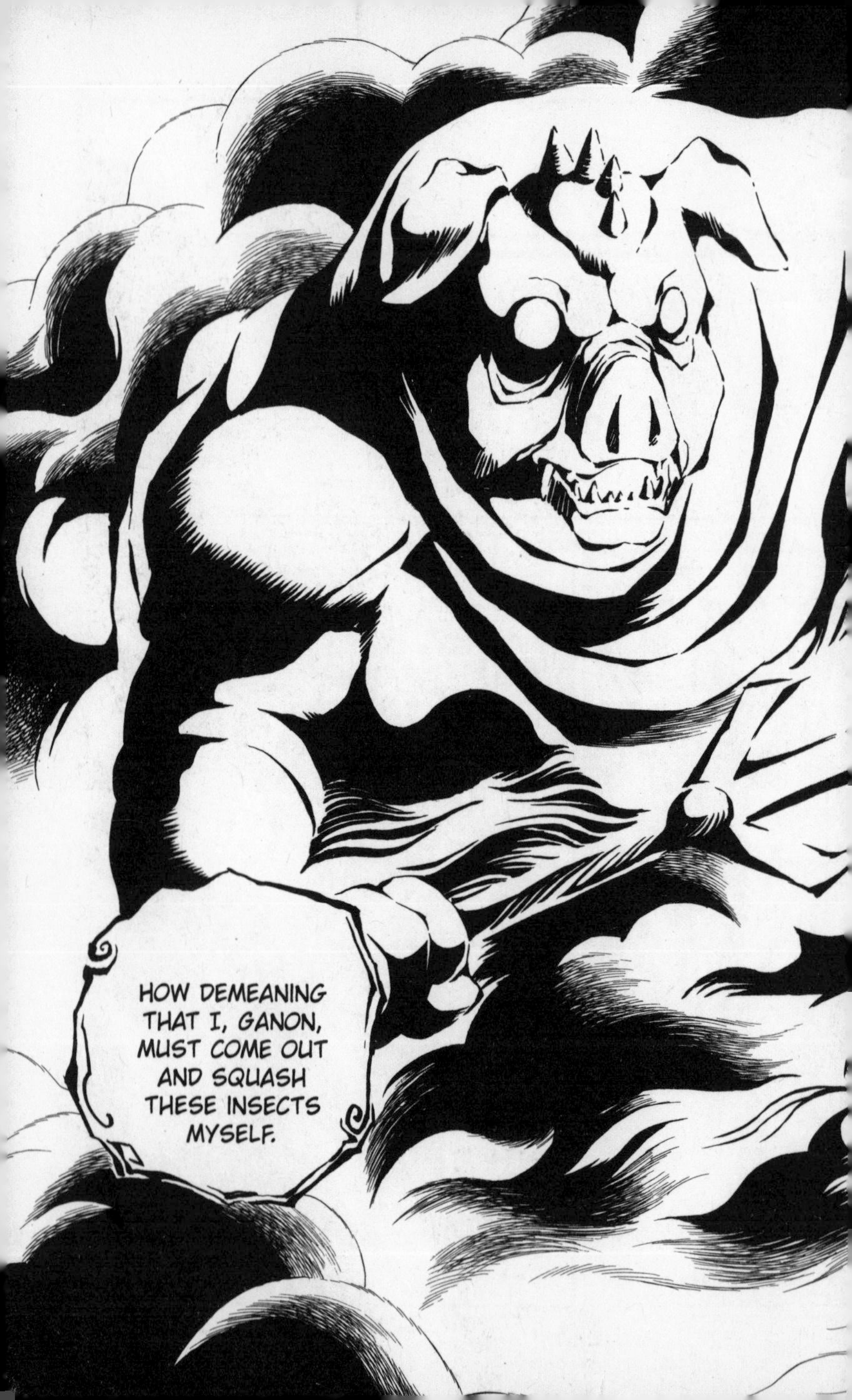
HOW DEMEANING THAT I, GANON, MUST COME OUT AND SQUASH THESE INSECTS MYSELF.

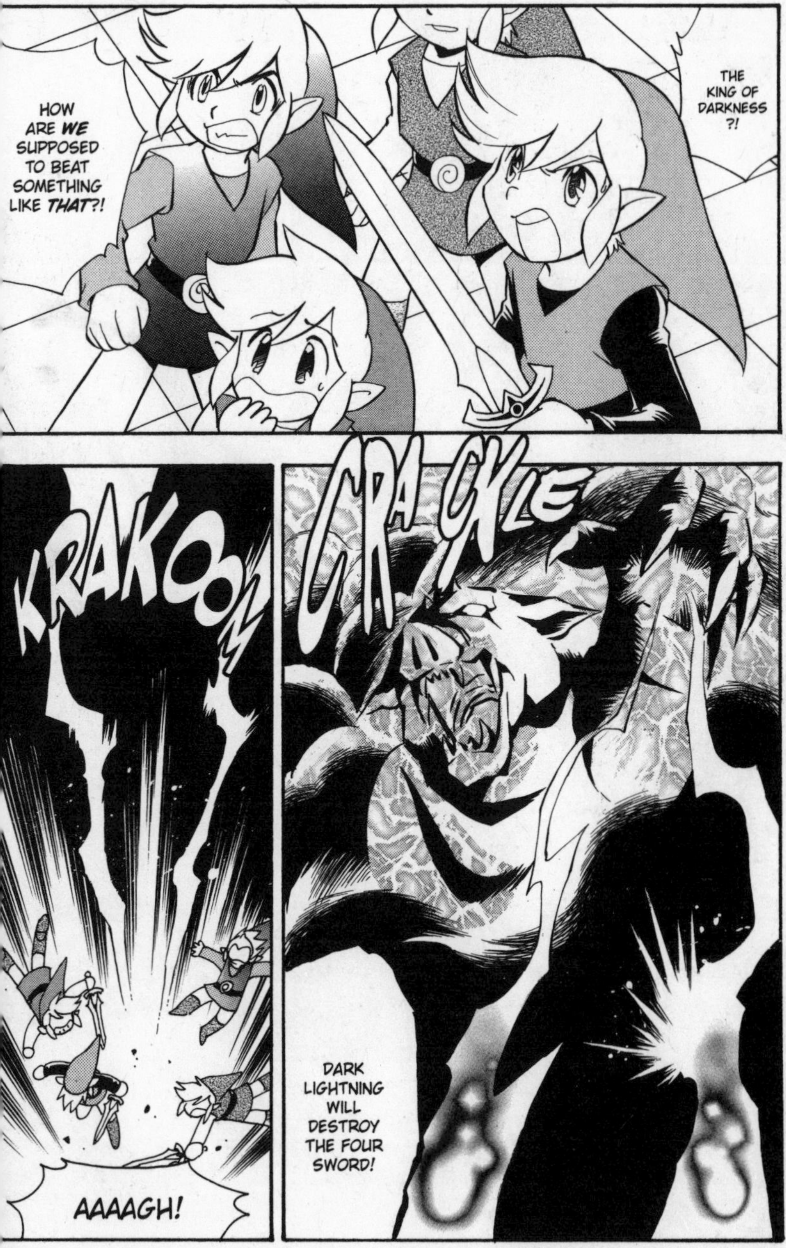
THE KING OF DARKNESS ?!
HOW ARE *WE* SUPPOSED TO BEAT SOMETHING LIKE *THAT*?!
CRACKLE
DARK LIGHTNING WILL DESTROY THE FOUR SWORD!
KRAKOOM
AAAAGH!

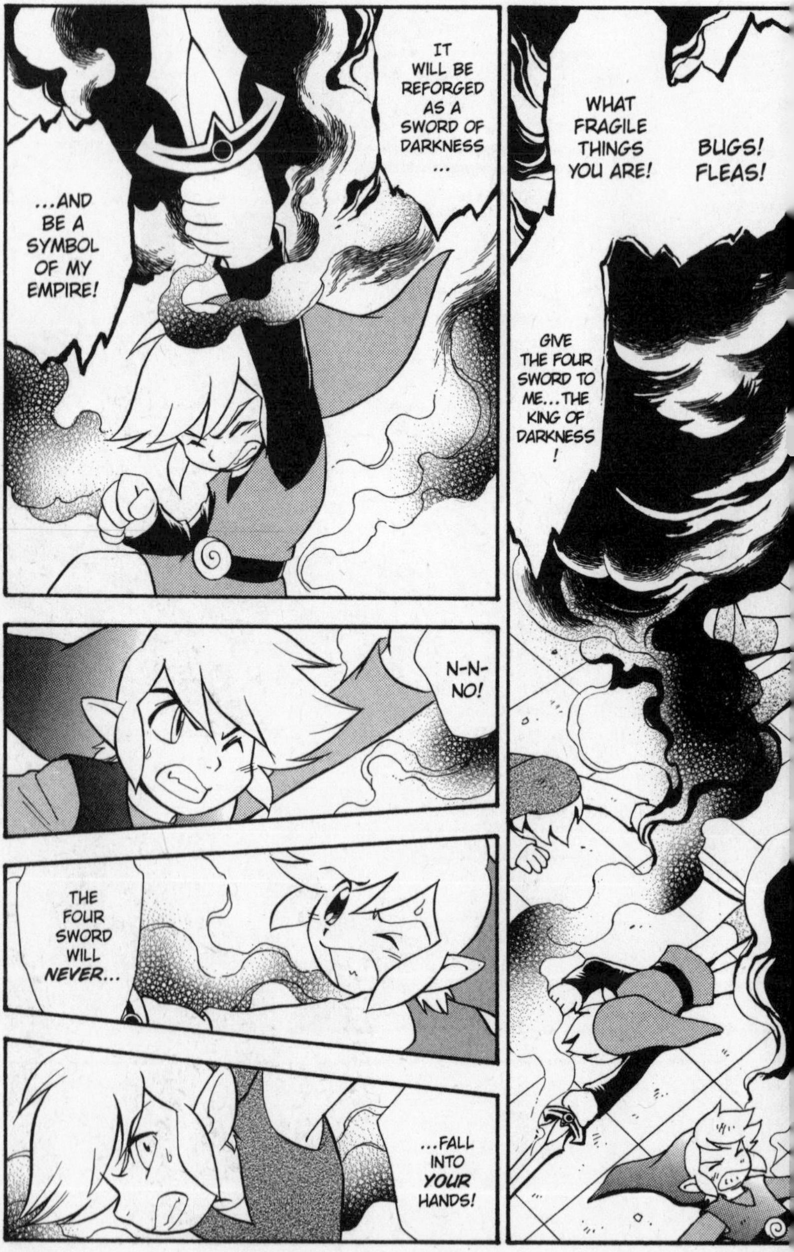
BUGS! FLEAS!
WHAT FRAGILE THINGS YOU ARE!
GIVE THE FOUR SWORD TO ME...THE KING OF DARKNESS!
IT WILL BE REFORGED AS A SWORD OF DARKNESS...
...AND BE A SYMBOL OF MY EMPIRE!
N-N-NO!
THE FOUR SWORD WILL ***NEVER***...
...FALL INTO ***YOUR*** HANDS!

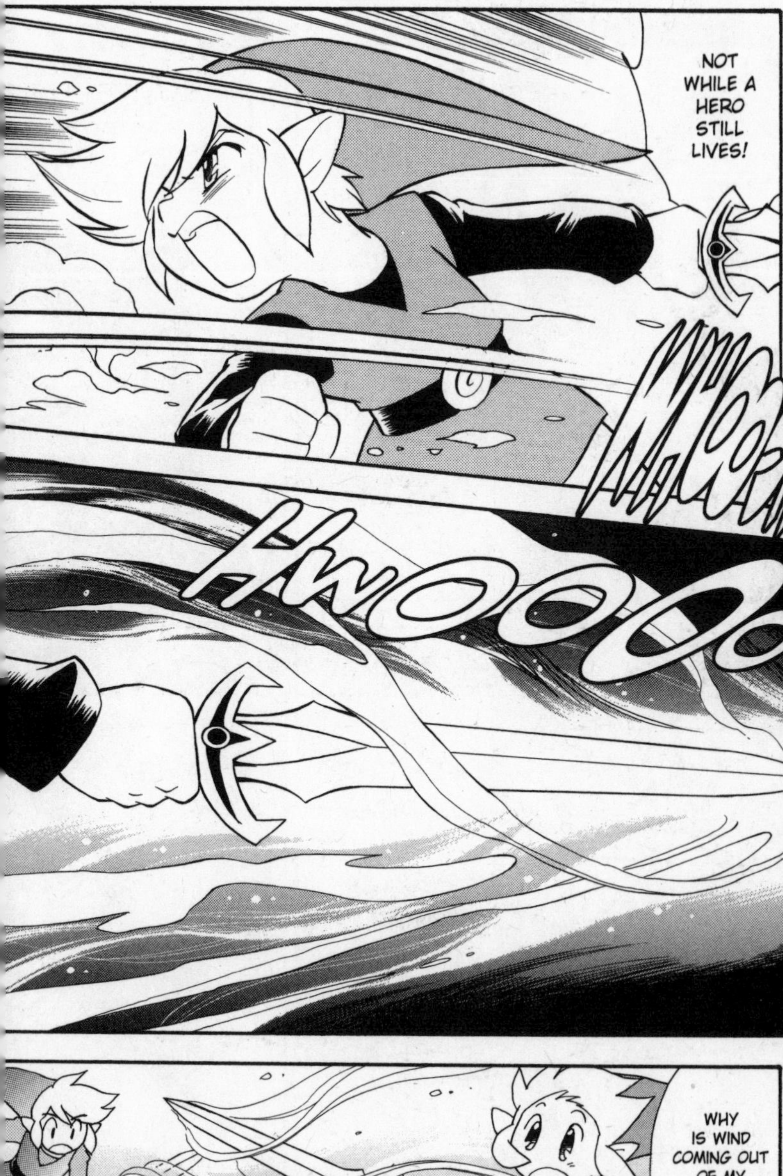
NOT WHILE A HERO STILL LIVES!
HWOOOO
WHY IS WIND COMING OUT OF MY SWORD?

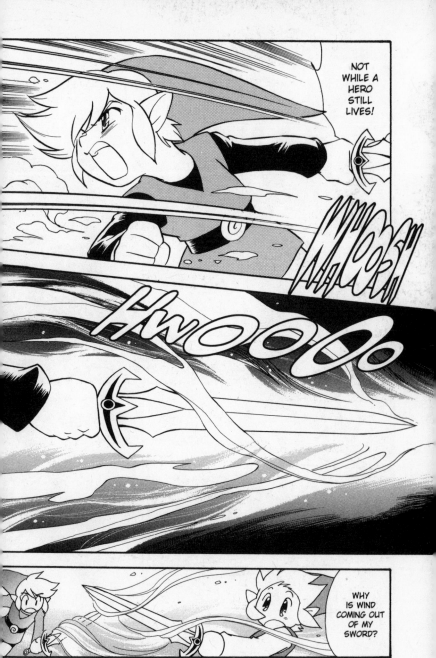

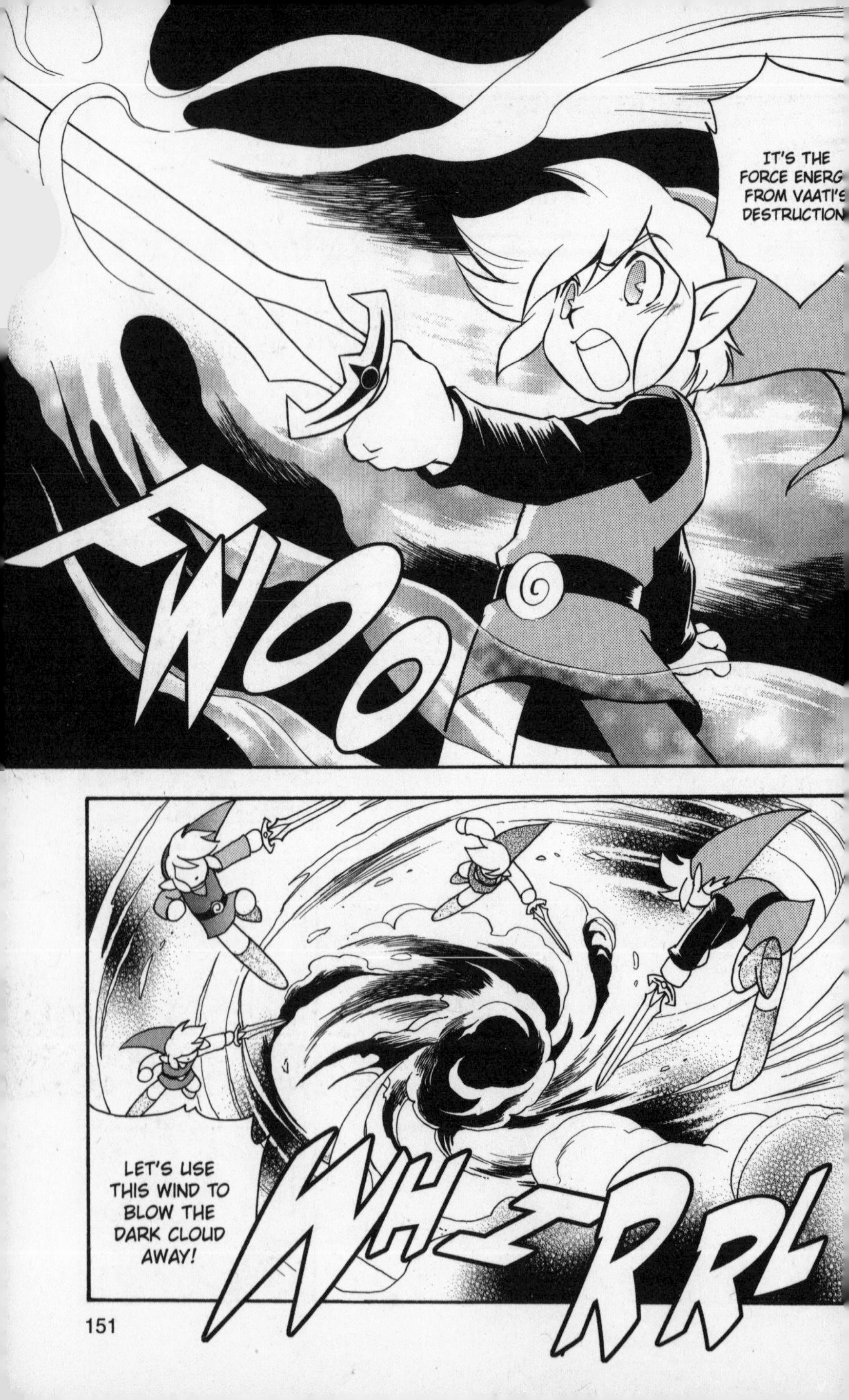
IT'S THE FORCE ENERG FROM VAATI'S DESTRUCTION
FWOO
LET'S USE THIS WIND TO BLOW THE DARK CLOUD AWAY!
WHIRRL

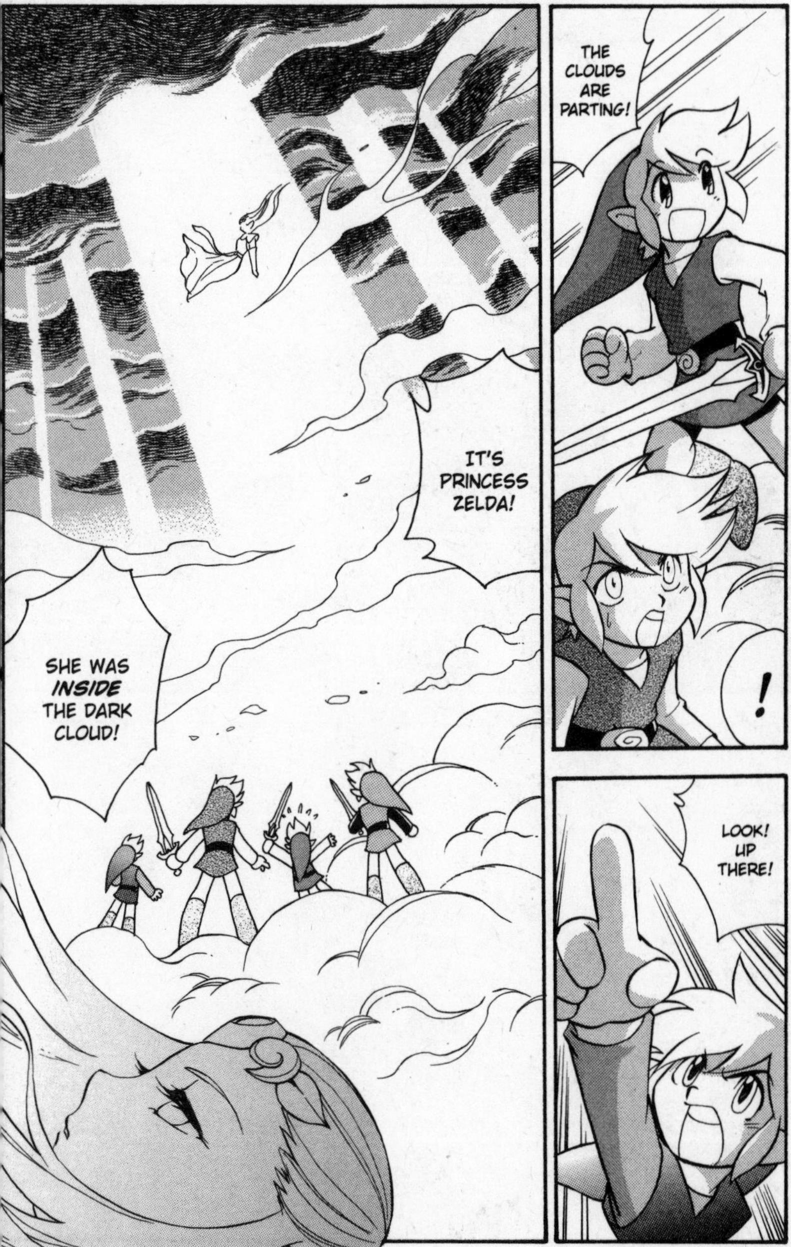
THE CLOUDS ARE PARTING!
!
LOOK! UP THERE!
IT'S PRINCESS ZELDA!
SHE WAS *INSIDE* THE DARK CLOUD!

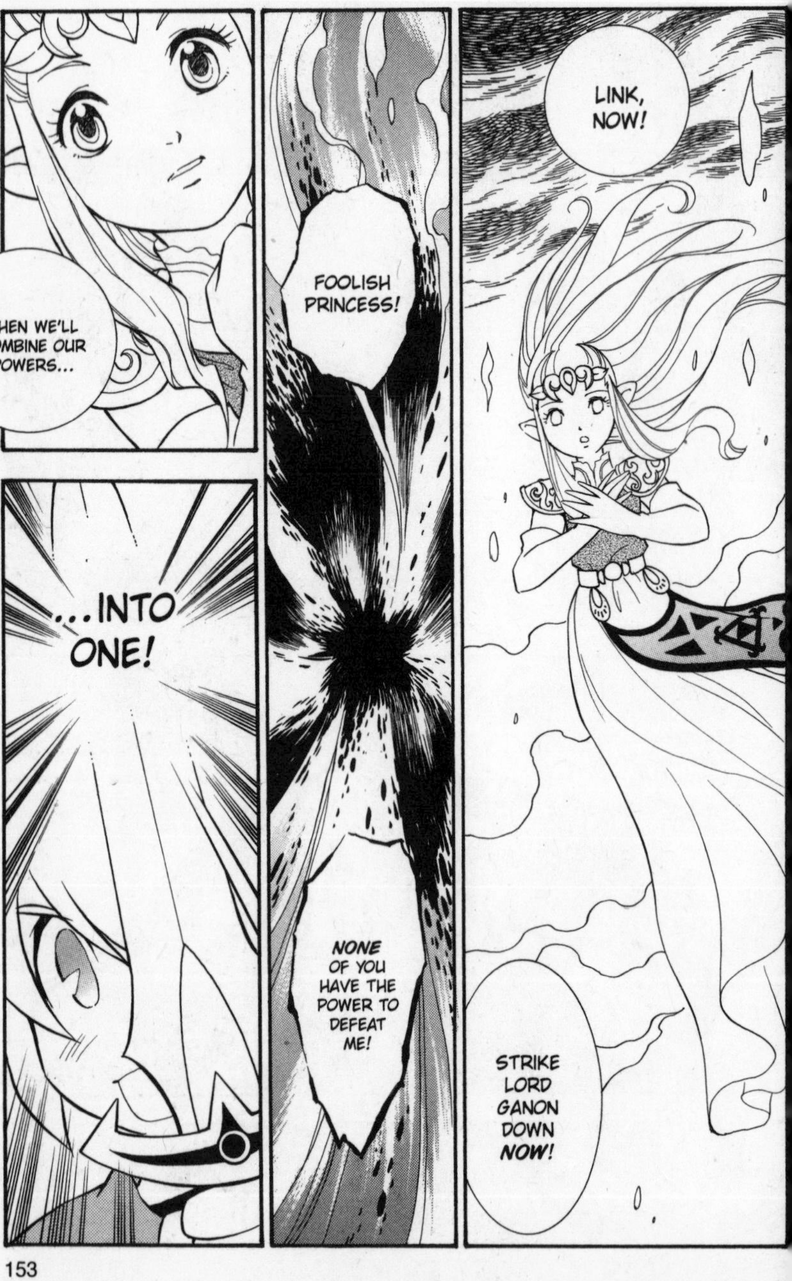
LINK, NOW!
STRIKE LORD GANON DOWN NOW!
FOOLISH PRINCESS!
NONE OF YOU HAVE THE POWER TO DEFEAT ME!
THEN WE'LL COMBINE OUR POWERS...
...INTO ONE!

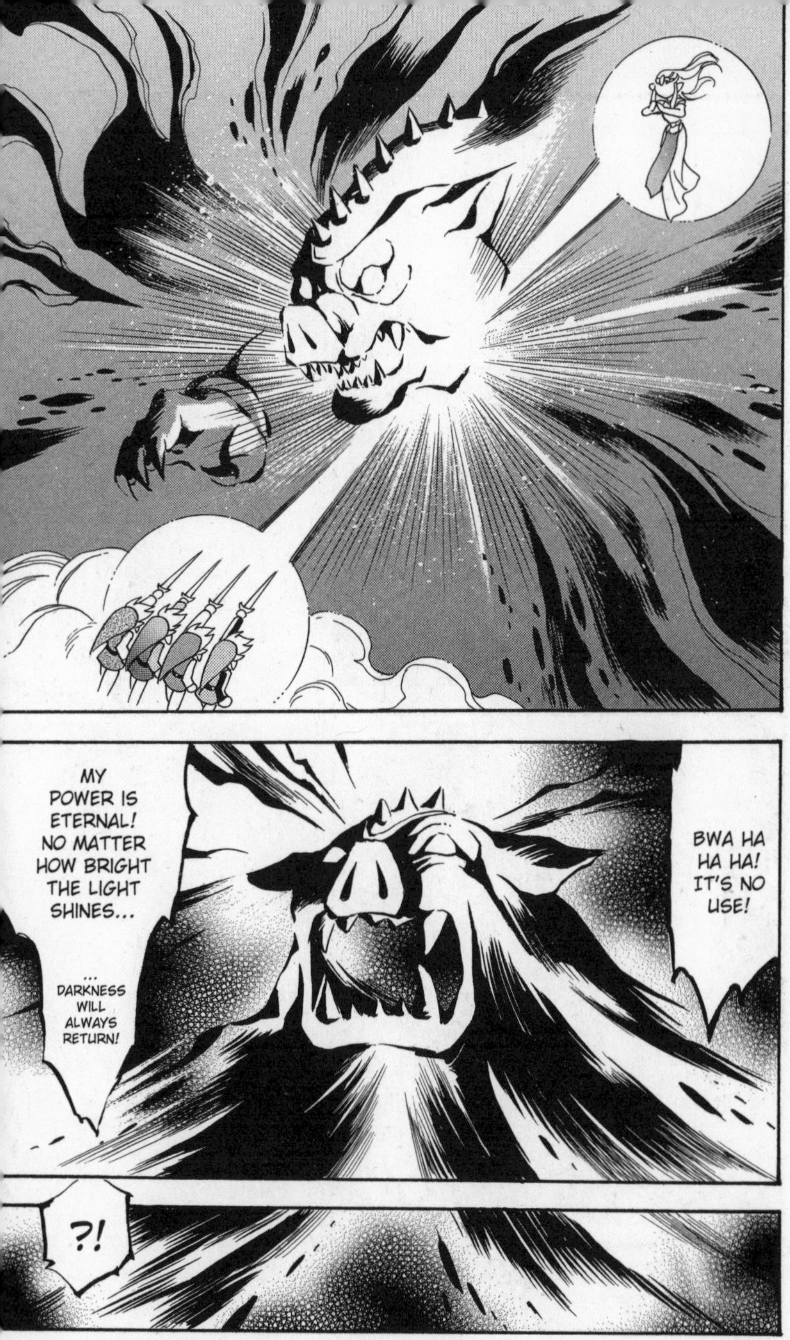
BWA HA HA HA! IT'S NO USE!
MY POWER IS ETERNAL! NO MATTER HOW BRIGHT THE LIGHT SHINES...
...DARKNESS WILL ALWAYS RETURN!
?!

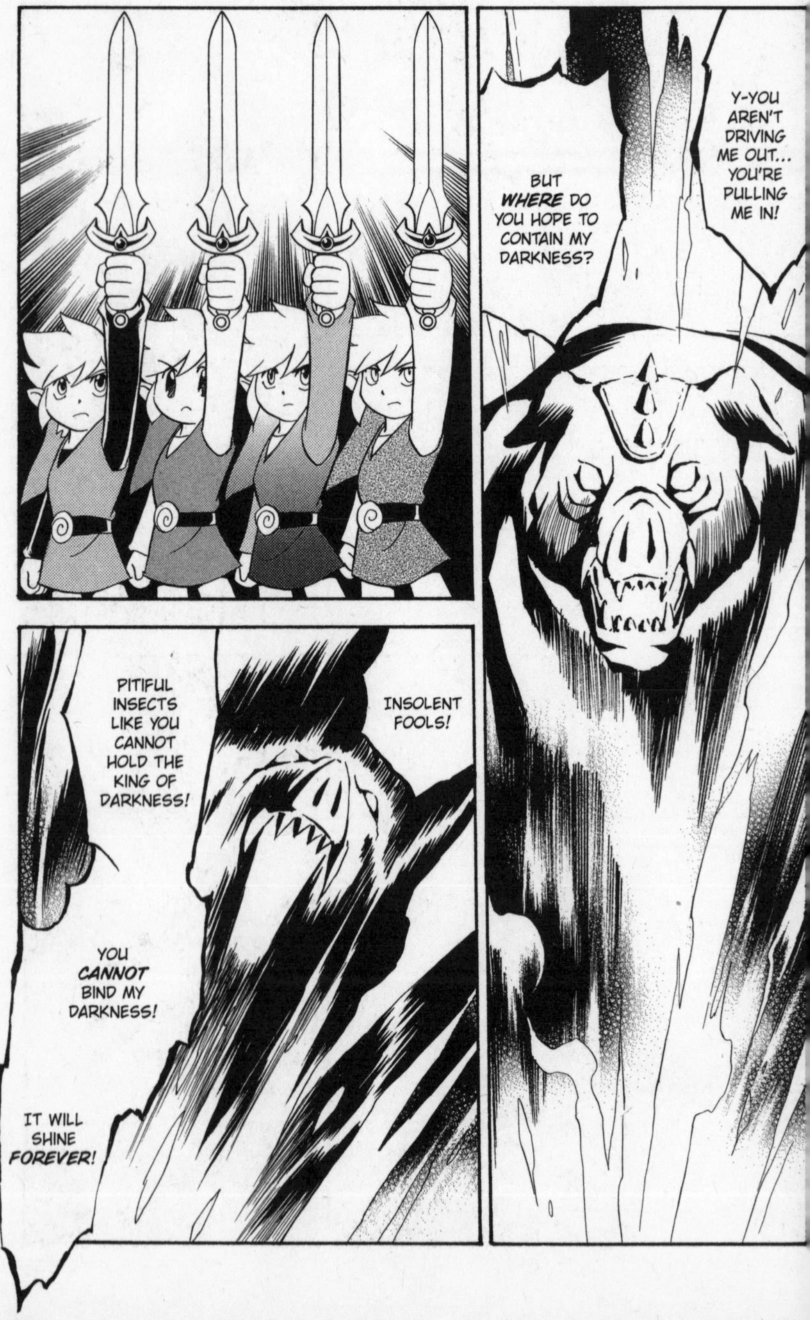
Y-YOU AREN'T DRIVING ME OUT... YOU'RE PULLING ME IN!
BUT *WHERE* DO YOU HOPE TO CONTAIN MY DARKNESS?
INSOLENT FOOLS!
PITIFUL INSECTS LIKE YOU CANNOT HOLD THE KING OF DARKNESS!
YOU *CANNOT* BIND MY DARKNESS!
IT WILL SHINE *FOREVER*!

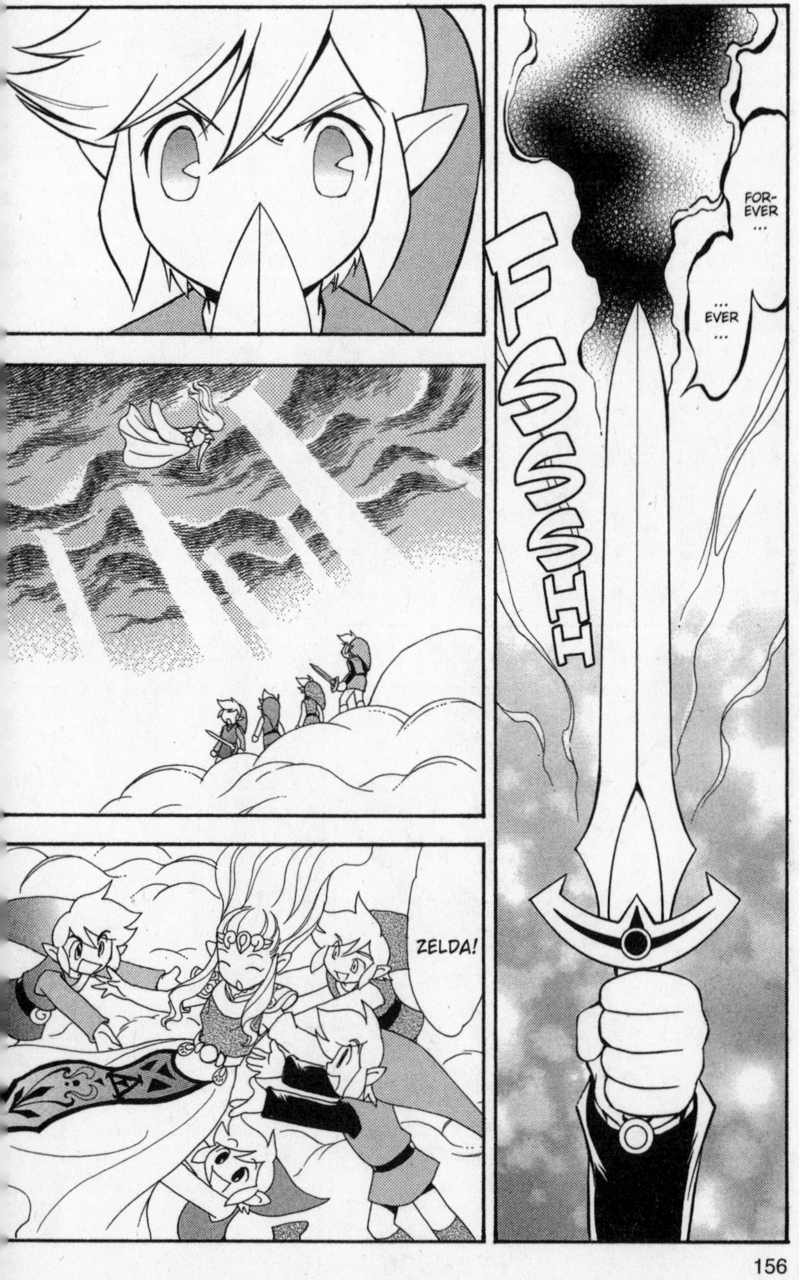
FOR-EVER ...
... EVER ...
FSSSHH
ZELDA!

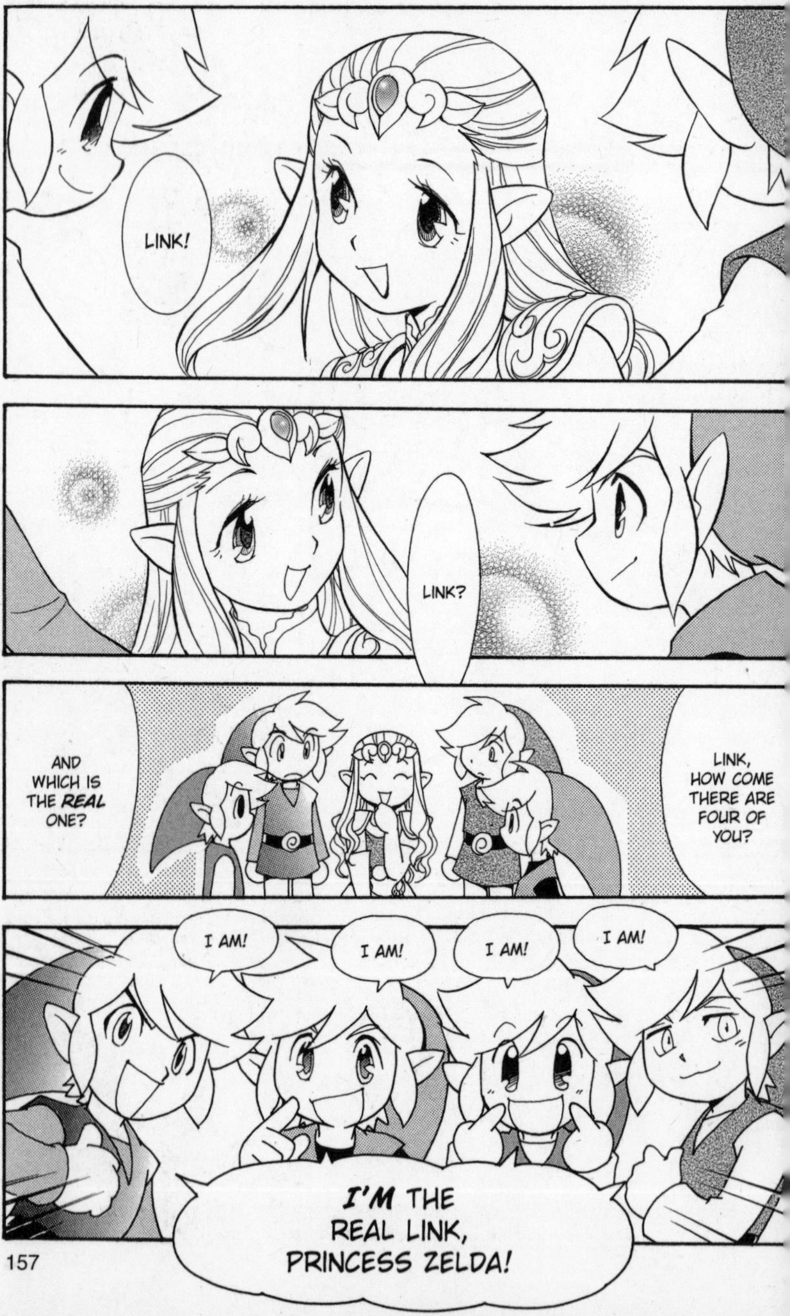
LINK!
LINK?
LINK, HOW COME THERE ARE FOUR OF YOU?
AND WHICH IS THE *REAL* ONE?
I AM!
I AM!
I AM!
I AM!
I'M THE REAL LINK, PRINCESS ZELDA!

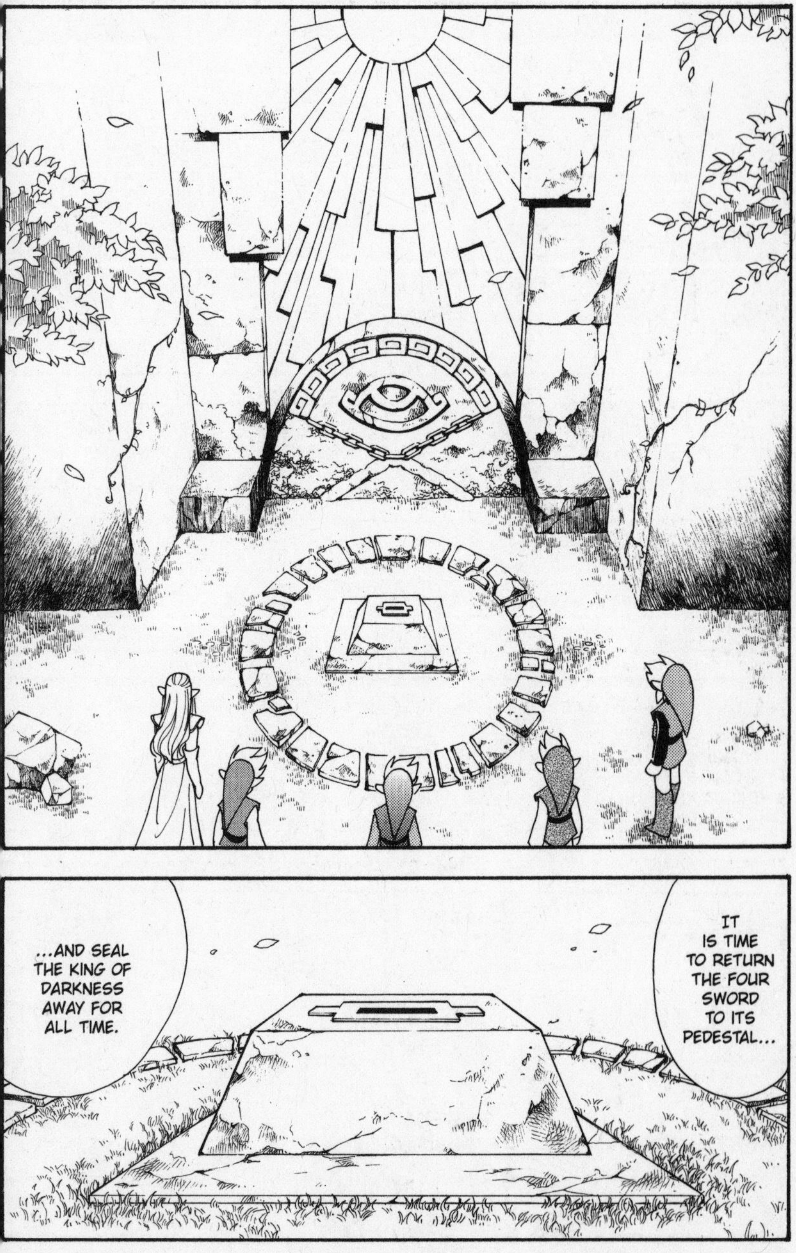
IT IS TIME TO RETURN THE FOUR SWORD TO ITS PEDESTAL...
...AND SEAL THE KING OF DARKNESS AWAY FOR ALL TIME.

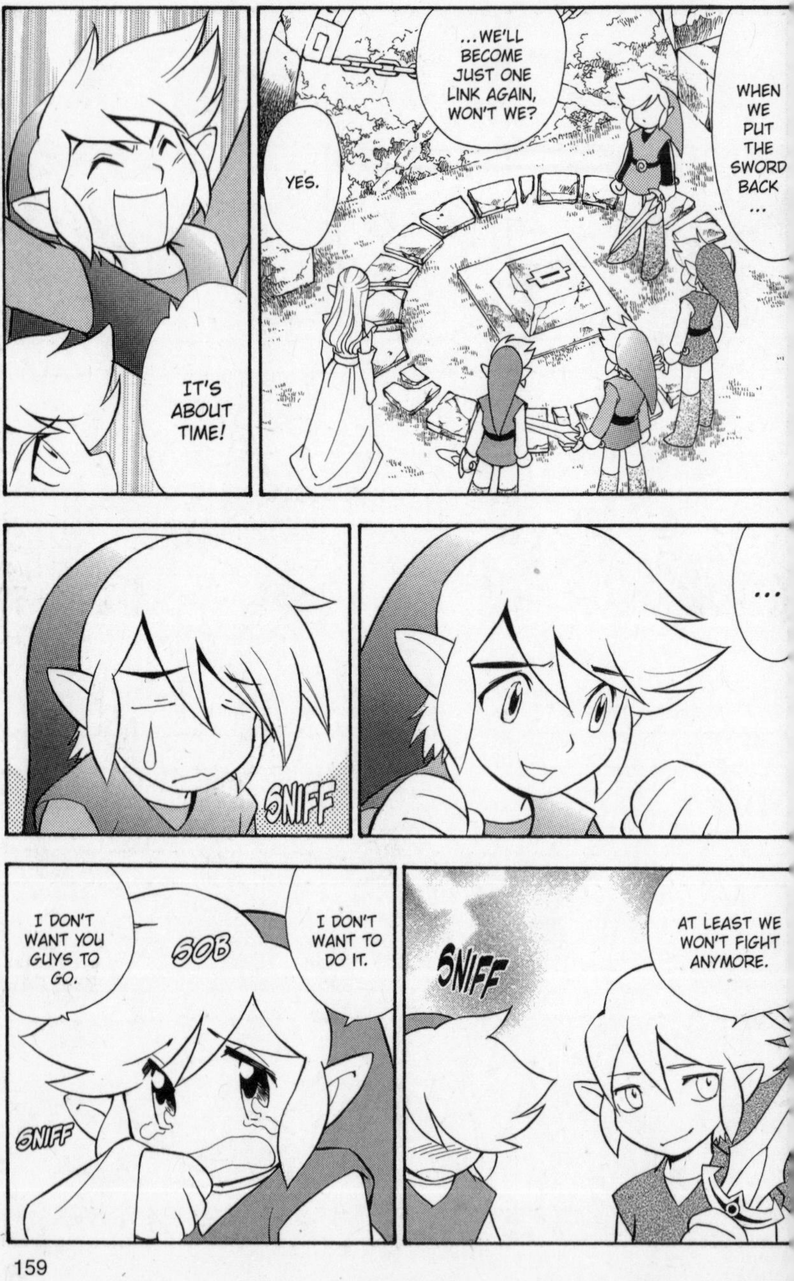
WHEN WE PUT THE SWORD BACK...
...WE'LL BECOME JUST ONE LINK AGAIN, WON'T WE?
YES.
IT'S ABOUT TIME!
...
SNIFF
AT LEAST WE WON'T FIGHT ANYMORE.
SNIFF
I DON'T WANT TO DO IT.
SOB
I DON'T WANT YOU GUYS TO GO.
SNIFF

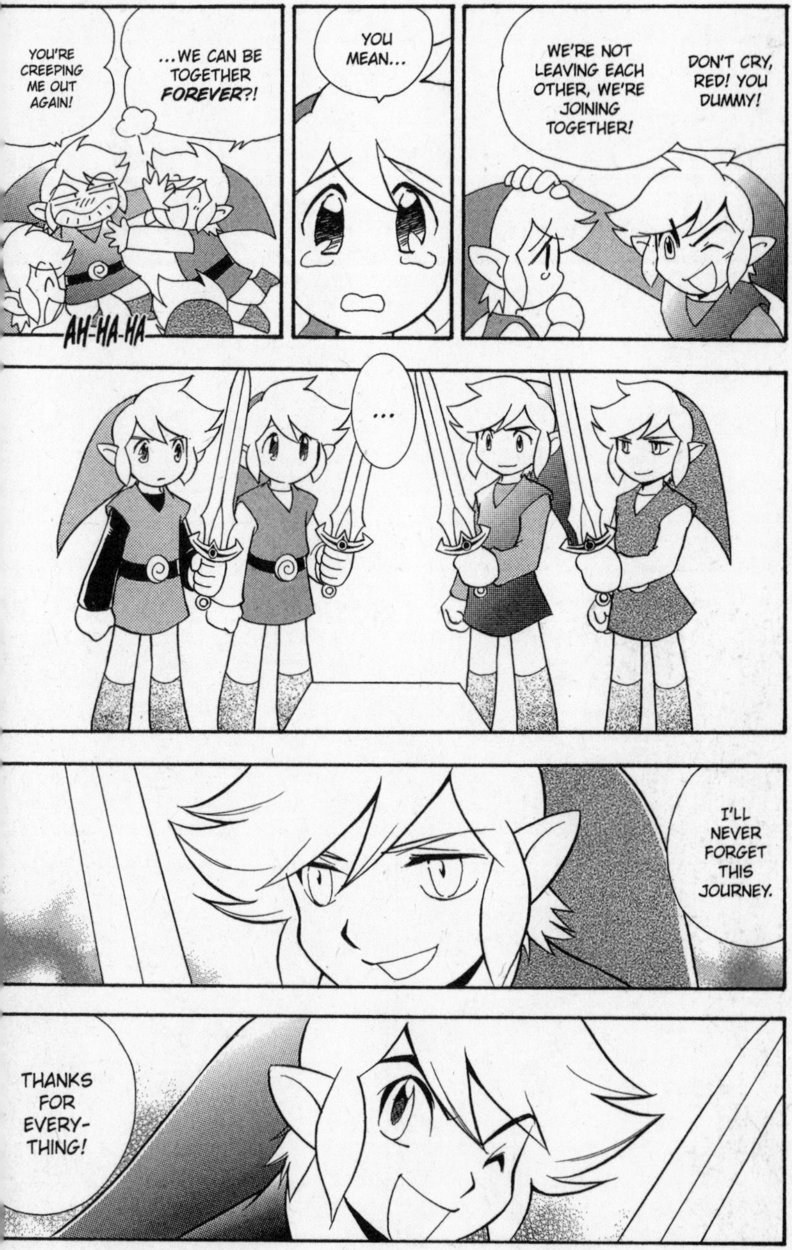
DON'T CRY, RED! YOU DUMMY!
WE'RE NOT LEAVING EACH OTHER, WE'RE JOINING TOGETHER!
YOU MEAN...
...WE CAN BE TOGETHER *FOREVER*?!
YOU'RE CREEPING ME OUT AGAIN!
AH-HA-HA
...
I'LL NEVER FORGET THIS JOURNEY.
THANKS FOR EVERY-THING!

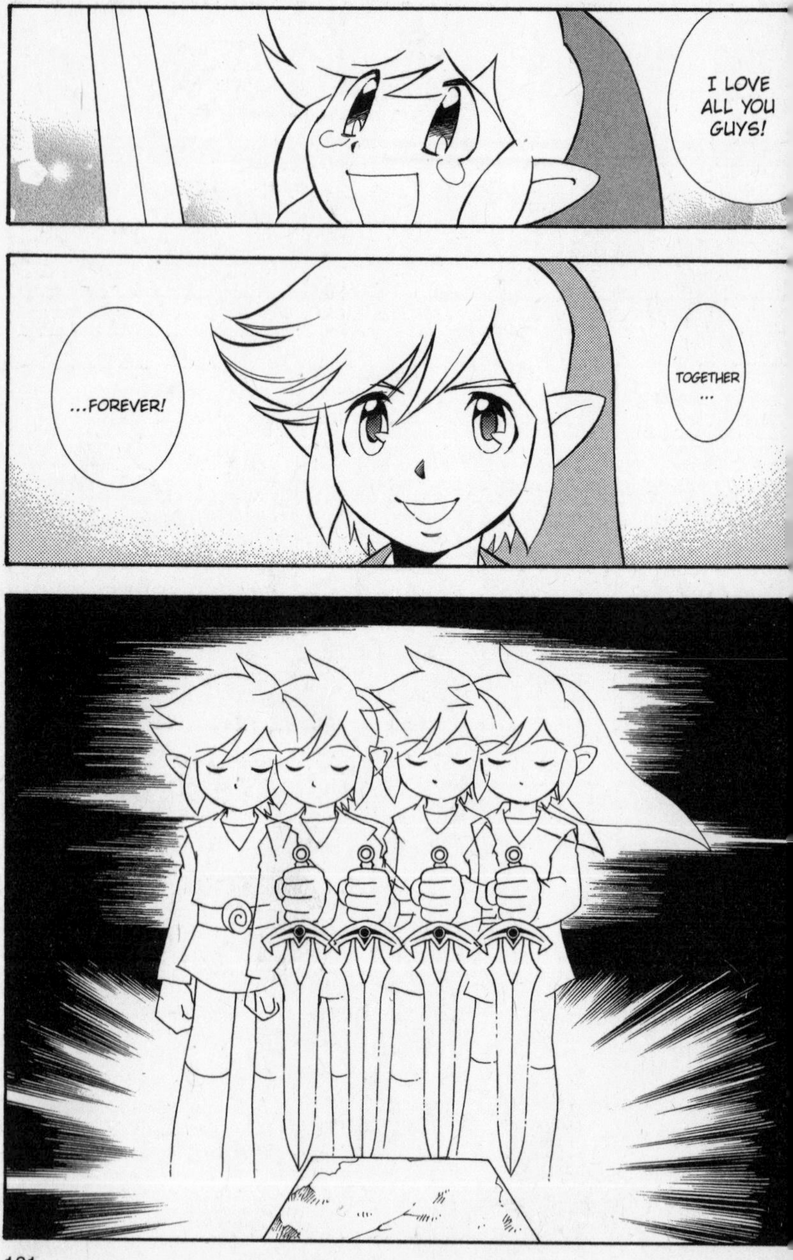
I LOVE ALL YOU GUYS!
TOGETHER...
...FOREVER!

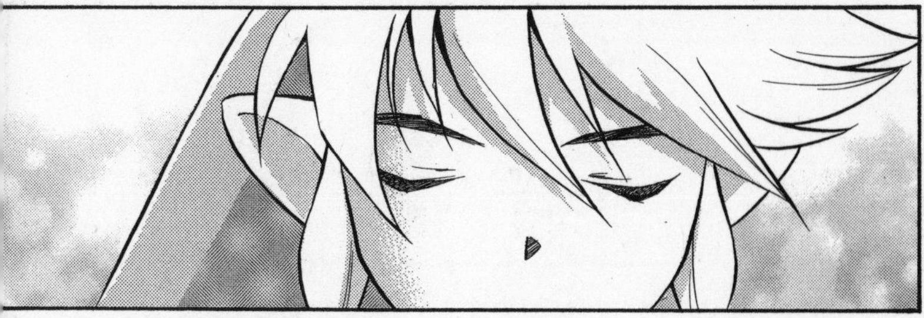
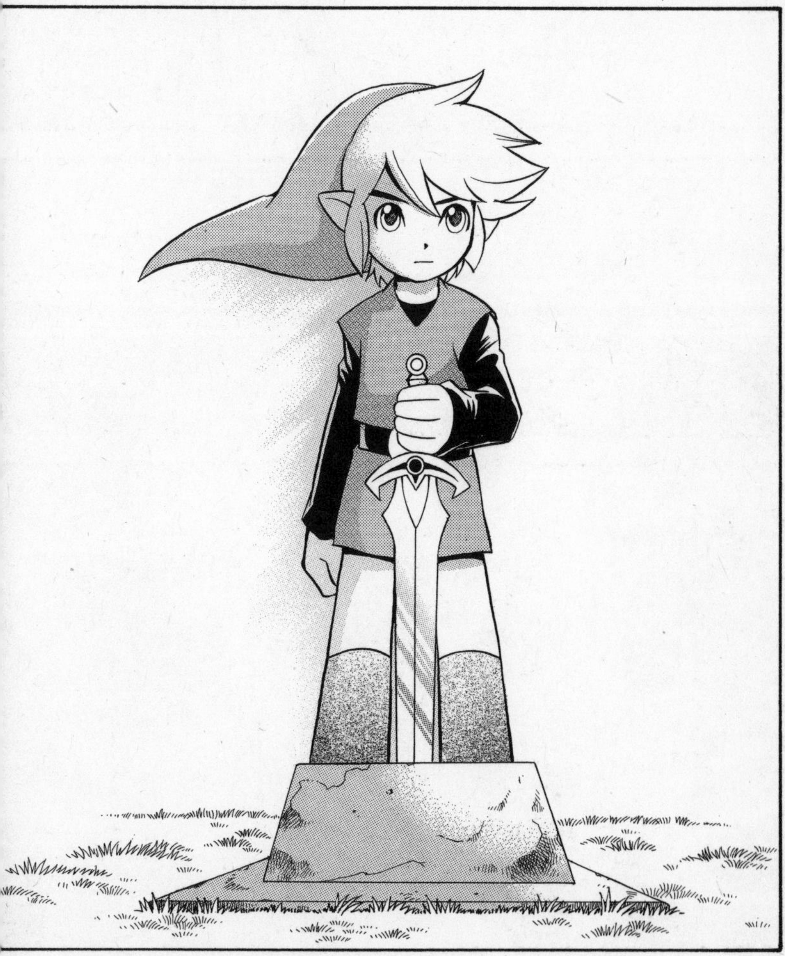

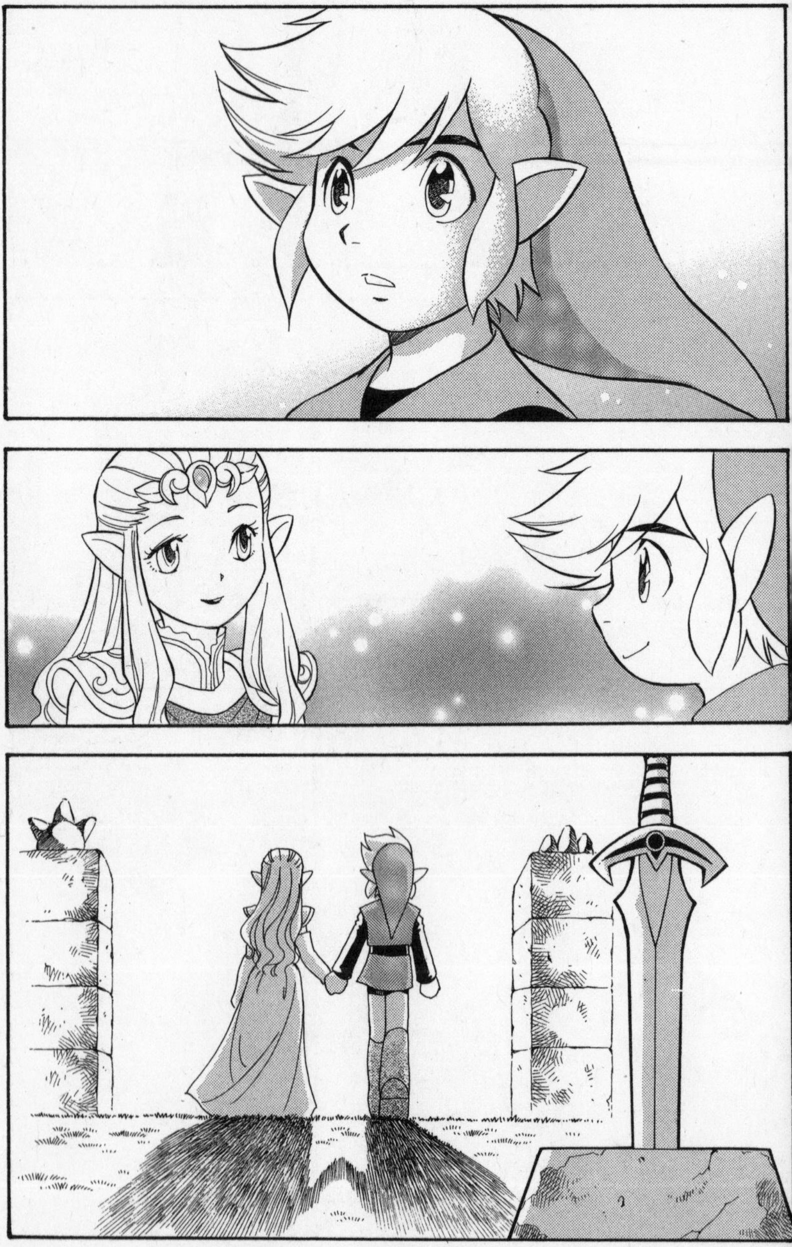

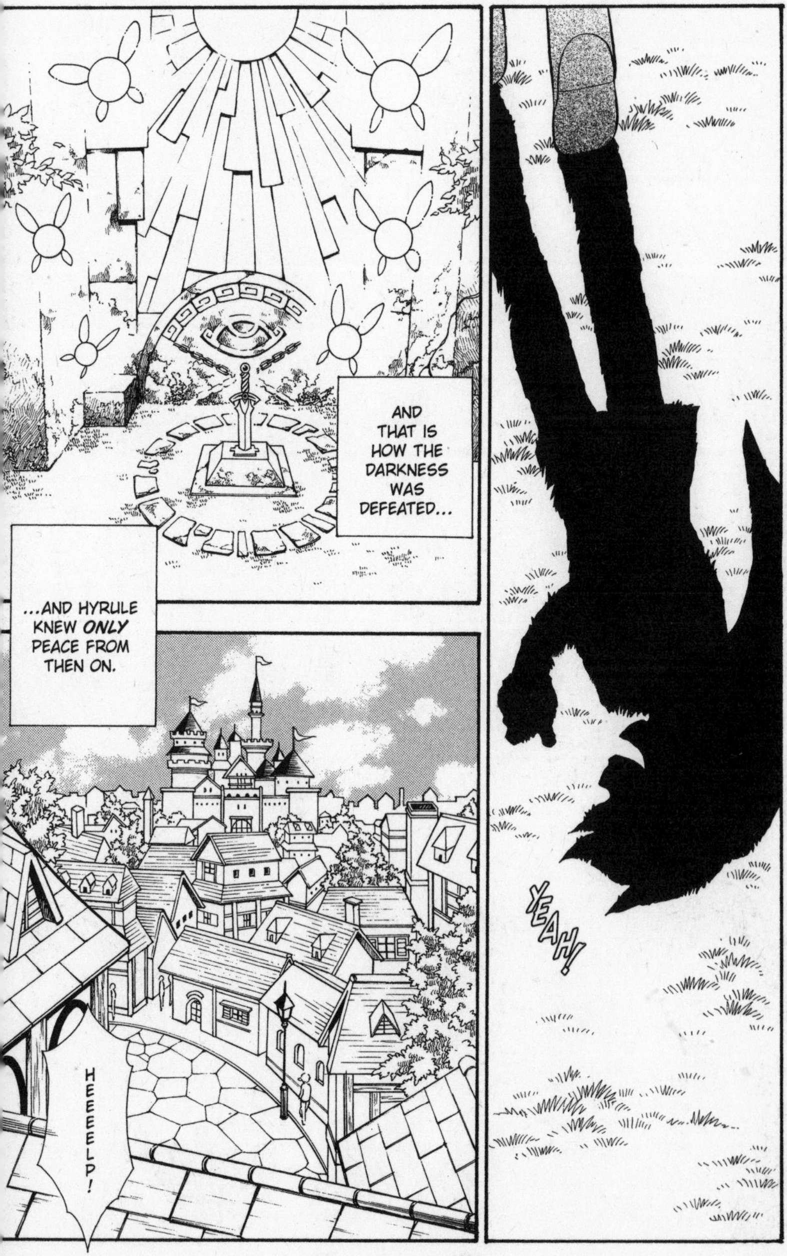
YEAH!
AND THAT IS HOW THE DARKNESS WAS DEFEATED...
...AND HYRULE KNEW *ONLY* PEACE FROM THEN ON.
HEEEELP!

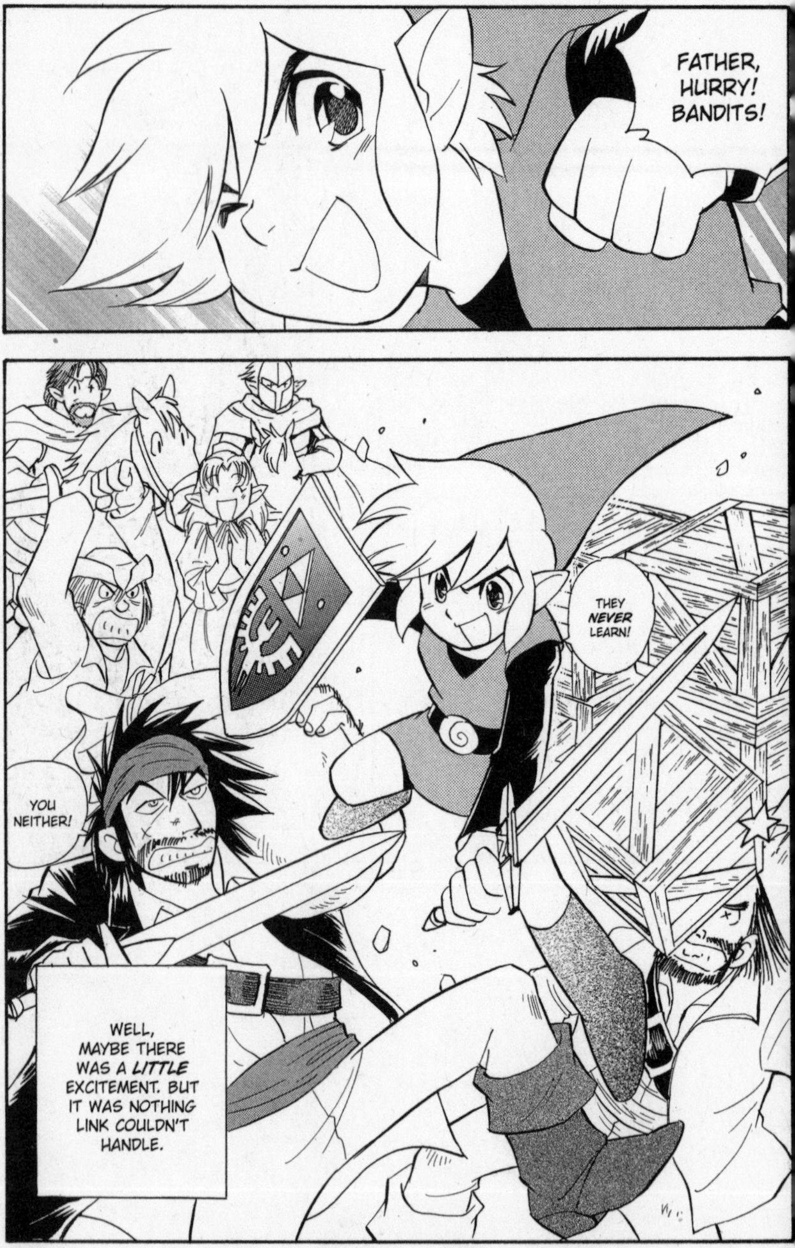
FATHER, HURRY! BANDITS!
THEY *NEVER* LEARN!
YOU NEITHER!
WELL, MAYBE THERE WAS A *LITTLE* EXCITEMENT. BUT IT WAS NOTHING LINK COULDN'T HANDLE.

■ THE END ■

BONUS MANGA

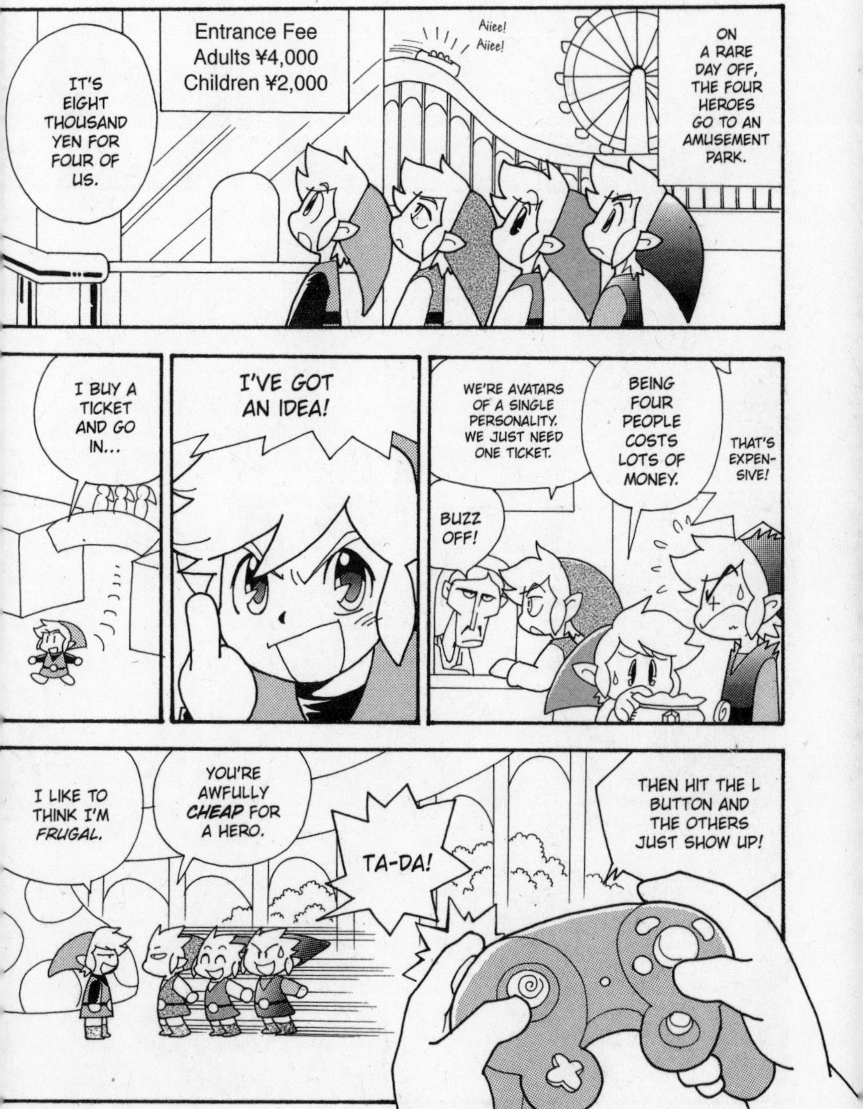
ON A RARE DAY OFF, THE FOUR HEROES GO TO AN AMUSEMENT PARK.
Aiiee! Aiiee!
Entrance Fee
Adults ¥4,000
Children ¥2,000
IT'S EIGHT THOUSAND YEN FOR FOUR OF US.
THAT'S EXPEN-SIVE!
BEING FOUR PEOPLE COSTS LOTS OF MONEY.
WE'RE AVATARS OF A SINGLE PERSONALITY. WE JUST NEED ONE TICKET.
BUZZ OFF!
I'VE GOT AN IDEA!
I BUY A TICKET AND GO IN...
THEN HIT THE L BUTTON AND THE OTHERS JUST SHOW UP!
TA-DA!
YOU'RE AWFULLY *CHEAP* FOR A HERO.
I LIKE TO THINK I'M *FRUGAL.*

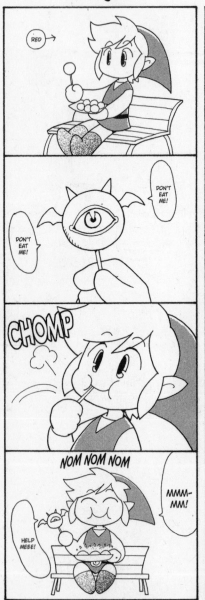

It's a Small Compulsion

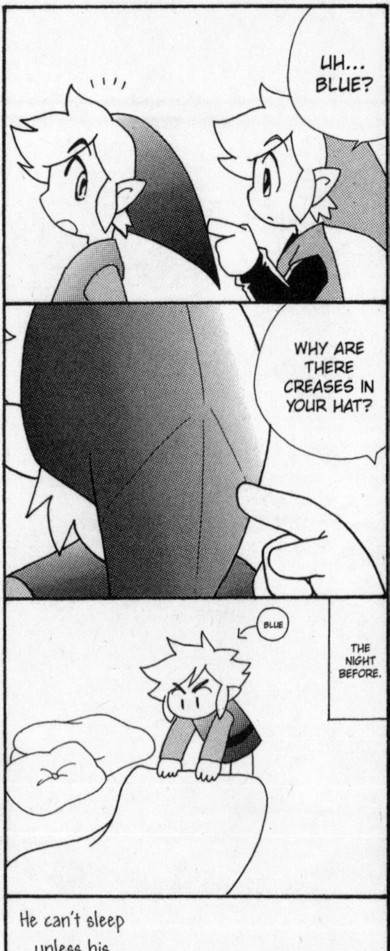
UH... BLUE?
WHY ARE THERE CREASES IN YOUR HAT?
THE NIGHT BEFORE.
BLUE
He can't sleep unless his clothes are neatly folded.
TIDY

Takoyaki*

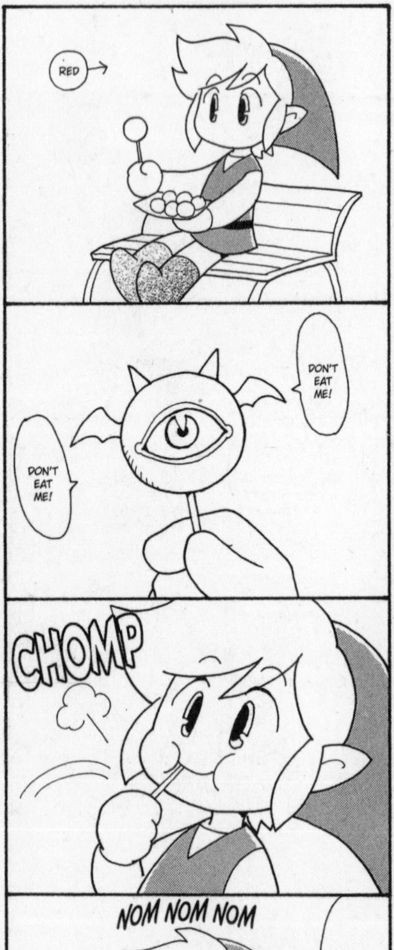
RED
DON'T EAT ME!
DON'T EAT ME!
CHOMP
MMM-MM!
NOM NOM NOM
HELP MEEE!

*TAKOYAKI ARE PIECES OF OCTOPUS, BATTERED AND FRIED.

It's Not Easy Being Purple

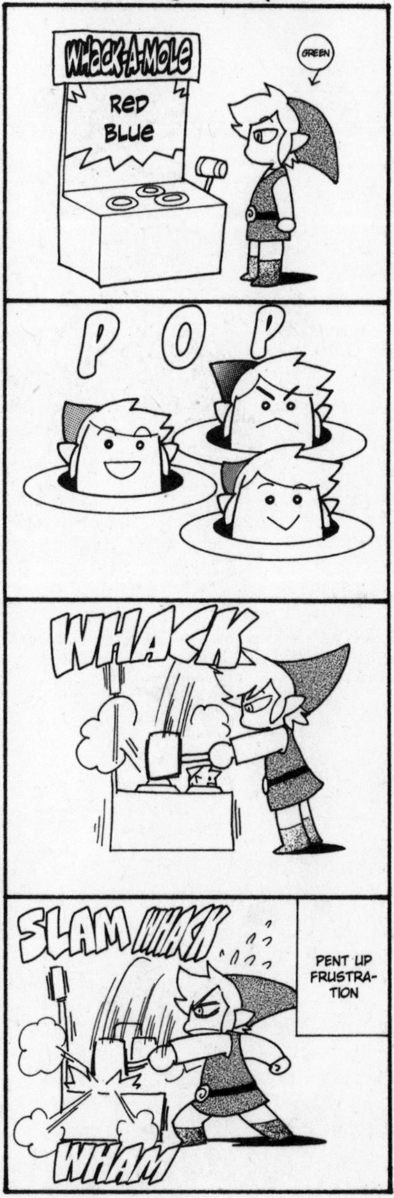
WHACK-A-MOLE
RED
BLUE
GREEN
POP
WHACK
SLAM
WHACK
PENT UP FRUSTRA-TION
WHAM

About That Time

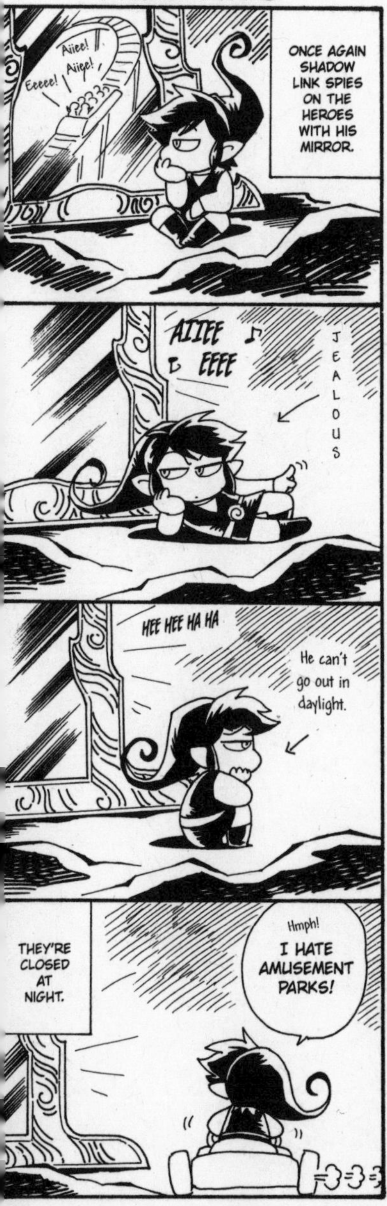
ONCE AGAIN SHADOW LINK SPIES ON THE HEROES WITH HIS MIRROR.
Aiiee!
Aiiee!
Eeeee!
JEALOUS
AIIEE EEEE
He can't go out in daylight.
HEE HEE HA HA
THEY'RE CLOSED AT NIGHT.
Hmph! I HATE AMUSEMENT PARKS!

Shadow Link's Blog

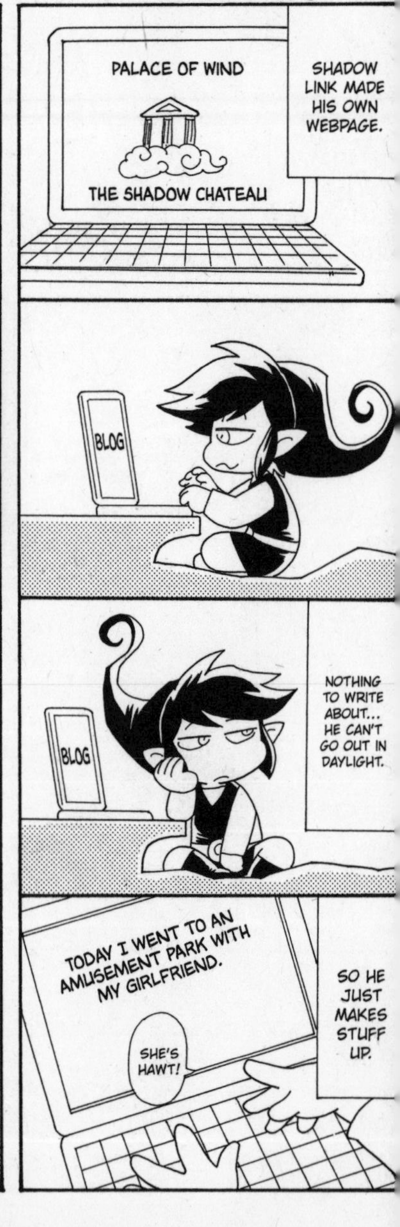
SHADOW LINK MADE HIS OWN WEBPAGE.
PALACE OF WIND
THE SHADOW CHATEAU
BLOG
NOTHING TO WRITE ABOUT... HE CAN'T GO OUT IN DAYLIGHT.
BLOG
SO HE JUST MAKES STUFF UP.
TODAY I WENT TO AN AMUSEMENT PARK WITH MY GIRLFRIEND.
SHE'S HAWT!

Shopping Online

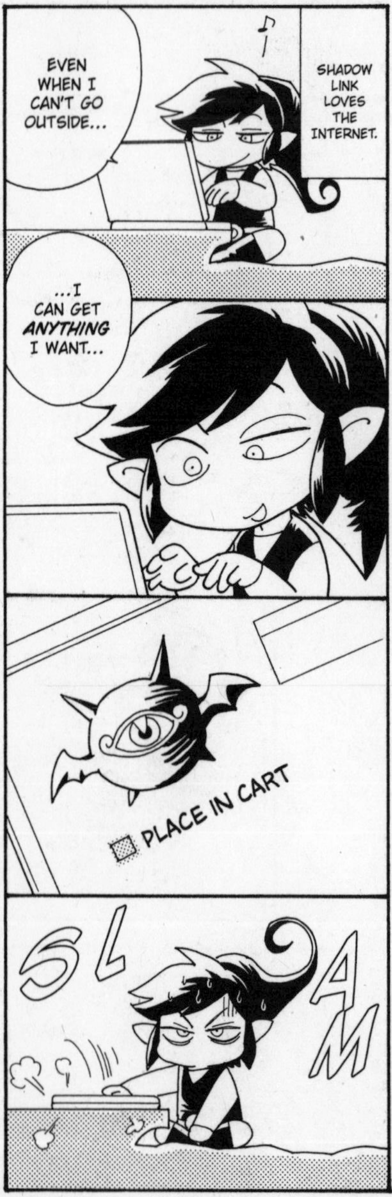
SHADOW LINK LOVES THE INTERNET.
EVEN WHEN I CAN'T GO OUTSIDE...
...I CAN GET *ANYTHING* I WANT...
PLACE IN CART
SLAM

Actually, He Was There

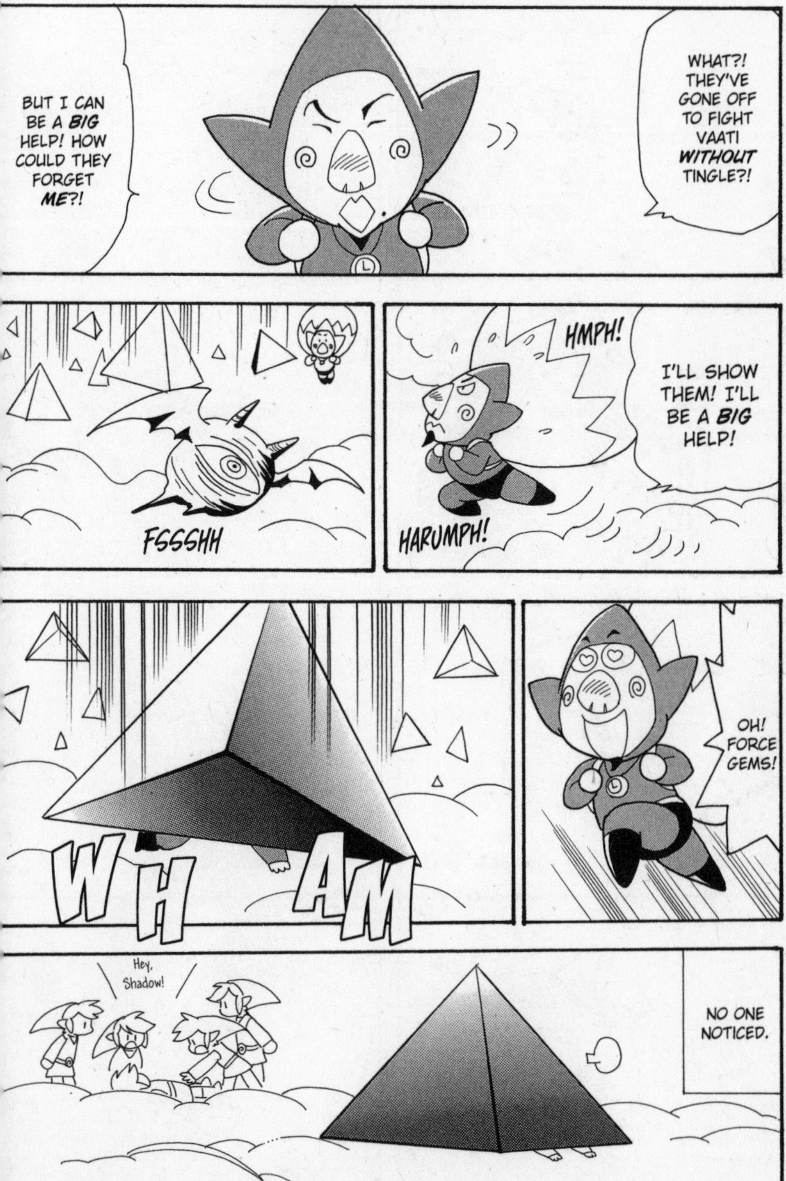
WHAT?! THEY'VE GONE OFF TO FIGHT VAATI *WITHOUT* TINGLE?!
BUT I CAN BE A *BIG* HELP! HOW COULD THEY FORGET *ME*?!
HMPH!
I'LL SHOW THEM! I'LL BE A *BIG* HELP!
HARUMPH!
FSSSHH
OH! FORCE GEMS!
WHAM
NO ONE NOTICED.
Hey, Shadow!

Sukiyaki Day

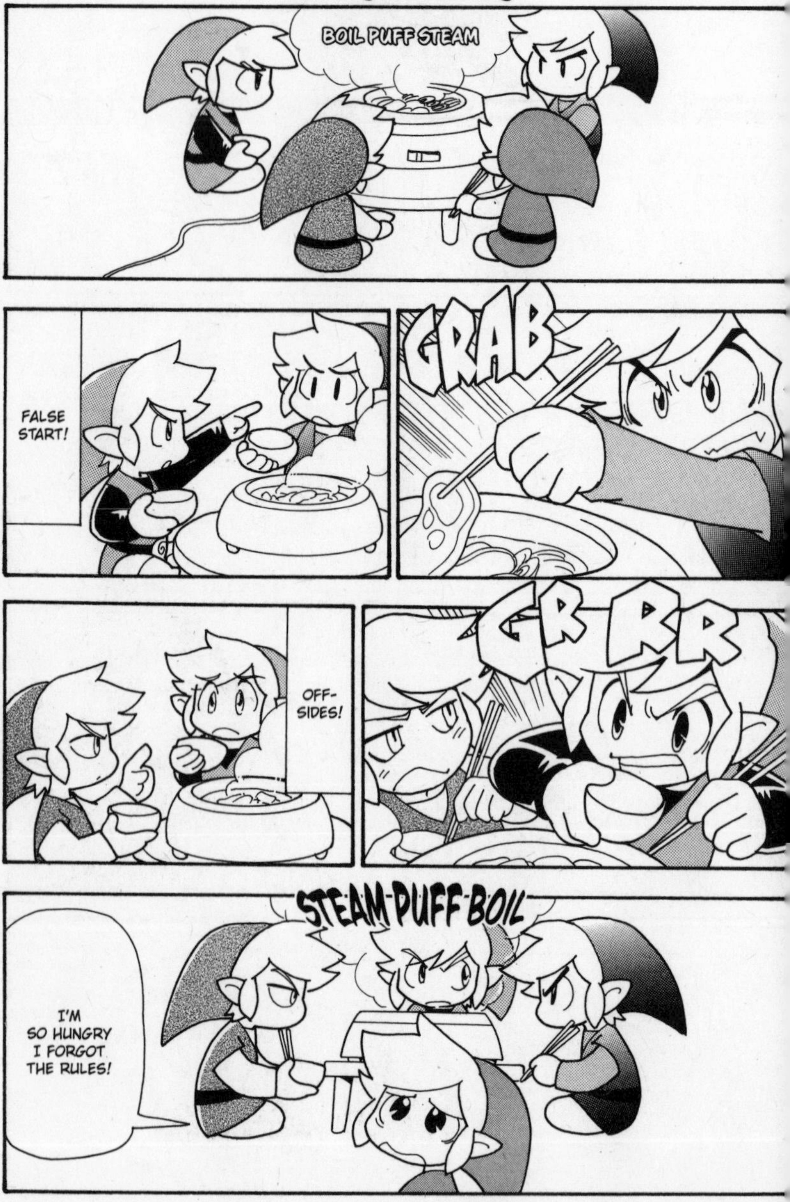
BOIL PUFF STEAM
GRAB
FALSE START!
GR RR
OFF-SIDES!
STEAM PUFF BOIL
I'M SO HUNGRY I FORGOT THE RULES!

Fear Like Never Before

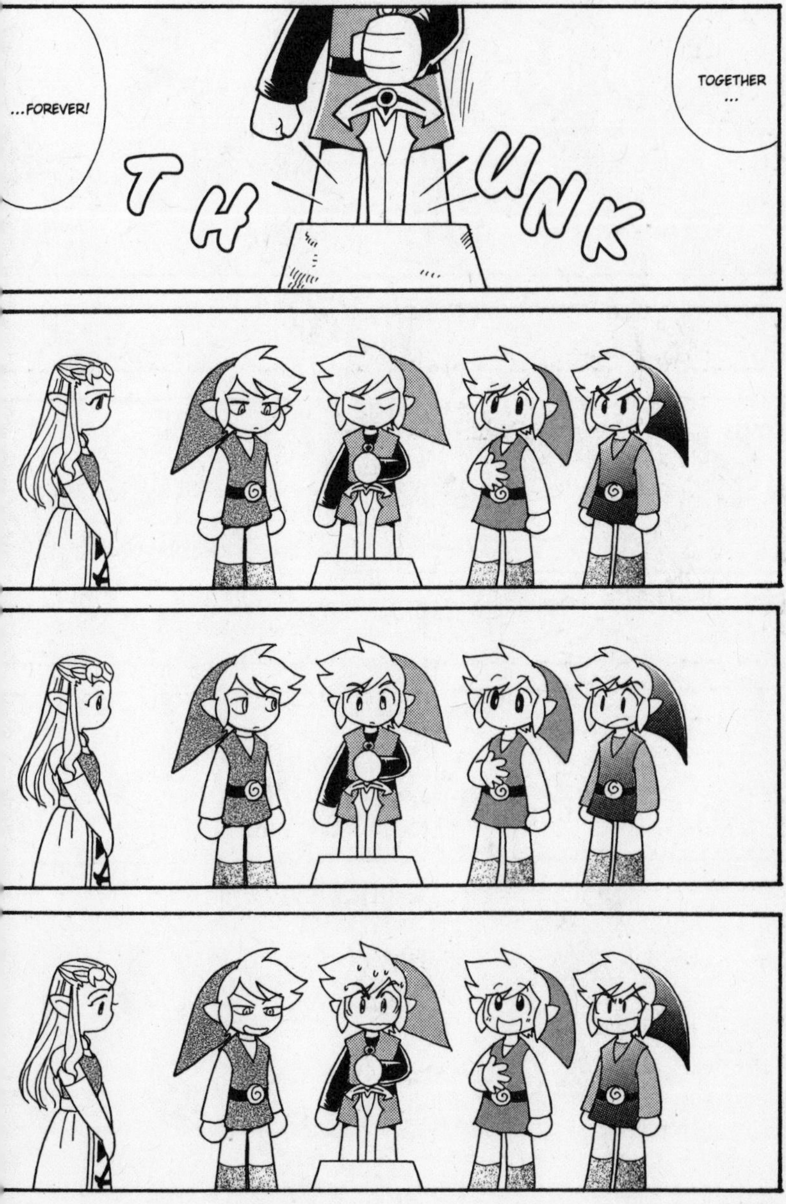
TOGETHER ...
...FOREVER!
THUNK

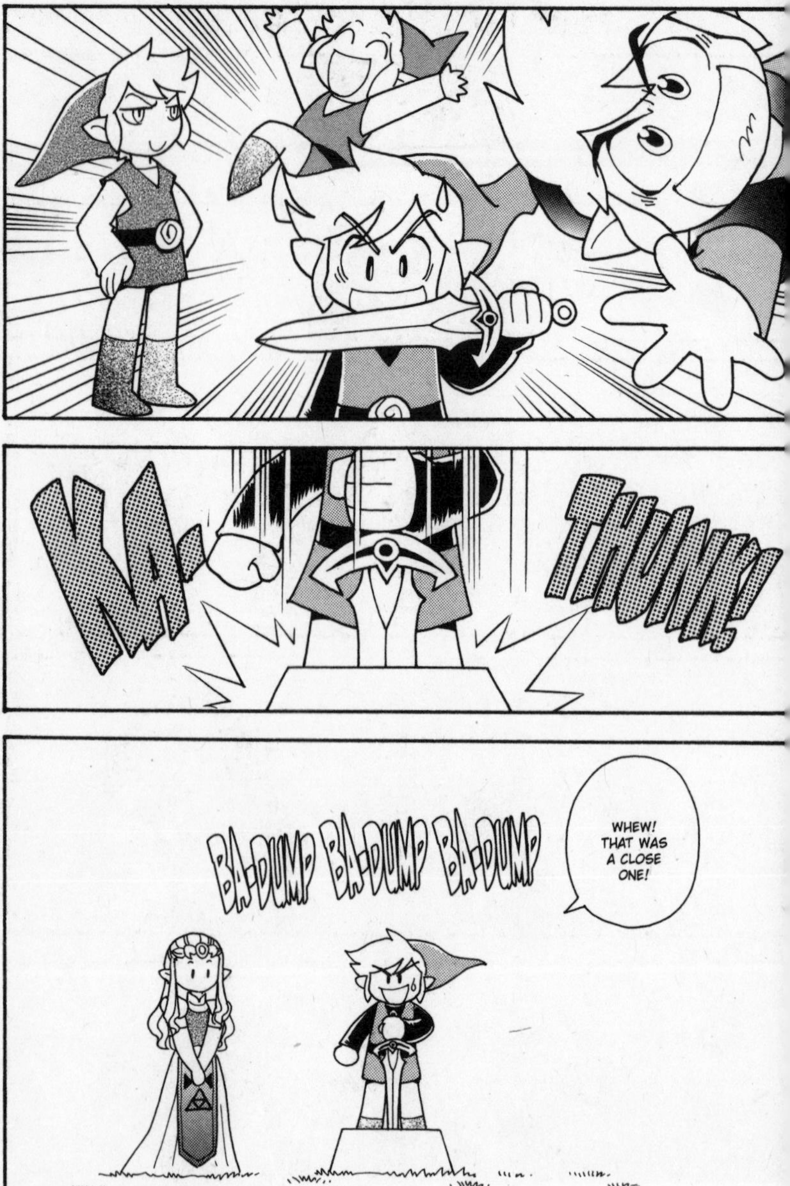
WA-
THUNK!
WHEW! THAT WAS A CLOSE ONE!
BA-DUMP BA-DUMP BA-DUMP

THE END

Coming Next Volume

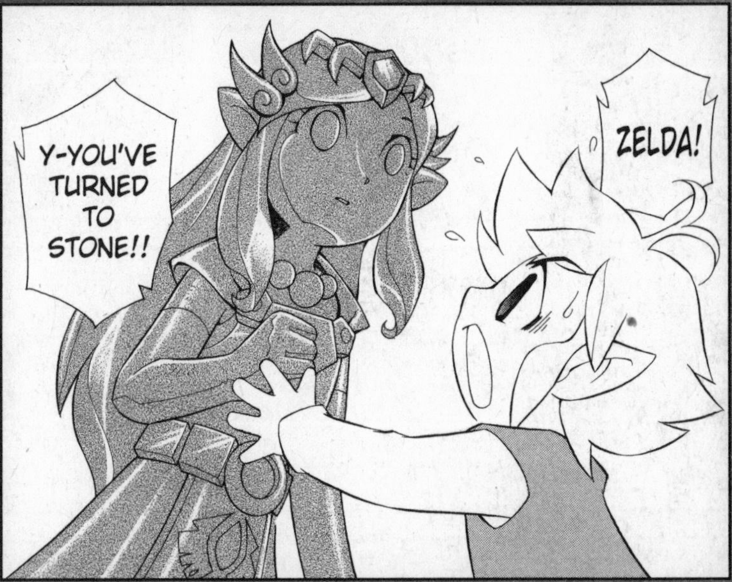
ZELDA!
Y-YOU'VE TURNED TO STONE!!

On the day of the Picori Festival, Link and Princess Zelda go to watch the sword-fighting tournament. The winner is a strange man named Vaati, who has come to claim the Light Force that is sealed within the Bound Chest. When it turns out the Light Force is not in the Bound Chest, he turns Princess Zelda to stone! To save his friend, Link needs the power of the Picori Blade, but only a certain master swordsmith can reforge it. Can Link find the pieces of the broken sword before Vaati does?

AVAILABLE NOW!

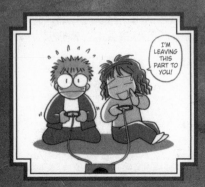

I'M LEAVING THIS PART TO YOU!

AKIRA HIMEKAWA

We're still beginners when it comes to skill at video games. On *Four Swords* we can work together, so we cruise through the difficult parts by leaving them to whichever of us is better at them. Boy does that feel good! But sometimes we can hold each other back...

Akira Himekawa is the collaboration of two women, A. Honda and S. Nagano. Together they have created nine manga adventures featuring Link and the popular video game world of *The Legend of Zelda*™, including *Ocarina of Time, Oracle of Seasons* and *Four Swords*. Their most recent work, *Legend of Zelda*™ : *Phantom Hourglass*, is serialized in *Shogaku Rokunensei*.

THE LEGEND OF

— FOUR SWORDS —

PART 2

Perfect Square Edition

STORY & ART BY
AKIRA HIMEKAWA

TM & © 2009 Nintendo.
© 2005 Akira HIMEKAWA/Shogakukan
All rights reserved.
Original Japanese edition
"ZELDA NO DENSETSU – YOTTSU NO TSURUGI PLUS – GE"
published by SHOGAKUKAN Inc.
English translation rights in the United States of America, Canada,
United Kingdom, Ireland, Australia and New Zealand
arranged with SHOGAKUKAN.

Translation/John Werry, Honyaku Center Inc.
English Adaptation/Stan! Brown
Touch-up Art & Lettering/John Hunt
Cover & Interior Design/Sean Lee
Editor/Mike Montesa

Printed in the U.S.A.

Published by VIZ Media, LLC
P.O. Box 77010
San Francisco, CA 94107

11
First printing, October 2009
Eleventh printing, March 2016

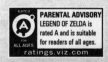

PARENTAL ADVISORY
LEGEND OF ZELDA is
rated A and is suitable
for readers of all ages.
ratings.viz.com

www.viz.com

www.perfectsquare.com